ROUTLEDGE LIBRARY EDITIONS: ETHNOSCAPES

Volume 13

TRADITION, LOCATION AND COMMUNITY

TRADITION, LOCATION AND COMMUNITY

Place-making and Development

Edited by
ADENRELE AWOTONA
AND
NECDET TEYMUR

LONDON AND NEW YORK

First published in 1997 by Avebury (Ashgate Publishing Ltd)

This edition first published in 2025
by Routledge
4 Park Square, Milton Park, Abingdon, Oxon OX14 4RN

and by Routledge
605 Third Avenue, New York, NY 10158

Routledge is an imprint of the Taylor & Francis Group, an informa business

© 1997 Adenrele Awotona

All rights reserved. No part of this book may be reprinted or reproduced or utilised in any form or by any electronic, mechanical, or other means, now known or hereafter invented, including photocopying and recording, or in any information storage or retrieval system, without permission in writing from the publishers.

Trademark notice: Product or corporate names may be trademarks or registered trademarks, and are used only for identification and explanation without intent to infringe.

British Library Cataloguing in Publication Data
A catalogue record for this book is available from the British Library

ISBN: 978-1-032-86590-4 (Set)
ISBN: 978-1-032-84608-8 (Volume 13) (hbk)
ISBN: 978-1-032-84625-5 (Volume 13) (pbk)
ISBN: 978-1-003-51416-9 (Volume 13) (ebk)

DOI: 10.4324/9781003514169

Publisher's Note
The publisher has gone to great lengths to ensure the quality of this reprint but points out that some imperfections in the original copies may be apparent.

Disclaimer
The publisher has made every effort to trace copyright holders and would welcome correspondence from those they have been unable to trace.

New Series Introduction to
RLE: Ethnoscapes

The neologism *Ethnoscapes*[1] was created by David Canter and David Stea in 1987 when they happened both to be in Yogjakarta at the same time. They wanted a term to cover the rapidly emerging multidisciplinary field of research into many aspects of how individuals, groups and cultures interact and transact with their surroundings. It was derived as follows:

Ethno (combining form) indicating race, people or culture.

Scape (suffix-forming nouns) indicating a scene or view of something.

Ethnoscapes (plural noun) Scholarly and/or scientific explorations of the relationships people and their activities, have with the places they create and/or inhabit; historical, psychological, anthropological, sociological, and related disciplines that study the experiences of places, attitudes towards them, or the processes of shaping, managing, or designing them. The term was subsequently used to provide an umbrella for a series of books. These cover topics that are so multidisciplinary that they do not sit comfortably in any of the constrained silos of academic and scholarly research. As indicated on the opening page of the first book in the series, many disciplines "have developed marauding sub-groups who move freely across each others' borders, carrying ideas almost like contraband, without declaring that they have crossed any disciplinary boundaries."

They include domains labelled as Behavioural or Perceptual Geography, Environmental/Architectural Psychology, Urban History, Social Ecology, Behavioural Archaeology, Urban Planning, Behavioural Architecture, and Landscape Architecture. There are also many other areas of research and practice that, whilst not being overtly psychological, social, or cultural, do explore and act on the built and natural environment in a way that recognises the importance of the human transactions with those settings. These professions include interior and product design, comparative linguistics, and even aspects of criminology and mental health providers.

Like all such implicit and explicit transactions between different domains, a community of interest and support has emerged in which those who cross the boundaries often find they have more in common with other transgressors than with their mother disciplines. This has given rise to common means and forms of communication, with a shared understanding of the issues and approaches that are of value. Although, of course, these are not always understood in the same way by all those involved,

The *Ethnoscapes* series of books provides a forum for these multifarious, cross-disciplinary, determinedly international, studies and practices. Each of the books takes on board one or more of the environmental challenges that that individuals, societies and cultures are facing. Emphasising a social perspective, rather than the dominant 'hard' science viewpoints embedded in physical, geological and climate changes.

It may now be regarded as rather prescient that it was over three decades ago that the need and importance was recognised of bringing together the many strands of environmental social research and practice. But there is no doubt that there were academics and professionals exploring Ethnoscape topics, going back to the 1960s, often in isolation and with little recognition, that are today front-page, and podcast, news. The challenges in the environmental social sciences that Ethnoscapes explores are just as pertinent now as they were when initially identified.

The series, in essence, deals with four challenges the environmental social sciences embrace.

>1. Addressing "the awareness of governments and public alike of the problems of environmental degradation and pollution."

This includes the challenge of providing acceptable housing and related environmental conditions that also encompassed the support for environmental and related cultural heritage. It also requires detailed consideration of the assessment and evaluation of designs and design proposals as well as background research on policy related issues.

>2. Developing ways of conceptualising human interactions with the physical surroundings.

This may seem somewhat abstract but has practical implications. The dominant view that people are passively controlled by their surroundings supports a paternalistic, management of what it is assumed people need. That ignores the active way in which people make sense of their environment, drawing on cultural and historical influences. This recognises the importance of user participation in decisions about built and natural settings. That, in turn, requires a much richer understanding of how people interact with where they are or want to be.

3. A much wider range of ways of exploring people's transactions with the environment is needed to contribute to policy and practice as well as developing richer insights into human experiences.

The stock in trade of surveys, or the inevitably artificial laboratory-based experiments, whilst of value for some explorations, need to be augmented by methodologies that enrich an understanding of what the experiences are of being in, acting on, and developing places. They need to connect not just with the endeavours of individuals but also with how cultures and societies express these transactions.

4. Finding ways to enable practitioners and researchers to express their own encounters with the contexts they are influencing or studying.

Much of the research that is carried out in what are curiously called 'Ivory Towers', even when it is studying the big wide world, allows the pretence of distancing from the direct experiences of the issues being studied. Yet the challenges of moving across disciplinary boundaries are as much personal challenges of finding new ways of thinking, communicating, and acting, as an academic demand to develop more effective intellectual systems. The Ethnoscapes series recognises the value of exploring these challenges by hosting a variety of formats. Many of these go beyond the staid and limited formulations that academic discourse assumes to be the norms.

The Ethnoscapes series brings together a vibrant mix of cutting-edge explorations, from all over the world, of human transactions with the built and natural environments. This includes, for example, consideration of vernacular architecture that contrasts with the architecture and urbanism of the colonial enterprise, the meaning of home, aesthetics, well-being and health, and consideration of how environmental psychology has become 'green'. All of these topics, and more, provide an exciting basis for dealing with current challenges in the environmental social sciences.

Note

[1] Not to be confused by the term *Ethnoscape* later concocted by Arun Appadurai in 1990, to refer to **human migration**, the flow of people across boundaries. This includes migrants, refugees, exiles, and tourists, among other moving individuals and groups, all of whom appear to affect the politics of (and between) nations to a considerable degree. Ignorant of the lexicographical origins of the term 'scape' he rather confusingly added it to many ideas of flow, such as the flow of technology – technoscapes and the flow of ideas ideoscapes. Appadurai, A. (1990). "Disjuncture and difference in the global cultural economy." *Theory, Culture and Society* 7(2–3): 295–310.

Routledge Library Editions: Ethnoscapes

1. *Environmental Perspectives* David Canter, Martin Krampen & David Stea (Eds) (1988) ISBN 978-1-032-81616-6

2. *Environmental Policy, Assessment, and Communication* David Canter, Martin Krampen & David Stea (Eds) (1988) ISBN 978-1-032-81635-7

3. *New Directions in Environmental Participation* David Canter, Martin Krampen & David Stea (Eds) (1988) ISBN 978-1-032-81646-3

4. *Vernacular Architecture: Paradigms of Environmental Response* Mete Turan (Ed.) (1990) ISBN 978-1-032-82023-1

5. *Forms of Dominance: On the Architecture and Urbanism of the Colonial Enterprise* Nezar AlSayyad (Ed.) (1992) ISBN 978-1-032-84164-9

6. *The Meaning and Use of Housing: International Perspectives, Approaches and Their Applications* Ernesto G. Arias (Ed.) (1993) ISBN 978-1-032-84781-8

7. *Placemaking: Production of Built Environment in Two Cultures* David Stea & Mete Turan (1993) ISBN 978-1-032-86434-1

8. *Environmental Psychology in Europe: From Architectural Psychology to Green Psychology* Enric Pol (1993) ISBN 978-1-032-83324-8

9. *Housing: Design, Research, Education* Marjorie Bulos & Necdet Teymur (Eds) (1993) ISBN 978-1-032-86388-7

10. *Architecture, Ritual Practice and Co-determination in the Swedish Office* Dennis Doxtater (1994) ISBN 978-1-032-81774-3

11. *On the Aesthetics of Architecture: A Psychological Approach to the Structure and the Order of Perceived Architectural Space* Ralf Weber (1995) ISBN 978-1-032-82034-7

12. *The Home: Words, Interpretations, Meanings and Environments* by David N. Benjamin (Ed.) (1995) ISBN 978-1-032-86411-2

13. *Tradition, Location and Community: Place-making and Development* Adenrele Awotona & Necdet Teymur (Eds) (1997) ISBN 978-1-032-84608-8

14. *Aesthetics, Well-being and Health: Essays within Architecture and Environmental Aesthetics* Birgit Cold (Ed.) (2001) ISBN 978-1-032-86577-5

Other Ethnoscapes series titles also available:

Integrating Programming, Evaluation and Participation in Design: A Theory Z Approach Henry Sanoff (1992) HBK 978-1-138-20338-9; EBK 978-1-315-47173-0; PBK 978-1-138-20339-6

Directions in Person-Environment Research and Practice Jack Nasar & Wolfgang F. E. Preiser (Eds) (1999) HBK 978-1-138-68674-8; EBK 978-1-315-54255-3; PBK 978-1-138-68677-9

Psychological Theories for Environmental Issues Mirilia Bonnes, Terence Lee & Marino Bonaiuto (Eds) (2003) HBK 978-0-75461-888-1; EBK 978-1-315-24572-0; PBK 978-1-138-27742-7

Housing Space and Quality of Life David L. Uzzell, Ricardo Garcia Mira, J. Eulogio Real & Joe Romay (Eds) (2005) HBK 978-0-81538-952-1; EBK 978-1-351-15636-3; PBK 978-1-138-35596-5

Doing Things with Things: The Design and Use of Everyday Objects Alan Costall & Ole Dreier (Eds) (2006) HBK 978-0-75464-656-3; EBK 978-1-315-57792-0; PBK 978-1-138-25314-8

Rethinking the Meaning of Place: Conceiving Place in Architecture-Urbanism Lineu Castello (2010) HBK 978-0-75467-814-4; EBK 978-1-315-60616-3; PBK 978-1-138-25745-0

Tradition, Location and Community
Place-making and Development

Edited by
ADENRELE AWOTONA
University of Newcastle upon Tyne
United Kingdom

NECDET TEYMUR
Middle East Technical University
Ankara, Turkey

Avebury
Aldershot · Brookfield USA · Hong Kong · Singapore · Sydney

© Adenrele Awotona 1997

All rights reserved. No part of this publication may be reproduced, stored in a retrieval system, or transmitted in any form or by any means, electronic, mechanical, photocopying, recording or otherwise without the prior permission of the publisher.

Published by
Avebury
Ashgate Publishing Ltd
Gower House
Croft Road
Aldershot
Hants GU11 3HR
England

Ashgate Publishing Company
Old Post Road
Brookfield
Vermont 05036
USA

British Library Cataloguing in Publication Data

Tradition, location and community : place-making and
    development. - (Ethnoscapes)
    1. Community development 2. Human settlements
    I. Awotona, Adenrele II. Teymur, Necdet
    307.1

    ISBN 1 85972 320 9

Library of Congress Catalog Card Number: 96-79944

Printed and bound by Athenaeum Press, Ltd.,
Gateshead, Tyne & Wear.

Contents

Figures	ix
Tables	xiii
Plates	xv
List of Contributors	xvii

Introduction   1

Section One: Theoretical and conceptual explorations on place-making and development

1   Some thoughts on people, place and development   7
Amos Rapoport

2   'Uneven development' of people and places: Outline of a theory of built form   27
Necdet Teymur

3   Development alternatives of the human ecosystem: An integrative and comprehensive approach   35
Anis-Ur-Rahmaan

4   Ecological community planning: Concepts and principles for eco-community development   47
Yung-Jaan Lee

5   The 'Enablement' approach and settlement upgrading in South Africa   59
Adenrele Awotona and Michael Briggs

Section Two   Case Studies

6	In search of a spatial culture *Amr F. Elgohary and Julienne Hanson*	81
7	Location and development: People, place and power in Alexandria's inner-city neighbourhoods *Amr El-Sherif*	121
8	Planning and designing rural settlements: The Algerian experience *Lamine Mahdjoubi and Adenrele Awotona*	141
9	Gender and structural adjustment: A case study in North-Eastern Ghana *Mariama Awumbila*	161
10	Societal values in development process: Place-making in Sokoto, Nigeria *Umar G. Benna*	173
11	Community self build in Britain: The potential and the reality *Christine Holman*	189
12	Understanding user transformation of public housing *Rafik Salama*	205
13	The making of territories: A case study in South Africa *Maano F. Ramutsindela*	225
14	Upgrading of townships in South Africa after apartheid *Ola Uduku*	235
15	Modernist housing policy and tradition *Peter King*	251
16	A study of a house type with an open space *Aysu Baskaya and Martin Symes*	261
17	Is informal housing the destiny of the urban poor? *Gülsün Saglamer, Hülya Turgut, Meltem Aksoy, Arda Inceoglu and Nurbin Paker*	281

References 293
Index 311

Figures

Figure 1.1	Relating expressions of culture to the Built Environment - the width of arrows approximates feasibility and ease of relating the various elements.	12
Figure 3.1	Prismatic framework providing for the interaction of seminal determinants of socio-physical development.	36
Figure 3.2	Cyclical interaction between the seminal determinants of the socio-physical development process.	36
Figure 3.3	Salient parameters of the determinants of socio-physical development.	38
Figure 3.4	Parametric variation due to cultural, technological, climatic and topographic changes.	39
Figure 3.5	A conceptualization showing the desirability of using an inductive approach for the generation of explorative, and a deductive approach for the selection of feasible and normative alternatives.	45
Figure 6.1	Map of El-Hekr and Northern City Sector, Ismaïlia.	83
Figure 6.2.1	Architectural plans of traditional houses. House Nos. 1-18.	86
Figure 6.2.2	Architectural plans of traditional houses. House Nos. 19-24.	87
Figure 6.2.3	Architectural plans of traditional houses. House Nos. 25-29.	88
Figure 6.3	Syntactic symmetry: symmetrical configurational relationship between two spaces A & B.	94
Figure 6.4	Syntactic asymmetry: asymmetrical configurational relationship between three spaces A, B & C.	94

Figure 6.5	Drawings of plans, spatial functions and justified graphs from various points for house 11.	96
Figure 6.6	Justified graphs of the 41 Cases.	97
Figure 6.7.1	Rank order of integration values of spatial functions and genotypes of 41 cases. (1 of 4 **diagrams**).	100
Figure 6.7.2	Rank order of integration values. (2 of 4 **diagrams**).	101
Figure 6.7.3	Rank order of integration values. (3 of 4 **diagrams**).	102
Figure 6.7.4	Rank order of integration values. (4 of 4 **diagrams**).	103
Figure 6.8	Drawings for house 20: plan, justified graphs from exterior and integration values.	110
Figure 6.9	Drawings for house 22: plan, justified graph from exterior and integration values.	110
Figure 6.10	Drawings for house 8: plan, justified graph from exterior and integration values.	111
Figure 6.11	Drawings for house 28a: plan, justified graph from exterior and integration values.	112
Figure 6.12	Drawings for house 28: plan, justified graph from exterior and integration values.	112
Figure 6.13	New plans, proposed by designers.	114
Figure 6.14	Justified graphs of the new housing prototypes.	114
Figure 6.15	Rank order of integration in the new prototypes.	115
Figure 7.1	The plan of the Gomrok district.	122
Figure 7.2	An example of Double houses in the Gomrok district.	124
Figure 7.3	Plan of El-Shemerly and El-Halwagy area.	127
Figure 7.4	The difference in living conditions between the residents of the harah and the residents of the street.	128
Figure 7.5	A model to understand the relationship between people and place in El-Shemerly and El-Halwagy area.	130
Figure 8.1	Plan of an Arab house.	147
Figure 8.2	View of an Arab village.	149
Figure 8.3	A general view of a Socialist village.	155
Figure 9.1	The Area of Study.	162
Figure 10.1	Conceptual **model** for the analysis of Sokoto's Development.	174
Figure 10.2.1	Caliphate system of cities.	181
Figure 10.2.2	Colonial system of cities.	181
Figure 10.2.3	Post-colonial system of cities.	181
Figure 10.3	Sokoto urban area in 1960s.	184
Figure 12.1	List of projects by order of size of transformation activity.	213

Figure 12.2	Different layout patterns used in the surveyed projects.	219
Figure 12.3	Different extension profiles develop from different block designs.	220
Figure 12.4	Different design configurations observed in the surveyed sample as a result of transformations.	222
Figure 13.1	Creation of ethnic territories.	229
Figure 13.2	Resettlement of the North Sotho.	230
Figure 13.3	Ethnic and racial magisterial districts.	231
Figure 16.1	Different uses of open space.	261
Figure 16.2	Traditional and contemporary organisation of space.	264
Figure 16.3	Schematic drawings of the house types in Gaziantep.	265
Figure 16.4	The evolution of the house type from ancient times till the present.	267
Figure 16.5	The evolution of the house type given by Dato.	268
Figure 16.6	Example of the house type in Ortigia.	269
Figure 16.7	Typology of the house type in Ortigia.	270
Figure 16.8	Section showing the relation of domains.	271
Figure 16.9	Position of main entrance.	272

Tables

Table 3.1	Morphological analysis for the generation of development alternatives of human ecosystem.	44
Table 6.1	Integration Min., Max. & Mean values for main functions.	105
Table 6.2	The physiography of 4 main integration genotypes (syntactic typology).	108
Table 7.1.1	Factors affecting the perception of the place by the residents of the El-Shemerly and El-Halwagy area.	133
Table 7.1.2	Factors affecting the perception of the place by the residents of the El-Shemerly and El-Halwagy area.	134
Table 9.1	Income -earning activities of women, Zorse, 1984 and 1991.	167
Table 9.2	Average daily time spent on reproductive work, Zorse 1984 and 1991.	168
Table 9.3	Seasonal differences in average daily time used in Zorse, 1984 and 1991.	170
Table 11.1	Self build schemes in 'Northern' England, July 1995.	195
Table 11.1	Self build schemes in 'Northern' England, July 1995. (continued).	196
Table 14.1	Access to electricity amongst South African households.	250
Table 14.2	Inadequate sanitation and water supply in South Africa.	250
Table 16.1	Ownership of households.	273
Table 16.2	Original place of households.	273
Table 16.3	Number of families residing in each block.	273

Table 16.4	Number of families around the open space on the ground floor.	274
Table 16.5	Use of open space.	275
Table 16.6	Use of balcony.	275
Table 16.7	Use of roof.	276
Table 16.8	The things which the inhabitants do not like.	277
Table 16.9	The type of house in which they would like to live in in the future.	278
Table 17.1	Pinar settlement by years.	287
Table 17.2	Akatlar settlement by years.	289
Table 17.3	Educational level of the inhabitants.	291
Table 17.4	Employment status.	291

Plates

Plate 8.1	A general view of a Berber village.	145
Plate 8.2	Provision of high rise buildings as a new approach to rural housing.	157
Plate 12.1	Kitchen used as a workroom.	207
Plate 12.2	Variation in balcony enclosure.	207
Plate 12.3	Roof top extension.	208
Plate 12.4	Underground extension.	208
Plate 12.5	Ground floor extensions used as shops.	209
Plate 12.6	Upper floor extensions.	210
Plate 12.7	Multi-storey extension.	211
Plate 12.8	Individual transformations.	211
Plate 12.9	Collective transformations.	212
Plate 12.10	Narrow spaces in Ahmed Helmi have limited the scale of extension activities.	218
Plate 14.1	Shanty housing in Port Elizabeth.	249
Plate 17.1	General view of Pinar.	288
Plate 17.2	General view of Akatlar.	290

List of contributors

MELTEM AKSOY is a research and teaching assistant in the Faculty of Architecture of Istanbul Technical University. She is currently a Ph.D. candidate and has recently participated in the Med-Campus Housing Network. She has designed several architectural projects and co-authored many published papers on architectural design, housing and shape grammars.

ADENRELE AWOTONA, who was educated at the Universities of Newcastle and Cambridge, is currently the Director of the Centre for Architectural Research and Development Overseas (CARDO) and the Director of Postgraduate Studies in the Department of Architecture at the University of Newcastle in the United Kingdom. He has been on academic assignments to all the continents of the world and has published extensively in international journals. He frequently participates in international conferences and workshops. Amongst his research interests are housing for the low income, resettlement planning, architecture and development, reconstruction after disaster and urban development planning.

MARIAMA AWUMBILA, B.A. and Graduate Diploma (Population Studies), University of Ghana; Ph.D. Geography, University of Newcastle upon Tyne. At present she is a Senior Assistant Registrar, University of Ghana Planning Unit. She also lectures part-time at the UN Regional Institute for Population Studies, and teaches and examines Postgraduate Courses on Population, Gender and Development. She has lectured in Newcastle and Middlesex, UK and California. She has published and presented several papers at conferences in the field of Gender and Development, Demography and Educational Planning.

AYSU BASKAYA is a graduate of Gazi University, Ankara and received her Masters of Restoration degree from the Middle East Technical University, Department of Architecture, Ankara in 1991. She is a doctoral candidate in the School of Architecture, University of Manchester. She was a practising architect before her present position as a research assistant at the Gazi University. From 1990 to 1992 she took part in rehabilitation and regeneration projects in the south eastern Turkey and in Ankara. Her research focuses on urban form analysis, culture and space types.

UMAR G. BENNA is an Architect/Planner and was, until recently, the chairman of the Department of Urban and Regional Planning at King Faisal University, Dammam, Saudi Arabia. His teaching and research interest is in integrated community design.

MICHAEL BRIGGS gained his Bachelor of Social Science and BA Economic History, at the University of Cape Town; and his MA Regional Planning at the University of Natal, Durban. He has worked as a part time lecturer of Town and Regional Planning at ML Sultan Technikon, Durban; part time Researcher and Assistant Planner for consultants; lecturer (Dean's Assistant) at the Department of Town and Regional Planning, University of Natal, Durban (1994-1995) working in Planning techniques and Project work; and Consultant researcher for 'Urban Strategies' unit of Durban City Council. Most recently he worked as a Research Associate in CARDO, University of Newcastle upon Tyne, UK.

AMR F. ELGOHARY, BSc Hons.Arch., MSc, MPhil, is a lecturer in the Department of Architecture at Ain Shams University, Cairo, Egypt. He is a qualified architect who has practised in the Middle East and is based in Cairo. He has completed the refurbishment, restoration and conservation work of the Egyptian Cultural Office in London. He has lectured and taught at undergraduate and postgraduate levels at Ain Shams University and in various academic institutions in the UK including UCL and Huddersfield. He has written and published extensively in the field of spatial culture in housing and development architecture.

AMR El-SHERIF is an architect and urban designer. He is an Assistant Professor and lecturer in Urban Design and Planning in the Department of Architecture at Alexandria University, where he gained his BSc and MSc degrees, and has a PhD in Urban Design from Oxford Brookes University. He is currently the managing officer of the Alexandria Preservation Trust. He has participated in a number of conferences related to both development practices and environmental design. He is the co-editor (with Nabeel Hamdi) of the book *Educating for Real* (Intermediate Technology Publication, 1996).

JULIENNE HANSON, DipArch, MSc, PhD, Vice-Dean of the Faculty of the Built Environment, Bartlett Graduate School, UCL, has for twenty years been an experienced teacher and educator in Built Environment education at all levels at the Bartlett. She has designed, organised and delivered a variety of postgraduate academic Master's courses for the construction industry, including an MSc

Programme in Advanced Architectural Studies and a Distance Learning Diploma in Higher Education Studies. She is co-author, with Professor Bill Hillier, of The Social Logic of Space, CUP, 1984, and the author of a forthcoming book on the Social logic of Houses.

CHRISTINE HOLMAN teaches housing policy at the School of Urban and Regional Studies, Sheffield Hallam University. She is a member of the management committee of the Community Self Build Agency and is actively involved with community self build groups in the north of England.

ARDA INCEOGLU is currently a research and teaching assistant and a Ph.D. candidate in Istanbul Technical University Faculty of Architecture. He graduated in ITU, and gained his Master of Architecture degree in the School of Design, North Carolina State University, USA. His research is about the housing problems of the low income groups in Turkey. He has led workshops in Gökçeada and in Cyprus. He is an assistant in the Med-Campus Housing Network. He is currently working on the perception and the meaning of the house in a cross-cultural context.

PETER KING is a senior lecturer in housing studies and a member of the Centre of Comparative Housing Studies at De Montfort University, Leicester. He is currently undertaking research on the control of housing and on housing need and capability. He has a Ph.D. in political philosophy from the University of Bradford.

YUNG-JAAN LEE is an Associate Professor in the Department of Land Economics at the National Chengchi University, Taipei, Taiwan. He qualified at the national Cheng Kung University, Taiwan and obtained a Master of Civil Engineering degree at the National Taiwan University, going on to gain his Master of Urban Planning and Ph.D. in Environmental Planning at the University of Michigan, USA. His research interests focus on environmental planning, environmental psychology, and conservation behaviour.

LAMINE MAHDJOUBI graduated as an architect from the University of Constantine (Algeria) and obtained his M. Phil. from the University of Newcastle. He was a Lecturer in the Department of Architecture at the University of Setif, worked as an IT training consultant at Computer Forum in Newcastle, Research Associate at the Department of Architecture, University of Newcastle; and is currently a Lecturer in Construction Management and IT at the University of Wolverhampton. His main areas of interest are planning and design during the process of rapid social changes, and the application of IT for construction.

NURBIN PAKER is a research and teaching assistant in the Faculty of Architecture, Istanbul Technical University doing her Ph.D. degree on 'Creativity in Architectural Design Education'. She received her master's degree from the same faculty. She has worked on different research projects and is a research assistant in the Med-Campus Housing Network. She has undertaken various architectural projects and received architectural design awards. She is the co-author of several published papers on architectural design, housing and shape grammars.

ANIS-UR-RAHMAAN teaches urban and regional planning in the Department of Urban and Regional Planning of the King Abdul Aziz University, Jeddah, Saudi Arabia and in other international institutions.
He studied at the University of the Punjab, Lahore; AA School of Architecture, London; University of Illinois; and the University of Wisconsin. He is a civil engineer, architect and city and regional planner and has experience in urban planning in Pakistan; as United Nations' Advisor in Saudi Arabia and as a United Nations' Consultant to the United Arab Emirates and Pakistan. His publications include numerous articles and research papers.

MAANO F. RAMUTSINDELA is a lecturer in the Department of Geography, University of the North, South Africa. He has done research on boundaries, forced removals and ethnic perceptions in South Africa. His research work has been presented at national and international academic conferences.

AMOS RAPOPORT is Distinguished Professor in the School of Architecture and Urban Planning at the University of Wisconsin-Milwaukee. He teaches Vernacular Design, Behavioural Factors in Housing, Behavioural Factors in Urban Design and Design for Developing Countries.
He is one of the founders of the new field of Environment-Behaviour Studies. His work has focused mainly on the role of cultural variables, cross-cultural studies, and theory development and synthesis. He is the editor or co-editor of four books and several monographs and the author of approximately 200 papers, five books and several monographs. His work has been translated into many languages.

GÜLSÜN SAGLAMER is a Professor of Architecture in Istanbul Technical University and the vice rector from 1992 to 1995. Her main research areas are: Low-Income Housing, Computer Applications in Architecture and Simulation of Parametric Design Procedures. She has published over 60 papers. She was a member of The Scientific and Technical Research Council of Turkey between 1990-1994. She was a visiting Scholar at the Martin Centre, Department of Architecture, Cambridge University between 1975-1976 and in 1991. She was a Visiting Professor at Queen's University of Belfast from 1993-1995.

RAFIK SALAMA, BSc. Arch., M.Arch., studied architecture at Alexandria University in Egypt and McGill University in Canada. He has been practising as an architect in Montreal and has been active in research for the last few years.

MARTIN SYMES is Professor of Urban Renewal at the University of Manchester. In 1980 he was Visiting Fellow at Princeton University, in 1985 he held the Nell Norris Fellowship at the University of Melbourne and in 1990 he was Monbusho Visiting Professor at the University of Tokyo. He has published books and papers on urban design, architectural practice, and architectural education, specialising in the development of case methods. From 1984 to 1993 he was co-editor of 'The Journal of Architectural and Planning Research'. Martin Symes has professional experience in Britain, North Africa and New Zealand.

NECDET TEYMUR studied at METU, Ankara, Bouwcentrum and Liverpool University, worked in Arne Jacobsen's office and has taught mainly in British Universities. Until recently he was Director of the Centre for International Architectural Studies in Manchester. He is presently a Professor of Architecture at METU, Ankara. He is the author of *Environmental Discourse* (1982) and *Architectural Education* (1992) and co-editor of *Rehumanizing Housing* (1988), *Culture, Space, Society* (1990), *Housing: Design, Research, Education* (1993) and a forthcoming one, *Architectural History in the Studio*.

HÜLYA TURGUT is an Associate Professor in the Faculty of Architecture of Istanbul Technical University. She received her master's and doctorate degrees in Architecture from ITU. She has won several competition prizes and published papers on architectural design and housing. Her current research aims to clarify the temporal, cultural and spatial transactions in squatter settlements for designing and upgrading purposes in developing countries. She was recently the assistant Coordinator of the Med-Campus Housing Network.

OLA UDUKU, formerly a Smuts Research Fellow at the African Studies Centre, University of Cambridge, is currently lecturing at the Department of Architecture, University of Liverpool. Research interests are in school design in the sub-Saharan Africa, and social infrastructure provision world-wide.

Introduction

Adenrele Awotona

This book is the outcome of an international symposium on *People, Place and Development* which was organised and hosted by the Centre for Architectural Research and Development Overseas (CARDO), University of Newcastle, UK. It was held in December 1994 and was an International Association for People-Environment Studies (IAPS) network activity. The two-day symposium covered a number of themes including the following: theoretical issues and methods; place and people's behaviour; place-making processes; tradition, continuity and change; places for special needs; concepts and strategies for place-development; women, housing and development; rebuilding communities after disasters; physical development standards; and agencies for development. The central view which the international gathering overwhelmingly noted, as reflected in the numerous papers that were presented, was that shaping places for people should not only be in conformity with their individual needs and aspirations, but should also be a means for social and economic progress. By strengthening these relationships, shaping places becomes a developmental process of multifarious dimensions: socio-economic, cultural and physical. This process aims at enhancing cultural identity and providing adequate living environments, as well as maximising the use of resources and encouraging income generation.

The structure of the book

The book brings together the selected papers of seventeen architects, social scientists and planners who were amongst the 109 delegates from 23 countries who attended the symposium. It offers a range of original perspectives on the relationship between the design and habitation of the built environment on the one hand and social and cultural development on the other. As an archival volume, it attempts to present a mixture of cross-disciplinary and cross-cultural perspectives.

It explores the view that planning and design (the organisation of the physical/built environment) which follow from the rapid transformations wrought by development must respond to, and be based on, the wants and needs of the people affected; that is, it must be in accord with their notions of environmental quality.

The book is divided into two sections. The first section has five chapters which explore the theoretical and conceptual aspects of *place-making and development.* Section 2 consists of twelve chapters each of which presents a case study.

In Chapter 1 Amos Rapoport uses an approach and framework based on environment-behaviour research to provide a structure for thinking about the three key terms of the theme of this book - *people, place and development.* In Chapter 2 Necdet Teymur presents a theoretical setting which introduces the composite idea of *uneven development in social space, built form and built culture.* Amongst the issues which he investigates are some cases of *'unevenness'* in science, culture, history and the built form; a theory of *unevenness* pertaining to built form; and key axioms for an n-theory and multi-theory of *complex, integrated and glocal unevenness.* In Chapter 3 Anis Ur-Rahmaan attempts to generate a number of explorative alternatives for the development of the human ecosystem by carrying out a morphological analysis of its basic determinants and their parametric typologies and inherent variations. In Chapter 4 Yung-Jaan Lee puts forward a new planning concept: *Eco-Community Planning* (ECP). First, he examines some critical issues of environmental degradation in community development as a result of the economic policies of the Taiwanese government over the past four decades. The second part of the chapter explores the connections between ecology and community. In the third part he describes the loss of community. In the fourth section, he lays out six values of effective activism. He then outlines his proposed approach to sustainable planning. In Chapter 5 Adenrele Awotona and Michael Briggs attempt to answer one of the central questions concerning housing development in South Africa: *Can the 'enablement' approach provide a framework for 'settlement upgrading'?* They do this by examining the factors which led to the emergence of the 'enablement' paradigm; and the distinctive characteristics, and the important critiques, of this approach amongst others.

The twelve case studies in Section 2 come from Africa, Asia and Europe. In Chapter 6 Amr Elgohary and Julienne Hanson examine the ways in which significant social and cultural values, household practices and lifestyle choices are embodied in the spatial layout and interior design of homes which ordinary people build for themselves. They explore these issues through a configurational analysis of 29 traditional dwellings from the 'informal' Egyptian settlement of *El-Hekr,* which lies to the north of the city of Ismailia. Chapter 7 by Amr El-Sherif reports on an investigation into the interaction between the socio-spatial systems of the urban environment and the political and economic constraints on development in *Elshemerly* neighbourhood in the inner area of the city of Alexandria in Egypt. In Chapter 8 Lamine Mahdjoubi and Adenrele Awotona recount the results of an investigation into why both the French and Algerian governments' programmes of rural development in Algeria (during the process of rapid social change between 1956 and 1989) failed to meet the requirements and aspirations of the rural inhabitants. In Chapter 9 Mariama Awumbila analyses the data which she obtained in the fieldwork which she undertook in Zorse, a village in north-eastern Ghana. The study examines the relationship between the World Bank-sponsored structural adjustment policies and the feminisation of poverty. In Chapter 10 Umar Benna uses the concepts of tradition, continuity and change to analyse the development of Sokoto in Nigeria, a non-Arab Muslim city. In Chapter 11 Christine Holman looks at two self built housing projects in England (one in North Tyneside and the other in South Yorkshire). The study explores both the potential and reality that these schemes have for creating housing, employment and community for their participants. In Chapter 12 Rafik Salama examines the development of transformations in different public housing projects in Egypt and attempts to identify some of the implicit factors that control change at both dwelling and community levels. In chapter 13 Maano Ramutsindela analyses how the apartheid South African government used the law, as well as other methods, as instruments of place-making. In Chapter 14 Ola Uduku looks at the physical development standards in South Africa's townships. In chapter 15 Peter King addresses the way in which traditions are linked to location and the formation and maintenance of community within the dwelling process. He also analyses the character of modernist housing policy and suggests that its basic nature is the problematisation of housing. In chapter 16 Baskaya and Symes use a typological approach in examining the vernacular housing conditions in Sicily. In the study, they place special emphasis on the analysis of the process leading to the organisation and use of private and semi-private open spaces. They also investigate how the house type with an open space fits cultural requirements. Finally, Gülsün Saglamer, Hülya Turgut, Meltem Aksoy, Arda Inceoglu and Nurbin Parker in Chapter 17 assess the present informal housing situation in Istanbul, Turkey. Amongst the issues examined are the squatterisation and land ownership patterns in two different squatter settlements in the city - Pinar and Akatlar.

Acknowledgement

In the preparation of this book the editors are grateful to the secretary at CARDO, University of Newcastle, Maggie Warford, for her work in getting the papers ready for publishing.

Section 1
THEORETICAL AND CONCEPTUAL EXPLORATIONS ON PLACE-MAKING AND DEVELOPMENT

1 Some thoughts on people, place and development

Amos Rapoport

Introduction

In this chapter I propose a framework for thinking about the theme of the book which implicitly proposes that the three terms -- People, Place and Development -- are necessary and sufficient to define the domain under discussion. One, 'development', refers to certain processes which are taken to be typical of particular 'developing' countries. Another, 'people', refers to those who initiate and sustain development processes and who are also affected by them (these are not necessarily the same). The third, 'place', presumably refers to a particular sub-domain that is of particular interest to this group -- which I take to be what is broadly called the 'physical' or 'built' environment.

My argument hinges on the premise that although these three terms do potentially define the domain, they do not do so in practice. This is because they are too vague to be usable either to analyse issues and problems, or to suggest responses once problems are identified.

I argue that two of these terms are vague due to excessive broadness or generality, 'people' (i.e.. humanity!) and 'development', and that the third, 'place' is inherently vague and generally inappropriate. In discussing all three (and others) I follow the principle which I wish to emphasise as a primary point of this chapter: that terms must be precise, clear and as unambiguous as possible because they are not useful unless they can be clarified sufficiently to become capable of being related explicitly to other variables. Clear and well-defined terms are essential so that they can discriminate among entities (Rapoport, 1990a, 1994a). The concepts that terms stand for must be characterised as fully and precisely as possible and these must be seen as ongoing activities. Moreover, in constraining and characterising such excessively broad terms and concepts it is essential to identify those of their dimensions, characteristics and attributes which play a major role in the particular domain being investigated.

In all cases I argue that a useful way to define, specify and operationalize terms and concepts is through analysis or dismantling. In so doing I continue a major theme in my recent work, which I have applied to concepts such as environment, culture, vernacular, tradition, privacy and others (some of which I will discuss below). In doing this I use a framework and an approach developed over a number of years and try to show that they are relevant to the topic in question. This represents two further aspects of my work: first, an ongoing synthesis and simplification of the approach; second, applying this synthesis using prior work and concepts to deal with new problems, often given to me e.g. children, elderly, capital cities etc.. In this way I am trying to develop a single approach which becomes generally applicable by using the relevant specifics. Identifying these specifics in itself involves carefully specifying the domain in question (Rapoport, 1990e). A major question then becomes for example: which aspects of 'people' and 'development' are relevant to the problems of the design (in the broad sense) of the built environment/cultural landscape 'place'? I thus assume, and will try to show that development is of interest in the present context to the extent that it affects the physical environment, which it always does -- often in unintended ways, and how this in turn, affects people, the users.

After I have clarified and constrained these terms by analysis and dismantling I bring the three terms together again in order to suggest some implications of the analytical framework. Note, however, that even in the three analytic sections, although I have tried very hard to discuss each term in isolation, some cross-referencing and overlaps are unavoidable. The synthesis thus becomes easy and follows 'naturally'.

In some sense the process of thinking and analysis, the approach which emphasises the need to clarify and define terms and characterise concepts is as important as (or even more important than) any specific conclusions. Although I clearly believe that the proposed framework is valid and useful, or I would not propose it, others are certainly possible. For example, I largely omit a range of economic, political and implementational aspects which I see as modifying factors -- in other words I deal with an ideal x model, (Rapoport, 1983a Figure 11, p. 267). Even so, it should be emphasised that I do not attempt to present a comprehensive review of the topics discussed. Rather, I try to provide a conceptual framework for the themes and problems addressed, and to give some sense of how they might be approached.

Underlying this approach is the conviction that what is not understood cannot be controlled or guided, i.e. design cannot achieve predictable results (which it must do) without understanding environment-behaviour relations (EBR). It is the function of environment-behaviour studies (EBS) to provide this understanding and my approach is based on an emerging explanatory theory of EBR.[1]

'People' - an analysis

Although there are 'designers' who deny that design has anything to do with users i.e. people, I take it as a given that we all accept that planning and design, in the broadest sense of any change by anyone to the face of the earth, whether in development or otherwise, is precisely about people.

It may seem that the use of the term 'people' is unproblematic. After all, being people we should know about people via empathy, einfuhlung and the like. However, this is a dangerous approach, because the term is so broad, and hence vague, as to be unusable in any real sense.

The themes of this book imply that one is interested in people as they relate to the built environment -- cultural landscapes, settlements, neighbourhoods and the like, and settings and systems of settings of all kinds -- under conditions of development. However, one does not know a priori which aspects or attributes of people are relevant -- human characteristics have proved to be a complex topic to say the least. It follows that an explicit analysis is essential, based on the empirical findings of the great variety of disciplines which are and are becoming relevant -- a larger range of disciplines than is commonly used in EBS.[2]

Clearly, however, one cannot be expected to define what it is to be human, or even to define a set of necessary and sufficient attributes of people regarding the built environment. All one can do is to discuss a few of the more important attributes as examples and to illustrate the approach. The range of these characteristics can be seen from what I call the first of three basic questions of EBS. I usually formulate question 1 as: what are the bio-social, psychological and cultural attributes of people, as members of a species, as individuals and as members of various groups from dyads to cultures and societies, which are relevant and in design should be relevant to the ways built environments are organised, structured and shaped. One can expect some to be constant, species-specific and pan-cultural; others to be highly variable across cultures, although possibly within evolutionary constraints and constant processes and mechanisms. The question then becomes: which are especially important in connection with development?

From an EBS perspective questions 2 (Rapoport, 1977, 1983a, b) and 3 (Rapoport, 1983b) are also relevant, further broadening the issue and making an explicit discussion essential. Question 2 asks: what effects do which aspects of what environments have on which people, under what circumstances and why? An environment may then be inhibiting for some, supportive for others and a catalyst for yet others, depending on who they are, and on whether the environment is chosen or imposed. Note that environments are rarely determining except in a negative sense that they can be so inhibiting as to block desired behaviour. Apparent positively determining environments are then catalysts, making possible behaviour which was previously blocked (Rapoport, 1983b). People differ in the extent to which they are affected by environments. For example, under conditions of 'reduced competence' (ageing, physical disability, rapid culture change etc.), which lead to increased criticality, the effects of environments are greatly magnified. Environments which may be merely inhibiting under conditions of low criticality may become negatively determining, and even destructive in extreme cases, under conditions of high criticality (which often apply in developing countries, as we shall see below (Rapoport, 1977, 1983b)). Under such conditions environments may need to be so highly supportive as to be considered 'prosthetic' (Rapoport, 1983b).

Question 3 deals with the mechanisms that link people and their behaviour and environments, making possible their mutual interaction. Among these are perception, cognition, action, affect, evaluation and preference (and hence choice), meaning, supportiveness and so on. Note that these are attributes of people - mechanisms are in people. In understanding behaviour (e.g. preference and choice, modification, activity systems and so on) it is most important to recognise the primacy of latent aspects, and hence affect, meaning, ideals and images -- and hence wants rather than 'needs'. Latent aspects and wants tend to be more variable than instrumental aspects and needs, so that variability becomes an important consideration as do 'perceived' i.e. cognized aspects of reality. However, in terms of question 1, one would expect some important patterns, regularities and constancy even behind the great and striking variety of cultures and environments. This implies that general models, characteristics and mechanisms are expressed differently in their specifics and in detail.

One can thus discuss evolutionary and constant aspects, event constraints behind cultural variability which derive from their evolutionary origins. This is central to my current work on theory development, and may be important in the present context e.g. in suggesting the need to search for regularities and patterns behind diversity and variety. At that level one can argue that cultural differences are less important than the underlying constancy. In the present context, however, it is the existing situation of both group and environmental variability and specificity which seems important.

Using the distinction between 'ultimate' and 'proximate' explanations, the latter starting point may be more relevant in the present context. Cultural and environmental differences exist however they came to be, and whatever their underlying 'deep' bases and these need to be considered and used if appropriate, because it is, of course, possible that some cultural and environmental patterns may now be inappropriate, or even maladaptive having evolved under very different conditions. Thus, although this is a very complex issue theoretically, pragmatically cultural and environmental specifics are a useful starting point.

The variety of environments which is so striking is apparently reduced by development. This may or may not be a problem (see section on 'place'). One source of worry may be the disappearance of what I have called a 'cultural gene pool', a laboratory or repertoire of solutions from which one can learn (Rapoport, 1982a, 1990a, e). Other sources of worry have to do with identity, with supportiveness, with a loss of the richness and complexity of the world in terms of ambience and perceptually (Rapoport, 1977,1989, 1992a, c).

Differences in environments, as they relate to people (and to development) brings up the issue of groups -- since traditional environments are group-specific. This, in turn raises the question of which groups are relevant or useful for given domains or problems. How one goes about defining the nature of the appropriate groups for particular sets of problems is a rather difficult question because it is a topic that has been grossly under-researched. It is also a most important topic because one cannot research, plan or design for individuals. The groups often used in the development context, such as 'developing countries' or 'the urban poor of the Third World' are much too broad to be useful -- the variety of groups involved is clearly very great. There are major differences among countries, among different regions in one country, often even within a single city, and these groups and their characteristics, requirements and wants need to be specified for environmental planning and design.

Historically groups have been defined (by themselves and by others) in terms of race, occupation, caste, religion, ethnicity, language, ideology, class and so on. All of these, and culture, can be shown to be relevant for environmental design to the extent that they produce different values, lifestyles and activity systems, and also various specific social expressions such as kinship and family structure, roles, institutions and the like. This, in effect, involves dismantling another notoriously broad and excessively general and also abstract term ('culture') and an attempt to characterise it in ways useful in environmental design (Rapoport, 1993, Figure 1, p.16, in press b). Note that 'environment' also needs to be dismantled (Rapoport, 1977, 1983a, in press). I will discuss this briefly in the next section.

In this connection, it is my suggestion that social and cultural variables are critical. They help to define the nature of relevant groups, describe their values, lifestyles and activity systems and their social characteristics. From these, preferences can be derived which can help define appropriate environmental quality for these groups. It is because, from this perspective, social and cultural variables are central in design, and design therefore highly culture- and group-specific, that one cannot generalise for a given country, region or even city either in developing countries or elsewhere, let alone for 'people'.

In terms of my previous discussion of question 2, recall that groups differ in the extent to which environments affect them, and hence what effects environments have on people. Under conditions of 'reduced competence', criticality goes up and members of groups become more vulnerable, magnifying effects of environments and needing highly supportive, possibly prosthetic, environments. One such influence is the rate of change (to be discussed under 'development'); another is what I call 'cognitive distance', the difference between the lifestyle of a particular group and the lifestyle it needs to adopt. It then becomes possible to

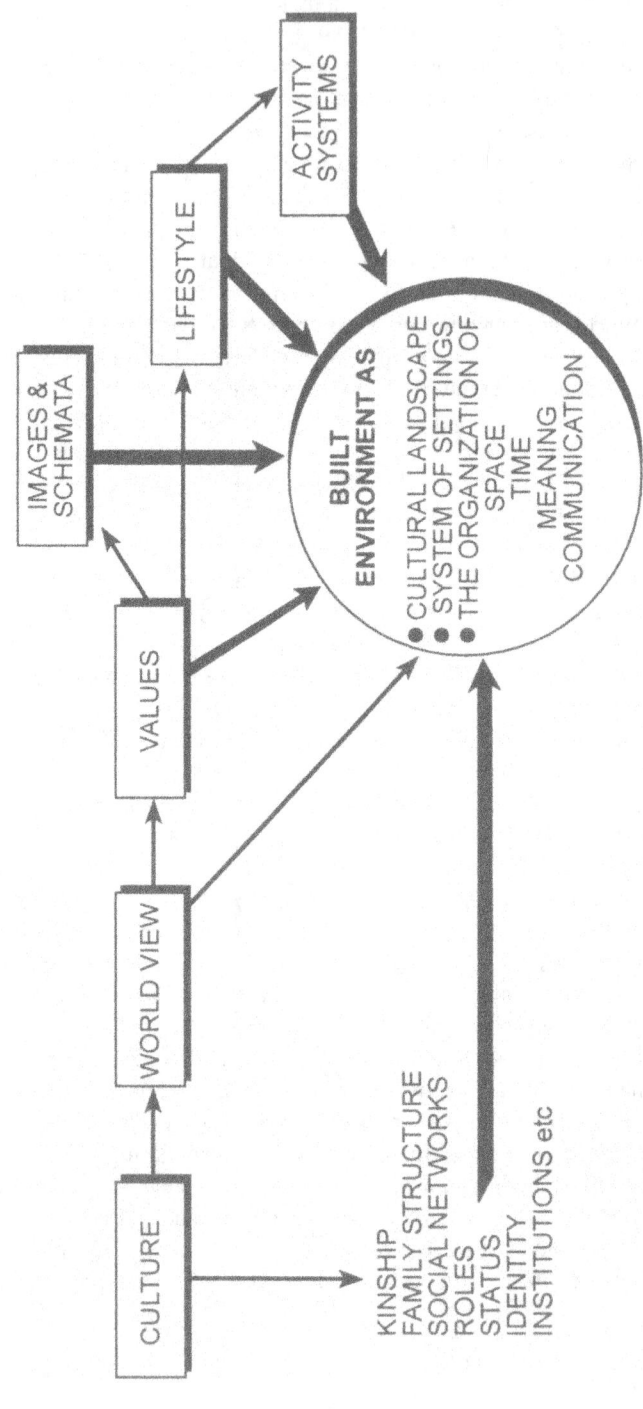

Figure 1.1 Relating expressions of culture to the Built Environment – the width of the arrows approximates feasibility and ease of relating the various elements. Based on Rapoport, 1993, Figure 1, p16 and in press b, Figure 3.

predict problems, for example that it will be more different for nomads to urbanise than it is for members of a group with urban traditions, with peasants intermediate, and that a role may be played by the existence of 'ready-made' units (Rapoport, 1983a, pp. 263 - 265 and Figure 10).

All these characteristics of 'people', and the many not discussed, become variably relevant and important depending on the situation, context or problem, in this case design for development in a given locale. In all cases, however, ideally these characteristics are reflected in and translated into environments through choices and actions of members of particular groups. In this, aspects of the Three Basic Questions interact, showing the usefulness of starting with them. For example, starting with the relevant human characteristics (question 1) and mechanisms (question 3), one can discuss the choices made regarding environments (whether migration, modification or design de-novo) - which are an aspect of the effect of environment on behaviour (question 2). The link is provided by supportiveness of the system of settings for both instrumental and latent aspects of activities, with latent often being the more important. Activity systems, as expressions of lifestyles and values and ultimately of culture, vary for different groups. As a result there are differences in the environmental quality selected by, and appropriate for, groups described by environmental quality profiles (Rapoport, 1990d). These may be groups as discussed so far, or the same group at different times (Rapoport, 1977, Figure 2.14, p.106; Sastrosasmita and Nurul Amin, 1990). Since design is intended to achieve 'better' environments or at least good ones, there is an immediate link with the physical environment and with design, as discussed later in this chapter. Note, finally that it is not at all self-evident what is a 'better' environment, and a similar process of analysis and dismantling, and use of empirical data is essential (Rapoport, 1983c, in press a).

'Place' - an analysis

Unlike the other terms which are difficult to use because they are vague due to excessive breadth and generality, the term 'place' is inherently vague and not useful. In fact I believe that despite its great and growing popularity it is not merely not useful but actually counterproductive. Since I have recently developed this argument in considerable detail (Rapoport, 1994a), I will merely summarise it here. I will also suggest an alternative, already existing framework and set of concepts which are more useful, can achieve whatever the use of 'place' is meant to achieve, and can do so more effectively.

Because of its growing popularity the term 'place' has been applied rather indiscriminately to extremely varied sets of situations. Not only has there been no advance or development in clarity but a deterioration, as ever new layers of meaning are added. The term is never clearly defined and when definitions are found they are illogical; the various dimensions or attributes of the term are never explicitly articulated; rather strangely, the physical environment, its qualities and ambience are neglected. Even worse, the physical environment and various reactions to it (cognitive, evaluative, affective, meaning etc.) are not clearly distinguished, and the term is used in many different, idiosyncratic and often inconsistent ways which makes it and any results confused and confusing. It is also used emotionally, subjectively and normatively, meaning whatever any given author wants it to mean. Essentially, it seems to describe individuals' (typically not users') personal preferences for, and evaluations of, particular locales, portions of cultural landscapes or systems of settings. Those liked become 'places' those disliked are described as 'placeless' or 'nonplaces'. This is both irrelevant and not useful, because one is not particularly interested in a given analyst's subjective interpretations and preferences. Moreover, 'placelessness' or 'nonplace' are an impossibility; those so described are merely environments that a given observer does not like, does not understand or regards as inappropriate, as is also the case with 'chaotic' environments (Rapoport, 1984, 1992a).

These are assertions and will not be supported here; the reader is referred to the rather detailed analysis mentioned earlier (Rapoport, 1994a). The conclusions of that analysis support the assertions above: that the term 'place' seems to be inherently ambiguous, and therefore vague, that it is unable to identify a clear, consensual concept or theoretical construct, even one requiring a polythetic definition (Rapoport, 1988, 1989, 1990a). Moreover, whatever attributes begin to emerge seem to be disparate and diverse, and do not 'hang' together, being inconsistent and belonging to different analytical categories.

In spite of the term being so flawed that, in my view, it should be given up, the interest in it suggests an attempt to get at something important. It seems that the term was introduced because of a feeling that something was missing when space, setting, milieu, street, plaza, dwelling or other terms were used. What seemed to be missing was a set of relationships between people and various systems of settings, whether these were sacred sites, landscapes, dwellings or neighbourhoods, a city or a country; or a work setting; or objects in these.[3] Such relationships can also be with 'mythical' or non-empirical environments, including ideal ones.

'Place' thus seems to be used primarily to draw attention to certain aspects of locales, spaces and settings which lead to people's affective, psychological, social, cultural, behavioural or meaning relationships with these environments. Yet the term 'place' commonly refers both to the space, setting or physical element and to people's evaluations of it, reactions to it and relationships with it. This confusion between physical environments and affective reactions or relationships various people might have with them at various times, creates an impossible situation. There is confusion between product and process, with 'place' referring to both. This usage actually interferes with the goal of drawing attention to these processes. At the same time the physical aspects of 'place', the objective environment, are also neglected.

Thus the intention of using 'place', to refer to particular environment-behaviour relationships, is made more difficult if not impossible, because such usage obscures and interferes with this goal. If the purpose of all this commotion about 'place' was to show that settings evoke responses in users, then it may be useful but is nothing new, and hardly worth the commotion. In my own work, for example, without ever using 'place',[4] it has proved possible to deal with ideal schemata represented in non empirical environments which often underlie the creation of physical environments; with the role of modification, personalisation and semi-fixed elements in establishing relationships between people and settings; with the communication of status and identity through cues and attributes which often add up to ambience (Rapoport, 1990, 1992c); with perception cognition, evaluation, preference and choice, and hence affective responses, with meanings; with activity systems including their latent aspects; with social and family relationships and networks as they influence and are influenced by physical environments; and with many other topics. It seems to be the case that everything necessary can be achieved without introducing the term 'place' which only confuses things. The use of the term can be interpreted as merely restating very unclearly my long-standing argument about the importance of associational aspects of the environment, about the centrality of latent functions (so that meaning may be the, or a, most important function), and about the primacy of affective responses.

There is, an alternative, more useful existing conceptual framework, which I have developed over the years. First, the term 'environment', also being too broad and too vague, needs to be dismantled. There are various ways of doing this: as the organisation of space, time, meaning and communication, or as sets of relationships between objects and objects, objects and people and people and people (Rapoport, 1977, 1983a, 1994b, in press b). Here I will use the concept of setting which, contrary to proponents of 'place', I regard as far more useful. The definition of setting itself needs elaboration, but I will use a minimal definition based on Barker and his followers, of a physical milieu with ongoing behaviour which is linked to cues in the milieu by cultural rules. In doing so I use the term generically, and combine Barker's approach with those of Goffman and others (Rapoport, 1990f.). It is also important to emphasise that the same space can be many different settings at different times. Such sequential use of space as different settings, and the co-occurence of multiple activities and behaviours within a single setting are typical of traditional societies and developing countries (Rapoport, 1989, 1994b; Payne, 1979). With the increase in scale and social and occupational complexity, settings become more specialised and often restricted to a single activity. There are, therefore, many more settings, separated one from the other and this process is most important in development (Rapoport, 1990b, 1992a; Kent, 1991; Sancar and Koop, 1989; Yellen, 1985). Under these conditions, but also more generally, settings cannot effectively be studied singly but only as systems of settings. This is because as activity systems occur in them, what happens or does not happen in some settings determines what happens or does not happen in others (Rapoport, 1986c, 1990b). The extent of such systems of settings must be discovered not assumed by following the systems of activities (Rapoport, 1990b), what has been called 'progressive contextualization' (Vayda, 1983). The specific settings involved, their centrality or importance, their sequences, linkages and separations, and the rules that apply (as well as the cues that communicate them), all need to be discovered and are highly culture-specific.

It then becomes necessary to identify the particular system of settings as physical entities embedded in the larger system of settings. The use of systems of settings has two major advantages in addition to being conceptually essential. First, it naturally and inevitably links different settings with one another: domestic, commercial, recreational, health, work and other settings. Second, it does so at different scales, from parts of buildings, through buildings, building groups, neighbourhoods, settlements and even regions, and emphasises the critical role of transitions. The arrangement of both then responds to the cultural specifics of the ways in which activity systems are distributed among settings.

The next step in this alternative to 'place' involves identifying the attributes of the resulting cultural landscapes and their corresponding ambience or character. One can then concentrate on the processes that relate these systems of settings to members of groups, explicitly defined and identified, in which one is interested. This is done, as described earlier, in terms of lifestyles, activity systems, social variables and other operational aspects of culture. These processes include perception, cognition, evaluation and action. Evaluation involves identifying the desired relationships between members of the group(s) in questions and the system of settings in terms of instrumental supportiveness, meanings, values, norms, ideal schemata and the like. This leads to the environmental quality of the particular system of settings being judged as positive, neutral or negative. As a result of these affective responses, certain decisions, choices, modifications etc. are made, and relationships established with these systems of settings, some of which may be those partly subsumed by 'place'.

More specifically any locality (place!) has a cultural landscape with a particular, more or less distinctive ambience or character which distinguished it from others and gives it some identity (Rapoport, 1992c). Note also that this identity of the environment may be linked to cultural or group identity (Rapoport, 1981; Duncan, 1981). The preservation of identity may be important -- and evidence of this concern, and the meaning and affect it carries, as well as its role in defensive structuring (a way in which groups respond to long term stress, which, if it can be achieved through the environment may avoid less desirable forms (Siegel, 1970; Rapoport, 1977, 1983a, 1990fl) suggests that it is important. This then makes it an important issue in dealing with development, and in this sense 'place' is linked to 'people' in terms of culture and identity (Rapoport, 1981, 1992c).

Once identified, the ambience or character of locales can be studied, as can the ways in which particular groups develop affective reactions to these, after evaluating them (not necessarily consciously) against values, norms, ideals, images, schemata and the like. Groups may know this locality only indirectly, through writings or illustrations -- or it may even by mythical. Group members can also experience such systems of settings as a function of their activity systems in the larger environment. Various characteristics of these comprise home ranges, core areas, territories and jurisdictions within which particular systems of activities occur within particular systems of settings. The totality of these various systems is what makes up the cultural landscape of the locality and its particular ambience.

Cultural landscapes and their particular ambience, once evaluated in terms of their environmental quality, have various meanings and may express group or individual identity or status. They also elicit positive or negative affective responses so that, in some cases members of some groups develop attachment to these locales or specific elements of them (settings, dwellings and possessions; associational aspects such as history or modernity and so on). One can then ask which causes communicate these various meanings, for example identifying a setting or system of settings as being 'place', having a 'spirit of place' or being 'homelike'. This often involves identifying the ideal schema, so that attributes of settings can be matched against it. Research can identify those attributes that communicate particular meanings (i.e. those subsumed under 'place'). Note that this process is highly general since all environments are evaluated.

The evaluation of some setting systems as positive is then what some call 'place' (or 'home', a particular type of place), but it is preferable to study the different relationships between the things being evaluated (dwellings, sites, spaces, landscapes, settings, etc. and their semi-fixed and non-fixed components, i.e. material culture) and occupants, i.e. the different groups at specific times, and what actions by designers might make such evaluations more positive. One can study change over time -- culture change, changes in lifestyle, values, ideals or images, so that historical and cross-cultural studies become possible. These are essential, since the things evaluated, the evaluations and hence also the relationships established are highly variable, even though the processes and mechanisms may be the same.

In other words, having defined the systems of settings and the group (at a given time) one can then study the interaction processes and resulting relationships such as evaluation, preference and choice, attachment and other psychological links, relation to status and identity, role of semi-fixed objects such as furnishings, decoration and other personalization, landscape elements and so on. One can thus study what kinds of relationships which people have to what attributes of which settings, why and through which mechanisms. Any such study then becomes a specific case of the three basic questions of EBS which greatly helps with cumulativeness and theory building. The use of already existing concepts is also extremely important for theory building, for unifying different bodies of literature and to maintain clarity and rigour.

This approach also avoids the confusion endemic to the literature on 'place' where processes and relationships, such as affect, are confounded with what the affect is directed to. Also, it enables negative affect to be studied, an aspect which is neglected by the literature which seems concerned only with positive affect. Yet there are certainly locales, settings, landscapes and ambience which are evaluated negatively and their attributes merit study rather than being dismissed as 'nonplaces' or examples of 'placelessness.'

'Development' - an analysis

In this section I return to a type of vagueness which is not inherent in the term, but which results from its excessive generality and broadness. The term 'development' can refer to, and be used in, a number of domains (embryology, psychology, exercise physiology, rhetoric etc.) Even in the domain under discussion it can have many different meanings. For one thing, although it tends to be applied to 'developing countries' it can be (and is) also applied to areas in developed countries e.g. the South of Italy, the North of Britain, parts of France or the United States; or to groups in such countries e.g. indigenous inhabitants of North or South America or Australia. The primary meaning seems to be economic, although with that are associated technological marketing, legal, political or infrastructural aspects. These latter begin to address the physical/built environment which I take to be our concern. But there is another way to look at development which is potentially of greater interest and utility for the theme of this book and for the framework which I am developing.

From the perspective of EBS, and given the emphasis on cultural variables and the culture-specific nature of environments, there is one characteristic common to developing countries although by no means restricted to them. From that perspective, 'development', 'modernisation' and other similar or related terms (which I will not discuss further) can all be seen as examples of culture change. More specifically, from my perspective, problems of development and modernisation can be seen as related not to change itself which is inevitable and hence 'natural' but with radical, abrupt and frequently excessively rapid culture change and change that often spans excessively large 'cognitive distances' in much too short a time. Such culture change is inherently stressful, as is the consequent need to change values, ideals, lifestyles, activity systems, meanings, images, ways of resolving conflict, social structures, institutions and roles; ways of working, time use and organisation, privacy norms, etc.. Rapid change is particularly stressful.

At the same time many, particularly new, environments in developing countries are notoriously stressful even in more general bio-social and psychological terms. It can also be shown that cultural variables are a very important although neglected aspect of stress (Rapoport, 1978). Moreover, because of the greater criticality of the situation in developing countries due to rapid culture change - other forms of stress, minimal resources and so on - environments play a more important role than elsewhere (Rapoport, 1983a, b).

Note a most important point. In terms of the model of culture-environment relations in section 1 (Figure 1.1) culture change can be conceptualised most usefully in terms of changes in lifestyles and activity systems related to values on the one hand, and in roles, family and kinship structures, institutions and other social variables on the other. Since changes in these although possibly slower and less drastic, and hence of lower criticality also occur in developed countries, this means that development is not a unique problem, but merely a more extreme example of a more general process. Recall also that with development and culture change the number of settings and their specialisation tend to increase. As a result systems of settings change. This means having to learn new cues and meanings, new rules about behaviour appropriate in given settings and hence new ways of behaving, new ways of organising space, time, meaning and communication, all of which add further to stress.

It follows that an important aspect of responding to development is then to modulate stress by modulating rates of change through manipulating the built environment. It should be noted that this position is not universally accepted. One view is that rapid change is not only acceptable but essential in order for transformation to the modem world to occur (Okoye, 1979; Meier, 1980). Another view is that the whole idea of culture-specific design is misguided, that people are adaptable and there is no need to worry (Sonnenfeld, 1976). If however my position is accepted, and I believe that the bulk of the evidence supports it, then, from the point of view of environmental design, this modulation of rates of change might be achieved by providing appropriate, i.e. highly supportive, possibly prosthetic environments. These may then play a key role in development as culture change.

The notion of cultural specificity also a plays a role in the process of culture change itself. I would suggest that the result of such change and hence of the resulting environments will not be, and should not be, to tend to a single model which is a 'copy of developed countries. Rather, such change should be (and typically tends to be if allowed, encouraged and helped) some form of cultural syncretism or creative synthesis which may often have counter-intuitive notions of appropriate environments and environment quality.[5]

Good environments for development are then best conceptualised in terms of supportiveness. This concept can be clarified by asking:

a)   What is being supported?
b)   By what is it being supported?
c)   How is it being supported i.e. the mechanisms involved?
                      (Rapoport, 1983a, 1990e, Part lll)

The answers to these questions are in turn related to bio-social, psychological and cultural characteristics of people. For our present discussion, as already suggested, the latter are those most directly involved and thus particularly important. In other words, it is the specifics of what is being supported, by what it is being supported and how, in a situation of culture change. This is not to minimise biological and physiological aspects such as pollution, dust, water quality, garbage and waste, nor bio-social and psychological aspects such as crowding, noise, perceptual and other considerations. These are generally important and often disregarded particularly in development. This also applies to cognitive and many other aspects.

To answer these questions and hence define or evaluate whether environments are supportive and hence desirable, one needs to identify the relevant group, describe and analyse its important characteristics and understand how these interact with various specified elements of the built environment. In general, what is supported are lifestyle and activity systems as well as social structures: kinship and family groups, institutions, rituals, language, food habits and many others including what are called 'intermediate institutions' or 'intermediate structures'. These are supported by various physical elements and settings at a variety of scales. It thus becomes necessary to identify the cultural specifics involved, over and above any more general aspects of supportive environments related to bio-social and psychological variables. The task then becomes to establish some crucial relations between aspects of culture and of supportive environments. It seems intuitively likely that in any given case certain aspects of culture will be more important than others. In any given case it is pragmatically necessary to establish some hierarchy and to deal with the most important aspects since one cannot deal with all. In all cases latent aspects - wants meanings and affect - must be considered.

It is, therefore, essential to be able to identify the most important, central elements of the culture. These could be called the elements of the culture core: those elements essential to the identity of the group both to itself and to others and hence to its continuity. There are also peripheral elements. Not only is it important to be able to distinguish between core and peripheral elements, one needs to identify those elements of the built environment which are supportive of the core cultural elements. Having identified the relevant group or groups in any given case, one needs to describe important characteristics of each and to try to understand how these interact with various components of the physical environment. In each case the question is: which elements of the culture core are supported? by what are they supported? how are they supported? In effect, the objective is to specify the environmental quality characteristics or profile and how that matches the lifestyle characteristics or profile of the group.

People, place and development - a synthesis

Note how at the end of the last section I had moved to 'design' i.e. the synthesis of the three terms. We have already seen at several points in this chapter that the three terms inevitably overlapped, although I tried to keep them separate. This shows how this approach and framework, through the particular process of analysis, dismantling and clarification seems to lead easily, inevitably and almost 'naturally' to synthesis. This seems significant and encouraging, and I will explicitly try to synthesise the three terms and trace some of the implications of the approach and develop the framework further. This will be rather brief because, as already emphasised, there is no attempt to be comprehensive. Furthermore, the analysis can be taken further and connections traced among the variables by anyone interested.

One thing that brings the three terms together is a normative position implicit in the theme of this book: that planning and design, the organisation of the physical/built environment that is 'placemaking', which follows from the changes wrought by development or in the context of the process called 'development' must respond to and be based on the wants and needs of the people affected; that is it must be in accord with their notions of environmental quality. Although this seems self-evident to some of us and to most of those reading this book it is, in fact, rather a radical position. In practice most design generally, and most development have almost completely neglected the human aspects of the built environment. Above all, they have neglected the potential stress-modulating and supportive role of the built environment under conditions of rapid change and high criticality. They have also neglected the cultural specificity of problems and solutions. Strangely, even when the cultural-specificity of certain agricultural, technological, health and other aspects of development are acknowledged, this is not reflected in issues of cultural landscapes and systems of settings i.e. dwellings, work settings, educational, health, recreational and other institutions. Neither are questions raised about how these are linked into culture-specific, supportive units -- building groups, neighbourhoods, settlements, systems of settlements and regions.

Yet, as I have tried to suggest, if one conceptualises the human aspects of development as culture change, and becomes aware both of the attendant stresses and possible modulating and supportive role of built environments, certain consequences follow which not only promise more humane environments for users. They may even have economic implications: there are at least some indications that settings properly organised may provide the extreme supportiveness in certain critical parts of the system that may help economic development where possibly supportiveness is more difficult (Boxer, 1969; Eidt, 1971) although I am not convinced that it is not possible even in the latter, and research is needed on culture-specific approaches and solutions there also.

As I have argued, this requires the preservation of culture-core elements, (social and cultural and their supportive physical settings) and their synthesis with, and possibly expressed in terms of, new peripheral elements. This is because of the high value given to modernity and its imagery, the cues such as building types, materials, technology etc. that communicate it; instrumental aspects of improved comfort and health, increased mobility and so on. It also requires a consideration of culture-core aspects at the larger scale of regional organisation (Adams, 1973), the role of the culture-specific ambience of locales in communicating group identity that is 'place' v 'placelessness'. This may also have implications for the riches of larger landscapes and even for economics through tourism (Rapoport, 1992c). It follows that development need not inevitably lead to the loss of identity which seems to be a fairly common concern, and not only in developing countries. As is common, developing countries merely provide a clearer example (Rapoport, 1983a; Barnard, 1984; Hakim, 1994; Akbar, 1988).[6] Another core element may be religion, and a consideration of such aspects of landscapes and sites, and even of land tenure may be most important (Tipple, 1987). Also critical may be not only how units at various scales are linked but the nature of the transitions between them which are often highly variable and culture-specific. There is also the possibility of using what I have called 'ready made' units, both physical and social such as Kampungs, Barangays and the like which are themselves more supportive (Rapoport, 1983a). They also allow for different, and possibly less destructive, more supportive and even more efficient forms of urban growth (Rapoport, 1977, Esp. Ch. 5 and Fig. 5.3, p.261, 1986b, 1987).

To reiterate, the relation among development, people and environments through design properly understood leads to culturally-specific i.e. variable solutions. These are a result both of the different cultural traditions as well as differential retention of old elements, selection of new elements and hence new syntheses. This is an aspect of development when seen within the proposed framework and, from this perspective, a critically important one, which has been almost completely neglected. In terms of my previous discussion this means that different groups will have different wants and possibly needs and will, therefore, choose different environmental quality profiles and, as a result, different provisions, standards and so on. These groups may be the ones I have been discussing e.g. 'cultural' groups. They may also be the same group at different stages and times in the development process. This has been little studied, but there is some recent empirical evidence in support of this position, from Jogjakarta, Indonesia and Australia which shows how highly group-specific approaches need to be (Sastrosasmita and Nurul Amin, 1990; Morel and Ross, 1993).

This clearly has implications for design in terms of open-endedness: Further and continuing change is part of the process and must be part of the solution as is the case more generally (Rapoport, 1990/91). Once again one finds that this approach to design is general, so that responses to development are only more 'extreme' than responses to other, more general problems. This point has already been made and is a most important aspect of this approach and I will discuss it briefly below.

Given all this, why have these issues been almost completely neglected. There are various reasons for this. One is the emphasis on purely economic aspects of development in the decisions and choices made (which=design). This goes hand-in-hand with a neglect of environment-behaviour considerations, and a lack of knowledge of how to use environment-behaviour information in design, and how to learn and derive precedents from what exists whether vernacular (Rapoport, 1982a, 1990a), from the past (Rapoport, 1990e), from spontaneous settlements (Rapoport, 1988) or from tradition (Rapoport, 1989).[7] This lack of knowledge is also due to the lack of developed theory in EBS generally, and based on this approach specifically. There are also some possible economic impediments and constraints as well as implementational ones. The latter are due both to users (Rapoport, 1983a, the chapter mentioned in fn.8) and to political decisions. I will discuss some of these very briefly in the conclusion. At this point I wish to make two other points.

The first has to do with the more theoretical implications of the approach. Without going into detail, it seems clear that by approaching the topic in this way, major insights can be gained which are relevant to EBS generally and in turn, make EBS relevant to this topic (c.f. Rapoport, 1990). This is a most important outcome. It means that mutual learning can occur from a great variety of situations, and that case studies and research from all of those become relevant and, as a result much stronger. Thus a single model is being developed which can be applied to all situations, as any real theory must do, as long as the relevant specifics are identified and introduced.

For example, the study of spontaneous settlements benefits from the study of vernacular design and in turn provides insights for understanding vernacular (Rapoport, 1988). Both of these, together with traditional high-style environments and those resulting from development, and an analysis of cultural landscapes, lead to very significant generalisations about planning and design in their broadest sense as the application of systems of rules, and raises questions about the sources of such rules (Rapoport, 1992a; Hakim, 1986, 1994; Akbar, 1988). It also raises questions about the distinction between selectionist processes typical of traditional environments and the instructionist processes typical of development and most contemporary built environments generally (Rapoport, 1986a, 1992b, in press a). It also raises further questions about whether and if so, how design might be understood in terms of designing rules and rule systems rather than designing environments directly, with implications for participation of users (Rapoport, 1992a). This is not the place to elaborate on this except to trace one further implication which I have already discussed. Developing countries raise problems which are general and, at the level of theory, concepts and process which apply elsewhere. This means that in addition to their intrinsic importance, the high criticality and severity of problems, they also have extrinsic importance. They make things clearer because situations are more extreme and, in this way, studying human aspects of built form in situations of rapid culture change and scarce resources that is development, provides a good point of entry into the study of EBR more generally as is also the case with vernacular (Rapoport, 1983a, 1990a).

The second point to be made in concluding this section is to discuss how EBR-based planning and design aspects of development might be carried out. Since this chapter is already too long, I can do no better than to refer to Rapoport, (1983a, pp.257-258). Although even there I do not deal with specific methods involved in discovering the information needed, with methods involved in programming or participation, with open-endedness and hence the design of frameworks, with how to handle transitions among subsystems of settings and scales, and so on. However, work on these topics with which I am familiar fits quite well and easily into the framework proposed. The synthesis can go on.

Conclusion

A great deal has been left out, but in the conclusion I very briefly address a topic which I explicitly excluded: economic, political and other implementational aspects. Not only are they not my area of expertise, but the chapter is already long and complex enough.

However, one is left with a question: this is all very well and good, but is it feasible, can it be implemented? My own very limited experience is not very encouraging. The few consulting reports along these lines were never acted upon or even considered. In being rejected, the views of users were not considered, yet there is evidence that users may reject many of the core elements which I have suggested are so critical. They may not want culture-specific design because of image, wrong materials, wrong spatial organisation (Martin, 1984) and so on. It may well be that the rejection of tradition is even more complete than at least I expected (Rapoport, 1983a, 1986a p.172ff, paper mentioned in fn.8). This may be because these core elements are at odds with the new peripheral elements. Under these conditions these core elements may need to be made more palatable by being expressed differently and, as it were 'stuck in'. I also sense a possible change in attitudes. A greater interest in, and concern with culture-core elements, questions of identity, of culture-specific institutions and environments. It is the duty of those working in this field to encourage such changes and developments without imposing them; there are even ideas for how this could be encouraged that could be generated, developed and tested. Research on these topics is also badly needed.

Among other reasons for rejecting this approach is the fear of the difficulty of actually doing it. This raises issues of teaching and research, of creating new types of practitioners. There is a need for researchers and for designers who are both willing and able to use such approaches and information, who think differently (Rapoport, 1986a, p.172). I might add that the course I teach on this approach, discussed briefly in Rapoport, 1983a suggests that difficulty is not a major problem.

Another possible impediment is, I suggest, economic. It is assumed that a concern with such matters will lead to delays because of research, analysis and the like and greater costs. Whether this is indeed the case and, if so whether there are ways of overcoming these are researchable questions and require research.

The major problem is, I suspect, political and ideological. It is widely held that 'different' means 'unequal', so that any approach which emphasises different environments for different groups is inherently unacceptable. Neither governments nor international agencies are prepared to accept different environments on ideological grounds; nor are they feasible politically. Furthermore, culture-specific planning and design imply group-specific i.e. homogeneous areas which seem to be even less acceptable or feasible. There is also a fear of generating group conflict and interfering with building national identity -- a major problem in many developing countries.

But let me conclude by tackling a somewhat easier question, that of 'different means unequal'. I have recently begun to speculate, on the basis of pretty total ignorance, about a possible solution which also relates to current issues of group identity, local control and so on. I propose it merely as something to be discussed and possibly worthy of research by those competent to do it.

Assume that there are various groups 'people' in a development situation which, in terms of my version of the theme of this book, require rather different environments 'places'. Assume further that they must be seen as being treated equally. Would it be at all feasible to make sure that each group receives the same level of funding per-capita, but is allowed to allocate it differently in creating appropriate specific systems of settings/cultural landscapes, expressing different meanings, wants, needs, choices and priorities: different environmental quality profiles?

This seems to me to be a question worthy of consideration and investigation if the basic premises of this chapter are accepted. It raises one immediate problem: it does not solve the issue of homogeneous areas mentioned above. It also raises other interesting and no doubt difficult questions about how such varied environments might fit into larger regional, super-regional and national frameworks both physical i.e. infrastructure and legal i.e. codes, standards and regulations, as well as how homogeneous areas will 'add up'. But this is inevitable - this is the nature of research, and I will leave you with these questions and, I hope, others that my approach has generated.

Notes

1. This I propose to discuss in a book in progress, *Theory in Environmental Design*.
2. There are a number of reasons for the need for such explicit, disciplinary analysis (Rapoport, 1990c). One which is significant here, but which I cannot elaborate, is the change from selectionism to instructionism which is characteristic of the change from traditional to contemporary ways of creating environments (Rapoport, 1986a, 1992b, in press a).
3. Note that terms such as sacred, landscape, dwelling, neighbourhood or city also require clear definition, dismantling and operationalisation (Rapoport, 1977, 1982b, 1990b, 1992a).
4. I actually did use it once (Rapoport, 1975) because the question was posed in these terms. It would be easy to rewrite that paper without using 'place' and without any loss.
5. Note that there is a literature on the possible outcomes when two cultures meet and development as culture change can be thus conceptualised. These outcomes can be listed, discussed and studied; this I will not do in this paper.
6. Thus, for example, government policy in France in the 1970s, which was intended to redress regional economic disparities, led to a loss of regional identity, as I pointed out during discussions there at the time.
7. There are many problems with learning from tradition which I will be discussing in a keynote paper at the conference in Tunis, December 16-20. 1994.

2 'Uneven development' of people and places:
Outline of a theory of built form

Necdet Teymur

Introduction and summary

It is quite proper to *associate* social, economic and cultural development of societies with changes in built form, space and settlements. However, it is a demonstrable fact that, contrary to a commonly held tendency to separate out these two domains in order to correlate them afterwards, the latter are *intrinsically*, but also *inevitably*, related to the former. Moreover, they are often inseparable instances or components of each other.

A basic recognition of this integral 'association' is obviously preferable to either of the two opposite, but equally untheorized, notions prevalent among architects, urban planners and policy makers: the first notion is that buildings and cities are *autonomous* works of design(ers) and have little to do with society The second is that buildings and cities *reflect* society. In either case, the types of relationship believed to prevail are considered self-evident, not needing proof or argumentation. Additionally, because of the causal model that they subscribe to, both positions fail to give adequate accounts of changes and developments in these societies and their physical components. For, the societies, their components and elements and the changes in them are fundamentally *complex, integrated, glocal, unequal and 'uneven'*.

The five concepts referred to constitute the basis of a theoretical framework introducing the composite notion of *uneven development in social space, built form and built culture*. In outline, this theory suggests that as complex and contradictory systems, architectural and urban forms as well as the whole range of social phenomena are *unevenly* constituted, they *unevenly* change and *unevenly* interact within themselves and with respect to other systems.

The implications of this formulation (the social side of which has been around for a long time in social and political theory) are not confined to the theoretical or critical discourses alone. A shift of thinking in that direction might enable us to understand, analyze, study, teach and represent socio-spatial reality on a more rigorous footing. It might even have some influence on problem definition, policy formulation, decision making, planning, design, education and research on localities, built forms, space and social formations!

Some cases of *'unevenness'* in science, culture, history and the built form

• **Case 1:** History is full of examples of societies in different periods making significant advances in various technological, scientific, political and artistic areas. What is not, however, equally recognized is that the so-called 'rise and fall' paradigm of historical discourse tends to ignore the geographical, chronological, sectoral and epistemological *unevenness* inherent in the way the 'rises' and 'falls' take place.

To put it simply,

i. no society has ever been *equally* advanced in all aspects of life, or
ii. developed or undeveloped at equal speeds in every location and at all levels,
iii. nor have the particular elements or aspects of these societies ever developed or declined internally in an even manner.

Added to this complexity is the fact that the definitions of what is and is not 'development', 'advancement' or 'decline' are themselves culturally and historically relative.

The well known case of the ancient Greek society embodying within it some extraordinary achievements in art and science coexisting with a slave society can be extended to today's 'developed' even 'post-industrial' societies displaying unbelievable strains of primitive thought, lack of education and wisdom and most anti-social social behaviour.[1]

For more current examples, one need not go further than the *unevenness* of the contemporary civilisation that produces, harbours and condones the (un)peaceful co-existence of such things as the unprecedented quantity and sophistication of knowledge that is only accessible to and benefiting a small proportion of humanity; racial, economic and urban apartheid, virtual reality, consumerism, mass starvation, pollution, electronic wars, ethnic cleansing, chronic unemployment, well-endowed high culture and poverty of all sorts - all these accompanied by broken pediments and lots of broken promises.

• **Case 2:** Specific scientific and technological developments, including some in building production, contribute to but also hinder each other. However, there is seldom a temporal or locational correspondence between the occurrence of knowledge, theories, inventions, innovations, availability of tools, realisation of theories or designs, normalisation of prototypes and inclusion of the new into the mainstream.

For example, a number of theories about the universe (e.g. Theory of Relativity) had to wait decades or longer until adequate tools of observation and calculation could emerge for their *empirical* confirmation. Computers have indeed been designed in the 19th century but could not be built without the calculating power and precision of modern computers as well as the methods of computer-controlled manufacturing of components making the building of a computer designed in the 19th century possible. [2]

• **Case 3:** Societies which, at various stages of their histories, managed to establish highly developed urban settlements called 'cities' may be finding the burden of the heritage too complex, difficult and expensive to continue planning, maintaining and operating them comprehensively in ways that would equally benefit all the inhabitants. Even as the originators and builders of these artifacts, 'developed' urban societies may now be lacking adequate knowledge and competence to cope with the *complexities* of such cities, the resources to invest in them and a vision to plan them forward.

Furthermore, the technologies of urban life too tend to embody some inherent contradictions which increase the discrepancy referred to. While, for example, what appears to be 'primitive' by today's standards might serve urban life with a high degree of economic, cultural and aesthetic sustainability, most up-to-date interventions might lack those qualities. The cast iron service lids or man-hole covers from the Victorian times, which still serve electric and gas installations in the streets of London, competing with cheap plastic ones put in place for advanced fibre-optic cables (- and that through shoddy workmanship) is a case in point.

From a very different historical perspective, the experience of new mega-cities that emerged in 'less-developed' countries demonstrate the same principle: superficially attaining the size, scale or the appearance of the big cities in 'developed' countries, or in part sheltering life styles and consumption patterns reminiscent of those in richer countries, these cities are even more unknowable, unplannable and unresourcable than their 'developed' counterparts.

In both cases, whatever interpretations of the past and the present of particular cities might be offered and whatever architectural styles or control technologies might be highlighted as evidence of achievement, what is self-evident is the determining presence of the *unevenness* in built form, spatial settlement, social organisation, urban technologies, ecological balance, planning techniques, management and urban culture within themselves and with respect to each other.

• **Case 4:** Even the most cursory experience of living in a modest building or a small city - let alone designing, planning, building or studying one, would confirm the obvious fact that buildings, hence settlements, cities and built form in general are complex, complicated and multi-layered objects. This obvious fact, however, is not borne by the ways in which built form are represented, written about, evaluated, discussed, taught and designed. Even when the complexity is recognised, there is often an underlying attitude dominated by generalities, reductionism and minimalism treating built form as easily knowable, classifiable, designable or buildable.

Against this, the physical and social reality of built objects suggests a profound unevenness in the make-up, composition, history, change ageing, interaction of their *whole* as well as their *parts*. To put it graphically, the bricks, the concrete, the plastics, the pipes, the wires, the insulation, the carpet, the columns, the spaces, the inside and the outside of even a simple building are of different order and complexity. They are subject to different laws of nature; they are the objects of different modes of appropriation, are represented in different media and known in different terms, and are ultimately *understood* within different cultural, disciplinary and professional paradigms which themselves are not equally developed.

Any change in one part or component of any built object not only makes many historical, stylistic or discursive generalisations redundant, but each change exerts effects on all other aspects differentially.

In short, built forms remain uneven phenomena by their very nature even when they are referred to by simple generalisations such as 'Architecture', 'Classical' or 'Post-Modern'.

From cases to a theoretical tool

Examples can be extended in order to draw attention to the fact that they are all around us if we can or want to see them. In a field where borrowed local theories, absence of theories, anti-theoretical attitudes and journalistic scholarship variously dominate our discourse and partly our education, a concise, non-local theory could be what we may need to advance our thinking and research. The theory that is presented here is *a theory to think with* and *by* rather than one to solve untheorised socio-technical problems associated with ill-defined objects and objectives. It is applicable to our thinking, argumentation, research formulation, teaching practice and design activity in a way that operates at unconscious as well as at meta levels.

A theory of *unevenness* pertaining to built form

To start theorizing the relationship between developments in social and built phenomena we need concepts such as *complexity*, *integratedness*, *glocalism*, *unequalness* and *'unevenness'*. It is then necessary to identify the most basic ontological and epistemological characteristics of the objects in hand. These would be the premises of what I call the *'multi-theory of built form'* (*m-T*) and *'n-theory of built form'* (*n-T*). n-T acknowledges and deals with the n-dimensions and n-elements of the built form while m-T is the theory of multiple disciplines, paradigms, methods and media not however as an after-thought but by its very constitution.[3]

It must be noted that unlike many theories of nature or of knowledge, the more the following propositions appear to be obvious, simple and commonplace, the more likely it is that we are onto something worth pursuing, for if they are already agreeable premises, all we then have to do is to build our discourse upon them.

Key axioms for an n-theory and multi-theory of *complex, integrated* and *glocal unevenness*

I

- Nothing is even. Everything is uneven - including our understanding of them.
- Nothing is pure, in a 'primitive' state, uncontaminated, undiluted or original.
- Nothing is simple. Everything is complex.

II

- No two things are the same.
- Nothing and no built form is absolutely unique.

III

- Everything belongs both (not *either*) to a place and (not *or*) to other places at the same time. In other words, everything is *'glocal'* that is, *both* local *and* global.[4]
- No two localities are the same, nor are they completely different.
- The localities and their properties, elements and aspects change, evolve, get transformed and develop *unevenly*, that is, at different speeds, rates and in different directions.
- Different localities contextualize and affect different aspects of different phenomena differently. This contextualization is itself *glocal* and *uneven*.

IV
- 'Architectural', 'urban' and other built objects are made up of, or come about as a result of the combinations of, *n number* of elements, agents, forces, intentions, objectives, representations and relations which *are at different degrees of complexity and development* and *at different orders* with respect to *each other and to other objects or systems* in their *locality, globality* and *glocality*.
- The elements, components, agents, forces, representations, ... can themselves be described in terms of the *n-theoretical* and *multi-theoretical* characteristics outlined above. In other words, each element of the built object or other objects and their contexts and relations are themselves *not* pure, even, simple etc.
- ....

From meta-theory to a theoretically informed research, education and design

The conceptual space provided by the axiomatic theory above is as much theoretical as it is practical - to use a traditional dichotomy. Being a meta theory, it carries with it neither the built-in limitations of local theories borrowed from particular disciplines such as sociology, anthropology, physics, biology, etc. nor the pragmatic requirements of practical occupations such as architecture, planning or engineering.

A meta-theory of built form that highlights the complexity of the objects and the unevenness of their development enables the practitioners of design, research and education to think about built form and society in terms of ever-increasing possibilities. I call this *'epistemological maximalism'* (or, in education, *'pedagogic maximalism'*). This is in marked contrast to *professional* attitudes to design, planning, research and education that favour solving given problems with as little knowledge and with as few questions as possible. I call this *'epistemological minimalism'* or, *'professional minimalism'*. [5]

Once *complexity, integratedness, glocality* and *unevenness* are recognised and are made the parameters of our perception and thinking, the problems might become somewhat less easily solvable, yet more *appropriate* to the phenomena in hand. In research, knowledge would be produced in an open-ended fashion without either looking over one's shoulder or watching out report submission dates. In an educational context teaching and learning would go beyond narrow professional goals and become more *educational*.

A conclusion

A conclusion of the sort expected of traditional academic papers would be a contradiction in terms in an intellectual paradigm, a research programme and a pedagogic ideal informed by an *n-theoretical* and *m-theoretical* understanding of our objects and their development as outlined above.

Notes and references

1. The paradoxical nature of the Ancient Greek society and its art has been pointed out and the concept of 'unequal development' has first been used 140 years ago by Karl Marx in his *A Contribution to the Critique of Political Economy*, 1859, Lawrence & Wishart: London, 1971, pp. 214-17). Similar cases of stupendous achievements of societies that would be considered 'undeveloped' by today's standards keep puzzling us.
2. For a brief description of Charles Babbage's 'Difference Engine' of the 1820s and 'Analytical Engine' of the 1830s, later called 'calculating machine', see *The New Joy of Knowledge Encyclopaedia*, Oriole Publishing Ltd.: London, 1989, v.2, p.84 and v.20, pp.1176-77.
3. *'n-theory'* and *'m-theory'* are concepts that I have been developing for some time and am hoping to articulate further in a book being prepared for publication.
4. *'Glocal'* is a concept first introduced in Teymur, N., *Architectural Education*, Question Press: London, 1992, pp.39-48.
5. cf. Teymur, N., 'Learning Housing Designing: the *home-less* design education', in Bulos, M. and Teymur, N. (eds), *Housing: Design Research Education,* Avebury: Aldershot, 1993, pp. 3-27.

3 Development alternatives of the human ecosystem:
An integrative and comprehensive approach

Anis-Ur-Rahmaan

Introduction

The human ecology is concerned with the interrelationship among people and their spatial setting. The pertinent literature does attempt to detail the various aspects of human ecosystem in terms of its basic elements, viz., population, social organisation, environment, technology and social-psychological factors (Gist and Fava, 1974, p.151). However, most of these endeavours are descriptive rather than prescriptive or therapeutic in nature and therefore, have limited applied utility for socio-physical development. These conceptualisations highlight the dynamics of the ecosystem generically, and fall short of incorporating the interactive planning and development mechanism into a single framework.

In order to increase the applied utility of the interactive development framework, three imperatives manifest themselves. First, due to the complex nature of the ecosystem development, the framework should be developed hierarchically; second, the apex of the hierarchy should be composed of the seminal determinants dealing with both the potential and procedural aspects of socio-physical development; and third, the framework should provide for the mutual and iterative interaction of the seminal determinants.

The ensuing portion of this chapter has been divided into four parts. Part one attempts to modify the salient elements of the human ecosystem into the seminal determinants of socio-physical development, and form them into an integrative framework. Part two attempts to identify various parameters of each determinant of socio-physical development and their inherent variations. Part three attempts to generate a number of explorative alternatives for the development of the human ecosystem, and also deals with their feasible and normative dimensions. Finally, part four highlights the salient conclusions of the study.

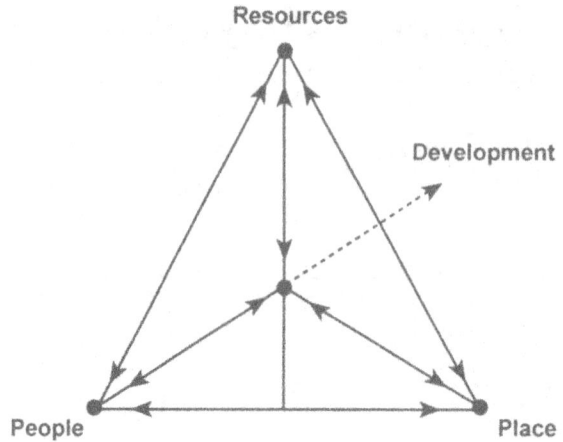

Figure 3.1 Prismatic framework providing for the interaction of seminal determinants of socio-physical development.

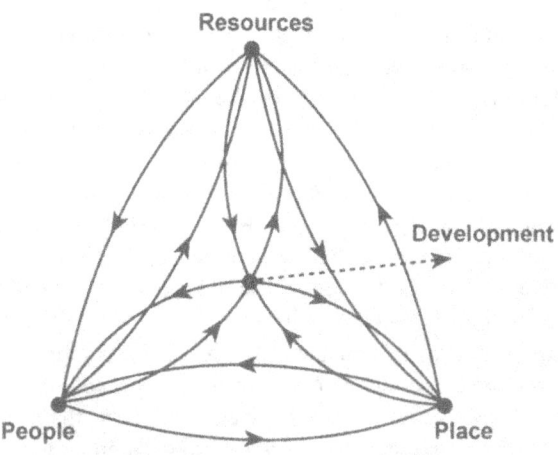

Figure 3.2 Cyclical interaction between the seminal determinants of the socio-physical development process.

An integrative framework for socio-physical development

The generally accepted five basic elements of the human ecosystem, mentioned in the preceding section, though important in their own right, do not provide for the processes of planning and development per se. These elements need to be modified and rearranged into an integrative hierarchy providing for the mutual and iterative interaction of the seminal determinants of socio-physical development.

The determinants of socio-physical development have been identified as 'People', 'Place', 'Resources' and 'Development'. Figure 3.1 shows that a prismatic framework is best suited for the integrative interaction of the four determinants because each of these determinants is directly linked with the remaining three determinants. It may, however, be pointed out that Figure 3.1 presents an oversimplified version of the mutual interaction between these determinants. In the real world, each of the determinant is interlinked with the other through a cause and effect relationship. Each of them influences and is influenced by each other, either implicitly or explicitly; for instance, the functions of the inhabitants (people) and the form of the habitat (place) iteratively assume cause and effect roles. On some occasions it appears that form is following the functions, and on others functions appear to be following the form; and sometimes, they appear to be interlinked by the phenomenon of circular causation! The same is true of the interaction between other determinants. Figure 3.2 presents the cyclical interaction between the four seminal determinants of socio-physical development.

Parameters and typologies of developmental determinants

The nature, magnitude and speed of socio-physical development is a function of a function. Although it appears to be the direct outcome of the four interacting determinants, yet each of these determinants is dependent on their respective sets of parameters. For illustrative purposes Figure 3.3 indicates three salient parameters of each of the four determinants of socio-physical development. For instance 'People' can best be understood in terms of their salient parameters such as social organisation, social-psychological factors and population density/size. All these parameters are interactive: social organisation is a function of social-psychology which in turn is influenced by population density/size in a given cultural setting; and population density/size also interacts manipulatively with the social organisation.

Likewise, 'Place' which is the receptacle of all human activity systems may require a variety of physical media including land, water and space. Similarly 'Resources' are of no less importance and may be better visualised in terms of human, financial and technological potentials of a social system.

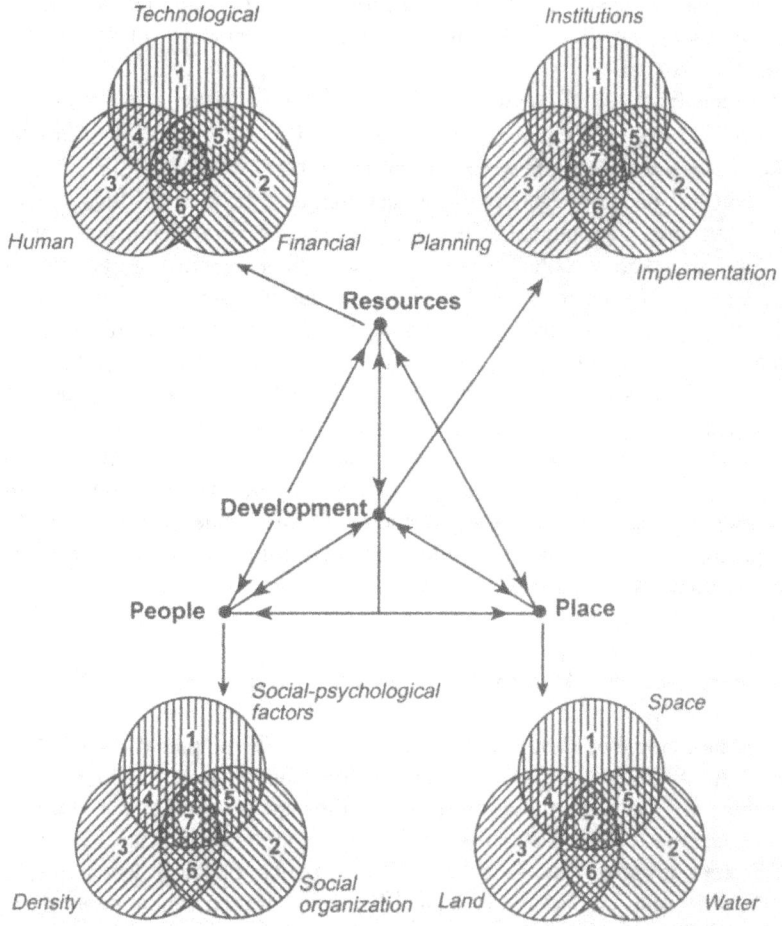

Figure 3.3 Salient parameters of determinants of socio-physical development.

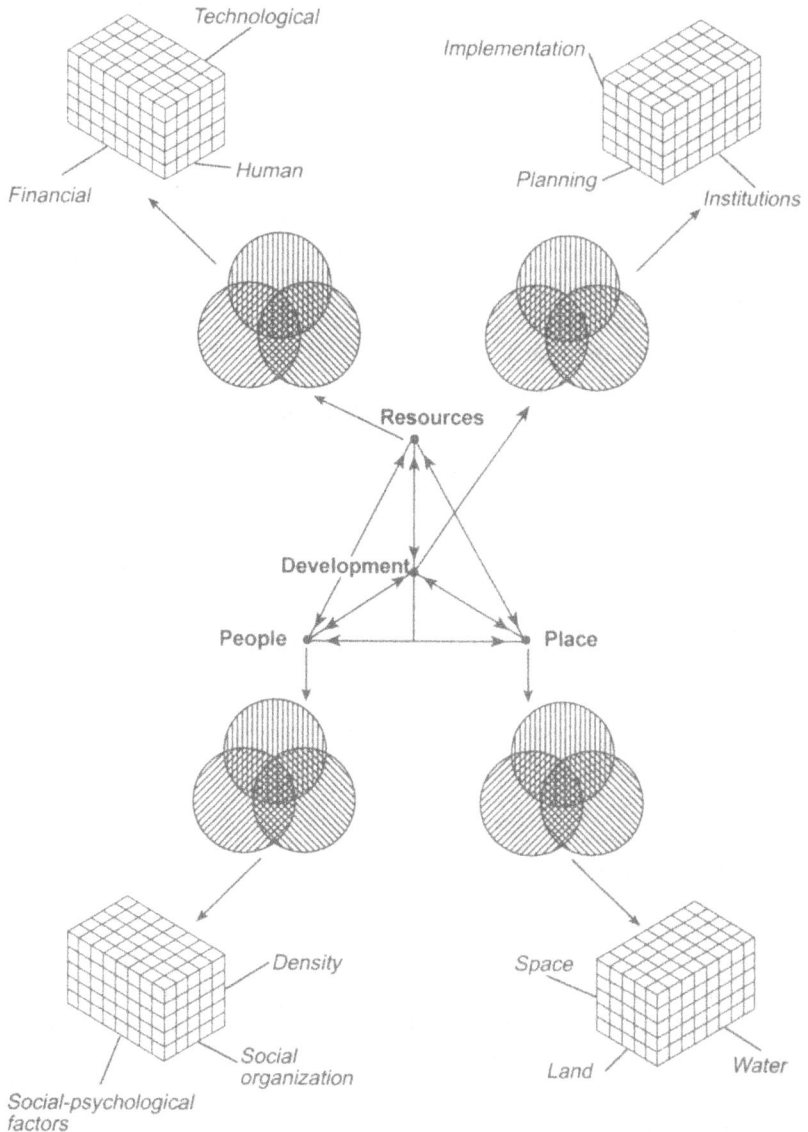

Figure 3.4 Parametric variation due to cultural, technological, climatic and topographic changes.

Lastly, 'Development' could be conceptualised as the actualisation of the planning process through the institutional set-up, and reflects the political ambitions of a community or its power elites. The salient parameters of 'Development' have therefore, been identified as: Planning, Implementation, and Institutional Set-up. The various sets of interacting parameters influence the determinants either severally or in a combination of two or even jointly. These parameters variously dominate each other and differentially affect the socio-physical development of a human ecosystem. Depending on their nature and extent of their availability or otherwise they may prove to be either a potential or a constraint. As illustrated in Figure 3.3 each set of three parameters results in seven typologies, leading to a total of twenty eight parametric typologies pertaining to the four determinants of socio-physical development.

The situation is further complicated by the fact that each parameter undergoes variations due to cultural, technological, climatic and topographical changes. An idea of the number of parametric variations may be formed by considering a hypothetical case. An assumption that each parameter undergoes five variations would be subjected to 125 variations in each of the four parametric sets as indicated by the cubes in Figure 3.4. Each of the smaller 125 cubes represents a set of parameters which would further lead to seven typologies due to their several, combinational and joint interactions. One hundred and twenty five variations coupled with seven typologies in each parametric set would amount to 875 inputs for each of the four determinants of socio-physical development.

This was, however, an oversimplified hypothetical example which dealt with only three salient parameters and only assumed five variations in each of them. In a real world situation, with numerous cultural settings, climatic zones and technological levels, the number of parametric typologies and their inherent variations would generate manifold increase.

Development alternatives of the human ecosystem

Having conceptualised an integrative framework for socio-physical development, and highlighted the dynamics of its parameters in the last two sections, this section will attempt to generate development alternatives of the human ecosystem. The technique of morphological analysis[1] will be used for the generation of various alternatives. This technique provides for 'identifying, indexing, counting and parametrizing of a wide range of variations' (Ayres, 1969, p.72). In this technique different options are generated by combining various attributes of a number of mutually exclusive sets of parameters.

The advantage of generating explorative alternatives is that they afford access to a large number of options which would have otherwise been ignored and that the 'process of synthesising alternative solutions in morphological analysis is systematic, the biases and prejudices held by the person using the tool are avoided while generating ideas'(Delp, 1977, p.10).

The list of various determinants and parameters developed in the previous section has been further enlarged and scrutinised for its mutual exclusiveness. Variations for each of the parameters have also been further refined. Table 3.1 shows the revised list of mutually exclusive parameters of socio-physical development along with their variations. Parameters 1-5 represent one or the other functional aspects of 'People'; 6-8 deal with 'Place'; 9 deals with 'Resources'; and 10-12 deal with 'Development'. Twelve parameters and their respective variations, shown in the table lead to 1,959,552 explorative alternatives. However, many of these combinations may be physically, if not theoretically, impossible or meaningless. However, sometimes 'even illogical combinations may trigger feasible solutions'(Delp, 1977, p.11).

Although it is not possible to describe such a large number of alternatives, much less to evaluate them for their feasibility or otherwise for a specific real world situation, yet it may be worthwhile to pick-up at least one alternative and highlight its attributes. The dotted line in the table indicates the parametric attributes of the selected alternative. It represents an ecosystem which will be intensive as well as extensive in its physical character with a mix of high, mid and low-rise structures, built on the ground as well as underground, and extending into the sea semi-submerged, with detachable floating suburbs, and orbiting industrial satellites in space, augmented by outstations on Mars.

The social organisation of the selected ecosystem will be based on the principle of universalism rather than communalism or pluralism. Functionally, it may be characterised as socially integrated rather than socially segregated; and therefore, the controversial concepts of 'exclusionary' or 'inclusionary' zoning will become meaningless. As the entire ecosystem will work as one community, economic activities would locate on the basis of absolute rather than comparative advantage,[2] and as a consequence, the economic base of the various nuclei of the ecosystem will be specialised rather than diversified. Although the ecosystem will be interplanetary in nature, yet due to a revolutionary breakthrough in communication technology, the friction of distances will be reduced to a minimum. Due to the erosion of the friction of distances, the locational contiguity of human activity systems will lose its significance, and therefore the physical development may follow a pattern which may be described as 'decentralised concentration'.

The various units of the ecosystem will be integrated by means of a very efficient electronic mail network. People will not have to move every time they change a job - it will simply require a change of computer terminal (Toffler, 1982, p.204). The various districts of the ecosystem will be endowed with a surplus of energy due to uninterrupted solar radiation in the space colonies and atomic fusion on various planets. The problem of solid waste disposal would also be obviated as most of it would be recycled. Peak hour traffic will no longer pose a problem as the places of residence and work are going to be combined in the electronic cottage (Toffler, 1982, p.195); and even the universities may start imparting education electronically.

Obviously the scenario of the selected human ecosystem appears highly utopian. But the same impression was created by most of the innovative development concepts propounded in the fifties and sixties. However, due to the accelerative pace of technological advancements, some of these concepts have either already been surpassed or are being outlived. For instance, Frank Lloyd Wright's proposal for a mile high city put forth in the fifties for Chicago's Lake Front (Blake, 1956, p.129) has already been dwarfed by the 'Volcano City' project proposed to be built by the Japanese on an artificial island approximately four miles in diameter. The volcano-shaped city, inspired by Japan's Mount Fuji, would allow its inhabitants in the upper levels to look down on the clouds below them. Exceeding the height of 2.5 miles, the one building city would accommodate up to 700,000 people. Facilities housed above the one-mile mark would include a nature and space observatory, an energy plant and a resort. The lower levels would hold marine resorts, as well as marine-based farms to make the facility more self-sufficient. The building comprises three circular frames: the outer frame would be used for residential facilities, the middle for business and commercial needs, and the inner to serve as a headquarters for administrative personnel (Conway, 1993, p.30).

Likewise, Doxiades' transnational and non-racial 'Ecumenopolis', which envisaged that the world's population will live in one universal city by the end of twenty-first century (Doxiades, 1986, pp.377, 430), will perhaps start spilling over into the sea and into space much before the end of twenty-first century. Some of the incipient concepts, mainly tabled by the Japanese are already on the horizon. For instance, the Japanese are suggesting floating islands which could serve as an alternative to creating new coastal space by landfills. One such proposed project, called Floating Station 'Jonathan' could be moored in deep water and accommodate scientific and recreational facilities, including a 1,000-room luxury hotel. Another artificial island proposed by Japan's Taisei Corporation could be used in relatively shallow waters. The man made island, nicknamed 'Never-Never Land' would rest on the sea floor and be accessible by either boat, helicopter, or an underwater tunnel connected to the mainland (Conway, 1993, p.32). Commenting on the supercities, Conway has opined: 'Whether the super macro engineering projects of the future tower past the clouds or brave the ocean depths, neither the sky nor the deep may limit the potential of tomorrow's supercities'(Conway, 1993, p.33)!

Viewed against the backdrop of the aforementioned innovative projects currently in the pipeline, and the accelerative technological advances, the development alternative of the human ecosystem, described in this section does not appear as theoretical as it did at the outset. It may indeed be one of the feasible alternatives for the Universal City of the twenty-first century, and perhaps an up-dated version of Doxiades' Ecumenopolis!

Conclusions

This chapter takes a holistic view of the development of the human ecosystem by visualising it as a composite of four determinants: People, Place, Resources and Development and employs the technique of morphological analysis for generating the explorative development alternatives of the human ecosystem. Table 3.1 shows the parameters of socio-physical development and their respective attributes and indicates that combinations of the various attributes lead to 1,959,552 explorative development alternatives of the human ecosystem. The chapter does not go into the specifics, such as the feasibility and normative analyses of highly theoretical development alternatives of the human ecosystem. However, that was neither the purpose nor it is possible to carry out any pragmatic analysis without detailed information about the culture, social organisation, physical environment, resources, institutional set-up and political aspirations of a given social system.

The main thrust of this chapter is conceptual rather than empirical. It provides an approach rather than a solution. Solutions, indeed, should be the last thing which planners should look for. Although the fact of the matter is that the planners, in their desire to achieve the goal, become impatient and resort to the deductive approach which is based on convergent thinking. The deductive approach is indeed scientific, mathematical and logical. Nevertheless in the process, unconsciously or subconsciously, planners end-up projecting the future incrementally rather than creating it and advocate solutions which are rather subjective. At worst they act like politicians and decision makers and at best, they act like Churchill's scientific advisor who, due to his subjectivity, failed to recognise the potential of the V-2 rocket which was identified by the morphological analysis and had already been secretly developed by the Germans.[3] The pursuit of the inductive approach, which involves divergent thinking, is also not right because it leads to artistic, less orderly and theoretical solutions which may be remote from reality. Planning being a scientific art, needs to combine both the approaches. As rightly pointed out by Faludi, 'when combined, convergent and divergent thinking enable truly creative responses to an ever changing environment in a way which neither of the two would be capable of providing on its own' (Faludi, 1976, p.118). Figure 3.5 provides the desired combination of both inductive and deductive approaches in order to identify innovative solutions which will not only be feasible and normative but also acceptable to the decision makers.

Table 3.1 Morphological analysis for the generation of development alternatives of human ecosystem.

	Determinants/Parameters	Variations (attributes)						
1	Social organisation	Communalism	Pluralism	Universalism				
2	Social-psychological aspects	Socially integrated	Socially segregated					
3	Density of population	Low	Medium	High				
4	Size (hierarchical level)	Village	Town	City	Metropolis	Megalopolis	Gigalopolis	Ecumenopolis
5	Economic base	Diversified	Specialized					
6	Place	Land based	Underground	Floating on water	Underwater	Space	Planets	Land & water	Land, water & space	Land, water, space & planets
7	Density of development	Low-rise	Mid-rise	High-rise	A mix of L, M & H-rise			
8	Pattern of development	Concentration	Decentralis-ation	Decentralised concentration				
9	Technological/human & financial resources	Low	Medium	High				
10	Planning	Normative	Functional					
11	Implementation	Turnkey project	Phased development	Phased programme				
12	Institutional Set-up	Public	Private	Autonomous	Semi-autonomous			

Number of alternatives = 3 x 2 x 3 x 7 x 2 x 9 x 4 x 3 x 3 x 2 x 3 x 4 = 1,959,552

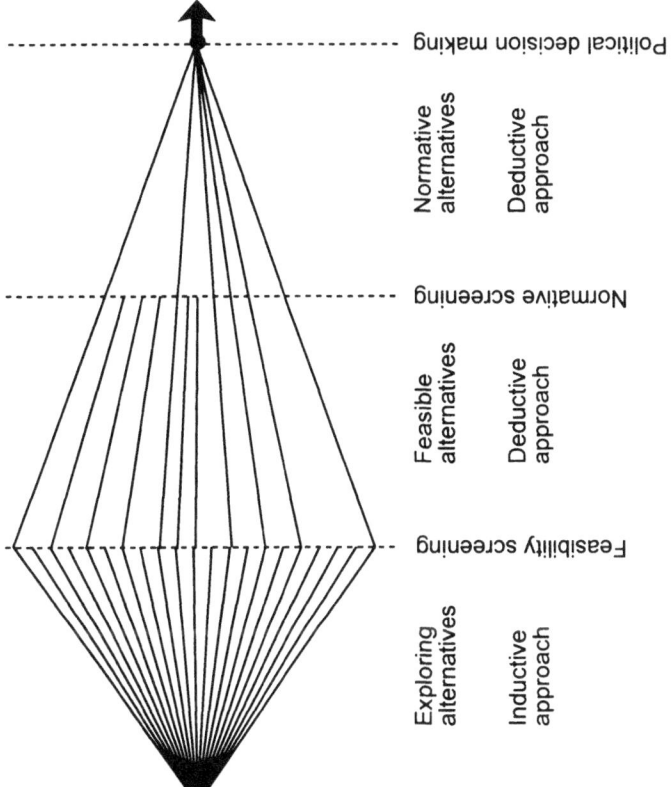

Figure 3.5 A conceptualization showing the desirability of using an inductive approach for the generation of explorative, and a deductive approach for the selection of feasible and normative alternatives.

Notes

1. The *morphological method* was developed by Zwicky, a well known Swiss astronomer working at the Mount Wilson and Mount Palomer Observatories in California, as long ago as 1942 (Jantsch, 1967, p.175).
2. Countries compete in the international markets on the basis of comparative advantage, whereas regions within a country compete on the basis of absolute advantage (Hirschman, 1975, p.152).
3. The simplest and perhaps purest example of morphological analysis comes from Zwicky; he focused attention in great detail on the totality of all jet engines containing simple elements only and being activated by chemical energy. As a result of morphological analysis Zwicky identified 36,864 distinguishable combinations. However, due to some internal restrictions the number of possible jet engines appeared to be 25,344. An evaluation in 1943, on the basis of fewer parameters, indicated 576 possibilities which correctly included the then secret German pulse-jet powered aerial bomb V-1 and V-2 rocket. The fatal failure of Churchill's Scientific Adviser to recognise the potential of the V-2 even when he was shown photographs has been explained by Jantsch as 'his preoccupation with solid propellants, leading to a stubborn rejection of the idea of liquid propellants' (Jantsch, 1967, pp.177 & 178).

4 Ecological community planning:
Concepts and principles for eco-community development

Yung-Jaan Lee

Environmental stresses in Taiwan's community

Taiwan, known as 'Ilha Formosa', Portuguese for 'Beautiful Island', has become an economic power-house in the post-war era. Since 1951 the island's annual economic growth has averaged about 9 percent (Republic of China, 1993). In 1994, the per capita income will approach $11,000, bringing Taiwan into line with the other members of Asia's industrial elite.

The most tangible cost of modernisation and industrialisation is environmental. From Taiwan's highest point, the summit of 3,997 metre Yu Shan (Jade Mountain), to the coastal crags of Lungtung, the landscape looks like one big fouled nest. 'Taiwan is filthy rich' as a local reporter puts it. The following describes some environmental stresses vis-à-vis Taiwan's community development.

The exploitation of slopeland

For the past forty years economic development has been the primary goal for Taiwan. As great as the economic success has been, it has not occurred without compromising the environmental integrity of the landscape. The growing population and successful economy have lead to increasing demand on slopeland, that is land over 100 metre elevation and over 5% slope, which results in serious misuse and exploitation. For example, over-use of forest land has now exceeded 58,000 hectares (Taiwan Forestry Bureau, 1993). On the other hand, increases in cropped areas in recent decades have often drawn cultivation onto marginal lands which are vulnerable to erosion. The exploitation of slopeland is even worse in places near urban areas. Most of the slopeland near urban areas is used for residential developments.

Due to the lack of comprehensive environmental planning these developments have become new 'urban ghettos,' and have caused serious environmental problems such as soil erosion, deforestation and water pollution caused by the overuse of agricultural chemicals.

Solid waste pollution

According to the Taiwan Environmental Protection Administration (Taiwan EPA) in 1975 Taiwanese generated 1.81 million tons of MSW (Municipal Solid Waste); this number has grown to 8.00 million tons, or 1.09 Kg per person per day in 1992, which is 10% higher than that in 1991, and twice that in 1975 (Taiwan Forestry Bureau, 1993). According to Taiwan EPA 90.1% of MSW are landfilled with 66.7% sanitary landfilled and 23.4% open dumping. However, on a national scale, it was estimated that among the 316 counties and townships, legal landfills in 217 counties and townships have red-light status, that is no more waste can be disposed; 28 have yellow-light status meaning that there will be not enough room for waste disposal within two years, and only 71 are still usable (Taiwan EPA, 1990).

Water pollution

The total waste water produced per day by cities and towns is over 4 million tons. In 1992, the percentage of population served by waste water treatment plants was only about 3.55% (Taiwan EPA, 1993). The untreated waste water along with the industrial waste have polluted major rivers in Taiwan: 40.9% of 21 major rivers are polluted, and according to Taiwan EPA, half its drinking water comes from polluted sources (Taiwan EPA, 1993).

Deforestation

During the 1930s and 1940s the forest in Taiwan had been heavily cut and cleared by the Japanese due to the Second World War. In the 1950s and 1960s the Government started to reforest the cut-over areas and the forest area increased steadily. By 1967 over 62% of the total area of Taiwan was in forest land use. However, during the last two decades, because of industrialisation and urbanisation, the total forest area has decreased to 52% of the total land area (Taiwan EPA, 1993).

Loss of wildlife habitat

A small island to begin with, Taiwan's continued expansion of industry, agriculture and urbanisation has made habitat destruction the primary threat to wildlife. One of the most interesting of Taiwan's rare species is the land-locked salmon or Taiwan trout. Originally in several upper tributaries of the Ta-Chia River, habitat damage and pollution have narrowed its range to only a 3 mile section of a single mountain stream. Another example is the Formosan clouded leopard. Little is known about these cats. They are partly arboreal and prey upon monkeys, deer, muntjac, and serow. The last official sightings occurred in the early 1980s, and it is uncertain whether the Formosan clouded leopard still exists in the wild.

Ecology and community

Communities are shaped by many forces: the determinants of nature that is biophysical processes and climate; the culture and history unique to each place and time; the role of a political and economic authority whose decisions impose an organisational structure on the landscape.

Traditionally, planners and policy makers in Taiwan have only concentrated on economic, political, social and to some extent cultural and historical forces, while neglecting the environmental factor. It is time we looked into the relationship between ecology and community.

Defining community

The term 'community' is used widely around the world nowadays. It is applied to such usage as the 'business community,' the 'social community,' the 'community of nations,' and others. By contrast, understood in a more traditional way as communities have flourished in the past and around the world, they have had very specific attributes. They are characterised by 'common attitudes and objectives that develop out of shared experiences and common social beliefs' (Swaney, 1990, p. 456).

Eric Fromm, in his book *The Art of Loving,* outlines love as having four characteristics: care, responsibility, respect, and knowledge. These four attributes might also define a sound relationship of people with one another and with the Earth in an ecologically sound community. 'Care is active concern for the life and growth of that which we love'. Responsibility entails 'my response to the needs, expressed or unexpressed, of another'. Respect is the ability to see and value a person on the basis of unique individuality. Finally, knowledge, 'to know a human being objectively ... in his ultimate essence,' provides the foundation on which care, responsibility, and respect can be constructed (Fromm, 1965, pp. 22-

26). Only in a sustained and lived connectedness can a healthy community be found. One must look closer to home for that sense of community, particularly for a community that joins people in a caring relationship to the Earth. The knowing that Fromm finds necessary to care for another person is also required to care truly for the Earth. As Murray Bookchin has written, it is 'only within a locally oriented political community that the uniqueness of the natural environment can be fully experienced in all its intimacy' (Bookchin, 1987, p.266).

Three orders of open space

Historically nature helped set out both the physical boundaries and the unique characteristic of each place of the community. Now smog, toxic soil, deteriorating ecologies, and polluted water contribute to the destruction of neighbourhood and community in the widest sense. Understanding the qualities of nature, expressing it in the design of neighbourhoods and communities, integrating it within our cities and towns, and respecting its balance are essential components of making the community sustainable.

The effort to create sustainable communities must be complemented with three orders of open space: those that define the edge and limits of the city region, those that form a large-scale connecting network within the city region, and those that provide identity within a community (Calthorpe, 1993). Each should respect the pre-existing ecology, and each can be a primary form-giver to the region, city, community or neighbourhood.

At the regional scale, the physical environment should fit into larger natural systems. City growth boundaries should be limited to preserve major natural resources at the edge of the city region. This line should be large enough to accommodate growth for future generations but small enough to encourage redevelopment at the city centre. Within this regional boundary major natural features should establish an internal structure of park-like linkages throughout the city region. Such open space elements should link and limit individual communities.

At the scale of community and neighbourhood, parks and open space should be used as formative elements, providing the focus and order of the community and neighbourhood. Neighbourhood parks should be smaller and more accessible, and have a strong local character. Every person should be able to walk safely to a neighbourhood park, a park that need not be 'naturalist' but should be of the place, socially and ecologically. Such parks can become the basis of a memorable and unique public domain for each neighbourhood, community or town.

Bioregionalism: the homeplace

An ideal of eco-community is important to the extent that it arouses our imagination and motivation, but the problems of our times require more than a vague imagination. They require a practical understanding of the dynamics of community, the obstacles and opportunities for eco-community building, and definite ways in which the principles of an ecological community can be applied to healing the relationship of humanity with the Earth.

The movement in environmental awareness that best captures the sense of place, of commitment and of homeplace is bioregionalism (Coleman, 1994; Register, 1987). The ecological issues that seem remote and impersonal or merely philosophical when described at the national or global level become immediate and personal when addressed at the local or regional level (Sale, 1985). For the bioregionalist, the very concept of homeplace is 'from which we go out and to which we return. It is our membrane - something to be cared for, nurtured with energy, love' (Mueller, 1990 p.88). Hence the concept of homeplace must be changed from a saleable commodity to a place where one puts down roots, a place once calls one's own.

The loss of community

Throughout human history until the dawn of the modern era, the selling and buying of land was a rarity. Aboriginal peoples generally comprehended the land as part of a web of life that included animal and plant species as well as humans of past and future generations. The Ashanti of Ghana have a saying that 'land belongs to a vast family of whom many are dead, a few are living, and a countless host are still unborn' (Coleman, 1994, p.83).[1]

The purchase or sale of human labour also has been a rare event. Although some people's labour was taken from them in the form of slavery, even then the ability to work was not considered as separate from the rest of a person's life. Generally, a person's labour was concentrated on meeting the needs of his or her family and the community. These communities depended on the common work and interdependency of their people.

Before the capitalist era, land and labour were not even understood as entities separable from the life of the community (Polanyi, 1944). Once land and labour have been commodified, the institutions and traditions that characterised pre-industrial society are devalued and ultimately lost in a society now organised around commodity exchange.

Enclosing the common

Land ownership is a recent concept. Heilbroner points out that 'as late as the fourteenth or fifteenth century there was no such thing as land in the sense of freely saleable, rent-producing property' (Heilbroner, 1980, p.25). Land was not subject to sale or purchase, and its use as well as any right of property were decided by a complex of institutional regulations and traditions (Polanyi, 1944). The commons were protected by an ethic of preservation and stewardship and were self-renewing without human intervention.

From the late fifteenth century through to the early nineteenth century, a process known as enclosure changed the landscape of the Europe, destroying the commons and the traditions that surrounded them. The history of enclosure is best known in England where, as textile manufacturing became more complicated, there was a need for an increased supply of wool. Peasants were driven off the formerly common lands, which were 'enclosed' and turned over to pasture land for sheep. The land appropriated by enclosure had often previously been held as common land (Marx, 1906). The new landlords tried to turn their property over to new forms of profitable enterprise and thought nothing of the brutal destruction of homes and communities.

Land as commodity

The difference between land as commodity and land as community was well expressed by the environmental pioneer Aldo Leopold who wrote that 'we abuse land because we regard it as a commodity belonging to us. When we see land as a community to which we belong, we may begin to use it with love and respect' (Leopold, 1968, p. vii).

Once land is treated as a commodity, its use is subject to short-term profit criteria. Its fertility and other characteristics can be depreciated just like any other form of capital (Lee, 1994). The result is that, for example, by the late 1970s, soil erosion exceeded soil formation on about a third of US cropland, much of it in the midwestern agricultural heartland (Brown, 1987). In Canada, soil degradation has been costing farmers $1 billion a year (Standing Committee on Agriculture, Fisheries and Forestry, 1984). In Africa, soil erosion could reduce agricultural production by one fourth between 1975 and 2000 if conservation actions are not adopted (Food and Agriculture Organization, 1983).

In an ecological society this conflict would not happen since all parties would feel a fundamental devotion to the well-being, sustenance, and sustainability of the broader community (Daly, 1989).

Twentieth-century enclosures

Enclosure has erased the moral economy that characterised most of human history. Commodification is the result of and further enhances the narrowing of values to the simple destructive measure of profit. Furthermore, commodification basically is incompatible with the participation of people in a democratic process of deciding their fate as a community.

To reverse this process of commodification a new sense of community must be created. This will not be a merely human community, but an ecological community in which society is embedded in harmony with its natural environment. Such a community will depend on the democratic participation of its people in its definition, sustenance and development. A clear articulation of sustainable, life-affirming values will be fundamental to such a community. Above all, since the obstacles confronting such a community are appalling, attaining it will require committed effort and sustained organising. Since the final form of such a community is unknown, an active imagination, a willingness to experiment will be needed in order ultimately to achieve an ecological community. The following sections will propose these steps.

The values of effective activism

This section will layout four key values as the foundation of a movement toward an eco-community. The claim is not that this is the only, or the best, statement of values. However, these four values are understandable, feasible and relevant in that they are already widely recognised around the world.

Sustainable development

Sustainable development provides the keystone for eco-community building. Sustainable development uses a whole systems approach to design, bringing together local and global, short term and long term and environment and development. It argues the need for action *now* to defend the future. It is a means by which 'economic and social progress could be achieved without compromising the integrity of the environment' (National Academy of Science, 1990, p.7).

Sustainability implies that 'a given modification or development within the living landscape is so designed as to cause no significant long-term stress to the natural systems'. (Simonds, 1994, p.50). In eco-communities, the physical, social and economic environment is arranged so that quality time with family, friends and community is possible. Leisure, recreational and civic activities along with work and family life are within walking or short non-polluting commute distance. The needs of a population and the flow of resources needed to support it are in dynamic balance (Van der Ryn, 1992). In short, sustainable development allows us to meet our needs without diminishing the ability of future generations to meet their own needs.

Decentralisation

An ecologically responsible society will be decentralised so as to be sensitive to environmental, social and economic diversity (Coleman, 1994). Decentralisation ensures that those living closest to environmental conditions have the best knowledge of them and should have the power of stewardship and policy-making. To be effective, the principle of decentralisation must be applied to political and economic power as part of a movement of revived grassroots democracy. National organisations in an ecologically responsible society must be redirected to support the development of organisational forms that allow direct grassroots democracy to function at the local, regional or even the global level.

Grassroots democracy

For eco-community building to be successful, it must discover the power to influence both public policy and the organisation and development of political and economic life. Therefore, grassroots democracy is more than a strategy for affecting government. It entails an active citizenship that transforms the character of the citizen through the process of participation in the public life of the community. Grassroots democracy transforms our usual top-down approach to public policy on its head, giving local residents and communities the power and chance to decide their ecological, social and economic destinies. It empowers people to search for an environmentally and socially healthy way of life. Grassroots democracy is the principal of the key values, the enabling force through which the broader vision of the eco-community can be fulfilled.

Community-based economics

Community forms the basis for democratic self-controlled economic activity, the basis for political life and the foundation of an ecological society. Community-based economics suggests co-operative enterprise, workers' self-control and human-scale organisation fitted to the ecological characteristics of the particular locale (North American Bioregional Congress (NABC) Economics Committee, 1989). An ecologically responsible, community-based economy will emphasise democratic self-control to promote environmental stewardship and social responsibility.

Sustainable planning principles for eco communities

Most planners and architects have paid little attention to the ecological aspects of the Earth on which their planning and design impact (see Bell, 1992). This is now changing to some degree. However, for the most part, plans and design designed to address ecological concerns have helped little toward making our society more ecologically sustainable. The reason for this problem is that planners, along with the rest of us, have very little knowledge about how our Earth's life support system functions, or what it costs us when our behaviour causes damage to it. Moreover, planners lack the crucial tools which will help them layout more ecologically appropriate planning options.

To help in identifying both of these issues, a new approach to community planning called Ecological Community Planning (ECP), is advocated. ECP is a proactive planning method based on the premise that human built infrastructures are ultimately dependent on the ecological basis upon which they rest. ECP also expands the realm of planning considerations beyond the limits of a specific project to include local, regional, national, and global concerns.

The goal of ECP is to design communities that satisfy human needs and basic values in ways which:

1. Use local resources sustainably.
2. Maintain the integrity and diversity of local ecosystems by maximising the preservation of native plant and animal communities.
3. Minimise the use of imported resources and only use them if they are harvested, procured and processed in ways that are ecologically sustainable.
4. Improve the quality of community and family life at all income levels.
5. Encourage public participation.

Based on the ECP concept and goals, eight sustainable planning principles are proposed as follows.

1. Conserve the natural environment
2. Use land more efficiently in order to reduce the need for cars and motorcycles, and to minimise the loss of farmland and wetlands.
3. Develop mixed-use eco-communities
4. Use advanced transportation, communication and production Systems.

5. Establish recycling programmes and recycled/recyclable materials industries.
6. Increase the supply of affordable housing.
7. Reduce the total volume of waste stream.
8. Change attitudes and behaviour by encouraging increased participation.

Changes needed for ecological community planning

In order to reduce the environmental impact to a rate and scale that can be accommodated, in the following section we lay out briefly what we consider to be the major changes in development strategies that will be needed in eco-community building in Taiwan. In fact, this means broadening the goal of the existing physical planning system to include the relationship *between* the built environment and the natural ecosystems. The criteria for making policy choices should at least include the objectives for natural resources, energy, trash and land use and transportation.

Natural resources

An eco-community should create an inventory of natural and physical aspects of its community, and initiate formal agreements with surrounding communities to share inventory information and call for city-wide and regional action to protect area ecosystems. An eco-community should also protect and restore cyclical processes, biodiversity, and natural beauty. Furthermore, the government should develop equitable land preservation and restoration agreements through fair market acquisition and development rights transfer.

Moreover, because of the lack of parks and open space throughout large parts of cities and communities in Taiwan, every redevelopment plan needs to make some provision for trees and other vegetation to add visual delight and to help increase the total biomass in city regions. The use of permeable paving materials around new planting will help maintain it as well as reducing excessive rainwater run-off. In addition, more use could be made of open rainwater channels leading to streams and ponds in open spaces as part of the growing network of natural features that is needed for greening the community. The reduction in road traffic will provide space for many more tree-lined streets, especially in areas that have re-acquired a sense of local identity and community.

Energy

Since these are the areas where age and obsolescence often combine to require either complete redevelopment or major renew works, there will be scope both for reducing total demand for energy and for increasing the share of renewable energy.

In order to build an eco-community, the government should redirect the energies and power of the old industrial/consumerist system into emerging sustainable systems. The government should also provide economic incentives for water, energy and materials conservation, for driving more efficient small cars and using alternative fuels, for working within the home and/or community where walking or cycling replaces most vehicle uses.

Trash

Reducing the total volume of the trash stream is a prime requirement through changess in packaging habits and greatly-enlarged recycling. At the community level, sufficient land needs to be allocated for recycling facilities and programmes such as community drop-off and buy-back centres, and toxic substance collection stations. Careful siting will be necessary in predominantly residential communities for materials which generate noise in handling. At a city authority level, a materials recovery and processing facility will be needed for all recyclable waste, including industrial waste, where this is the appropriate scale. For some materials--such as tires--only one or two facilities nation-wide may be required. Residual waste can be incinerated for district heating.

On the other hand, the government should create economic and policy incentives that encourage the use of non-toxic biodegradable materials, and that help create strong markets for recycled/recyclable materials and facilitate siting of local recycling industries. Furthermore, the government should support the establishment of regional facilities to recycle bulk materials thus diverting them from landfills.

Land use and transportation

Typically, the focus is to be on correcting the deficiency in local community facilities, and creating a variety of housing types and sizes, suited to different income levels, life-styles, cultures and age groups. Some regrouping of business uses may be necessary to eliminate nuisance and to provide the more up-to-date operating conditions which are essential if the compatible mixed-use character of these communities is to be kept.

One objective will be improved accessibility; but new traffic management plans must be designed to reduce the excessive road traffic. Through traffic will have to be re-routed and traffic reducing instruments widely used to create larger areas with safer, quieter streets and less polluted air. Networks of safe and attractive routes for walking and cycling then become easier to develop, adding to accessibility and further reducing the need for vehicle trips. These restraints on road traffic must be accompanied by major improvements in public transportation with more use of electric vehicles to reduce noise and pollution further.

Where existing buildings are too old and decayed for rehabilitation to be practicable, urban renewal schemes must be employed to introduce better environmental practices, replacing old polluting factories and energy-inefficient housing and providing improved routes for public transportation.

The government should create community centres composed of public buildings and spaces for governance and the arts that will generate a sense of place. The government should also create neighbourhoods that encourage walking and cycling.

Conclusion

As Leopold points out 'that land is a community is the basic concept of ecology, but that land is to be loved and respected is an extension of ethics' (Leopold 1968, pp.viii-ix). Such a view of land and people is subject to distortions of bias and personal experience. However wherever the truth may lie, this much is apparent: Taiwan is now so obsessed with its own economic progress as to have lost the capacity to remain ecologically sustainable. The whole society is so greedy for more 'economic miracle' that it has lost the sustainability necessary to build it. As Swaney puts it: 'Future generations are entitled to the environmental functions, so we do not own the natural environment. We are not free to discount what we do not own' (Swaney, 1990, p.458). Maybe it is time we stop causing the deterioration of future generations' environment, and start to build an ecological sound community for this and future generations.

Note

[1] This section was presented at the 1st International Seminar on 'Towards the Sustainable Use of Land Resources in the 21st Century,' 15-16 August 1994, Taipei, Taiwan.

5 The 'Enablement' approach and settlement upgrading in South Africa

Adenrele Awotona and Michael Briggs

Introduction

This chapter explores the implications of the 'Enablement' approach to housing and human settlement for research aimed at providing foundations for policies on settlement upgrading in South African townships.

Assessment and critique of the 'Self-Help' experience and shifts in general approaches to Urban Development are identified as key factors underlying the emergence and crystallisation of the 'Enablement' approach. Distinctive features of 'Enablement', it is suggested, include an emphasis on the creation of 'enabling environments', the shift from 'project-based' to 'programmatic' approaches, and the importance ascribed to partnerships. Key critiques outlined refer to the limitations of 'Enablement' in meeting the needs of the poor, operational constraints, and the need to shift the focus of 'enabling' strategies to assisting householders in their relationships with small contractors. The limitations of 'Enablement' approaches in addressing urban environmental considerations are also highlighted and an argument is made for the specific incorporation of spatial concerns into research and policy formulation if qualitative dimensions of shelter and settlement are to be addressed.

The scope for differences of interpretation and emphasis is found to be a key factor in addressing the question of whether 'Enablement' can provide an appropriate framework for settlement upgrading strategies. In this regard conceptualisation of implementational issues and of the relationship between 'enabling' and 'empowering' strategies are identified as important arenas of debate.

Finally, an outline is provided of key research themes which arise from an exploration of shifts in thinking about housing and human settlement in 'Developing Countries'.

The emergence of the 'enablement' approach - factors leading to crystallisation of the approach

In December 1988 the United Nations General Assembly issued the proclamation on the '*Global Strategy for Shelter to the Year 2000*' which heralded the emergence of a new 'Enabling' approach to housing and shelter policies.

Two key factors which shaped the approach were the assessment of the 'Self-Help' experience, and broader paradigmatic shifts in approaches to urban development.

Assessment of the 'self-help' experience

Cohen (1994, pp.117-118) suggests that the World Bank assessment of policies implemented in the 1970s and 1980s is a crucial factor shaping new approaches. In this regard neighbourhood interventions, particularly site and service and slum upgrading projects of the 1970s, as well as Municipal development and Housing Finance programmes of the 1980s, are assessed as having limited and rare city-wide impacts and as being inadequate in the sense that the pace of urban growth exceeded the scale of the urban Programme. The critique asserts that an approach of replicable pilot projects cannot produce adequate numbers of houses, and needs to be replaced by a sustainable process of shelter delivery in order to scale up housing programmes (Sheng, 1995, p.3). The implication (Cohen, 1994, p.118) is that a shift is needed towards 'city-wide policy reform' involving institutional development, and high priority investment - or in more general terms, a shift to 'enabling' strategies.

Paradigmatic shifts in approaches to urban development in the late 1980s and 1990s

In the arena of urban development policy a number of closely related threads of concern have been at the centre of new thinking since the late 1980s. Key amongst these has been a concern with 'urban productivity' and the conceptualisation of cities as 'engines of economic growth'. Attempts to frame strategies aimed at achieving higher levels of 'urban efficiency' and a focus on the need to develop 'urban management' capacities have been closely related to the central theme of 'productivity'.

The Lille International Meeting of 6-10 November 1989 (attended by 200 experts, donors and international organisations) signalled an important reorientation in thinking on urban development. The meeting concluded that 'urban growth lies at the very heart of the development process' and viewed the 'town as the powerhouse of economic and social development in the third world' (UNCHS, 1990, pp.6-7). This represented a major shift from previous thinking which had viewed cities as 'consumers' of resources in a paradigm centred on the objective of achieving 'urban-rural' balance.

Burgess (1994, pp.9-16) identifies two key urban development policy thrusts characteristic of the 1990s. The first emphasises the enhancement of urban productivity and efficiency, the second focuses on poverty alleviation.

According to him, strategies for enhancing urban productivity typically include the following:
- Withdrawal of the state from direct provision;
- Market oriented strategies to encourage private sector provision of infrastructure and services;
- The 'Enablement' of markets and privatisation;
- Deregulation and reform of regulatory regimes;
- Decentralisation of authority and popular participation;
- Institutional and management capacity building on a city-wide Programme and sectoral basis.

Poverty alleviation measures have emerged in the light of an assessment of the impact of structural adjustment and sustained economic recession on the very poor. It is widely acknowledged that increased unemployment, a decline in real wages, the removal of consumer subsidies and decreased public expenditure in various areas have had severe consequences for the quality of life of the poor. Criticism of the effects of structural adjustment measures in particular has led to an exploration of poverty alleviation strategies in the 1990s. Within the urban productivity framework Burgess (1994, p.15) identifies the following bundle of poverty alleviation strategies:
- Improve the productivity of the poor through improving 'Human Capital Resources';
- Increase the intensity of productive investment;
- Increase access to employment;
- Remove constraints on the informal sector and micro enterprises;
- Increase the labour force participation of women;
- Improve household access to land, infrastructure, building materials and finance;
- Increase access of the poor to: basic education, health facilities, nutrition, vocational training;
- Create safety nets and compensatory measures for the most vulnerable.

In his summary of the World Bank's 'redefinition' of the 'urban challenge', Cohen (1994, p.118) concurs with Burgess regarding the centrality of concerns with the productivity of the urban economy and the need to alleviate constraints on productivity. He also notes the concern with alleviating urban poverty, and that the World Bank approach asserts that the productivity of the poor should be enhanced by increasing the demand for labour and improving access to basic infrastructure and social services.

The shifts in thinking outlined above were significant in shaping the 'Enabling' approach to housing. Most important in this regard was the coherent conceptualisation of the role of government as 'enabler' primarily concerned with creating 'environments' for the efficient operation of market-driven processes. The centrality ascribed to the goal of 'urban productivity' has also been significant in that it has become the pivot around which other strategies turn.

Distinctive features of the 'enabling approach'

The 'Enablement' approach involves the reiteration of key dimensions of the 'Self-Help' perspective and as Jones and Ward (1994, pp.33-35) have noted there is a current of philosophical continuity in dominant approaches to housing from the 1970s through to the 1990s. Continuity is reflected in attempts to orient housing strategies towards market forces, and in the central notion that the state should not be directly involved in the 'provision' of housing for the poor, but should rather support people's efforts to house themselves.

The latter perspective is sometimes described as if it were a unique feature of the 'Enablement' perspective, whereas it has actually been clearly and consistently articulated since the emergence of the 'Self-Help' perspective in the early 1970s. Furthermore it has centrally informed the policies of key international agencies and many national governments over the last two decades. Renewed calls for the withdrawal of government from direct involvement in the provision of housing, as well as infrastructure and services, should be understood in the light of the vigorous ascendancy of radical liberal ideology in the 1980s, and in the context of 'structural adjustment' imperatives requiring reductions in government expenditure.

Despite the continuity alluded to above it is certainly possible to illustrate that the emergence of the 'Enablement' approach has marked a new orientation in approaches to housing and settlement. Hundsalz (1994, p.2) has described these changes as 'fundamental'. Distinctive features of the new approach are reflected in an emphasis on the creation of 'enabling environments', the shift away from 'project-based' approaches and in the importance ascribed to partnerships as a tool for achieving housing and urban development goals.

Emphasis on the creation of 'enabling' environments

At the core of the 'Enabling' approach is the notion of a 'radically' new role for government in creating 'enabling environments' (Hundsalz, 1994, p.3). The UNCHS (1990, p.25) quotes the Global Strategy for Shelter as follows:

It is becoming increasingly clear that national governmental policies which affect shelter delivery require co-ordinated action at the highest national level on a considerably broader range of issues than simply housing production. The fundamental policy change will need to be the adoption of an 'enabling' approach whereby the full potential and resources of the participants in the shelter production and improvement process are mobilised, but the final decisions on how to house themselves are left to the people concerned.

Characteristically proposals aimed at creating such 'enabling environments' concentrate on the following arenas (UNCHS, 1989, p.11):

- National economic policy aimed at encouraging investment in shelter and property development;
- Institutional, legal and financial reform aimed at expanding private land tenure and removing restrictive controls which discourage investment in shelter.

The influence of a broader paradigm which emphasises the link between urban development and wider economic processes is discernible in the pursuance of housing goals and objectives through macro-economic policy instruments. Where 'Self-Help' approaches are centred on fairly direct forms of support to individuals and communities engaged in housing processes, the emphasis under 'enablement' is on indirect measures aimed at creating 'environments' for the efficient operation of market-driven housing processes. Government becomes a number of steps further removed from the 'bricks and mortar' dimension of the housing process. The emphasis on 'decentralisation' and local government development within the 'enabling' approach is related to this further withdrawal of central government from direct involvement in housing processes (UNCHS, 1989, p.11).

The move towards 'programmatic' approaches and away from 'project-based' approaches

The emergence of the 'Enabling' approach is associated with a shift, beginning in the late 1980s, away from 'project based' strategies and towards more sector and policy oriented programmes.

'Programmatic' approaches are concerned with broad measures such as policy reform and development and capacity building, which are aimed at creating 'environments' in which people can effectively meet their housing needs and requirements. This contrasts with the 1970s and most of the 1980s when 'Self-Help' policies were carried out primarily through the implementation of a series of 'Site and Service' and 'upgrading' projects.

An emphasis on partnerships

The 'enabling' approach places a strong emphasis on establishing and nurturing 'partnerships' between key actors in the housing process. Hundsalz (1994, p.4) sees partnerships as 'the key to the enabling approach'.

Enabling perspectives typically call for 'a national shelter drive with the people and supported primarily through the people's (the private sector, communities, householders, NGOs) own resources' (UNCHS, 1989, p.11). The 'Global Strategy' is, 'founded upon the realistic perception that central governments have a vital managerial function which should enable others - local government in partnership with the private sector, formal and informal, community groups and individual families - to develop shelter more efficiently'.

Within this perspective, the public sector role is to take facilitating measures to encourage formal and informal business sectors, non-governmental organisations and community groups to optimise their contributions to the housing process. In other words 'to mobilise the resources of other actors and to facilitate their deployment for efficient provision of all types of shelter for all target groups' (Sheng, 1995, p.3).

Critique of 'enablement'

Three important critiques of 'Enablement' are outlined below. The first highlights the limitations of 'Enablement' policies in addressing the needs of the poor. The second asks important questions about the operational viability of 'Enablement' strategies in countries where urban management capacities are inadequate. The third suggests that the emphasis - carried over from the 'Self-Help' paradigm - on turning householders into 'self-builders' is inefficient and unrealistic. Two arenas of debate within the 'Enablement' perspective are also briefly outlined. The first concerns the place of 'Self-Help' strategies within the framework of 'Enablement'. The second deals with questions of power and contest and how these relate to 'enabling' strategies.

The limitations of 'enablement' in meeting the needs of the poor

Hundsalz (1994, p.6) states that 'the introduction of enabling strategies implies a change from policies of intervention to policies of liberalisation'. Key elements of this process are aimed at achieving security of tenure for the poor, the removal of restrictive legal and bureaucratic controls and creating incentives for private sector involvement. Hundsalz cautioned however that 'If governments decide to liberalise human settlements policies without including safeguards to ensure housing for the poor, the housing options of the poor will not improve substantially because they might be excluded from access to essential inputs, especially land and finance'.

Hundsalz argues that in a number of cases the introduction of enabling strategies has actually damaged the housing choices of the poorest groups. At the level of the individual settlement, upgrading often drives out those who cannot afford the costs imposed by higher housing standards and service charges. Land sharing, rehabilitation and resettlement programmes often have negative effects on the ability of very poor families to remain in an area where shelter and the environment are improved and commercialised. Significantly Hundsalz (1994, p.4) suggests that 'those cases where the very poor have benefited have come about only through deliberate action on the part of the government or the community concerned, usually in the form of direct subsidies or special assistance. This implies going beyond the "enabling" strategy to delineate Government's role as providers...' One implication of this critique is that a combination of 'enabling' strategies and 'provision' is necessary to meet the needs of the very poor.

Sheng (1995, p.3) also critiques 'enabling' policies in terms of their impact on the housing situation of the poor. His reflection on their application in Thailand is particularly apt, as this is often seen as a country 'where the impact of an enabling housing strategy is most visible'.

Sheng explained that the private sector contribution to housing stock in Bangkok is large, and is also increasing in other Thai cities. Furthermore, the private sector is able to provide housing 'at prices affordable to ever larger segments of the population'. Remarkable improvements in housing delivery have been made possible by rapid economic growth, dynamic private sector involvement, and effective government support policies. Sheng's strong critique highlights the fact that, despite positive trends, 50% of people in Bangkok can still not afford private sector housing. De-regulation of the housing market and other 'enabling' strategies allow the growing middle class in Thailand to access home ownership. However, the housing market is still unable to provide housing for the poor, and 'Enablement' policies do not change this fact. On the contrary, Sheng (1995, pp.6-7) has suggested that government assistance can result in 'formalisation' of situations and the removal of the informality which protected the poor. For example, deregulation can result in the poor being pushed out of favourable locations in the city, as it removes barriers between formal and informal sectors and 'informalises' the formal sector, putting the 'formal' sector and the poor into direct competition for land.

Sheng's (1995, p.8) argument suggests that the Global Strategy for Shelter through equating 'enabling' with 'facilitating', defined as making actions easier through the removal of obstacles, does provide a useful framework for encouraging private sector participation in housing provision. However, for the urban poor 'the problem of housing is not only a matter of removing obstacles, but also a problem of a lack of power, if only purchasing power'. He argues that the 'empowering' dimension of 'enabling' generally receive far less attention than the 'facilitating' dimension, and that the building of partnerships between government, community and NGOs is key. (He refers to the case of the Community Action Planning Approach of the National Housing Development Authority in Sri Lanka and the Collaborative Katchi Abadi Improvement Programme in the province of Sidh based on the approach followed by the Orangi Pilot Project in Karachi, both in Pakistan).

Enablement sounds good in theory but is unrealistic in operational terms

An important critique of the 'Enabling' approach identifies key limitations in the implementational realm. To be implemented effectively 'enabling' strategies require flexible, proactive planning and management by various tiers of government - particularly local government. In contexts where urban management capacities are limited and where inappropriate legislative frameworks and institutional stagnation are a reality, it is questionable whether complex 'enabling' strategies can be sustained.

Acioly (1994, p.1) critiques the new 'Enabling' approach through a critical appraisal of programmes in the city of Bissau in the Republic of Guinea-Bissau. His main point is that 'in theory, the shifts advocated by the new agenda(s) can be considered as coherent proposals but in practice, when confronted with the situations typically found in the countries of sub-Saharan Africa, they become unrealistic or difficult to operationalise'. In this regard he refers to: lack of local government capacity, scarcity of financial resources, outdated legislation, and institutional stagnation. For Acioly this means that the organisation of basic municipal services and public administration is necessary before 'enabling' strategies can be considered.

He also finds that 'enabling' strategies 'disregard agendas and priorities set by the grassroots' and that policy approaches concerned with city-wide problems dilute 'the needs and problems of the poor'. He argues that 'integrated neighbourhood upgrading' is 'one of the instruments to alleviate urban poverty, because it enables significant improvement of the living conditions of the inhabitants' (Acioly, 1994, pp.9-10). In this sense he directly questions the abandonment of 'project-based' approaches and the shift to sectoral policy oriented approaches. Central to his conceptualisation of 'integrated neighbourhood upgrading' is the notion of a 'minimum habitat condition', in the absence of which further neighbourhood development is severely constrained. Key dimensions of the approach, as implemented in a neighbourhood of Bissau, include: the provision of basic infrastructure, the formulation of a settlement plan, participation strategies and the provision of credit facilities.

The need to target enabling strategies more appropriately

Tipple (1994, pp.4-13) argues that 'Enablement' strategies currently focus on the interface between the householder and the house, and that the focus needs to shift to the interface between the householder and the contractor, as well as the interface between the small contractor and the house. This suggests that strategies aimed at assisting the individual or household in building and improving a house are misguided and wasteful of resources. These resources could more effectively be directed towards assisting the householder in conducting interactions with small contractors and other actors, and towards developing the delivery capacity of contractors. In many senses Tipple's critique echoes early criticisms of the 'Self-Help' approach which highlighted the hidden costs caused by materials wastage, building failures and time wasted by inexperienced builders.

Debates within 'enablement'

The polarised debates on 'Self-Help' which were a feature of the 1970s and the first half of the 1980s have given way to a pragmatic consensus on the importance of strategies in support of people's own efforts to house themselves (Mathey, 1992, p.386). In part this reflects the development and modification of the 'Self-Help' perspective in response to criticism and project assessment. For example, from an early emphasis on people's own labour input into the house building process, Turner shifted to an emphasis on people's 'self-organisation' as the key input. In response to criticisms accusing him of a 'laissez-faire' approach which exposed the poor to the vagaries of the market, he also clarified and developed his position on the state's responsibility for 'enabling strategies' (Mathey, 1992, p.381). In its more developed formulations, Turner's approach envisaged a three-dimensional process including: community decisions, a state role aimed at ensuring access to land, energy and tools, and a role for 'intermediate agents' (the 'third system') clearly described in 1988 as a role played by NGOs and CBOs.

While a broad consensus exists on the need for 'enabling' approaches, debate over the forms which 'Enablement' strategies should take reflects important differences in underlying perspectives and agenda. At one level there is on-going debate over questions of implementation. Various authors have attempted to identify possible areas for improvement in the implementation of 'Self-Help' and 'Enablement' strategies. Gilbert and Ward (1985), for example, asserted that the key problem with 'Self-Help' was that not enough projects had been implemented to have widespread effect. Laquian (1983) stressed the need for good professional backing in support of 'Self-Help' strategies. A more fundamental set of differences relates to questions of power within the 'Enablement' process. 'Self-Help' and 'Enablement' are viewed by some authors as arenas of contest where the interests of structurally disempowered groups might be advanced. In this sense 'Self-Help' and 'Enablement' are seen as potential strategies for 'empowerment'. Fiori *et al* (1992) saw possibilities for transferring resources from affluent to poor sectors of society through the implementation of 'Self-Help' strategies. Others (Martin, 1977) have reflected positively on the scope for popular participation in 'Self-Help' schemes.

An important dimension of the 'empowerment' perspective is the assertion of gender concerns (Moser, 1995; Chant, 1995). It is suggested that women, despite the fact that they are often the principal consumers, have least rights and benefits in the housing process. This is reflected in limitations on access to credit, exclusion from tenure arrangements and property ownership, and the fact that women's interests and concerns are often not taken into account in the location or layout of settlements, or in housing design.

The physical and spatial environment and housing

'Self-Help' and 'Enablement' policies and strategies focus primarily on intervention into housing 'processes' and on shaping the economic and institutional 'environments' within which housing processes occur. They seldom deal directly with the physical and spatial environment in qualitative terms (Kellett, 1995, p.33). In Burgess's (1994, p.47) terms, urban planning has been 'despatialised' and 'deterritorialised', and housing 'dematerialised' by neo-liberal theory with its emphasis on aspatial sectoral policy. Nevertheless, it is possible to trace important trends reflected in the treatment of specifically physical and spatial dimensions of shelter provision and settlement development over the last three decades. This period has seen important shifts in thinking and practice with regard to both 'the dwelling' or 'shelter', and with regard to 'settlement' or the 'urban environment' within which housing solutions are sought.

The dwelling

Until the late 1960s conventional housing policies focused primarily on the construction of whole standardised housing units in planned 'new settlements'. Informal housing solutions were seen as highly problematic and generally subjected to bulldozing and forced removal. Concurrent with the emergence of the 'Self-Help' approach from the 1970s, the 'package' of what was provided under conventional housing schemes progressively diminished from a complete house, to a 'outer shell' or 'core house', to a 'wet' core, and finally to serviced plots with no attempt actually to 'provide' a dwelling or part of a dwelling. Paralleling this withdrawal from actual 'provision' was the growth of strategies aimed at supporting people's own housing efforts. These strategies included the provision of information, financial support, building materials supply and skills transfer (Tipple, 1994a, p.3).

Besides powerful economic imperatives of cost and affordability the move away from government driven mass housing projects was also based on arguments which questioned the notion that 'formal' mass-housing necessarily provided the best shelter alternative in qualitative terms, and arguments which suggested that under certain conditions 'self-built' housing had relatively high performance potential. A closely linked perspective highlighted the progressive and continuous nature of the process through which shelter is constructed, consolidated, improved and extended over time (Dewar, 1993, p.16).

The shift from provision of standardised formal units to support for informal and progressive housing processes is significant. Equally significant perhaps is the fact that throughout the period under review in South Africa and other 'Developing Countries' the dominant ideal has been that of an individual free-standing, detached house on an (ever-shrinking) plot. This has meant that other forms of housing such as high rise and various forms of single and multi-storey attached dwellings have often been excluded from serious consideration. This has severely constrained the achievement of high densities and limited the range of housing options available to people. Of course people have often responded creatively to these limitations by, for instance, letting out rooms and informally adapting housing stock to suit this purpose.

Settlement

Conventional 'neighbourhood' planning (the modernisation period)

In the conventional 'modernisation' paradigm housing provision was tied up with a particular set of planning concepts at the level of the whole settlement. Key amongst these, and underlying the planning of many new residential townships, was the notion of 'neighbourhood'. This approach, rooted in idealist notions of 'community', advocated the creation of planned, orderly, primarily residential settlements in which people's reproductive needs would be met. The following features were typical of the dominant approach:

- A primary school catchment area often defined the neighbourhood unit for planning purposes;
- land-use separation through planning and regulation was seen as important;
- there was a strong emphasis on the provision of green (in theory) open spaces;
- the movement structure of neighbourhoods was geared towards vehicular access to all individual lots, and at the same time to preventing the through-flow of traffic in residential areas;

- the detached housing unit in a small garden was seen as the ideal, leading to low built densities.

The use of this approach in 'Developing Countries' has been criticised as an imposition of derived and inappropriate models based on unrealistic assumptions about climate, vegetation and other elements of the bio-physical environment; culture, values and ways of living; household characteristics and structures; incomes and access to resources.

More broadly the approach has been severely criticised in terms of an assessment of the kinds of environments produced around the world. Typically, a critique will argue that traditional neighbourhood planning has created residential areas which are poorly integrated into city-wide flows and concentrations of activity and opportunity especially for those without cars and in the absence of good public transport networks; are monofunctional and lacking in diversity and hence opportunity; are sterile and aesthetically uninteresting; are inadequate in terms of spatial quality especially lack of spaces which adequately accommodate public activities; and are inefficient in that low densities and spatial extensiveness mean inadequate thresholds for cost-effective provision of services and infrastructure.

Settlement strategies under 'self-help' and 'enablement'

Settlement 'upgrading' and 'Site and Service' schemes implemented within the 'Self-Help' and 'Basic Needs' paradigm tended to focus in physical terms on defining and formalising lay-outs and cadastral boundaries in informal settlements; and addressing quantitatively defined backlogs and needs in shelter, infrastructure, and services. While these are clearly important arenas of intervention, the rather limited focus has meant that broader questions of urban environmental quality and performance have not received adequate attention.

A marked escalation in the deterioration of urban environments in the 1980s has forced a recognition of the importance of developing adequate policy responses. In this regard, the outcome of the United Nations Rio Summit (1992), in the form of the 'Local Agenda 21' initiative has been particularly significant (Grubb, 1993). It is not clear however that recognition of crisis in the quality of urban environments will lead to specifically spatial strategies to address these problems. The Neo-Liberal analysis of urban environmental deterioration emphasises aspatial causes of environmental problems such as deficient regulatory and institutional frameworks and weak management capacities and skills, and advocates primarily aspatial sectoral 'enabling' responses to these problems.

Sectoral, aspatial approaches do not really deal with the concerns of Rapoport (1977) and others with the quality of urban environments measured in 'terms of cultural supportiveness and perceptual quality' and other key measures of urban environmental performance. In this regard Dewar's critique of housing policy and projects in southern Africa is important in that it is precisely in the spatial and physical dimension of housing policy that he detects a critical failure. He argues (Dewar, 1994, p.1) that

> the record of southern African countries in relation to the challenge of overcoming the urban housing problem, appropriately defined in terms of the generation of positive, enabling, total living environments, has been ubiquitously poor.

He further argues

> that the heart of the issue is the way in which 'the housing problem' is defined. A narrow focus on the individual housing unit and the provision of shelter, which is the prevalent disposition, gives rise to a particular mindset and approach which ensures the generation of poorly performing, sterile environments.

Significant improvement, Dewar suggests, 'demands a paradigm shift which places collective spaces, institutions and facilities at the centre of the housing issue, not the individual housing unit'.

In this regard, he calls for an emphasis on the quality of the 'public spatial environment'. He also reasons that, particularly when people are poor, the full range of people's needs cannot be met within the individual house. He then further notes that 'properly made and celebrated public spaces enable poverty to be tolerated with some dignity' (Dewar, 1993, p.13). Public spaces, especially for the poor, he suggests, are 'probably the most significant form of necessary social infrastructure in urban areas and their emergence needs to become a non-negotiable part of housing policy'. The implication which he draws is that design, and directly spatial strategies need to be incorporated more centrally into the housing process.

Of course, it has been suggested above that 'the individual dwelling unit' in its physical form has all but disappeared from consideration within the 'Enablement' approach. In this sense, Dewar's characterisation might be amended slightly to reflect that it is quantities of 'dematerialised' housing units, served by more or less adequate infrastructure and services placed in a 'despatialised' urban environment, which are at the centre of currently dominant approaches to housing policy.

South African housing policy and the 'enablement' paradigm

The 'Enablement' approach has been highly influential in shaping the emerging South African housing policy. This is clearly reflected in the Department of Housing's (1994) *'White Paper on Housing'*.

Consistent with the emphasis of the *Global Strategy for Shelter* on rooting housing policy in an understanding of national economic growth determinants, the *White Paper* starts with an attempt to draw linkages between the housing sector and the macro-economy. The analysis of this intersection focuses on real side linkages including the impact of housing policy on such macro-economic variables as output, employment, income, consumption, savings and investment, prices, inflation and the balance of payments; financial linkages, that is the relationship between the financial sector - in particular those providing housing finance - and the demand for and supply of housing; fiscal linkages, that is the contribution of the government to the supply of houses through tax and subsidy policy; and socio-economic linkages such as the impact of housing policy on socio-political stability, productivity and attitudes and behaviour.

In addition to this methodological consistency with the 'Enablement' approach, the *White Paper* explicitly indicates that 'The approach adopted has been the search for enabling environments' centred around notions of partnerships, the creation of a climate for investment and the overarching theme of 'People Centred development' (Department of Housing, 1994, Preface). The *White Paper* emphasises the importance of the mobilisation of various sectors though partnerships. 'It is only by mobilising and harnessing the full diversity of resources, innovation, energy and initiative of individuals, communities, the State and the broader private (non-State) sector, that the challenges can be met effectively' (Department of Housing, 1994, p.4.1).

In line with broader paradigmatic shifts 'productivity' concerns are also central. The *White Paper* asserts that housing policies and delivery systems can contribute to employment creation and economic growth 'but cannot be the primary drivers of such growth. Housing policy will therefore favour the involvement of small and medium sized businesses and labour intensive approaches, in order to maximise the economic growth and employment impact of such policy'.

Can 'enablement' provide a framework for 'settlement upgrading'?

The move towards aspatial, sectoral approaches associated with 'Enablement' implies that upgrading projects will be de-prioritised. In this context it is necessary to ask whether the 'Enablement' approach can in fact provide a framework for settlement upgrading. Essentially this means identifying the potential and limitations of 'enabling' strategies as a means by which to achieve widespread settlement improvements discernible in significant advances in the quality of local environments. A key variable in this regard is the considerable scope for differences of interpretation and emphasis within the 'Enablement' approach. The actual content and form of 'enabling' strategies and the manner in which they are implemented in South African cities is likely to reflect some degree of contest and discussion at national and local levels. Six arenas of debate likely to impact on the potential for widespread settlement upgrading under 'Enablement' are identified and discussed below.

'Provision' and 'enablement'

'Enablement' is often presented as an alternative to the 'provider' paradigm. This is understandable in contexts where there is a need to promote a shift away from rigid and unrealistic approaches which fail to grapple with the realities of diverse housing needs and limited resources. However, the sharp juxtaposition of 'enabling' approaches and strong government involvement in delivery of key components of the 'housing' product creates a questionable dichotomy. An alternative conceptualisation is expressed in terms which emphasise the potential of 'enabling' strategies to encourage various actors to fulfil their potential contributions in the housing and settlement process. From this perspective the role of the government in 'providing' certain public goods might be dealt with on the basis of analysis of contextually specific priorities and capacities.

Tension exists therefore, between an approach which juxtaposes 'provision' and 'enablement', and one which accepts that 'provision' of certain public 'goods' by government might be conceptualised as one dimension of 'Enablement'. Significantly, recent perspectives on urban productivity and poverty alleviation, put forward by the World Bank and other international agencies, recognise that governments need to take responsibility for the provision of certain public goods.

A number of authors have suggested that cost and affordability limitations mean that a strictly market-oriented approach to 'Enablement' is unlikely to meet the needs of poorer sections of society. This implies that a government 'providing' role may be necessary if infrastructure and services are to be improved and measures taken to improve the quality of built environments in low-income areas. This may be compounded where low-income residential areas occur as large monofunctional townships which do not benefit from investment in the built environment related to concentrations of business activity or the presence of major institutions such as hospitals and tertiary institutions.

It is of course important to note that 'privatisation' of infrastructure and service delivery has different implications in areas where basic infrastructure is already in place, as opposed to areas where large backlogs exist. Furthermore, it is questionable whether market-driven approaches - even where large amounts of capital are mobilised - will adequately address such issues as the quality of collective public spaces, and the integration of activities and movement patterns.

How Proactive should 'enablement' be?

Tension regarding 'provision' reflects a broader tension within 'enablement' perspectives on how proactive government should be in creating 'enabling environments' and supporting people in the housing process.

At the one pole there is a push for the withdrawal of government from housing processes and an associated emphasis on locating the individual householder in relation to market processes. Within this perspective 'enablement' focuses on limited facilitating strategies aimed at removing obstacles constraining the effective involvement of various actors in the housing process. For example, unnecessarily complex regulations and restrictive legislation might need to be reformed in order to facilitate the involvement of the private sector in housing provision, and to encourage home ownership.

At the other pole is the argument for a reoriented but nevertheless interventive and proactive government role. The focus falls on strategies aimed at improving government's role as a facilitator and enabler. From this point of view government is often seen as having a basic responsibility for ensuring that adequate and appropriate service and infrastructure networks are provided. In this regard the UNCHS (1990, p.25) has suggested that 'the adoption of an enabling approach does not imply that shelter is no longer a government's problem or concern, nor that it can wash its hand of the issue by saying that people, especially the poor, can take care of shelter themselves. On the contrary, enabling necessitates a more challenging and also complex role for governments'. Suggested arenas for action and intervention include land tenure and building codes reform, informal sector development, and clear policies towards the construction sector in the national economy. Institutional reform and management is another key arena for government involvement. In this regard proactive strategies are needed to remove red tape, foster co-ordination, devolve authority and decentralise responsibilities to allow city and municipal authorities to link up with the private sector, both formal and informal. The government enabling role means responding to tensions and bottlenecks in the shelter production and delivery system; negotiating, regulating, making responsive modifications to legislation and regulations, and taking stimulatory actions. Governments 'now act as catalysts in a physical and economic environment in which all participants - local governments, the private sector, communities and citizens - work together to shelter all'.

Hesselberg (1994, p.7) has also pointed to tension within the 'enabling' approach regarding government intervention through his assertion that: 'the aim must be for governments to find the right balance between market liberalisation and deregulation on the one hand, and intervention on the other'. In a similar sense Graham Tipple (1994a, pp.3-4) has argued that 'enabling' strategies require strong and coherent government action so as to improve the functioning of markets which supply the five major components in the housing process, namely:

land, finance, skills of the labour force, infrastructure and building materials, and the regulatory framework.

A number of questions arise from these considerations. How much and what kinds of government intervention will encourage shelter consolidation and settlement upgrading processes? What obstacles need to be removed in order to allow improvements to occur, and what kind of proactive measures might be appropriate, beyond the removal of obstacles? These questions need to be addressed in relation to specific contexts.

'Enablement' and 'empowerment'

Where 'enabling' strategies are oriented primarily to facilitating the functioning of market-driven processes 'empowerment' of people is not a primary concern. Of course the removal of obstacles such as regulatory controls to certain kinds of economic opportunity might be interpreted as a form of economic 'empowerment'. In contrast to this rather limited view, some have emphasised that 'enabling' approaches offer considerable scope for the implementation of strategies aimed at empowering individuals and groups through development processes. One key dimension of 'empowerment' deals with increasing ordinary people's involvement in and ability to influence decision-making which affects their daily lives - and potentially the quality of their immediate living environments. In this regard public participation strategies can play an important role. Another key dimension of empowerment deals with questions of economic power and access to economic opportunity. In this regard key strategies might, for instance, be geared towards improving access to financial and other resources necessary to widen the scope of economic opportunity to which people have access.

Sheng's (1995) observation, regarding the extent to which poverty disempowers people and prevents them from responding positively to the opportunities created by 'enabling' strategies, is important. It illustrates a key limitation of 'Enablement' - and points to the importance of strategies geared towards empowering people to participate actively in the transformation of urban living environments. It also suggests that settlement upgrading strategies need to be integrally linked to strategies aimed at generating economic opportunity and the alleviation of poverty.

The shift away from local area project-based approaches raises some questions about the nature of community participation in settlement upgrading. How is participation to be conducted where upgrading programmes are defined in terms of city-wide, sectoral policies and strategies?

Partnerships

A key tool of 'Enablement' is the building of partnerships through which individuals and communities, local government, non-governmental organisations and community based organisations, and the private sector, build complementary and co-operative relationships. The building of such partnerships generally requires government or some other agency to play a strong role in bringing different parties together, and in facilitating the exploration of common ground and the scope for complementary or combined action.

The strategic priorities and actions of 'enabling' partnerships will generally be shaped by broader power relations and are likely to reflect some kind of compromise, or coalition of interests. In this sense the nature and composition of such partnerships will be an important factor affecting their potential as vehicles of settlement upgrading.

A number of questions arise in considering the implications for settlement upgrading strategies of an emphasis on 'partnerships': what is the potential for forging partnerships oriented towards settlement upgrading? can the private sector, for instance, be encouraged to recognise that their own interests might be served by settlement upgrading? who are the different actors with potential to contribute to such partnerships? at what geographic scale should partnerships focused on settlement upgrading be conducted? Again, these questions need to be addressed through an assessment of contextually specific conditions.

'Enablement' and specifically spatial strategies

Finally, there is considerable scope for debating how specifically spatial considerations might be incorporated into or related to 'enabling' frameworks.

In addition to limitations in terms of cost recovery and replicability, 'traditional' project-based approaches to 'upgrading' also failed in the sense that they tended not to address questions of urban performance beyond rather limited concerns with infrastructure and service provision. 'Enablement' approaches have also generally failed to deal adequately with questions of the qualitative performance of shelter and urban environments, primarily because of their aspatial orientation. An appropriate approach to settlement upgrading, in addition to recognising the potential of 'enabling strategies', might therefore also be based on a broad and holistic conceptualisation of the performance of urban environments. This would mean recognising that spatial design-based interventions are essential building blocks in the process of improving the quality of urban environments. Such an approach would seek widespread consolidation and improvement of shelter ('the dwelling'), and widespread improvements to the performance of urban environments as a whole. This would include efforts to ensure adequate infrastructure and service provision and well as strategies to improve the spatial quality of the 'public sphere' of the urban environment.

The limitations of 'Self-Help' and 'Enablement' approaches in addressing questions of spatial quality and performance suggest the following two questions: can strategies be developed which 'enable' appropriate design and spatial planning processes to occur in relation to broader 'enabling' frameworks? what measures can be taken to ensure that sectoral policies are adequately informed by analysis of the impact, or likely impact, of these policies on the physical and spatial quality of urban environments?

Conclusion

This study has identified a number of key characteristics of currently dominant approaches to housing and human settlement in 'developing countries'. It has suggested that within the broader framework of 'enablement' the 'Self-Help' paradigm continues to exert considerable influence. In particular, the idea that governments should not 'provide' housing but should rather support people's own housing efforts, is a broadly accepted view. The study indicates that the currently dominant 'enabling' approach is rooted in a conceptualisation which emphasises the links between urban settlement and housing processes, and broad macro-economic processes. A distinctive feature of the 1990s has been the shift away from 'project-based' interventions and towards aspatial policy and sector oriented programmes aimed at creating 'enabling environments'. Recent South African housing policy is found to be strongly informed by the 'Enablement' approach. In this sense the various critiques outlined are significant when considering the implications of 'enabling' strategies for policy on settlement 'upgrading' in South Africa. Similarly relevant are the reflections on the limitations of 'Self-Help' and 'Enablement' approaches in addressing issues of urban environmental quality.

Finally, the scope for debate and contest over differences of interpretation and emphasis within the 'Enabling' approach is found to be a critical factor determining the extent to which it offers a framework for the development of successful strategies for widespread settlement upgrading. In this regard, important arenas of debate have been identified and briefly explored.

Section 2
CASE STUDIES

6 In search of a spatial culture

Amr F. Elgohary and Julienne Hanson

The urban context

El-Hekr is a spontaneously-evolved urban area to the north of the city of *Ismaïlia*, on the shore of Lake Timsah in the north-east of Egypt, at the approximate midpoint of the Suez Canal. The founding of *Ismaïlia* in 1862 is inextricably bound up with the building of the canal, which remains to this day the largest employer in the region and which supports a thriving local economy based on maritime trade, shipbuilding, light manufacturing and service industries. The first settlers began to put down roots in the area which was to become *El-Hekr* during the 1930s, but the settlement was consolidated in its mature, fully-evolved urban form during the 1960s and 1970s. Ever since its inception, the majority of *El-Hekr*'s population has been composed of low-income rural migrants, many of whom were originally attracted to the city by the possibility of work. By the end of the 1970s the built up area of the settlement covered about 132 hectares and the local population was estimated to stand at around 37,000.

By this point in time, the informal township had begun to attract attention from the consultants responsible for the formal planning of the city of *Ismaïlia*. Plans were drawn up to improve the living conditions of the local community through a combination of environmental upgrading and the implementation of a 'sites and services' project, in what was to become an internationally-acclaimed transformation of the township. This has now been implemented, and the *El-Hekr* of the 1990s bears little resemblance to that of the 1970s. The 'ethnographic present' for this study is therefore set in the late 1970s, immediately pre-dating the transformation of the town and its constituent houses, and the account draws on cartographic records, house layouts and social survey data gathered during the period immediately prior to redevelopment. (Figure 6.1)

The first area of *El-Hekr* to be settled was the south-west quarter, abutting the northern edge of the town. The last area to be settled was the northern fringe of the township. The living conditions of the settlers and the material condition of the housing stock reflect *El-Hekr*'s northward expansion. Average land values in the south-west corner are the highest in the neighbourhood and it has the highest proportion of the solidly-constructed, traditional mud and red brick, single-storey family houses, known locally as *Beit*. The local residents tend to earn higher incomes and a greater proportion of the community is in steady employment in permanent jobs. Some plots in this part of *El-Hekr* have been converted from single-storey family houses to small three to five storey apartment blocks, or *Aimara*, reflecting the achievement of the landowner in capitalising on his original investment. Most owners of Aimara reserve an apartment for their own use[1] and let or sell the remainder of the block. Apartments tend to have a smaller floor area, but a better material standard of living than houses.[2]

Immigrants in the more-recently occupied parts of northern *El-Hekr* build more temporary homes from mud brick, concrete blocks or rammed earth. A smaller proportion of the local community is in regular employment and people's earnings tend to be much lower. According to the design consultants, incomers arriving in the city usually live for a short time in a tenement house whilst they take their bearings and find a steady job. Then they obtain a plot of land in *El-Hekr* and build themselves a house incrementally. At the same time, a significant percentage of the local population remains in a tenancy for life. This process not only takes a long time, but it is also subject to the many vicissitudes of life in a developing urban township - growing numbers of children and livestock, financial problems, job loss, the unforeseen death of a spouse, divorce, re-marriage, the housing demands of children who marry but have no home of their own and relatives requiring a roof over their head, the opportunity to make a little extra by taking in lodgers. The traditional houses of *El-Hekr* are capable of absorbing a great variety of living patterns, which makes them an attractive prototype for a rapidly-urbanising situation, but this also means that the terms family and household require a little more exploration than might be expected under more stable urban conditions.

This manifest variety in the traditional living arrangements of its occupants was one of the factors which led to the close scrutiny of *El-Hekr*'s traditional housing stock at the time of its redevelopment. It was still unusual in the 1970s for informal housing to be held in high esteem, but in this case the consultants to the master-plan engaged in a detailed survey of the local urban vernacular, apparently with the intention of using any principles which could be identified as a model for their proposed new housing types.

Figure 6.1 Map of El-Hekr and Northern City Sector, Ismaïlia.

The sample

All of the 29 houses which will be referred to in this study, and which are illustrated in Figure 6.2, were completed during the 1960s and 1970s. Twenty houses were originally surveyed in connection with research into the formation, spatial layout and social significance of urban cul-de-sac and cluster, Harah,[3] which had by this time become a characteristic of the local morphology of *El-Hekr*. Because of the nature of the original inquiry, social data is available for these houses. The remainder were recorded as typical examples of traditional housing by the consultants to the planned redevelopment of *Ismaïlia*.[4] These plans have been reproduced from their published reports but, unfortunately, comparable social information was not gathered for these examples so the composition of the households which inhabited them can only be conjectured.

The sample, though small, is broadly representative of *El-Hekr*'s current housing stock.[5] Of the 29 houses, over three quarters[6] are individual family houses or *Beit*, defining this as a single-storey, square or rectangular room arrangement grouped around a courtyard and which is the home of a man, his wife and their unmarried children.[7] This is the most common type of house found in El Hekr. It is capable of great plasticity of form and is able to mutate easily into either an *Aimara*, or into a *Rabaa*, which is a serviced block of rooms for rent to unrelated families.

Because this is so, it is often difficult to attribute a house unambiguously to a specific type of dwelling. Where more than one nuclear family is in residence, it is more accurate to describe with some precision the living arrangements of the households which occupy each home. For example, in two of the households, (Houses 21 and 28) the household head has more than one wife. In each case, his two wives have separate suites of accommodation, comprising one or more rooms together with a bathroom and kitchen, linked together by a courtyard. In House 28, the husband has provided for each wife contiguous but almost completely separate dwellings which have only a transitional entrance in common.

In two more cases, segments of an extended lineage share a home, but each segment has its own sub-complex within the curtilage of the property. House 18 is shared by a widowed mother living with one unmarried son, and one of her married children with his family. House 23 is also shared, but this time by two more distant male relatives. Each part of the family has its separate living accommodation but the entrance and courtyard are common. In House 25 a man shares his home with some of his married children, each of whom lives in a room and shares the common parts of the house. A more extreme case is where a house has been sub-divided into two completely separate premises, either to accommodate a close relative or to supplement the family income by offering a home for rent. This situation has happened in two examples, which therefore give rise to four separate small houses (Houses 2, 3, 4 and 10). In both cases, the courtyard has been retained by the owner.[8]

In yet other cases, (Houses 17, 19, and 27) rooms are offered for rent to other families by the original householder, who nonetheless retains part of the accommodation for his own use. House 29 has servants living on the premises. The degree of spatial separation of the rented rooms and accommodation for servants varies, with some tenants sharing an entrance, the courtyard and the domestic offices, whilst in other examples the tenanted rooms are more clearly separated in the plan from those areas occupied by the owner's immediate family. Although social data is available for only one of these dwellings, we can deduce that the owner lives on the premises because his part of the house is spatially differentiated by function, whereas the rented accommodation is simply labelled 'room'.[9] House 7 is an ambiguous case from the consultants' survey, and for which no social data exists. It has two 'rooms', implying two families sharing.

If these were related, or if one family owned the plot or sub-let a room, as seems likely, then it would be consistent to regard the house as a Beit. For the purposes of this study, all these dwellings have been classified as 'Beit with lodgers' rather than as serviced, tenement rooming houses or Rabaa.

The final two families live in flats in walk-up apartment houses (Houses 5 and 16) which have been included for the purpose of comparison. In these cases, the open-air stair well performs many of the functions which are normally associated with the courtyard in a single storey dwelling so it has been taken into account in mapping the layout of the accommodation.

Everyday life in the traditional houses of *El-Hekr*

The houses in *El-Hekr* are close-packed on their sites. This way of aggregating homes locally guarantees access to the dwellings and natural light and ventilation to those rooms facing onto the street. Windows are set small and high, so that the houses appear closed from the street. Corner sites and dual-aspect plots are rare, but allow for greater flexibility in planning the domestic accommodation including the provision of more than one entrance to the dwelling.

The courtyard, *Hawsh*, is such an important feature in the traditional domestic space culture of *El-Hekr* that it seems reasonable to deal with this space first, especially since it is one of the most frequently-occurring uses with 25 out of the 29 examples having some form of open, interior domestic court. An open courtyard within the curtilage of the dwelling is necessary in these close-packed living conditions to provide access, light and ventilation to the inner rooms, but this is clearly not its sole purpose for the courtyard is, above all, the locus of family life. The women do most of their household chores in the courtyard including the cleaning and the laundry, children play about as the washing hangs out to dry, and the entire household gathers there to share in the cooking and consumption of food. It is used for sleeping at night and for taking an afternoon

Figure 6.2.1 Architectural plans of traditional houses. House Nos. 1-18.

Analysed sample of 29 traditional houses

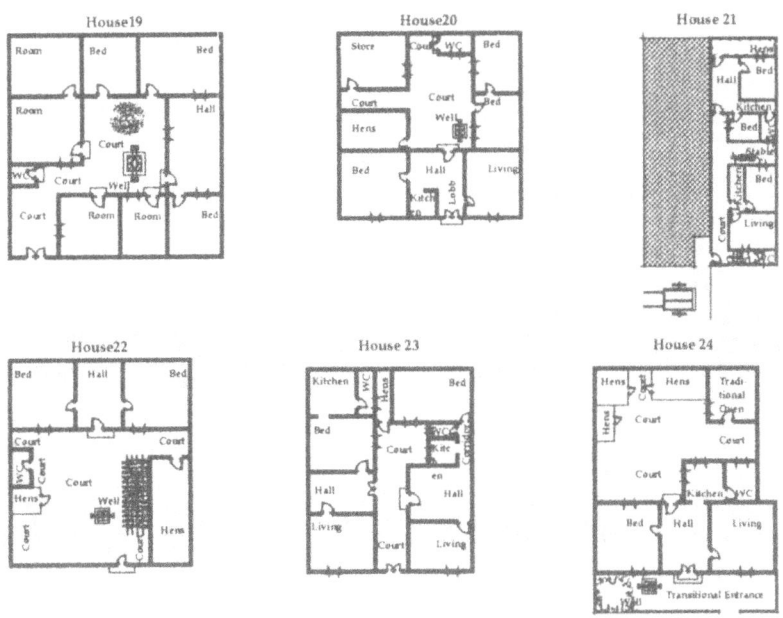

Figure 6.2.2 Architectural plans of traditional houses. House Nos. 19-24.

Figure 6.2.3 Architectural plans of traditional houses. House Nos. 25-29.

siesta. Relatives and close family friends are entertained in the courtyard on hot summer nights. Finally the courtyard is a focus for household gossip. The courtyard may contain a well (*be'er*) or a kitchen (*Matbakh*), and it may give access to a hen house (*Beit Firakh*) or the lavatory (*Hammam*). One house[10] has a donkey stable just off the courtyard and another[11] has a traditional oven for baking bread, cooking and sleeping during the winter time. Several houses[12] have a storage room which is often, though not invariably, associated with the courtyard.

Both the apartment buildings in this sample use the open stairwell as if it were a courtyard. For this reason, the stairs have been included in configurational analysis as part of the domestic interior. Two single-storey houses do not have their own courtyard. Both have arisen from the partitioning of a larger house. In each case, the owner of the land has retained the use of the courtyard and the rented portion has to make do with borrowed light. It can be safely assumed that preference had little part to play for these occupants in the decision not to have their own courtyard.

Three dwellings, including one of the examples which has arisen from the sub-division of a larger property, have a courtyard-like space at the front of the house as well as an inner court. This 'anterior court' is referred to as a 'transitional entrance' and this term seems to be reserved for a narrow, walled open area lying between the front door and the street.[13] Western architects would most likely interpret this as a 'semi-public' space as its main function seems to be to elaborate and shield the entry to the house from direct contact with the street. This may be an apposite interpretation of the part the transitional entrance plays in the configuration of the traditional house in *El-Hekr*, though it has also to be born in mind that in small houses like House 2, the transitional entrance acts as a courtyard,[14] and it may also contain external seating (*Takhtaboush*) which suggests that it can also play a linking role with the street. In two of the three cases which have a transitional entrance, the hall lies immediately within doors. In the case of House 28, the owner has used a transitional entrance to control his access to the separate premises of his two wives: one has an internal corridor and the other a covered passageway giving access to a pair of completely separate, private courtyards beyond.

Some houses have more than one courtyard. In House 28, each of the two wives has her own courtyard, but this is an exceptional case where a rich man is able to indulge his own, or his wives', partiality for a garden. The two courtyards of House 25 allow for privacy between the separate domestic offices of the owner and his married children. In House 4, two courtyards are left over from the conversion of the original premises into two, and the owner has chosen not to demolish the intervening wall. The minor courtyard in House 29 is devoted to hens. On the basis of this sample, one courtyard seems to be the accepted norm and the preferred way of arranging space since, even where a large plot could in theory have been sub-divided to separate incompatible functions, in practice the opportunity to do so has not been taken.[15]

At the same time, it is very rare for the courtyard of traditional *El-Hekr* houses to be an unitary, square or rectangular space. It is much more common for the courtyard of even the simplest houses to be convexly articulated, with a convex break-up varying between 2 and 5 convex segments. This occurs so often that it is unlikely to have occurred by chance. On the contrary, convex articulation of the courtyard enables a subtle fine-tuning of the outdoor space to take place. 'Polluting' functions like the lavatory and the hen house may be screened from the rest of the house by a chicane or a recess, so that these areas become deeper and marginally more private.[16] In other houses, the articulation of space is used to shield the entrance to the dwelling, so that it is not possible for a passer-by to see directly from the street into the main living space of the courtyard.[17] Occasionally, outdoor cooking is spatially differentiated.[18] Articulation of the courtyard can also introduce a degree of separation between the lodgers' or servants' rooms and the owner's house,[19] where the family home is shared.

In some houses, particularly where a small plot has been used to accommodate several segments of an extended family or to take in lodgers, the articulated courtyard is made up of a series of long narrow spaces which gives it the appearance of a corridor.[20] In other houses, the courtyard is clearly valued as a living space, and is elaborated by planting vines or fruit trees, or by decorative changes in the surface finish.[21] Another way of differentiating parts of the courtyard is by building a pergola, which may contain built-in seating.[22] Generally speaking, squarish courtyards with articulated recesses occur much more often than rectilinear, passage-like arrangements. There seems to be a cultural preference spatially to synchronise rather than to separate household members where they are not members of the same nuclear family, and even when they are unrelated. The concept of family privacy is clearly more 'elastic' in *El-Hekr* than it seems to be in many parts of the developed world.

Five houses in the sample have a space labelled 'terrace', which in all cases is a space directly adjacent to the courtyard.[23] This seems to indicate a relatively superficial distinction in the surface materials used, rather than a substantial differentiation of function: courtyards are surfaced in rammed earth and terraces are tiled and slightly raised areas which are usually roofed-over. In small houses which have no hall, the terrace may function as the informal living area or outdoor hall, thus assuming many of the functions of an indoor hall in a larger home. The terrace is immediately by the front door in House 6, between the courtyard and bedrooms in House 9, and House 18 has two terraces, one on each side of the courtyard. In House 8 the terrace is associated with a lobby, thus elaborating the entrance still further.

House 26 has a 'porch', which seems to perform a similar function to the terrace in insulating the deeper interior spaces of the house from the shallower entrance and courtyard. In House 12 the terrace runs right across the front of the property to separate the rooms which front onto the street from the public domain in the same way as a transitional entrance. The two apartment houses (Houses 5 and 16) have balconies, which are quite different from terraces in that they are the end-points of a sequence beyond the living room or bedroom, rather than intermediate spaces marking the threshold of the main entrance or the transition to the interior.

Some houses have a lobby or corridor as part of the domestic interior. This occurs so often (12 cases) that it seems to be yet another way of insulating one part of the dwelling from another. It will therefore be considered as such, along with the transitional entrance and porch. The entrance lobby to House 8 has already been mentioned and House 20 has a similar lobby to its entrance hall. In the remainder of cases, inner lobbies and internal corridors are used to separate the principal daytime living spaces from a WC,[24] kitchen or bedroom. The ubiquitous presence of these insulating devices suggests that the spatial elaboration of circulation routes within the home by the shaping of space through walls, convex articulation and surface differentiation, is an important constant in the space configuration of traditional *El-Hekr* houses.

One of the most-often cited room uses in *El-Hekr*, other than WC of which every house has at least one, is the 'hall' or *Saala*: 21 out of the 29 cases have a hall. It is used for everyday living and, in smaller houses where separate bedrooms are not a practical possibility, the children may sleep in this space. A corner of the hall may be set aside for cooking indoors. The relation of the hall to the other spaces of the dwelling, and especially to the space labelled 'living room' or *salon* is a significant clue to domestic space arrangements in traditional *El-Hekr* houses. However, 21 houses in the sample have a living room. The living room is also a multi-purpose space where food is occasionally consumed and where everyday living takes place. In the past, it was called the travellers' room (*Hogret Al-Mosafereen*) and traditionally, overnight guests are accommodated in this room. Children may also sleep here.

Out of the sample of 29 houses, only one case, House 1, has neither hall nor living room. This is the smallest house in the sample, and it has only one general purpose room. Another five examples[25] have only a living room. House 18, which a widow and her married son occupy as separate households, has a shallow and a deep living room for the mother's and son's sub-complexes respectively. Eight houses, only have a hall.[26] These include both small and large houses. In some cases, the hall is the first space off the street. It has one or more rooms accessed directly from it, and it also leads directly to the courtyard. In other cases, the circulation route is into the courtyard and then on to a deeper hall which also controls access to one or more bedrooms and ancillary spaces beyond.

The remainder of the sample, which includes the two houses with no courtyard and both the apartments, has both a hall and a living room. In 8 cases,[27] the hall is an entrance hall which is directly permeable to a shallow, end-point living room, one space deeper into the complex. In this case, the hall may also give access to front bedrooms, as well as to the courtyard beyond. A variant on this plan, House 13, has shallow bedrooms and a deeper living room at the rear of the courtyard. In 3 cases,[28] entry is into a shallow courtyard, and then to the hall and a living room beyond. All are non-conventional courts of a stairwell or corridor type. In House 5, the hall and living room are on a ring with the bedroom and the stairs. Finally, in House 21 where a man has two wives, one wife has a hall and the other a living room as part of the premises.

The relationship between the hall and the living room is significant for those houses which incorporate both functions,[29] but so is the relation between the hall and the means by which access is obtained to the dwelling. Of the 29 houses, a substantial minority of 12 cases[30] enter first into the hall, and then into the courtyard[31] which lies beyond the hall. The majority, 17 including the two apartments and 15 excluding them, enter the open courtyard from the street, either directly or through a transitional entrance, terrace, lobby, corridor or passage and then the circulation diffuses from the courtyard to the remaining rooms of the house.[32] In effect, cases 15 and 27 actually have the best of both worlds: a front door which gives onto the hall and a side door which opens directly into the courtyard. These are the only two examples which have a ring of circulation passing through settlement space. The overwhelming majority of houses have only a single front door. However, whether entry is into the hall or to the courtyard seems to be a substantial difference between homes which will be returned to later.

The category of space referred to simply as a 'room' gives an initial impression that domestic space in *El-Hekr* is highly flexible and multi-functional, but closer inspection has already suggested that this assumption would be erroneous. In all but the smallest houses, the use of the term room usually implies the presence of lodgers. Further evidence in support of this is that 26 out of the 29 houses have one or more spaces assigned as 'bedrooms' *(Nawm)* although this does not mean that the room is used exclusively for sleeping. However it does suggest that, where space allows, the married couple sleep apart from the male and female children. It is not considered necessary to provide separate bedrooms for each of the children and, despite the fact that the local residents tend to have large families, no house has more than three bedrooms. In those houses with only one bedroom, the children sleep in the hall. House 1, 7, and 17 do not have any labelled bedrooms. The first two are too small to have other than multi-functional rooms, and House 17 is a Beit with several lodgers so that the part reserved for the owner is likewise very small. Aside from those already noted, a further 5 houses[33] have multi-functional rooms within the premises which are occupied by married children and their families or by servants or unrelated lodgers. Traditional houses in *El-Hekr* are often described as having multi-functional rooms and this may indeed be so in respect of the actual uses to which space is put, but even so all spaces are labelled systematically and even spaces called rooms have well-defined uses.

Although much everyday food preparation, cooking and eating takes place in the courtyard, 22 houses have a separate kitchen indoors. This is invariably small, and is nearly always associated with the more 'polluting' domestic offices such as the WC. Where a house is occupied by segments of a lineage or by unrelated families lodging, it is usual for there to be more than one kitchen, one for the owner and his immediate family and another for the lodgers. This is also the case with lavatory and, in the absence of social data, it is one way spatially to deduce that several families are occupying one house.

Finally 13 households keep hens and one man stables his donkey at home. The chickens are usually located in an out of the way corner of the courtyard or close to the kitchen and WC, but some may be given what amounts to their own room within the main dwelling as merits their considerable contribution to the household economy.

However, space in architecture is only trivially a list of rooms and their uses, and the important thing about houses is that they from a pattern of space which is governed by intricate conventions about what spaces there are, how they are connected together and sequenced, which activities go together and which are separated out, how the interior is decorated and even what kinds of household object should be displayed in different parts of the home. To compare these *El-Hekr* houses with one another, we have to know what a space pattern is and how to tell one from another. We have to describe the space configuration as well as the individual spaces which make it up, and this task will therefore inform the next stage of analysis.

Analysing configurations

The remainder of this chapter will therefore draw on techniques of configurational analysis which have been developed at the Bartlett, UCL, over the last two decades.[34] By configuration, we mean something quite precise. Spatial relations exist where there is any type of link between two spaces. Configuration exists when the relations which exist between two spaces are changed according to how each is related to a third, or indeed to any number of spaces. For example, if we consider the simple building shown in Figure 6.3, comprising two rooms, A and B divided by a partition in which there is a doorway which creates a relation of permeability between them, then it is clear that the relation is symmetrical in an algebraic sense, since A is to B as B is to A.

Now consider Figure 6.4 in which we have added relations to a third space, C, which is in fact the space outside, but in two different ways so that on the left both A and B are directly permeable to C whereas on the right only A is directly connected to C.

This means that in the latter case, the relation between A and B has become asymmetrical with respect to C. We have introduced a configurational difference between the two small buildings.

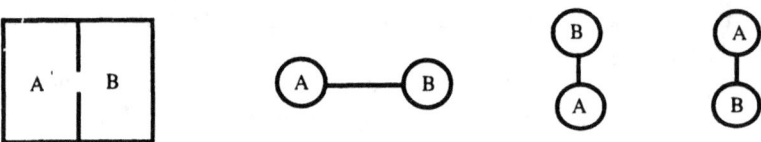

Figure 6.3 Syntactic symmetry: symmetrical configurational relationship between two spaces A & B.

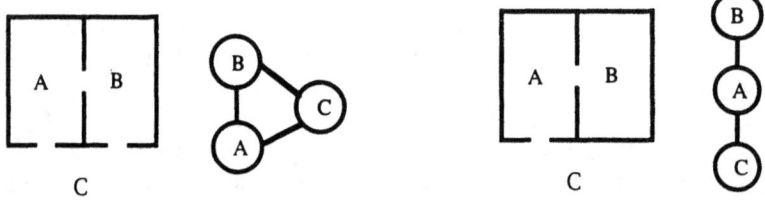

Figure 6.4 Syntactic asymmetry: asymmetrical configurational relationship between three spaces A, B & C.

We can show configurational differences rather neatly by a useful device we call a justified graph, in which we imagine ourselves to be in one space - the outside space C in this case - and align a graph of all the other spaces in the configuration up the page according to how deep or how shallow each space is from where we are. Justified graphs for small numbers of spaces tend to show configurational differences rather clearly. They capture significant properties of configurations in a visual way.

Justified graphs of houses, or indeed of any kind of space configuration from a building to a city, show that space is organised in relation to two parameters, depth and rings. There can be no more depth from a point in a configuration than a sequence, nor less than a bush. A tree has the least number of connections to join the configuration up into a continuous space pattern. Rings add extra permeability, up to a theoretical maximum where every space is connected to every other.

We can make these differences more precise by using measures of configuration - depth and rings - to capture the kinds of difference we find in houses. For example, if we take just one of the *El-Hekr* plans, House 11, and draw the justified graph from the courtyard, the hall and the WC, then we can see that the depth values of all the spaces in the graph change depending on the point of origin. The house does not just seem different from each of its constituent spaces: it actually is different. We can express this difference mathematically as the depth compared with a bush and a sequence for that number of spaces. We call this measure 'integration'.[35] Shallow graphs will be configurationally more integrated: deep graphs more segregated. The pattern of relative depth or integration of the house from each of its constituent spaces turns out to be one of the principal means by which houses embed cultural information. Different functions or activities tend to be assigned to different spaces, which integrate the complex to different degrees. If these numerical differences in function are in a consistent order across a sample of dwellings then we can say that a cultural pattern exists, one which can be detected in the configuration of space rather than in the way it is interpreted by minds. We call this particular type of numerical consistency in spatial patterning a housing 'genotype'. Integration values can be made more accessible to intuition by shading the plan in different shades of grey, so that the most integrating areas are shown in black and the most segregated areas in palest grey, as shown here for House 11, Figure 6.5. This house is cited by Hassanein[36] as the prototype for traditional *El-Hekr* houses. It remains to be seen how typical its graph and integration distribution are when these are compared with the sample as a whole.

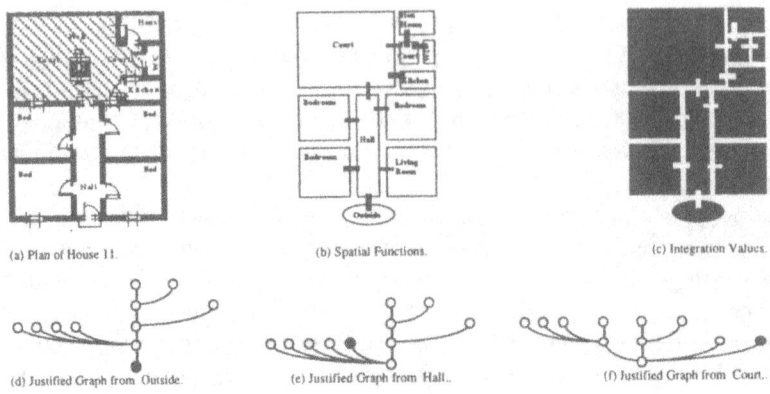

Figure 6.5 Drawings of plans, spatial functions and justified graphs from various points for house 11.

The puzzle of *El-Hekr* homes

A visual and descriptive analysis of the traditional houses of *El-Hekr* suggests that these homes have certain regularities but that they also present a puzzle which requires further investigation. It seems to be an important factor as to whether entry to the premises is effected through a hall or through a courtyard. This in turn seems to bear some, as yet undefined, relationship to whether the house has just a hall, or a hall and a living room, and also to how the hall fits into the overall pattern of interior space. The next stage of analysis therefore compares the houses as they unfold from the exterior, so see if any light can be shed on this puzzle. The houses are shown in syntactic size order, from the least to the most convexly elaborated, (Figure 6.6). The number of graphs is larger (41) than the number of houses (29) because, as will become clear later, six of the larger houses can also be considered as composed of two separate sub-complexes.[37]

The smallest examples (see Figure 6.6) have 5 convex spaces, and the largest has 23. The graphs have been arranged so that the visually shallower trees are on the left and deeper trees on the right (in most cases), with any ringy cases on the extreme right (where possible). This immediately clarifies the tree-like nature of *El-Hekr* houses. It is not only the case that only two houses[38] have more than one access from the street, but the interiors of the dwellings are also tree-like and sequenced. All shapes of tree are found. Some branch low: others branch deep.

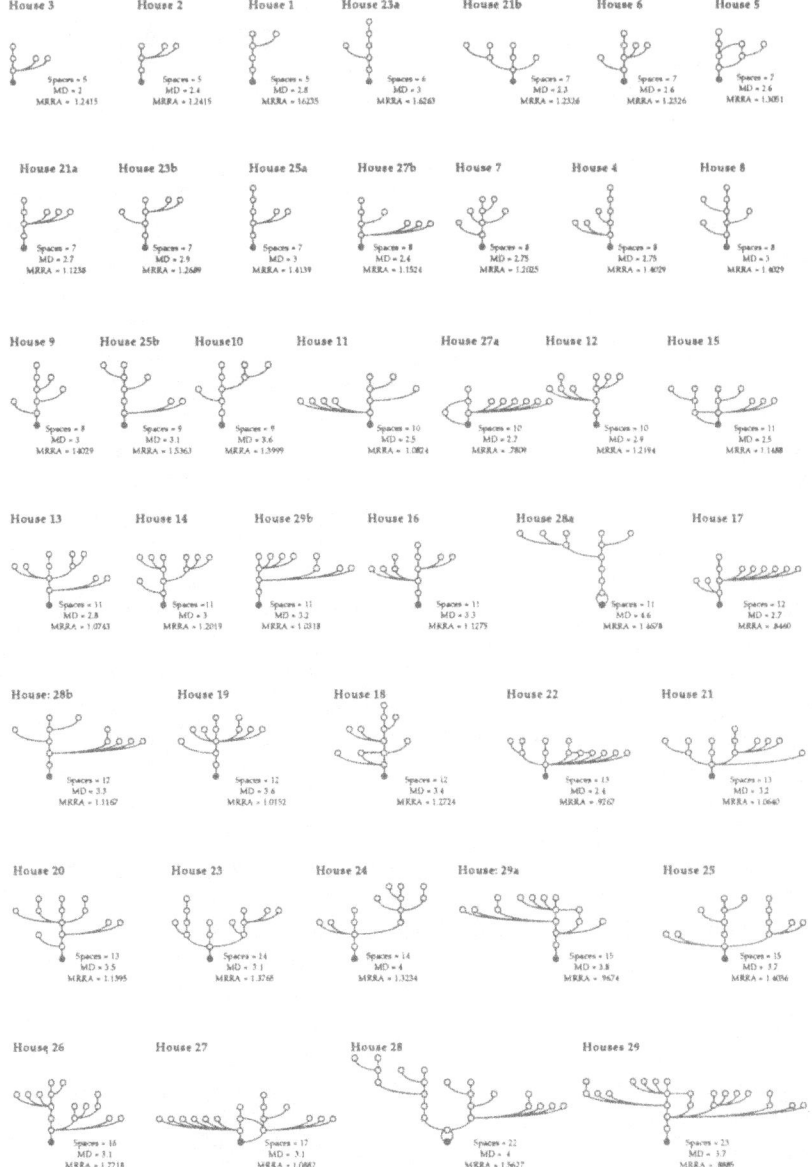

Figure 6.6 Justified graphs of the 41 cases.

MD = Mean depth
MMR = Mean RRA

Some almost take the form of an unilinear sequence, though a pure sequence is not found even amongst the smallest cases. Some have bushes springing out from a single fork: others have a long trunk with a branch at every level. Some have even, balanced groups of branches: others branch in an irregular, uneven manner. Looking just at the patterns of space and permeabilities traced by the graphs, there is very little duplication in space configuration. Only one duplicate space arrangement exists. Houses 8 and 9 are spatially identical. However, the majority of the houses are, spatially-speaking, highly individual. This is unusual in samples of traditional and vernacular architecture which, especially where the principle for growth is clear as it is here, tend to replicate examples of interior layout.

Very few houses have an internal ring. House 5 has a small ring passing through the stairwell, hall, bedroom and living room, but directly linking major spaces in this way appears to be very much the exception in *El-Hekr*. In practice, the door between the living room and the bedroom is always kept closed when visitors are welcomed into the home, and it is only occasionally used to serve refreshments to the guests. House 29 has a large ring passing through the hall, internal corridors and the courtyard. Other houses[39] have rings within the courtyard, but these tend to be a trivial product arising from the articulation of boundaries, rather than a way of offering significant route choice through the dwelling.

As the houses grow syntactically from small and simple cases, to large and ramifying courtyards, they tend to become deep, though there is an occasional exception. The average mean depth (MD) of spaces from the outside is 3.0. The minimum value for mean depth is House 3, which has a mean depth of 2.0, but this is a very small case and therefore not representative. House 28a has the highest mean depth of 4.6.

A considerable amount of depth in these houses is accounted for by the elaboration of courtyards, terraces, lobbies and the like, which is referred to earlier. The graphs clarify the way in which these separate and insulate the interior rooms from one another. Rooms appear as small spurs off the main circulation branches. Although rooms which accommodate major living functions are occasionally found in sequence, this way of arranging space in a matrix of interconnected rooms does not feature largely in the domestic arrangements of *El-Hekr*. Where rooms are accessed directly from one another then space tends to assemble a major and a minor function, such as bedroom and WC, bedroom and kitchen, bedroom and store. The hall is the exception to this rule, and in some homes it becomes the organising focus for a group of rooms.

Although there do not appear to be any formal rules in *El-Hekr* which systematically allocate specific living functions close to the street and others at the back of the plot, some consistent principles for patterning domestic space can be identified from the graphs. Courtyards penetrate all parts of the domestic interior. Rooms and bedrooms can be either shallow or deep in the plan, and may be located on short end-point spurs or, less frequently, on longer branches.

Living rooms tend to be an end-point space, one step deep from the main branches. Halls are usually well-connected. Both functions may be found either shallow or deep from the entrance. Kitchens, WC's and animal houses are nearly always in the deepest parts of the graph where they are much more discreet in relation to the main entrance to the home, though less convenient insofar as the disposal of waste is concerned.

The houses are all relatively segregated, though there are one or two notable exceptions (Figure 6.7). All but five examples have mean values above 1 (mean is marked in black) and the mean integration for the sample (mean of means) is 1.2233. The most integrated case is the owner's sub-complex from House 27 (27a) with a value of 0.7809, though the whole house including the lodgers' rooms is more segregated, at 1.0882. The most segregated example is House 23a, with a value of 1.6263. However, it is in the distribution of integration that the most consistent relations between configuration and space use are revealed, Figure 6.7, although as always there are individual exceptions to any rule. The most integrating spaces, which literally draw all the parts of the domestic interior together, are the courtyards, halls, transitional entrances, entrance lobbies, porches, pergolas, corridors and terraces.

The rank order of integration below the mean is dominated by these spaces in every case, although the courtyard is not always the most integrating space of all (24 cases). Sometimes the most integrating space is the hall (12 cases), which tends to feature quite strongly on the integrated side of the mean, for those houses which have a hall. Apart from courtyards and halls, no other function is found which consistently integrates the house, though where the hall is either the most integrated space or very integrating, the rooms to which it gives access may also be drawn shallower within the configuration. This is revealed in the rank order of integration for the individual houses in a tendency for examples with shallow halls also to have a room, bedroom, store or, very occasionally, a living room, WC or kitchen on the shallow side of the mean integration for the complex. The segregated side of the mean also has its consistencies though, as before, these are not absolutely invariant across all cases. The street is nearly always on the segregated side of the mean, and it so often appears as the most segregated space in the complex that it has to be concluded that *El-Hekr* houses systematically build privacy into the dwelling by segregating the interior from the street. This is so, even where the courtyard is directly permeable to the street. The bulk of living spaces in each house are also on the segregated side of the mean, thus confirming what has been already observed in the plans and graphs, that living functions are separated out within the interior and spatially insulated from one another. This is the case not only with the more earthy functions like the WC, kitchen and hen house, but of all indoor activities.

House No. **Integration Rank Order**

House No.											
1	2 Court .8595	>	Court 1.4325	>	Room WC 2.0055	>	Outside 2.5785				
2	Hall .2865	>	Trans.- Entr. .8595	>	Bed WC Living 1.4325	>	Outside 2.0055				
3	Hall .2865	>	Lobby .8595	>	Bed Living Outsid e 1.4325	>	WC 2.0055				
7	Court .4509	>	Court Hall .7891	>	Kitchen Room 1.2401	>	Court Room WC Outside 1.5783				
21a	Hall .2900	>	Court Kitchen .8701	>	2 Bed Hens 1.1600	>	WC Outside 1.7401				
23b	Hall Corridor .5800	>	Court 1.1601	>	Living Kitchen Bed WC 1.4501	>	Outside 2.0302				
14	Court .5106	>	Court Lobby .7658	>	Hall .8935	>	2 Bed Kitchen Hens 2 WC 1.4040	>	Living Outside 1.5317		
5	Hall Stairs .7251	>	Bed Living 1.0151	>	Kitchen 1.3051	>	Outside 1.5951	>	Balcny. 1.8852	>	WC 2.1752
6	Court .4350	>	Terrace .7251	>	Court 1.0151	>	Living WC 1.3051	>	Bed Outside 1.5951	>	Kitchen 1.8852
11	Hall .4521	>	Court .5275	>	Court .9042	>	Living 3 Bed Outside 1.1303	>	Kitchen 1.2057	>	WC Hens 1.5824

Figure 6.7.1 Rank order of integration values of spatial functions and genotypes of 41 cases. (1 of 4 diagrams)

N.B. > = Mean Integration value for the whole house.

House No.　　　　　　　　　Integration Rank Order

12	Hall 5275	>	Lobby Trans. Entrance 7506	>	Bed Bed 1.2057	>	Living 1.2810	>	WC Kitchen Bed Outside 1.4317	>	Balcony 1.6592
21b	Court 4360	>	Kitchen 7251	>	Court 1.0151	>	Stable Outside 1.3051	>	Bed Living 1.4951	>	WC 1.8892
25a	Hall 5600	>	Lobby 1.1601	>	Court 1.1601	>	2 Bed Kitchen 1.4301	>	Outside 2.0392	>	WC 2.1202
27a	Hall 1507	>	Court 5275	>	Outsid * 6782	>	Living 3 Bed Room Kitchen 8289	>	Court 1.0550	>	WC 1.2057
27b	Court 4509	>	Court	>	Room 1.1273	>	Court Kitchen WC Outside 1.2491	>	Room 1.3028	>	Room 1.9165
4	Court 6764	>	Hall 7961	>	Court 1.0146	>	Kitchen 1.4655	>	Bed Living Outside 1.5763	>	WC 2.3674
17	Court 2200	>	Hall 4849	>	Court 7149	>	3 Room Kitchen Store WC 8268	>	2 Room Outside 1.0968	>	Courts 1.3197
20	Court	>	Hall	>	2 Court Lobby Bed 4810	>	Hens 1.0671	>	Bed Kitchen 1.1532	>	Living Bed Store WC Outside 1.5376
29b	Court 9629	>	Court 5106	>	Court 9695	>	Store WC 1.0211	>	2 Bed Hens Room 1.1494	>	Room Outside 1.5315

Figure 6.7.2 Rank order of integration values of spatial functions and genotypes of 41 cases (2 of 4 diagrams).

House No.   Integration Rank Order

32a	Hall 7951	<	Bed 9814	<	Court 1.3799	<	Kitchen 1.5792	< Living 1.7665 < Outside 2.5853 < WC 2.5516
15	Hall	<	Court	<	Lobby/ Outside	<	Court 1.0211	< 2 Bed Living 1.0849 < WC Kitchen 1.4678 < 2 Hens 1.6593
16	4467	<	6382	<	8297	<		
	Hall 4467	<	Corridor 5744	<	Bed Stairs 9673	<	2 Bed Living 1.0849	< Kitchen 1.2126 < Outside Balcony 1.5955 < Balcony 1.7231
25b	Court .8182	<	Court 1.0000	<	Court 1.1818	<	Kitchen 1.5454	< 2 Room Outside 1.7222 < Court 1.8182 < Court WC 1.9090
27	2 Court	<	Hall Outside	<	Court	<	Kitchen Court 2 WC	< Room Living Kitchen 3 Bed < Room < Room
	.3079		.6198		.8678		1.0537	1.1157 1.3017 1.3657 1.7975
8	Terrace 6764	<	Court .7991	<	Lobby 1.0146	<	Court 1.3528	< Living 1.4655 < WC 1.5783 < Bed Outside 1.9037 < Hens 2.1419
9	Court 6764	<	Terrace .7991	<	Court 1.0146	<	Bed 1.3528	< Living 1.4655 < Bed 1.5783 < WC Outside 1.9037 < Stove 2.1419
19	Court .3290	<	Court .4049	<	Hall Room .8248	<	2 Bed Room .9048	< Court 1.0666 < WC 1.2097 < Bed Room 1.9037 < Outside 1.7046
28a	Court .7020	<	2 Court .9573	<	Court 1.0849	<	Court 1.3402	< Living Bed Pergola 1.9685 < Hens WC 1.8628 < Trans- Entrance 1.8628 < Outside 2.4940
13	Court .3629	<	Hall .6382	<	Court .7658	<	Court	< Bed Living 1.0211 < 2 Bed Outside 1.2764 < WC Kitchen 1.4040 < Stove 1.5317
24	Court .7222	<	Court Hall .7647	<	Court 1.1437	<	Kitchen Court Trans- Entrance 1.2320	< Bed Hens 1.3570 < Living 1.3710 < 2 Hens 1.6994 < Oven WC Outside 1.7843

Figure 6.7.3 Rank order of integration values of spatial functions and genotypes of 41 cases (3 of 4 diagrams).

House No. **Integration Rank Order**

28b	Corridor	>	Court	>	Bed Trans- Entrance	>	Court	>	Bed Living Store	>	Court	>	Outsid e Kitchen	>	Hens WC														
	.4309		.6049		.9348		.9688		1.0448		1.2097		1.5397		1.5947														
10	Court	>	Court	>	Hall	>	Kitchen	>	Court	>	Court	>	Bed Hens	>	WC	>	Outsid e												
	.6363		.8182		1.0000		1.1818		1.3636		1.5454		1.7272		1.9090		2.0908												
21	Court	>	Hall	>	Kitchen	>	Court	>	Kitchen Stable Outside	>	Hens 2 Bed	>	Bed Living	>	WC	>	WC												
	.4325		.5286		.8169		.9130		1.0091		1.1052		1.3935		1.4896		1.5857												
22	Court	>	Pergola	>	Hall	>	2 Court	>	Court	>	Court Hens Outside	>	Court	>	Bed Bed	>	WC	>	Hens										
	.2883		.6247		.6727		.7208		.7688		.8649		1.1052		1.2493		1.2974		1.6818										
25	Court	>	Court Hall	>	Court	>	2 Room Lobby Outside	>	Bed Bed	>	Court	>	Kitchen	>	Kitchen	>	Court WC	>	WC										
	.7208		.8725		1.1001		1.2519		1.4036		1.4795		1.6312		1.7071		2.0106		2.2382										
29a	Corridor	>	Corridor	>	Court	>	Hall	>	Court Hens	>	Kitche n Bed	>	Court 4 Bed	>	WC	>	Hens	>	Outside										
	.4173		.5311		.6070		.8346		.8725		.9484		1.0622		1.1381		1.4036		1.5933										
29	Court	>	Corridor	>	Corridor Court	>	Court	>	Court Room	>	Hall WC Store	>	Hens	>	Bed Kitchen	>	6 Bed Room Hens	>	Outside Room	>	Hens								
	.4056		.4636		.6760		.6953		.7919		.8306		.8499		.8885		1.1010		1.2169		1.2748								
26	Pergola	>	Pergola Seating	>	Hall	>	Court	>	Court	>	Store Room Lobby Outside	>	3 Bed	>	Hens	>	Court	>	Kitchen WC	>	Hens								
	.6491		.6833		.7858		.9566		.9807		1.1615		1.2982		1.4007		1.5032		1.6740		1.9131								
18	Court	>	Court	>	Terrace	>	Terrace	>	Court	>	Court	>	Kitchen	>	Kitchen	>	Living	>	Living Outside	>	WC	>	Bed						
	.6049		.6599		.8798		.9868		1.0998		1.2097		1.2647		1.3747		1.4847		1.5947		1.8037		1.9796						
23	Court	>	Hall	>	Hall	>	Lobby	>	Court	>	Outside	>	Bed	>	Living	>	Living	>	Bed Kitchen WC	>	Hens	>	Kitchen	>	WC				
	.6797		.8072		.8922		1.1046		1.1471		1.2320		1.2745		1.3595		1.4445		1.6569		1.6994		1.7418		2.2941				
28	Trans- Entrance	>	Corridor	>	Pergola Passage	>	Court	>	Court	>	Court	>	Bed	>	Outsid e	>	Store Living Bed	>	2 Court	>	2 Court	>	Kitchen	>	Living Pergola Bed	>	WC Hens	>	Wc Hens
	.9513		.9720		1.0133		1.1167		1.2408		1.2615		1.3649		1.3856		1.4062		1.5717		1.6751		1.7992		2.0060		2.0266		2.0473

Figure 6.7.4 Rank order of integration values of spatial functions and genotypes of 41 cases (4 of 4 diagrams).

However, two tendencies can be observed in the rank ordering of spaces. In some cases, courtyards create configurational differences between activities which appear as strong differences in the rank order of integration. In other cases, they homogenise functions so that they are separated from one another but not arranged with respect to each another.[40] This is particularly the case where a house has several rooms which fulfil the same or similar functions such as rooms, bedrooms, living rooms and storage.

This gives an interesting new slant to the concept of 'flexibility' or multi-functional space, for rooms which are configurationally identical can easily take on a new use without disturbing the principles of integration and segregation which dictate that some rooms act as foci for domestic life, whilst others are systematically separated out. This potential for syntactic inter-changeability seems to be one benefit which accrues from the tree-like principles of growth of these *El-Hekr* homes.

These strong tendencies in the layout of individual homes can be detected more easily at the statistical level, by comparing the mean, minimum and maximum values for each function with the overall values for the set of plans given earlier, (see Table 6.1). As might be expected from what has gone before, the integration values for courtyards, terraces and pergolas vary greatly - for courtyards from a minimum of 0.220 to a high of 2.011. The mean value is, however, 0.936 whilst the mean just for the most integrated courtyards in each house is 0.561. The terraces vary from a minimum of 0.676 to a maximum of 2.142, with a mean of 0.841, while the mean for the pergola is 0.971. There is also a considerable fluctuation in the values for the utilities of the house - kitchens, WCs, animal houses and stores and the like - from a low of 0.75 to a high of 2.142, but the number of cases with a value well above 1.0 is large, and the average value for kitchens, WC's and stores of 1.463 shows that they tend to be much more segregated than the average value for all spaces (1.155). Rooms and bedrooms are also more segregated, statistically. The minimum for rooms is 0.792 and the maximum is 2.006 but the average is only 1.233, a little above the mean for all the spaces in the house. Likewise for bedrooms, the minimum and maximum values are 0.829 and 2.006 respectively, but there is a preponderance of values well above 1.0 leading to a high, segregated mean of 1.240 for this function. Living rooms show a smaller range of numerical variability, with a minimum value of 0.829, a maximum value of 1.885 and a mean of 1.382. Halls also have a wide spread of values at the integrated end of the range, from a low of 0.151 to a high of 2.552, and hence the mean is 0.651, which shows that this function tends strongly to integration.

The most integrated halls, show the previous with a the maximum mean of 0.479 within the whole sample of functions. Finally, the values of the exterior range between a low of 0.620 and a high of 1.252, but the minimum value is clearly an exception. The next lowest value is 1.0849, and the prevalence of a segregated exterior leads to a high mean value of 1.526 for the sample as a whole.

Table 6.1 Integration Min., Max. & Mean values for main functions.

	Min	Max	Mean
Hall	0.151	1.000	0.651-most Int Hall=0.479
Court	0.220	2.011	0.936 -most Int Crt.=0.561
Room	1.009	1.305	1.157
Bed	0.829	2.006	1.240
Living	0.829	2.006	1.382
Kitchen/WC/Store	0.8112	2.5516	1.4956
Exterior	0.6782	2.5785	1.5892
All	0.6782	2.5785	1.5892

These consolidated values give rise to the following simplified rank order of integration: most integrated courtyard = hall > courtyard > room > bedroom > living room > utilities > exterior. This can be regarded as the underlying space 'genotype' on which all the *El-Hekr* houses are based, see Figures 6.6-6.7 and Table 6.1. The most integrated courtyard and the hall have almost the same value, and serve more or less the same informal everyday living functions. Houses which do not have a hall tend to use a terrace or courtyard as if it were a hall. As with many of the individual cases, all the domestic functions other than the courtyards and the hall in this statistically-derived domestic space genotype are above the mean integration value for all spaces. The values for rooms, bedrooms and living rooms are close to the mean value for all spaces, again underlining the relative configurational homogeneity and inter-changeability of these functions. As might be expected, the aggregate values show utilities: kitchens, WCs, stores and animal houses as highly segregated, but that the exterior is the most segregated space of all. The final outcome of the permutations and the combinations of functional locations within the home is a duality in spatial norms, i.e. a set of rules structuring the spatial house culture, resulting in a cultural stratification of certain functions, combined with a loose structure for some others. The previous forms the core of the spatial genotypes of domestic spaces in *El-Hekr*. This space genotype reflects consistencies in the patterns found in real cases, but not the many exceptions to the rule which makes these houses so much a set of individuals, each with different physiognomy.

From physiognomy to physiography

Seven cases[41] out of the original 29 plans are 'hall-centred', and twelve in the whole sample of 41 cases, in that the hall is the most integrated space in the complex. These include both the cases without a courtyard, and both the apartments where the stairs absorb the courtyard function. The remaining three cases are all small, single family houses with a shallow, well-connected hall either giving onto or very shallow to the street. This group also includes House 11, which is cited by Hassanein[42] as the prototype for traditional *El-Hekr* houses, though in fact, it is unique. House 15, which is superficially like it, is one of the two cases in the sample which are bi-permeable through the courtyard. If it had only one entrance, it would be configurationally very similar to House 11. House 12 is an interesting case where the physical and geometric relation between the court and terrace with the street is more like a transitional entrance than a conventional courtyard, and the terrace takes the function of a large balcony rather than the traditional terrace which is equivalent to an open-roofed hall. In the two of these 'hall-centred' houses,[43] the courtyard is the second most integrating space, except in house 12, where the transitional entrance and the lobby take the second most integrated position. Five of the subdivided houses are also hall centred.[44] Of these houses, the shallowest from the outside in four cases is the court,[45] which gives onto the integrating hall. Only one case has the outside giving onto the integrating hall with a deep court. The predominance here is for the shallow court which acts mainly as a transitional space. In the case of the deep court,[46] it is more of an active almost squarish court, with all the qualities of traditional functioning courts described earlier in the chapter. In three of these cases the court is the second most integrating space. The remaining three cases vary between bed corridor and lobby followed by court in all three cases.

The majority of the remainder of the houses are 'courtyard-centred' plans - sixteen in the original sample of 29 houses, and 21 in the whole sample of 41 cases - in the sense that the courtyard is the most integrating space in the complex. However, they unfold into three sub-groups: court-centred with shallow hall, deep hall and courtyard proper with no hall. The first group, with eight examples,[47] has a court centred plan with shallow hall. It comprises all those cases which, like the previous plans, also have a shallow, geometrically central hall either directly adjacent to the street, or only separated from it by a lobby or transitional entrance. In all these cases, the hall is almost as integrated as the courtyard. These houses are in other respects like the 'hall-centred' cases. Most are single family houses. House 17 has rooms for lodgers which are integral with the main courtyard. In the case of House 27, the layout of the complex is such that it can be disaggregated into two functionally independent premises - that of the owner and that for lodgers. If these are analysed separately, then the part belonging to the owner is clearly another example of a 'hall-centred plan' whilst that shared by the lodgers remains a 'courtyard-centred' plan.

The second group of eight examples,[48] has a courtyard centred plan with deep hall, a shallow, integrated courtyard. In these cases the courtyard and its ancillary spaces also control access to the street, with a deep hall. House 19 creates an interesting case, which represents the residential rental type of *Rabaa*, with almost all the rooms of lodgers opening onto the internal courtyard. The court controls all the access to the outside and the shared facilities. In a group of four houses,[49] the hall is nearly as well-integrated as the courtyard, but it is deep from the outside and geometrically located at the back or side of the plot. The cases of houses 21, 23, 25 and 29 have the same divided qualities of a shallow integrated courtyard, described earlier in house 27, splitting the house into two domains of owners and lodgers. The third group of ten houses,[50] has a courtyard centred plan with no hall, all small examples with only one family in residence. The exception is house 18. Yet, the main living spaces are at or above mean integration and the sequence of courtyard areas assemble the rooms together and link them to the outside world. The living activities performed by the hall are replaced by either a terrace or a living room. Otherwise the court performs almost all the living functions, if they are not done in the multi-functional rooms. The few remaining houses form another genotype that revolves around transitional spaces, with only three examples in the whole sample,[51] with mainly transitional spaces like corridors or transitional entrances being the most integrated spaces. The three examples are built very late in the development process, between the early and mid 1970s. The first two examples of subdivided houses 28b and 29a represent this phenomenon of the most integrated space being the corridor followed by the court. House 28 is a unique case of a man with two wives living on the same plot, yet it is divided into two domains, where the main integrated space is the transitional entrance, followed by the corridor, followed by the pergola then the court. The whole house has no hall. The chain of integrated transitional core shows the power exercised by the male member of the family, controlling the access to both domestic domains through transitional spaces thus segregating the two wives' daily activities and functional domains.

The final sample is a pattern genotype, what we may call the split type, with 6 examples[52]. Although the houses were categorised under the earlier described genotypes, they have a characteristic pattern of their own, within the locality of *El-Hekr*. This part of the sample contains all the larger houses that are shared by family segments, as well as the remaining case of a house with lodgers. For these homes the courtyard acts as a shallow filter and in each case the premises are actually made up of two sub-complexes which are able to function independently and can therefore be analysed separately.

When this is done, the results are striking. In House 21 where a man has two wives, the first wife's suite has a hall-centred plan whilst the second wife's domain is a shallow separating type of 'courtyard-centred' plan. House 29 with servants living-in, also breaks up into distinct sub-complexes comprising a corridor-centred plan for the owner and a shallow, separating courtyard centred-plan for the servants. House 23, in which two male relatives share a home, divides into two hall-centred plans. House 25, shared by a man and his children, splits into a hall-centred plan for the owner, and a courtyard-centred plan for the children. Finally, in House 28, one wife has a courtyard-centred plan and the other a corridor-centred plan, both with deep living rooms.

Table 6.2 The physiography of 4 main integration genotypes (syntactic typology).

Variables		Spatial Genotypes			
		Hall-Centred	Court-Centred	Transition-Centred	Split
	Cases	12	26	3	6
	Min.	0.151	0.220	0.417	0.406
	Mean	1.184	1.197	1.268	1.224
	Max	2.552	2.578	2.047	2.294
	DF	0.176	0.264	0.612	0.540

Variables		Sub-Groups			
		Shallow Hall	Deep Hall	No Hall	
	Cases	8	8	10	
	Min.	0.220	0.288	0.383	
	Mean	1.139	1.147	1.323	
	Max.	2.367	2.294	2.578	
	DF	0.308	0.410	0.472	

Total (*)	
Cases	41
Min.	0.151
Mean	1.155
Max.	2.578
DF	0.176

Min. = Minimum, Max. = Maximum, DF = Base difference factor.
N.B. - (*) Total is based on the overall of 41 cases.

House 18, which is shared by a mother and son cannot be disaggregated, and although it has two living rooms, both are deep and segregated.

When these differences in geometry and household form are taken into account, the puzzle of *El-Hekr* houses resolves itself into four general variations on the traditional *El-Hekr* house and 6 detailed ones. If the surface appearance is a physiognomy, and the rank order of integration a genotype, then interposing between the two is a physiography, or variations on a theme, which result from strategic choices in the organisation of the home, Table 6.2.

The first and most numerous variant is the hall-centred plan proper, with 12 out of 41 cases.[53] This type is characterised by a well-connected, (average 4-5 links) well-integrated, mean 0.463, and mostly shallow (depth 1-2) hall. The most-integrating hall in this plan type therefore is much more integrated than both the hall and the most integrated hall of the genotype for the whole sample, which is 0.651 and 0.479, respectively. The courtyard may be shallower or deeper than the hall, but the two spaces are always directly permeable to one another. The most integrating courtyard in this type is more segregated than in other plan types, with an overall mean of 0.860 across the whole sample, with a mean of 0.924, which is closer to the mean value for all courtyards in the *El-Hekr* space genotype, 0.936. Most examples have a living room, which is usually accessed from the hall and is relatively more segregated, with a mean of 1.264. Houses of this type tend to be small, with an average of 8 convex spaces. If these factors are coupled to the fact that the hall-centred plan nearly always results from the sub-division of a larger house or from the building of an apartment block, then it may be regarded as the most basic form of traditional home in *El-Hekr*. The focus of informal daily life here seems to be the indoor hall, whilst the living room is used as a more formal space and a reception room for guests. Hassanein's *El-Hekr* prototype, House 11 (in Figure 6.5) is a good example though it is not strictly-speaking typical, since it is one of the 3 cases which were planned this way from the start as opposed to having emerged from the process of redevelopment.

The second type is a courtyard-centred, shallow hall plan, with 8 cases.[54] This plan type is larger, with an average of 11 convex spaces. It has a courtyard which is deeper from the outside (depth 2-4). The courtyard mean across the type is 0.839, but the most integrating courtyard with a mean of 0.478, is considerably more integrated than the average value of the most integrating courtyards in the *El-Hekr* space genotype (0.561). The hall is also well-integrated, mean average 0.696, but this space is still noticeably less integrating than in the hall-centred plan. However, it is always shallower in the plan than the courtyard (depth 1-2). The courtyard is, on average, better-connected than the hall, with a mean connectivity of 5 as opposed to 4. In these houses, a visitor is received first into the hall, and can either remain there informally or be led into the courtyard to mix casually with the family out of doors, or to the more formal and private living room, with a considerably high mean of 1.359. House 20 is a classic case, (see Figure 6.8). The next group of houses, the courtyard-centred, deep hall plan, has 8 representatives, all from among larger homes. The average number of convex spaces of these homes is 13, in a ratio of 5 courtyard areas to 8 rooms, yet despite their size these homes are the most integrating plan type of all, with a mean of 1.147, Courtyard-centred, deep hall houses are characterised by shallow, elaborate courtyards with a sequence of several, most integrating (average 0.5167) and shallow spaces which span between steps 1 and 3 deep from the street. The hall is always deeper (average depth 4) and it is more segregated than in the previous types (mean integration 0.8267) but it is still the most integrated indoor living space. None of the deep hall plans has a living room. The courtyard is on average twice as well-connected as the hall, with a mean connectivity of 6. In these houses, the outdoor spaces seem to be associated more with informal living, whilst the deeper hall accommodates the more formal aspects of household life. House 22 is a typical case, (see Figure 6.9).

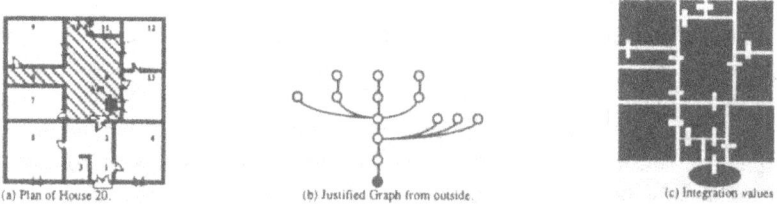

Figure 6.8 Drawings for house 20: plan, justified graphs from exterior and integration values.

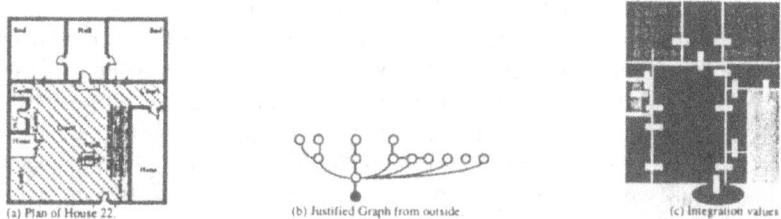

Figure 6.9 Drawings for house 22: plan, justified graph from exterior and integration values.

In the final group of 10 plans, the courtyard-centred plan proper,[55] the most integrating courtyard with mean value of 0.598 is invariably part of a sequence of between 2 and 6 small courts, terraces and lobbies, which begins at the threshold from the street and runs from shallow to deep in the house. Both the most integrated courtyard and the courtyard (mean 0.944) within the genotype, are also more segregated than the most integrated courtyard across the whole sample (mean 0.561). These houses clearly exploit the organising potential of a sequence and they are deeper than the norm from the outside, where other plan types tend to be more bushy. All the living spaces in this plan type are on the segregated side of mean integration, 1.323, and most are also at or above the mean depth from the outside. Overall, this plan type is the most segregated. Even more striking is that none of these houses has a hall. The terrace or the courtyard is the locus of everyday living. The principal room, if there is one - and half the examples do not - is a rather segregated, formal living room (mean value 1.501). All the examples of this plan type are small, with an average of 9 convex spaces. House 8 is a typical example of this plan (see Figure 6.10).

The fifth type that evolved very recently is a corridor centred plan, with the most integrated space being the corridor with a mean of 0.590, and the rest of the living functions being very segregated. It has only three representatives across the whole sample that mainly evolved out of the subdivision of existing houses.[56] It links most of the house spatial functions. Courtyards run either shallow or deep into the house. When shallow, they act as transitional spaces that give access to a hall. When deep, they are mostly associated with informal living - with no hall - but have a formal deep living room. House 28a is a good example for this type (Figure 6.11).

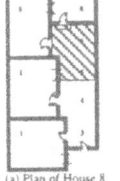
(a) Plan of House 8

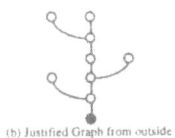
(b) Justified Graph from outside

(c) Integration values

Figure 6.10 Drawings for house 8: plan, justified graph from exterior and integration values.

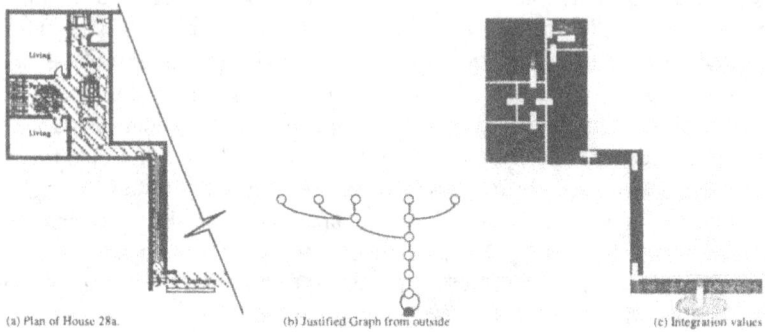

Figure 6.11 Drawings for house 28a: plan, justified graph from exterior and integration values.

The split houses combine the sixth type, it forms the twinning effect of two houses merged together through shared facilities. This type is more of a characteristic local pattern genotype. It has 6 representatives across the whole sample. The overall type is average in terms of integration, the mean of 1.224 is equivalent to the overall mean of the whole sample, 1.223. Usually the twin houses are not identical but each possess the individual spatial properties of one of the previous genotypes. The split twinnings have the largest average of 17 spaces. The hall is the most integrated function within the genotype with a mean of 0.758, followed by the transitional spaces (transitional entrances and corridors) with a mean of 0.834. The living room is the most segregated of them all, mean 1.454. House 28 is a good example for this type, (Figure 6.12).

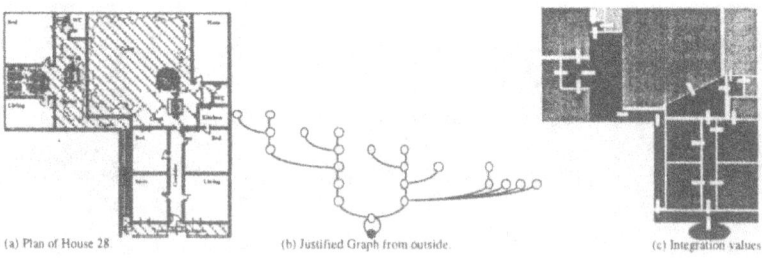

Figure 6.12 Drawings for house 28: plan, justified graph from exterior and integration values.

The new homes

The design of the new housing prototypes for *El-Hekr* seems to have taken place on a 'rational' basis which began by specifying the range of preferred plot sizes and frontages which it was felt could accommodate a wide variety of domestic functions, and then proceeded to set minimum space standards for the courtyard and for each of the constituent rooms of the house. The layout of the accommodation on the plot was treated as a secondary consideration, to be resolved in the most efficient way which satisfied modular plot sizes and preferred room dimensions, and was also capable of housing a six person household. Prototypes were developed for plot sizes ranging from 54 m. sq. (6m x 9m) to 144 m. sq. (12m x 12m), with the intention that any new provision should offer a wide range of choice to prospective inhabitants. The proportion of each type was set by balancing maximum affordability against minimising infrastructure costs, whilst at the same time catering for the needs of different household sizes and family structures. Four illustrative layouts of single storey house prototypes from the consultants' reports are presented here, for comparison with the traditional domestic space arrangements in *El-Hekr*, Figure 6.13. The permeability graphs are illustrated in Figure 6.14. They are broadly representative of the set of 25 housing layouts which were eventually adopted in carrying out the upgrading project.

The living patterns in these prototypes are more embryonic than in the real cases, where the pattern of permeability is unambiguous and where specific functions can be assigned clearly to rooms. In these prototypes, the positions of doorways can only be conjectured[57] and, for the most part, rooms are simply described as habitable spaces, without any specific assignment of function. However, the position of the living room, which occurs in all prototypes, and of the hall if one is provided, are known, as are the locations of the WC/bathroom and the pit latrine, which is normally provided separately.

Permeability graphs immediately show that these prototypes are also deep trees. However, on a number of variables, the proposed new homes appear more like each other than the traditional examples we have just looked at. First, despite the wide disparity in plot size from smallest to largest, the number of convex spaces remains constant at 12-13 spaces. Three of the four prototypes contain a deep sequence of six rooms which develops away from the exterior. The average mean depth of these cases is 3.5. The final case is shallower, with four steps of depth. However, because most of the rooms give off a deep internal courtyard, the mean depth of this case is still quite high at 2.9. The mean integration value of three of the four prototypes is likewise high, i.e. segregated, an average of 1.3651, whilst that of the final example is very low, 0.8780, compared with the traditional sample (max. 2.5785 and min. 0.6782 and mean 1.5892 respectively). The new prototypes seem to locate the extremes of the range around the means of traditional integration values, with a small range of variation.

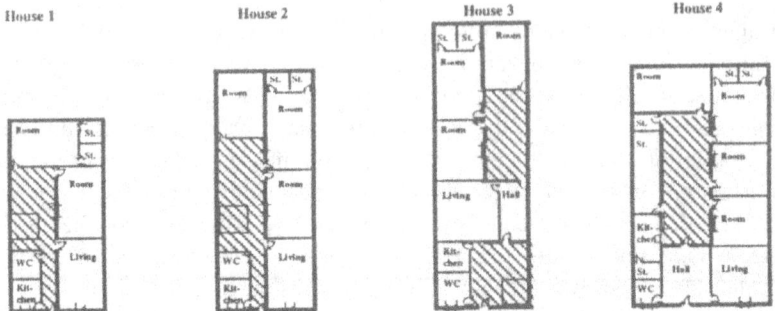

Figure 6.13 New plans, proposed by designers.

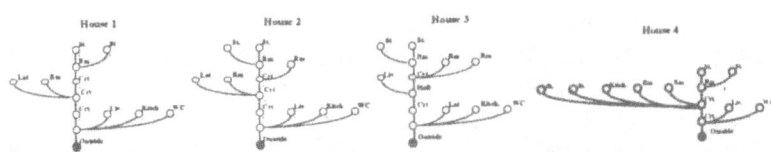

Figure 6.14 Justified graphs of the new housing prototypes.

This gives a clue to the way in which the proposed new houses incorporate daily living into the domestic space pattern, Figure 6.15. In Prototypes 1, 2 and 4, integration centres on the courtyard, and of these three 'courtyard centred' cases, two (Prototypes 1 and 2) have characteristics in common with the 'courtyard-centred' traditional plan. However, unlike in traditional plans, the most integrated part of the courtyard is quite segregated (0.7453) and the space is made less usable by the prominent position of the pit latrine. Neither has a hall, but these prototypes do have a deep, segregated living room like that in the traditional courtyard-centred plan. Prototype 4 is ostensibly a courtyard-centred shallow hall plan, with a courtyard having an integration value of 0.2549 and a hall at 0.5523. However, all the numerical values for the constituent rooms of this house are much more integrated than in a traditional home, and the rooms which the hall integrates - the living room and the WC - traditionally would not be given such prominence. In Prototype 3 the hall is the most integrated space but the room arrangement is not at all like a traditional *El-Hekr* hall-centred plan. Far from the hall's acting as a focus for indoor living, here it is permeable only to the living room and it is nearly twice as segregated as in the traditional hall-centred case, 0.7208 as opposed to 0.463.

Rank Order of Integration in house 1														
Court	›	Court	›	Court	›	Court	›	WC Room	≯	Room	›	Kitchen WC Living Outside	›	Store Room
Rank Order of Integration in house 2														
Court	›	Court	›	Court	›	Court	›	Room Room Room	≯	Room	›	Kitchen WC Living Outside	›	Store Room
Rank Order of Integration in house 3														
Hall	›	Court Court	›	Court	›	Room	›	Living	≯	Room Room Kitchen	›	WC WC Outside	›	Store Store
		Rank Order of Integration in house 4												
		Court	›	Hall	›	Room	›	Kitchen Store/ Store Room Room	≯	WC Living Outside	›	Store Store Store		

Figure 6.15 Rank order of integration in the new prototypes.

The prototypes which conform more closely to the traditional physiography are Prototypes 1 and 2, which are just about capable of absorbing a 'courtyard centred' living pattern. In its 'natural' state, this is favoured traditionally by smaller and poorer households, and by groups of unrelated residents like lodgers and servants who are perceived as having an inferior social status. Often it results from partitioning. Whilst this might indeed be the predictable outcome of a design process which concentrates on economic variables, all the evidence suggests that it is not a type which people would prefer in circumstances where they were able to build a new home as they chose. The other two prototypes do not conform closely to the types of traditional home in *El-Hekr*. Certainly, neither would be appropriate to residents with aspirations to social status. These prototypes would be quite difficult to modify so as to support a traditional lifestyle.

But there are more serious obstacles to the adoption of the proposed prototypes by the indigenous residents of *El-Hekr*. First, a particular difficulty encountered with all the prototypes is that, whilst these do have WCs and the entrance in the most segregated place in the rank order of integration, in the traditional morphology these are segregated and separated from one another, whilst in the new prototypes, they are segregated together at the interface with the street. This does not happen in traditional homes. The close physical proximity of these functions transgresses cultural concepts of modesty and pollution. A second difficulty is the fact that the arrangement of courtyards, halls and living rooms in the new prototypes does not offer choice in how formal and informal activities should relate to indoor and outdoor living, a factor which was so pervasive in the traditional dwelling types.

Conclusion

The genotypes discussed earlier are, it seems, the basic building blocks of the traditional domestic architecture of *El-Hekr*. The variety in plan physiography seems to relate to how formal and informal behaviours are modulated indoors and outdoors by different permutations of the hall, living room and principal courtyard. Larger houses occupied by several segments of an extended family tend to combine two types of plan. The sample is too small to draw firm conclusions but the evidence suggests that those plan types which incorporate a strategically-located hall as well as a courtyard, are more prestigious than hall-centred or courtyard-centred plans, which seem to be associated with house conversions and sub-divisions for rent, or to accommodate a second wife, married children, servants or lodgers.

Finally, and perhaps most important of all, despite the avowed intention of the designers to learn from the vernacular, the prototypes they have come up with would be impossible to modify so as to become the building blocks of separate sub-complexes, to house segments of a more extensive lineage. This is such an important constituent of the local culture that its physical denial would be likely to cause great hardship to residents in the new houses. Without wishing to stretch the evidence too far, it may be that had there been a widespread adoption of the new prototypes, over time this could have resulted in a more pervasive adoption of western-style patterns of household and family life. It may also go some way to explain why the prototypes were rejected wholesale by the local population.

Between the ethnographic present of this paper, which is set in the late 1970s, and the early 1990s, *El-Hekr* was indeed upgraded. The local residents were, for the most part, displaced. A new population of more affluent, middle class residents who could afford to buy or rent the newly-constructed properties, moved into the district which was redeveloped as apartment blocks. How much this may be attributed to economic or to cultural factors will never be known. Even so, *El-Hekr* does raise a question as to the ultimate purpose of reconstruction and upgrading. Here, economic considerations seem almost to be in opposition to cultural factors. Therefore, the final section has examined the designers' perceptions and their typological proposals for the upgrading project in comparison with the results arising from the chapter's analysis and findings. The aim was to measure how far are their proposals from the traditional domestic spatio-cultural structures.

As a matter of policy, it seems important to give a weighting to the extent that planned developments should respect traditional family patterns and lifestyle variables, and to make informed decisions as to role which these should play in dictating new housing prototypes tailored to local conditions. The paradox for design is that a failure to do this may destroy the independence of the culture which it purports to enhance.

By implication, the research maintains the belief that it is essential that a people's way of life should be respected in any attempt to give them a better material standard of living.

Notes

1   Or for their children after marriage.
2   The average floor area of house without lodgers is 120 m. sq. and the average size of house with lodgers is 220 m. sq., including the courtyard, whilst the average size of an apartment is 47 m. sq. excluding the stairs. The provision of utilities in apartment blocks is, however, high with 76% having piped water, and 90% having a connection to the public electricity supply and sewerage system. All these figures are based on a city-wide survey.
3   Hassanein, S, 1981-2, *Space Use in a Spontaneously Developed Urban Settlement : the Hai El Salam (El Hekr) Case Study*, Master's Thesis of

	the Catholic University of Leuven, pp 161 Houses 2, 3, 4, 6, 8, 9, 10, 11, 14, 15, 16, 18, 19, 20, 21, 22, 23, 24, 25, 26 and 28 come from this source.
4	Culpin, C. et al. 1978, *Ismailia Demonstration Projects,* Final Report to the Ministry of Housing and Reconstruction, Advisory Committee for Reconstruction, Arab Republic of Egypt and the Ministry for Overseas Development, United Kingdom, Vols. I and II; Davidson, F. and Payne, G. eds., 1983, *Urban Projects Manual : a guide to preparing upgrading and new development projects accessible to low-income groups,* Liverpool University Press in association with Fairstead Press, Liverpool; and Vandersypen, M. ed. , 1980, *Case Study : Ismailia*, a report to the United Nations Training Course for Housing Experts, at the Postgraduate Centre for Human Settlements in the Catholic University of Leuven. Houses 1, 5, 7, 12, 13, 17, 27 and 29 come from these sources.
5	A much larger random sample of 200 dwellings which was undertaken by the development consultants in 1977 showed the existence of 143 Beit without lodgers (72%), 40 Beit with lodgers (20%), 6 Rabaa (3%), 3 Aimaras (1%) and 8 unclassifiable 'mixed' houses (4%). This much smaller sample of 29 dwellings, comprises 23 Beit with a variety of family structures (79%), 4 Beit with lodgers (14%) and 2 Aimara (7%).
6	Houses 1, 6, 8, 9, 11, 12, 13, 14, 15, 20, 22, 24, and 25.
7	Those houses where married children are resident will be discussed on a case by case basis below.
8	Even though it is possible to conjecture the physical form of the original, unitary dwelling, the uses of rooms prior to partition is not known, so the alternative strategy of treating the house as one premises is not feasible.
9	As in House 1 which has only one room, and House 25 where each room was occupied by a married child.
10	House 21.
11	House 24.
12	Houses 13, 17, 20, 26 and 29. In House 9 the store is off a bedroom; in House 28 it is off the entrance corridor.
13	Houses 2, 24, 28.
14	Like the stairwell in blocks of flats.
15	House 10, 22, 24, 26, and 29 all have sufficient space for more than one courtyard.
16	Houses 11, 13,14, 15, 18, 20, 21, 22, 23, 24, 25, 26.
17	Houses 10, 19.
18	House 10.
19	Houses 17, 27, 29.
20	Houses 6, 12, 17, 21, 23, 25, 27.
21	Houses 10, 19, 22, 24, 26, 28, 29.
22	Houses 22, 26 , 28.

23	Houses 6, 8, 9, 12, 18.
24	Normally a pit latrine.
25	Houses 6, 8, 9, 18, and 28.
26	Houses 7, 10, 17, 19, 22, 25, 26, 29.
27	Houses 2, 3, 4, 11, 14, 15, 20 and 24.
28	Houses, 12, 16 and 23.
29	There is some evidence that the hall is a more traditional room, dating from a period where circulation and activities were spatially combined, whereas the living room can be associated with the separation of circulation and activity spaces.
30	Houses 2, 3 , 4, 7, 11, 13, 14, 15, 17, 20, 24 and 27.
31	Except for 2 and 3 which do not have a courtyard.
32	Houses 1, (5), 6, 8, 9, 10, 12, (16), 18, 19, 21, 22, 23, 25, 26, 28,29.
33	House 19 with 4 rented rooms, 26 with 1 room, 25 with 2 rooms for married children, 27 with 4 rented rooms, and 29 with 5 rooms for servants.
34	See for example, Hillier B and Hanson, J., 1984, *The Social Logic of Space*, Cambridge University Press: 281, and Hillier et al, 1987, *Ideas are in things : an application of the space syntax method to discovering housing genotypes*, Environment and Planning B, Volume 14: 363-385.
35	The integration value of a space expresses the relative depth of that space from all others in the graph through the formula : Integration value = $2(d-1)/(k-2)$ where d is the mean depth of spaces from the space, and k is the total number of spaces in the graph. This gives a value varying between 0 for maximum integration (no depth, a bush) and 1 for maximum segregation (maximum possible depth, a sequence). The integration value of a space therefore express numerically a key aspect of the shape of the justified graph from that space. These values are then adjusted by comparing each value with a that for a diamond graph for the same number of spaces. This takes account of the increasing unliklihood of the practical occurrence of a pure room sequence as complexes become larger.
36	Hassanein, op.cit.
37	Houses 21, 23, 25, 27, 28 and 29.
38	And therefore Graphs 15, 27, 27a.
39	Houses 18, 22, and 26.
40	We can accordingly safely conclude that the court performs as a synchronising controller, allowing multi-functions to operate at the same time independently.
41	Houses 2, 3, 5, 11, 12, 15 and 16.
42	Hassanein, Seifalla, *Space Use in a Spontaneous Developed Urban Settlement The Hai El-Salam Case Study*. Unpublished Thesis of

	Master's degree of engineering in architecture, University of Leuven, Belgium, 1982.
43	Houses 11 and 15.
44	Houses 21a, 23a, 23b, 25a and 27a.
45	Houses 21a, 23a, 23b and 25a.
46	House 27a.
47	Houses 4, 7, 13, 14, 17, 20, 24 and 27.
48	Houses 10, 19, 21, 22, 23, 25, 26 and 29.
49	Houses, 10, 19, 22 and 26.
50	Houses 1,6, 8, 9, 18, 21b, 25b, 27b, 28a and 29b.
51	Houses 28, 28b and 29a.
52	Houses 21, 23, 25, 27, 28 and 29.
53	Houses 2, 3, 5, 11, 12, 15, 16, 21a, 23a, 23b, 25a, 27a and 28b.
54	Houses 4, 7, 13, 14, 17, 20, 24 and 27.
55	Houses 1, 6, 8, 9, 18, 21b, 25b, 27b, 28a and 29b.
56	Houses 28, 28b and 29a.
57	Though this has since been established in conversation with the consultants.

7 Location and development:
People, place and power in Alexandria's inner-city neighbourhoods

Amr El-Sherif

Introduction

Places as living and working environments determine many aspects of the life and welfare of the urban poor, but they are never an isolated issue. A better place to live in is but one of a whole number of key concerns. To eat, to sleep, to be appropriately dressed, to obtain care, help and support in times of need and sickness, and the livelihood to provide the necessities of life are basic preoccupations of the impoverished everywhere. This means that studying the quality of the place, the physical environment, housing, streets, urban spaces, etc. should be situated within a larger contextual framework. The physical elements of the environment must be seen as being integrated with other aspects of life and as contingent on a number of factors at both the macro (external) and micro (internal) level. The larger context comprises factors of both production and consumption or use such as the economics and technicalities of control, management, administration and provision of services. The micro or intimate context is related to more elusive factors such as the values and aspirations that people have in life and their effects on the way they perceive the quality of the place in which they live.

The aim of this chapter is to discover the interrelations that associate people and places under constrained economic and environmental conditions such those of inner-city low-income neighbourhoods in Alexandria, Egypt. How the 'place' with its historical and locational characteristics on the one hand, and its present residents' interests and power on the other, influences positively or negatively people's options, choices and decisions concerning improvement of their living and working environments will be examined. In addition what the strategies are that people adopt to capitalise on the place's constraining or enabling characteristics in their drive for self-development and improvement of their quality of life will be considered.[1] In the following sections the chapter first

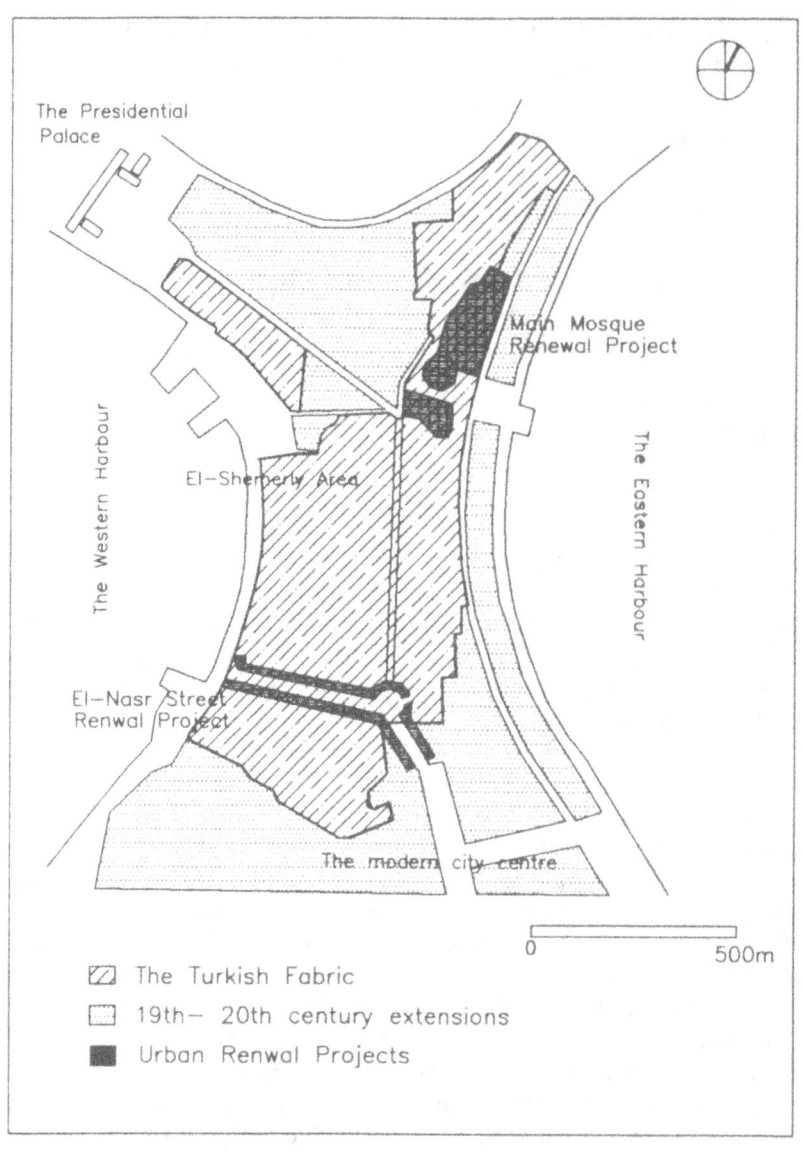

Figure 7.1 The plan of the Gomrok district .

describes the specific context of the place and the people examined in Alexandria in order to understand the actual relation between place and people that was observed among the Alexandria poor. Secondly, it identifies factors in the relations between people and place in the particular study area that have constrained its residents' developmental options and strategies.

The place: location and environmental setting

The study area, the Gomrok district, occupies the rectangular land which separates the Eastern and Western harbours centrally located in the metropolis (Figure 7.1). At the beginning of the nineteenth century the Gomrok was the only inhabited area of Alexandria which was left from the Turkish city, as named by the French expedition to Egypt in 1798. Located in the central part of Alexandria, the district enjoys an advantageous proximity to newly developed residential and industrial districts to the west of the city. Such location, ease of communication and integration in the physical structure of the city are a key attribute of its business activity as the main business and commercial centre for lower-income classes, in addition to its 'traditional' crafts, such as gold work, silver products, garments, wood works, printing and furniture manufacturing (ACMPP, 1984). This has also led to enormous economic and social pressures for redevelopment, through speculative developers and state-sponsored renewal projects which threatens its original historic urban form.

Against this pressure, the Gomrok district maintains a traditional intimate scale and sense of place which still give it an identity distinct from the modern 19th and 20th century parts of the city surrounding it, particularly the modern centre, once called the European quarter, which lies to the south east and which is currently the central business district of Alexandria. The change of identity can be felt when moving between the two districts along the longitudinal thoroughfares that connect them. The urban texture of the Gomrok district is still a homogeneous one, characterised by tight busy streets with continuous residential tissue mostly at an even height. Narrow main arteries within this tight urban grain make connecting links through the area and are intensively used, thus providing a clear differentiation from the mass of local streets (*harah*).[2] Large scale streets were constructed in the first quarter of this century to connect the modern city with the Western harbour and the Presidential Palace to the north west of the district. These streets have greater dimensions than the other streets and are fringed with commercial activity. Other commercial streets inside the district quarters are used as an open air market with a mix of some vehicles passing through the predominantly pedestrian throng.

High density has been a major characteristic of the district throughout its history and not because of a process of densification through migration in recent years[3]. Evidence from the study of the building types and the population of the area suggests the historic existence of a high density housing pattern. Reasons for this may be related to the scarcity of land and the prevailing housing types. Historic residential buildings in the area were of mainly two types: the house, *bayt*, normally used as elsewhere in Arab cities by a single extended family, with an inner courtyard or small light-well and entered from the street through a single doorway. This housing type is characterised in the study area by a unique vertical composition of two housing units which enable two families to live together on the same lot with two independent entrances (Figure 7.2). According to older residents in the area, sharing land between two houses was common. One resident said: *In the old times people used to invite relatives and friends to come and live on top of their houses. That is why houses are on top of each other.*

The other residential building type, *rab*, was used when shops occupied the lowest part of the building in a street, as is generally the case on major thoroughfares and in some *harah*s and bystreets. The superstructure is usually divided into distinct lodgings, separated from each other, usually comprising one big room and a little store area, and were let to families who could not afford the rent of a whole house.

Figure 7.2 An example of Double houses in the Gomrok district.

Not many houses of this type have survived but many *bayt* houses are used as a *raba* house by renting the individual rooms around the courtyard as separate dwellings. In addition to those two traditional types there are the newer 4-5 storey apartment buildings which replaced older houses in this century.

The people : the social and cultural conditions

> Although Midaq Alley lives in almost complete isolation from all surrounding activity, it clamours with a distinctive and personal life of its own. Fundamentally and basically, its roots connect with life as a whole and yet, at the same time, it retains a number of the secrets of a world now past.
>
> Naguib Mahfouz, Midaq Alley.

The study undertook an examination of the socio-economic context at a number of levels: central Alexandria as a whole, including the context of the old city and the specific zone of the study area. As a background for the reader it is important to emphasise that Alexandria - a part of Middle Eastern-Islamic society and culture, which in some respects is a civilisation primarily based on cities - has a long history of urban form which takes on various manifestations in the present-day city. Following a parallel classification of similar areas in Cairo (Abu-Lughod, 1971, pp.159-188), the Gomrok district would be a part of the section characterised as 'traditional urban' since it represents a continuity with the historic pattern of urbanism of the pre-modern Middle Eastern city. Abu-Lughod's modern-traditional descriptions are merely academic and not perceived as such by local people in everyday discourse. Other terms are commonly used which indicate a different perception of the city's districts. A particular term which is commonly used by both the public and professionals to describe the study area, and other similar areas according to its lifestyle, is the term '*ahya' sha`biyya*' meaning 'folk districts'. The term is derived from the word *sha`b*, folk or people, which has been stressed during the development of socialist ideology in Egypt from 1960 to 1974 (El-Hamamsy, 1982). The term refers to the majority of the city's districts as opposed to districts which are mainly inhabited by the elite.

Popularly, the area is called Bahari (from *bahr* which means sea) and considered by Alexandrians to be the origin of Alexandria's native local culture. It is a place where nostalgic stories of true Alexandrian customs often praise the behaviour of *awlad bahari* (sons of bahari). Those are characterised by their strong relations, solidarity, sense of belonging, voluntary help and hospitality to strangers. Such a reputation and local image, while it does not in reality currently correspond to particular practices of the poor residents of the area, gives the area a favourable reputation and makes its residents proud of living there.

Survey of living and housing conditions

Like Cairo, Alexandria is losing population in its centre and the growing population are mainly accommodated by peripheral expansion. Analysis of available census data shows a strong outward movement of the population from the old city, including the study area. The number of residents in the Gomrok district was 86,186 in 1897 and decreased for ten years until it was 77,545 in 1907 and then increased again up to 1960s when the central districts started to lose population. The Gomrok district lost 3.4% of its population between 1976 and 1986 while that of Alexandria as a whole increased by 25%. Therefore, the relative importance of the district's population decreased from 6.2% in 1976 to only 4.2% of Alexandria's population in 1986. This is due, as seen in a similar process in Cairo, partly to the transformation of the central city's upper income residential districts to commercial areas and partly to the flight of low-income groups from old, badly maintained, crowded housing to the more comfortable periphery (Antoniou et al, 1980).

A programme of field work was undertaken in the specific 'zone' encompassed by the two sub districts (*shiakhets*) El-Shemerly and El-Halwagy. Structured interviews with a sample of 120 residents and shopkeepers were also conducted. The aim was to provide a detailed picture of the people who live there and their conditions in order to establish how their needs relate to the requirements of change and development in the area. The sample area residents range from the unskilled and under-employed who are the poorest to the better employed but poorly paid teachers, government clerks, etc. with lower middle class aspirations.

As elsewhere in the Gomrok district, most residents interviewed live in rented housing. The district has a high percentage of tenants among its residents - 78.3% compared with 58.2% for the whole of Alexandria in 1986 (CAPMAS, 1990). Public housing does not exist (only .01% of the residents live in public housing). A small number of houses have an owner occupying one apartment and renting out the rest to others. Shared ownership between a large number of absentee owners is widespread and evolved over a long period and through inheritance into a very intricate pattern. It is common to find people owning a quarter, one eighth or smaller fractions of buildings (they are usually parts of 24 fold-divisions called *kirat*). In interviews, many did not know the identity of the other owners.

Housing in the area ranges from windowless traditional *rab* rooms (one to a family) and flimsy sheds on roofs to three-room apartments with self-contained utilities, proper windows, and sometimes a balcony. However, single rooms used as residential units are a major characteristic of housing in the district (23% in 1986). In reality the proportion of single-room households are much higher

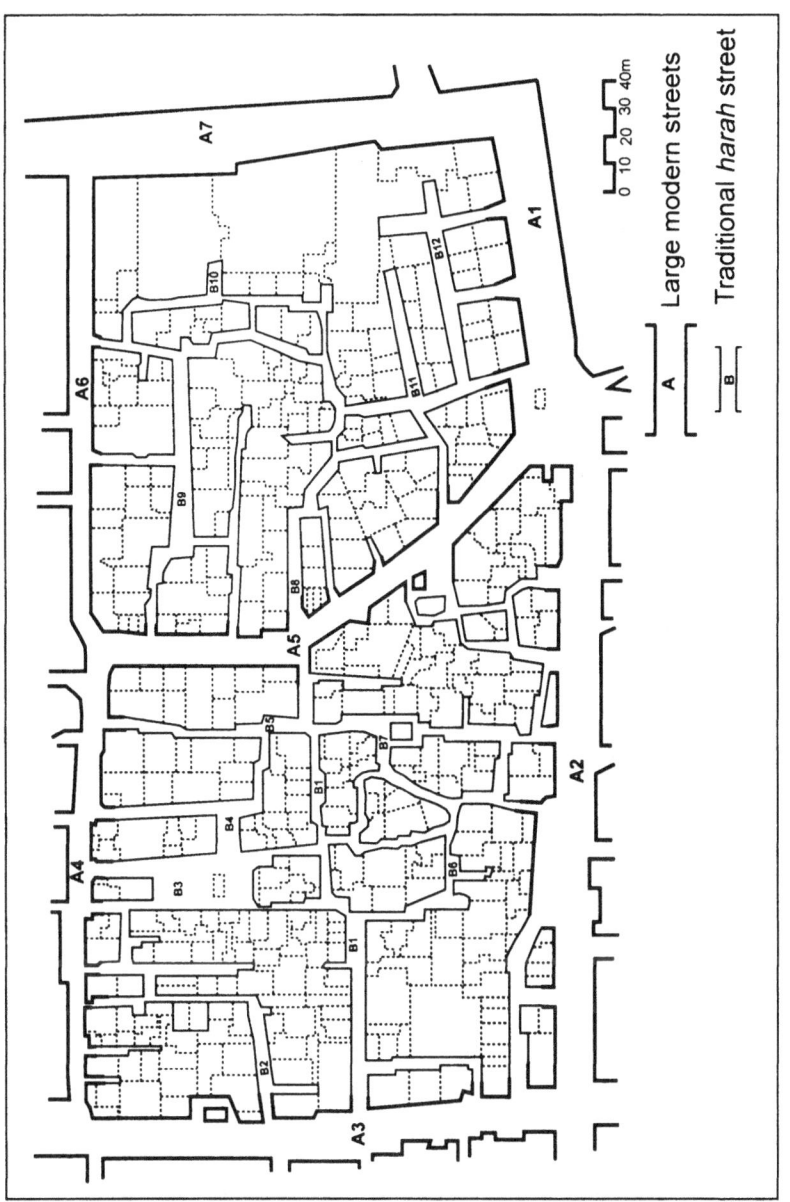

Figure 7.3 Plan of El-Shemerly and El-Halwagy area.

How many enclosed rooms in your dwelling unit?

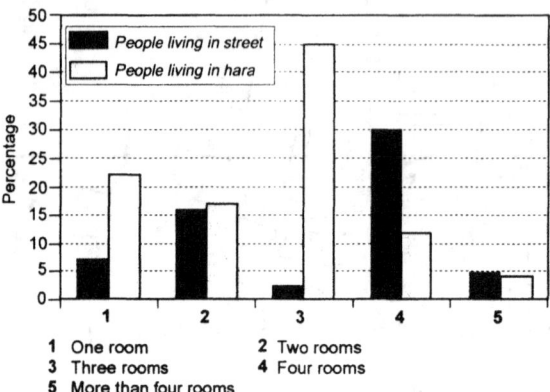

1 One room
3 Three rooms
5 More than four rooms
2 Two rooms
4 Four rooms

How are the utilities (kitchen and toilet) organized in your dwelling unit?

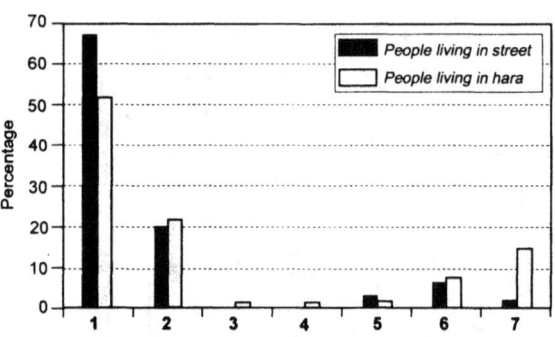

1 Selfcontained unit with separate kitchen and toilet
2 Selfcontained with single utility space (kitchen/toilet)
3 Have own kitchen and share the toilet
4 Have own toilet and share kitchen
5 Have own toilet and no kitchen in the flat or building
6 Share toilet and no kitchen available in flat or building
7 Share kitchen and toilet together

Figure 7.4 The difference in living conditions between the residents of the harah and the residents of the street.

because many families accommodate other families with them in their flats leading to families living in one room in these informally divided apartments. To understand the perception of the overcrowding as part of the quality of living, it is essential to explain some of the locally valid cultural premises and preferences. Such premises can constrain housing and lodging but also provide solutions for the urban poor where no other alternatives are available. Most households interviewed were putting up or had put up relations, in-laws or friends for weeks and months on end or these had become permanent part of the household. The aggregate result of these cultural premises, combined with poverty, is extreme congestion. On average the families interviewed had nearly two persons per single sleeping place. At the same time such overcrowding is considered a hardship and there are strong pressures to maintain a minimal separation of the sexes and privacy. Ideally children aged four and over should sleep in a separate room from their parents; brothers and sisters should sleep in separate rooms; unrelated male guests should be received in a room which does not serve as a bedroom for women.

A key finding suggested by the analysis is that the living conditions of the residents are not homogeneous. Residents of the *harah* street typology were poorer and living under worse conditions than those living on large streets (Figure 7.3). In the *harahs*, about one half of the families were living in conditions of severe over-crowding. Nearly half of those interviewed (42.5%) do not live in a self-contained unit and share at least the toilet or the kitchen and 16.7% of the households interviewed live in one room. It was found that sometimes families of nine people live in one room with an area of less than 15 m^2. Most of these are in traditional *rab* houses.

Association factors: internal parameters

The extensive association between people and the place is an outcome of both internal and external parameters. To examine people-place relations two key variables were identified: people's satisfaction with the physical aspects of the place and the perception of the place, and the perception of opportunities and limitations of the place (Figure 7.5). These variables were examined through both structured and unstructured interviews with the residents. Interviews with local authorities were also conducted.

Nearly two thirds of the interviewed residents were born in the same area, which contributes to the continuity of the social structure of the district despite the influx of migrants and movement of residents to other parts of the city. Reasons for choosing the area for people who were not born there varied. The main reason was that it has favourable living conditions (12.6%). Other reasons included place of work, availability of residence and because of no other area being available. However, evidence from interviews with older residents suggests that

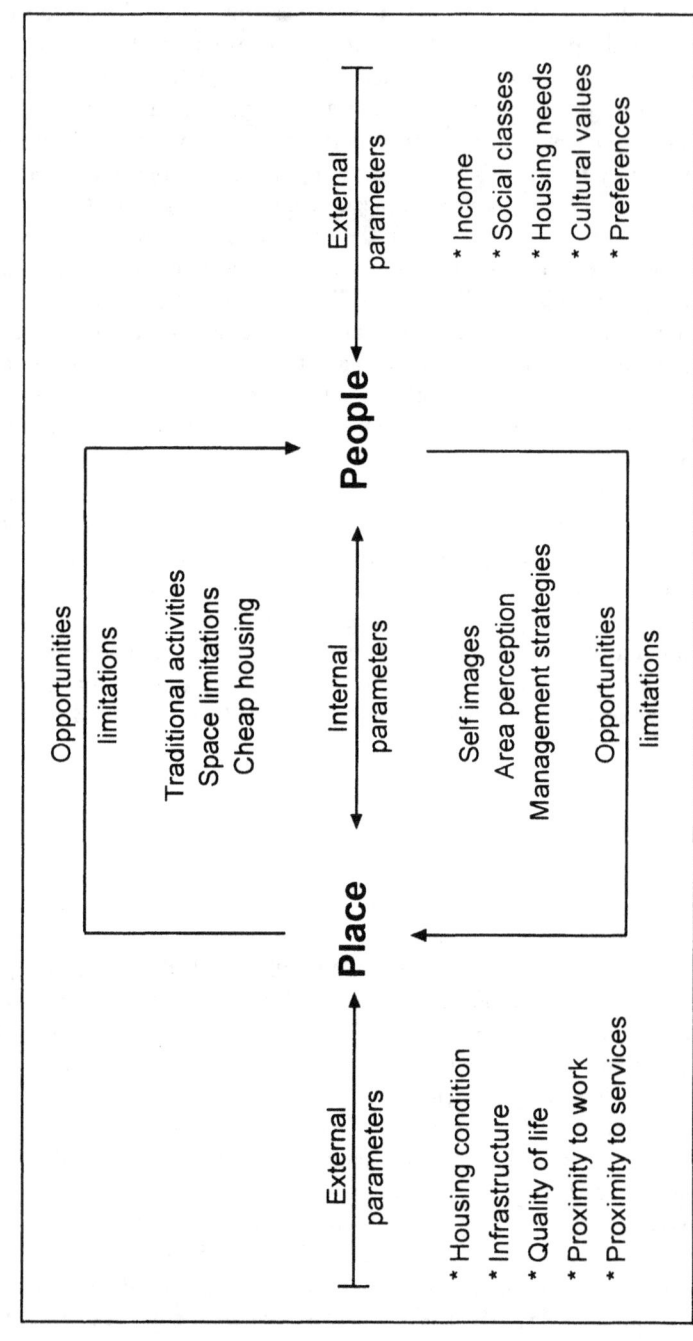

Figure 7.5 A model to understand the relationship between people and place in El-Shemerly and El-Halwagy area.

proximity to relatives was more important for earlier generations. The following personal history of one resident illustrates the pattern:

> Mohammed is a migrant resident of *harah* Zakariah-bek. He is originally from a middle Delta village. He came to work in Alexandria in 1939. He said 'all the people were immigrating when I came. I joined as a workman in the Gomrok with my uncle who was living in Zakariah-bek but lived in Raseltin (A district to the north). When the two rooms next to my uncle became vacant, I moved here and rented the two rooms for LE O.60 per month (in 1950; now he pays 1.20). Later I married his daughter and stayed here. I worked as a textile worker in a factory until I retired'.

As an indication of the perceived role of the place and its advantages or disadvantages for the residents of the area, respondents were asked to identify things that they like and do not like about their neighbourhood. It is possible to note some differences between such perceptions on the part of the people who are living in the large streets compared with those who live in the internal *harahs*. For the first group the advantages of the area are related more to their residential unit than to the overall advantages of the area. Using a score method to analyse the answers it was found that the cheap rent of the residential unit (15.4%) was followed by the advantages of the dwelling itself in terms of number of rooms and its size (10.6%) and ownership (5.6%). Factors related to the area such as the availability of shops and markets (7.5%) and the central location of the area and availability of transportation modes came second. Local area satisfaction was cited more by residents of the *harah*. Residents perceive their relationship as special to the area and as a main factor in the strong solidarity that characterises their neighbourhood and the Gomrok district or *Bahari* in general. Similarly to street residents, *harah* residents considered dwelling characteristics such as cheap rent (26.5%) a key advantage of the area, but they gave more emphasise than street-residents to other factors related to the area such as availability of markets (14.3%), proximity to relatives and friends (11.3%) and the particular neighbourhood relations (8.0%). Functional requirements provided by the area in terms of markets and shopping were also identified as key reasons for living in the area. The open air market suq-el-midan on the eastern side of the area is quite important for the livelihood of the residents, 45.7 % of them using it daily to buy their food and 30.5% do buy both their frequent and lasting consumer needs. The functional relation with other areas of the city is a main factor in constructing the residents' perception of their neighbourhood's advantages.

With regard to the disadvantages of the area, problems of illegal activities undertaken in the less-policed roads such as drug dealing were considered the most important in both streets and *harah*s (28.19% in streets and 33.59% in *harah*s). Residents put that before any other disadvantages in the dwelling or the area because such activities threaten the future of their children (Table 7.1). Most respondents considered that the appearance and the amenities and functions of their area 'have changed in the last few years' (the survey was conducted in 1992-3). Respondents were asked to identify any changes in their neighbourhood areas. People's assessment reflected the slow pace of change and the continuity of many older trends. However changes were felt more in the street than the *harah*. Although it was expected that the *harah* street typology would have more problems with privacy due to the narrowness of the street space, it was found that residents of modern large streets emphasised more the problems of overlooking and privacy invasion (62.9% in the street compared to only 42.1% in the *harah*). Evidence from interviews and observation suggest that the *harah*-people, as a result of a stronger social relationship with the neighbours, are more considerate towards each others' needs for privacy. Even if there is a physical possibility of overlooking, behavioural norms and customs in the *harah* prevent privacy invasion problems. In contrast, in the street, where fewer physical opportunities are available, people in opposite blocks are not obliged by any particular code of behaviour which results in a greater occurrence of privacy invasion problems. A key problem emphasised by the *harah* residents was the newly decreased level of security (15.8%) and the behaviour of the newcomers in relation to the public space of the *harah* (10.5%). In interviews *harah* people were afraid that the norms that ruled life in the *harah* are threatened. As one resident said: *There will be a time when no-one knows his neighbour.*

The role of external parameters: the effect of rent control

Some other external parameters should be also mentioned. In Egypt, all rents have been frozen by various government decrees since 1948. The original tenant, or his/her heir, pays the monthly rent originally fixed. If the apartment is vacated, on the other hand, the house-owner is allowed to set the rent at current market rates. In the most recent investigation it was found that in Cairo the average rent paid constituted, only 2% to 5% (compared with one-sixth or 17% in the early 1970s) of the average income of heads of households employed in the public sector. This proportional decline is due to the fixing of the rents (Melperri, 1986). Intended to aid the poor and undoubtedly serving their interests in the essential respect of keeping rents low and preventing exploitation, this policy of freezing rents is increasingly immobilising the established population, locking them into the particular apartment where they happen to be. Government regulation of rent has created an immobilised housing market for tenants, where personal history and economic advancement cannot be reflected in changes in tenancy and location. In addition, rent control acts as a disincentive to property owners to maintain or improve residential property. For most owners houses do not bring any profit. A house of 300-400 square metres would yield a rent of only LE 10-20^5. The disadvantages of these regulations, from the owner's point of

Table 7.1.1 Factors affecting the perception of the place by the residents of the El-Shemerly and El-Halwagy area.

		Street				Harah				Total			
What do you like about your neighbourhood area?		First in importance	Second in importance	Third in importance		First in importance	Second in importance	Third in importance		First in importance	Second in importance	Third in importance	
Owner of property	1	14.3% (6)	-	-		9.2% (7)	-	-		11.0% (13)	-	-	1
The dwelling is good (size & number of rooms)	2	21.4% (9)	7.1% (3)	2.4% (1)		13.2% (10)	1.4% (1)	2.8% (2)		16.1% (19)	3.5% (4)	2.6% (3)	2
Rent is cheap	3	23.8% (10)	19.0% (8)	7.1% (3)		39.5% (30)	16.4% (12)	4.2% (3)		33.9% (40)	17.4% (20)	5.3% (6)	3
Social environment of the neighbourhood is friendly	4	2.4% (1)	7.1% (3)	-		6.6% (5)	12.3% (9)	2.8% (2)		5.1% (6)	10.4% (12)	1.8% (2)	4
The social status of the residents are appropriate	5	2.4% (1)	2.4% (1)	11.9% (5)		3.9% (3)	8.2% (6)	6.9% (5)		3.4% (4)	6.1% (7)	8.8% (10)	5
The neighbourhood is quiet and clean	6	-	-	2.4% (1)		-	2.7% (2)	5.6% (4)		-	1.7% (2)	4.4% (5)	6
The availability of shops and markets	7	7.1% (3)	26.2% (11)	9.5% (4)		13.2% (10)	15.1% (11)	15.3% (11)		11.0% (13)	19.1% (22)	13.2% (15)	7
The area is central to other parts of the city	8	4.8% (2)	11.9% (5)	9.5% (4)		-	9.6% (7)	6.9% (5)		1.7% (2)	10.4% (12)	7.9% (9)	8
Easy transportation to other parts of the city	9	4.8% (2)	7.1% (3)	14.3% (6)		1.3% (1)	11.0% (8)	8.3% (6)		2.5% (3)	9.6% (11)	10.5% (12)	9
Proximity to schools	10	2.4% (1)	2.4% (1)	23.8% (10)		-	2.7% (2)	9.7% (7)		0.8% (1)	2.6% (3)	14.9% (17)	10
Proximity to workplace	11	9.5% (4)	7.1% (3)	7.1% (3)		3.9% (3)	11.0% (8)	12.5% (9)		5.9% (7)	9.6% (11)	10.5% (12)	11
Proximity to relatives and friends	12	2.4% (1)	9.5% (4)	4.8% (2)		9.2% (7)	9.6% (7)	20.8% (15)		6.8% (8)	9.6% (11)	14.9% (17)	12
The area in general is good	13	4.8% (2)	-	7.1% (3)		-	-	2.8% (2)		1.7% (2)	-	4.4% (5)	13
Other	14	-	-	-		-	-	1.4% (1)		-	-	0.9% (1)	14

133

Table 7.1.2 Factors affecting the perception of the place by the residents of the El-Shemerly and El-Halwagy area.

What do you not like about your neighbourhood area?		Street				Harah				Total		
		First in importance	Second in importance	Third in importance		First in importance	Second in importance	Third in importance		First in importance	Second in importance	Third in importance
Dwelling is unsatisfactory	1	5.9% (2)	-	4.0% (1)	1	17.4% (12)	3.1% (2)	5.2% (3)	1	13.6% (14)	2.2% (2)	4.8% (4)
Rent is expensive	2	2.9% (1)	-	-	2	1.4% (1)	1.6% (1)	-	2	1.9% (2)	1.1% (1)	-
Social environment of the neighbourhood is not friendly	3	38.2% (13)	3.6% (1)	24.0% (6)	3	17.4% (12)	17.2% (11)	13.8% (8)	3	24.3% (25)	13.0% (12)	16.9% (14)
A dropped social class	4	2.9% (1)	10.7% (3)	12.0% (3)	4	5.8% (4)	7.8% (5)	6.9% (4)	4	4.9% (5)	8.7% (8)	8.4% (7)
Lack of shops and market	5	2.9% (1)	3.6% (1)	-	5	-	-	-	5	1.0% (1)	1.1% (1)	-
Difficult transportation	6	-	-	4.0% (1)	6	-	-	1.7% (1)	6	-	-	2.4% (2)
Utilities are not sufficient (water/power outages)	7	5.9% (2)	3.6% (1)	-	7	2.9% (2)	1.6% (1)	-	7	3.9% (4)	2.2% (2)	-
Public facilities are not sufficient	8	5.9% (2)	25.0% (7)	4.0% (1)	8	8.7% (6)	10.9% (7)	3.4% (2)	8	7.8% (8)	15.2% (14)	3.6% (3)
A lot of noise and workshops	9	2.9% (1)	-	-	9	-	-	-	9	1.0% (1)	-	-
The area is not safe (a lot of thefts)	10	5.9% (2)	3.6% (1)	16.0% (4)	10	8.7% (6)	7.8% (5)	17.2% (10)	10	7.8% (8)	6.5% (6)	16.9% (14)
The area is full of illegal activities (drug dealing)	11	18.6% (8)	25.6% (11)	12.0% (3)	11	34.8% (24)	34.4% (11)	19.0% (11)	11	31.1% (32)	35.9% (33)	16.9% (11)
Far from schools	12	-	-	-	12	-	-	-	12	-	-	-
Far from work place	13	-	-	-	13	-	-	-	13	-	-	-
Far from relatives and friends	14	2.9% (1)	3.6% (1)	-	14	-	-	1.7% (1)	14	1.8% (1)	1.1% (1)	1.2% (1)
The area in general is not good	15	-	7.1% (2)	8.0% (2)	15	-	4.7% (3)	5.2% (3)	15	-	5.4% (5)	6.0% (5)
Other	16	-	-	16.0% (4)	16	2.8% (2)	11.0% (7)	25.8% (15)	16	2.0% (2)	7.6% (7)	22.9% (19)

view would make some of them resort to various techniques to force tenants to leave. Other factors specific to the district such as high land price and intensity of businesses encourage speculation and put more pressure on the owners to demolish existing houses and evict current poor residents.

While many houses are already so derelict that the owner can obtain permission to tear them down, residents always refuse to leave with the result that derelict flats are tenaciously occupied until they are condemned. It is not uncommon for people to be wounded or even killed when such houses collapse. For most families, shortage of supply, long waiting lists and favouritism make public housing practically unavailable to the poor, except as a replacement for houses that actually collapse or are demolished by the authority. Government provision of shelter for those staying in their houses until they collapse usually takes a long time to materialise and even then only under political pressure from some groups, or before election times. One respondent told me that people whose homes had collapsed stayed in a temporary shelter in the street for up to six years until they were given shelter when a member of parliament promised them this during his election campaign. After his election it took only six months for them to be allocated new homes in `Aimriah (An industrial estate on the western periphery about twenty kilometres west of the centre of Alexandria). One resident commented: *It was a poor shelter but they accepted it.* However this housing provided by the government is not always accepted by the people. Respondents described these new houses as animal shelters. Others called them a detention camp with no transport facilities. An example provided by one of the residents illustrates the difficulty of the choice.

> Ahmad is head of a family composed of his wife and three children in addition to his widowed mother. He came to live in the area 17 years ago when he got his job as a workman in the harbour at the edge of the area. He lived in the ground floor of an old house shared with another 7-person family who were originally there. He paid LE 2 per month as a rent. The room was too small for his large family and, after his marriage, he applied for a flat through a housing scheme for newly-weds sponsored by the governorate. After 15 years of waiting he was allocated a flat in Sidi-Abdelkader, a newly built social housing project 30 km to the west of the centre of Alexandria. He refuses to go because the area there is not fully serviced and has no secondary school for his children. He does not have the LE2,500 requested by the governorate and most importantly, his salary would not be enough since he needs LE3 for daily transport while his monthly salary is only LE120. He would like to leave the area for better housing but he can't at the moment. He is ready to pay half of his salary (LE50-60) to pay for a two bedroom flat that could be near his work, but that seems impossible. In the meantime he is repairing the room that he currently occupies in order to prevent the building from collapsing.

Development and coping strategies

According to government policies, the objective of development projects such as urban renewal and upgrading of the area are to increase the prosperity of the existing residential population and to improve their living conditions (ACMPP, 1984). However these objectives are viewed by both residents and local authorities as mere hypothetical concepts, since the means to achieve them are not to be found or provided by any governmental agency. Other factors which limit the ability of government to intervene and set up any formally sponsored improvement of housing conditions over the last few decades include fragmented ownership and lack of owner occupation, lack of government owned land for housing or social infrastructure and lack of political interest in the area. According to the authorities, people's refusal to leave the area is explained in terms of social and symbolic commitment to the areas where they were born and their relatives and friends are. However it is possible to suggest that the area's social and cultural, as well as political, conditions support the very poor of society better than peripheral development offered by the government. These factors have resulted in a voluntary or non-voluntary attachment of people to the place and an inability to leave. The poorer stay and the better off or more active economically leave to better their living conditions or move out and stay only to practice their business. The very central location of these quarters, close to schools, universities, markets, and other public facilities, actually establishes the strong relationship between people and the place.

For most respondents, their social, political and economic conditions have created a specific and complex association with the place. While many people are not satisfied with their residence or job, they think that they will not be able to move because of their low income on the one hand and because of the establishment of strong social and functional attachment to the place which in turn helps to reduce the intensity of their economic situation. A better dwelling unit is a long term aim of many residents. However, saving to have a proper apartment that has front doors that can be closed upon the world seems to be a distant objective for many of the residents. Instead, long term strategies for improvement are directed to investing their resources in their micro enterprise or children. Education of young members of families is seen as the key means of achieving such improvement. Families interviewed showed an impressive drive, farsightedness and commitment to 'investing in the future of their children' which they believe will result in the long term in a considerable improvement in their standard of living.

Maintenance of buildings is a major short term priority for all the residents and most of them undertake it independently or in co-operation with each other despite of their low level of income. When asked about the source of funds, respondents who carried out repairs on their building or dwelling unit (61 out of 99 tenants interviewed), depended mainly on their own savings. Forty five point nine percent of the respondents who carried out repairs on their dwellings depended on a collective saving method called *gam`iah*[4] with friends, relatives or neighbours, 44.3 % on their own savings or assets, and 6.6 % borrowed money from family or friends. Only one person depended on a particular kind of formal institution, which was his employer. To undertake such repairs, tenants tend to improve their relations with owners. Co-operation between neighbours is also indicated by sharing the cost of cleaning or maintaining common amenities that serve them. Most of the interviewed respondents (79.0%) said they share the cost of regular maintenance with their neighbours. Paying for refurbishing and changing of common facilities of the building such as the staircases and structural elements is a common practice for all the residents. Dependence on self help as a primary way of achieving improvement in relation to their dwellings and sometimes to other improvements which are related to the neighbourhood as a whole stems from the expectation of a weak role on the part of the authority with regard to these issues. Interviewed residents believe that to get the authority to achieve any of the needed improvement in their area, political pressure from what they called `important persons' whom the area lack is needed.

Conclusion

The urban environment should be seen within the dynamic and wide variety of lifestyles that they sustain and the correspondingly wide range of choices and development strategies that individuals have for improving their environmental and living conditions.

As a case study, inner Alexandria reveals many features that are commonly observed in traditional *madina*s of Arab cities (Vigier, 1987; El-Sherif, 1992). The development constraints of poverty, inability to mobilise state-sponsored development projects and lack of co-operation conceals many positive strengths that communities still practice in relation to making and adapting its spaces.

The investigation points to a significant divergence in views of the place between people living on the large modern streets and those who live in the small internal *harah*s. People living in the *harah*s share their low class and economic positions with millions of citizens of back streets in Egypt's two largest metropolises, Cairo and Alexandria (Wikan, 1990). The difference created in perception of the place is indicative of the way different people perceive differently what is a good quality of life and the priorities that they have for themselves. But such a difference is also caused by other external factors such as cultural changes in society, the socio-economic gulf between classes and even particular government policies, all resulting in complex place-people relations. The analysis of the relations between internal and external relations of both place and people indicates the interaction between many elements. These interactive relations are usually hard to grasp with normal indicators used to assess the living quality of urban areas in terms of their location, land value, rent and infrastructure resources. For example, policies of rent control have confused the relationship between income level or class and geographical area. In particular, the density of population and the long periods of residence in the area do not indicate people's preferences, since their level of choice is limited. Also government regulation of rents has created an immobilised housing market for tenants where personal history and economic advancement cannot be reflected in changes in tenancy and location (Wikan, 1990, p.125).

As the cases show, where residents have succeeded in improving their standard of housing, this reflects the effects of short term responses rather than rationally planned improvements. The modification of place to fit hard-to-change conditions of income and socio-cultural characteristics, as well as the adoption of new cultural patterns or their reorganisation is a short term strategy of development. Long term strategies for development are in most cases related to investing in the qualities of people, education being seen as the key element in achieving such improvement, which, however, is expected to take a generation to come to fruition. Currently development plans conceived by the authorities are considered by the residents to be part of the external relations of the place and not a changeable variable that can be influenced by them. A possible change of the role of the authority should however consider this set of relations. Improvement strategies such as renewal or greater intervention in the management of space in the area may be useful for the residents in some cases, such as in the improvement of municipal services, but it can be harmful for many informally operating income-generation and shelter activities which provide the poor with the opportunity for living and working in a central location, albeit at a substandard level.

Notes

1 The chapter draws on a research programme undertaken by the Joint Centre for Urban Design, Oxford Brookes University funded by The British Council's Foreign and Commonwealth Scholarships Programme.

2 *Harah* is the name used to refer to the traditional residential quarters in Arab cities but is currently used to refer to local old streets. In terms of its general physical structure, the study area contains a mix of traditional and modern morphological elements. The following two street types can be identified: A. Harah-type: older street types includes traditional *harahs* and their offshoots, with a maximum width of 3-4 metres but sometimes as narrow as one and half or 2 meters. B. Street type: Narrow streets of modern planning of 8-10 metres wide, and large wide streets of 10-20 metres. Characterised by the linear morphology of a modern street system, it has mostly a newer fabric. These are either developed as part

3   of efforts to open large streets or by *harahs* which are gradually transferred to this morphology through applying the set-backs stipulated in the building regulation.
3   The study area has a population of 134,659 (including Suq-el-Turk) living in an area of nearly one square kilometre (1986 numbers (CAPMAS, 1990)) making up a density of nearly 1,350 people per hectare.
4   A prototype of popular and usually female-run savings-clubs in which all members pay weekly or monthly contributions which are pooled, each member appropriating the whole amount once, in turns, people in severe need taking the first turn. Others in need are helped when others organise such clubs on their behalf. This social organisation of saving and the interest-free character of loans, deposits and instalments, proves a powerful tool for saving and investment in the hands of even the most economically marginal households.
5   One Egyptian pound is equal to £ 0.2 in 1993.

8 Planning and designing rural settlements:
The Algerian experience

Lamine Mahdjoubi and Adenrele Awotona

Introduction

This chapter deals with the problems of planning and designing settlements for rural communities during the process of rapid social changes. It postulates that planned change must be based on existing rural socio-economic patterns. This entails fully understanding communities' values, norms and attitudes and how they are changing. It also emphasises that ignoring the fundamental basis of rural life and peoples' attitudes towards change may have severe human and economic implications.

The Algerian countryside has known three periods of major changes. The first one was introduced by the French with the implementation of the policy of Regrouping Centres, as a result of the outbreak of the Algerian revolution in 1956. During the second period, the programme of '1000 Socialist Villages', was initiated by independent Algeria in 1971. The third period of settlement planning and design was instituted in the early 1980s, as a result of the failure of the Socialist Villages. The successive programmes of rural development aimed at creating attractive and supportive rural environments. However, this chapter demonstrates that people's attitudes towards change must be taken into consideration during the planning and design process, otherwise the projects may fail woefully. This requires an understanding of the way rural life has worked socially, culturally, economically and physically and how it is changing. As a starting point, it is important to examine the original settlement pattern of the native population.

Traditional rural settlements and communities

The study of traditional rural settlements is essential, as it shows the original pattern of the rural society against which change can be measured. On the other hand, it clearly expresses the relation between the rural settlements and local cultures. At the house level, it vividly demonstrates the relation between house form and family social structures. At the village level, it indicates the relations between the organisation of rural space and activity and behavioural patterns. It also reflects the link between the way families earned their livelihood and the rural settlement organisation and setting. The close relationship between rural settlement forms and patterns and the rural communities, before they were affected and in varying degrees transformed by the tidal wave of rapid urbanisation and a modern market economic system, is defined as traditional. A large part of the Algerian countryside is considered as traditional, as many of the pre-colonial characteristics of rural living are still prevailing today. For example, the technological and economic levels of development are still primarily geared towards self-sufficiency and self-containment.

The social cultures in Algeria

The population of North West Africa, or the Maghreb shares Muslim, Arabic and Berber civilisations. There are two linguistic categories: Arabic and Berber speaking. Over the centuries, two socio-cultures in Algeria (Arab and Berber) have co-existed, but each has retained its distinct identity and local customs. Islam, however, played a significant role in Algeria by creating a sense of unity amongst the various tribes. The superimposition of the Islamic culture on the ancient cults, and the ethnic mixture between Arabs, Berbers and other civilisations, gave the Algerian communities their distinctive identity and sub-cultural variety.

Organisation of rural settlements as a reflection of social and family structures

The social structure of both Arab and Berber communities is based on tribal and clan systems. Despite the great variations in the tribes' customs, there is a striking consistency in their ways of life (Bourdieu, 1962). The various social entities, from the extended family to the tribes, are all reflected in rural space. The house, the compound, the village and the settlement patterns - each scale is the physical expression of a social entity.

The structure of the extended family and house form

The extended family is the basic unit of socio-economic organisation. It is the fundamental social cell of the complex social structure as many extended families form the clan and many clans form the tribe. The Algerian family is of a patriarchal type. Each extended family comprises a member of conjugal families of married brothers and their children, the father, the married paternal uncles and the grandfather. The extended family organisation, as a cohesion of many nuclear families, has been physically expressed by all male descendants and their families living in the same big house or family compound. The compound is composed of many rooms, but each room shelters a nuclear family, so that it can be considered as a house in itself.

The houses are arranged around one or several courtyards. The interior of the compound is carefully organised so that each nuclear family can preserve a certain amount of privacy. Extensions are built onto the original house as the family grows larger, so that the compound may shelter twenty to sixty people of three or four generations. The relation between the extended family and the compound is so strong, that only one word refers to both of them. The Arabic word *Dar* means either the extended family or the compound, as does the Berber Kabyle word *Akham*.

The clan organisation and village layout

Beyond the extended family, the traditional rural settlements have a spatial organisation reflecting family and kinship structure. The way families are grouped into phalanxes, under fraction and clan, is physically expressed in the spatial organisation of the village. Various social units and tribes are formed as the extended family increases. The clan is the largest socio-economic and political unit still based on kinship ties. Its lineage is more or less pure, spanning five or six generations (Bourdieu, 1962). Often, all the members of this community share the same ancestral name. It includes several extended families of which the male members consider themselves to be 'sons of the parental uncle', without defining their precise degree of relationship. The plan of a village shows up as clearly as would a genealogical tree the subdivisions of the village community- the extended family, the lineage *takharroubt*, the clan *adroum*.

There are distinct differences between Arab and Berber villages. The clan members of Arab villages are grouped in the same village, distant from other clans. However, in Berber villages it is common to find two or three clans living in the same village, but each of them has its own autonomy and nearly lives a separate existence (Bourdieu, 1962). Up until recently, each clan had its *tajmaat* (*Djemaa*) its cemetery, its own section in the village, its fountains; sometimes its own festivals and customs; and even its own legend of its origin.

The tribe organisation and rural settlement patterns

The tribe is the association of many clans whose members claim descent from a common ancestor from whom they derive their name. The driving force of the tribe's solidarity is often adversity, but there is a common purpose that builds up intense socio-cultural relations between its members. The common name replaced the natural ties of blood relationship as a driving force of group solidarity and cohesion and, therefore, established its distinctive identity. Members of a tribe also share the same facilities: the well, the mosque, the assembly house. They often bury their dead in the same cemetery which has many ritual and symbolic aspects. At each social occasion female members of the tribe socialise while men travel to the same periodic markets where they meet and exchange news.

Activity and behavioural patterns and the rural space organisation

Rapoport (1976), suggested that 'activities are the most specific and may offer the most useful entry point into relating built environment and culture'. He also proposed (1980), that any activity can be analysed into four components - the activity proper, the specific way of doing it, additional, adjacent or associated activities, and symbolic aspects of the activity.

Rural families' territorial behaviour and space organisation

The examination of traditional rural settlement in terms of activities and behavioural patterns seems to show the presence of a hierarchy of use. Women's social space is only confined to certain areas within the village and men have specific settings to socialise. This segregation is mainly related to the need to regulate and filter the movement of people across marked or commonly known boundaries, according to criteria such as kinship, sex, family and so forth.

Pronshansky et al., (1970) labelled this phenomenon as 'territorial behaviour'. They argued that 'human beings, no less than lower organisms, define particular boundaries of the physical environment and assume the right to determine who can and who cannot move across these boundaries.' The stress on some mechanisms and not on others may reflect the degree of privacy required by each culture. In general, six main mechanisms are used to avoid unwanted interaction. These are: rules, psychological means, behavioural cues, structuring activities in time, spatial separation and physical devices (Rapoport, 1980). The intense desire for privacy is reflected at every level of the Algerian village.

Plate 8.1 A general view of a Berber village.

The house and the compound

The need for privacy is characterised by a division of space into private and public domains and a clear segregation between male and female spheres. The division of domains are accompanied by specific written and unwritten rules which are accepted unquestioningly. These rules govern behaviour and social interaction, thus decreasing social conflict within the community. Therefore it becomes important to live in such areas where rules and systems are shared and hence one knows when and where to do what; who 'owns' space; and how spaces, activities and times are organised (Rapoport, 1976). The stress and overload are further alleviated as most neighbours are related by blood ties. The division of space into male and female spheres is perhaps the underlying basis of privacy and this is often related to the position of women in each society (Rapoport, 1969).

In Islamic culture maximum segregation between the sexes is strengthened and stressed only outside the kin group, in so far as women are seen to be safe within their family group. The concept of privacy differs between Arab and Berber communities. Berber women carry out domestic activities away from the family compound. Although privacy is to a certain extent desired within the clan, it is however mainly emphasised outside it. Apart from male members of the agnatic group, the women are mainly insulated from males of other clans. This is probably physically expressed in the way in which the Berber villages have in general a close-knit layout as privacy is probably not a crucial issue within the clan (Plate 8.1).

However, in the Arab dwelling, women may only be seen by family members. Therefore their social space is limited to the house and its surrounding area. In this case the degree of privacy required is relatively more important, even within the clan. This is perhaps reflected in the way the extended family compounds are clustered and separated from one another and hence, privacy is achieved through distance. The courtyard houses seem to have mainly derived from a need to insulate the houses from the outside world. Along with space organisation, marked boundaries reinforce seclusion inside and outside the house. The front of the dwelling is surrounded by a low wall physically indicating the first threshold of the house. Beyond this wall, the space may be considered as semi-privately controlled. The front entrance may be considered as the second threshold dividing the semi-private and the private domains, the interior of the dwelling itself. Family members, close male relatives or female visitors are permitted to use this entrance as it leads to the sacred area of the family compound. Usually Islamic cultures reserve one room for male and the other for female visitors. Male visitors do not usually penetrate the sacred area of the dwelling. Therefore the male guest room has a separate door that communicates directly with the outside. This entrance leads to a hall called the *'Skifa'*. This space has many manifest and latent functions. It firstly ensures visual privacy. The mechanisms used to meet this purpose vary from one house to another. Generally, it is achieved by careful

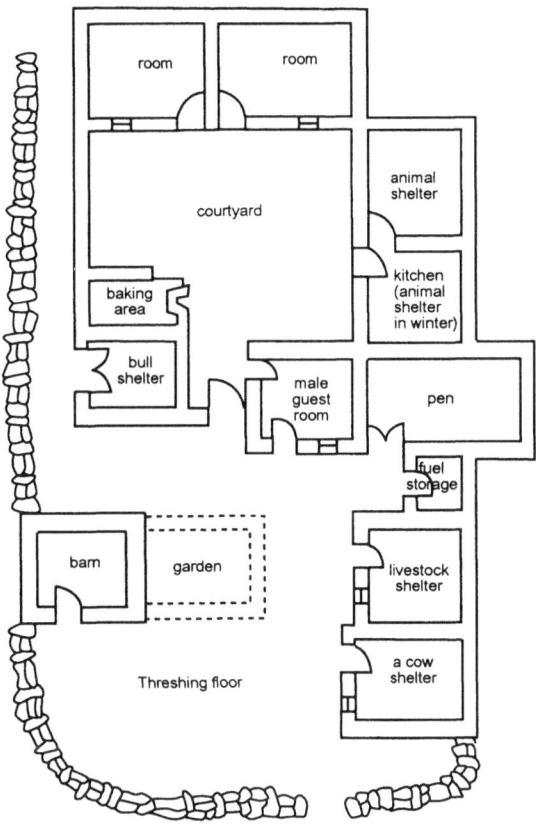

Figure 8.1 Plan of an Arab house.

design, which aims at obstructing direct visual contact between the exterior and interior of the compound. In most cases, it is reinforced by unwritten rules. It is an offence to glance into someone's house, as family members are taught never to open the door before ensuring it is safe to do so. The *'Skifa'* also serves as a shelter for the flock during the winter period. Privacy is also required within the family group. Therefore, the entrance of each nuclear family and the parents' house, is considered as the third threshold. This may have derived from the need to guarantee some privacy to each couple (Figure 8.1).

The courtyards and animal shelters, as well as the cooking spaces, may be considered as messy areas. Therefore, they are hidden from view. Hence, the courtyard is mainly used as a transition space as female visitors are primarily received in the parents' house, which is the tidiest and the best furnished place of the whole compound.

The village

The analysis of traditional rural settlements shows the concentration of various compounds forming a village - each village is spatially separated from the others. This need for clustering and sharing the same territory may have emerged as a result of various causes. It is, first of all, the spatial expression for the need for communality. This involves clustering of village buildings for mutual protection, convenience, social cohesion, economy and sometimes solidarity (Bunce, 1982, p.44).

However, in the case of the rural Algerian villages, the setting of marked boundaries prohibiting intruders may indicate that privacy was of utmost importance. Hence the village territory may be considered as a private collective realm; the family compound being its most private part. The facilities that are situated within the village (the well, the mosque, assembly house) are exclusively used by the members of the village. Therefore, the rural settlement pattern shows this need for privacy expressed at the clan level. This has been reflected in the way the members of the agnatic group are spatially insulated from members of other clans (Figure 8.2).

Social relations and rural space organisation

> The meeting of people is also a basic need, since man has been defined as a social animal. What concerns us is where people met whether in the house, the cafe, the bath or the street. This, not the fact of meeting itself, affects the form of the habitat (Rapoport, 1969).

Figure 8.2 View of an Arab village.

The specific setting where social meetings take place, the way they occur and who is involved in them, has an important impact upon space organisation. Understanding the relative importance of these meetings in relation to their settings, and how they are changing, may help us to create an informed basis for future rural settlement design. Such factors may facilitate and support these meetings rather than hinder them.

In North Africa and throughout the Mediterranean lands, culture and climate play a major role in the way people conduct their social lives. Algerian men spend most of their time outdoors either working or socialising. However women attach more importance to the home as they entertain friends and relatives. The courtyard is the setting for most domestic activities and is the favoured social meeting place for the female members of the family. Although their social space is restricted to the dwelling, they still spend much of their lives in the open air.

The social venue for women to meet varies from one community to another. Berber women meet by the well while undertaking their daily chores. The pathways leading to it are strictly out of bounds to men (Maunier, 1926)). However, in the Arab villages, women socialise only in the compound. This may vary with time. For instance, when men are absent from the family household, women circulate freely within the area surrounding the compound. Overall, rural women (as in most Islamic countries) are excluded from public spaces. Even Berber women, who move freely within their settings, avoid the places reserved for male gatherings.

Within the village, the social contacts between male villagers are the most frequent and are basically restricted to the clan members. They meet in the assembly house (the *Djemaa*) which is first of all a public space where judiciary activities are held. It is also the web of social life where the peasants begin and complete their daily routine. Men have to spend much of their time outdoors so that 'a man who has respect for himself should let himself be seen, should continuously place himself under the gaze of others, and face them (*gabel*). He is a man amongst men' (Bourdieu, 1973).

Traditional rural economy and its impact on design

The Berber and Arab communities' livelihood is principally based on agriculture and pastoralism. These dominant productive economic activities are principally geared towards the satisfaction of domestic needs. Each member of the extended family is allocated a definite task. The men undertake most of the heavier duties such as harvesting, ploughing and so on. Children are given charge of much lighter work (such as animal rearing and fetching water, amongst others). Women ensure, to a certain extent, the self-sufficiency of the family in terms of home produce: weaving and making clothes, to mention but a few activities. Only a few necessities are bought from the market. The family economic activities are reflected in house form and organisation. The house is divided into zones of transformation, storage of products and the sheltering of animals, domestic work and living. The allocation of spaces may change with time and seasons. The specific organisation of houses in relation to family economic activities can differ between Arab and Berber villages.

Socio-cultural and economic change and its implications for rural planning and design

The modern era has seen the integration of the formerly self sufficient and self contained societies into a modern market economy primarily oriented towards food production for national and World markets. These needs, combined with the need to improve rural living, have had far reaching effects which have influenced nearly every aspect of rural life. Agricultural change in Algeria involved three main programmes of settlement reorganisation: the French 'regrouping centres' policy of 1959, which involved the reorganisation of the traditional rural structures and the rehousing of the displaced families; the Algerian post independence Socialist Villages Policy, which was part of a comprehensive strategy of rural development; and, the recent rural planning and design policy. As a consequence of these interventions, various cultural, social, economic, political and locational changes were inflicted upon the rural society very suddenly.

Planning and design of the French regrouping centres

The early Regrouping Centres policy was primarily and exclusively a military action. Rural population was displaced to isolate the freedom fighters. Accordingly up to 3,525,000 rural dwellers had to leave their homes: 50 per cent of the Algerian peasantry, without any provision for rehousing those expelled (Cornaton, 1967). In 1959, the French decided to limit the damage done to the rural society by transforming the military population regrouping policy into a rural development programme. The policy of creating '1000 New Villages' was initially launched to convert some of the temporary centres and to create new villages. The siting, location and design of the new villages were in most cases dictated by military engineering, without any consideration for the human, physical and economic costs. The most common procedure often involved the regrouping of the population in the shade of the watch tower, near the military posts. It would have been more economical, and above all more humane, to relocate these posts (Lesne, 1960). As a result climate, soil conditions and topography were often ignored. Consequently, some villages were flooded as they were located too close to rivers, others were deprived of adequate drinking water (Lawless and Sutton, 1978); and in some cases, the sites were too constrained to allow future extensions (Lesne, 1960). Excessive distances between the fields and the settlements, combined with a strict control of mobility, led to the abandonment of the agricultural activities and a sharp decline in the cultivated area and crop production (Bourdieu and Sayad, 1964). Together with material degradation, the policy of new villages had dramatic socio-cultural implications.

Imposition of an alien environment

The design of the new settlements was heavily based on a centralised European village plan. Its spatial organisation resembled a French rural settlement implanted in the Algerian countryside. It was also influenced by technological and military imperatives by setting up a grid-iron layout to facilitate military control of population movement within the village. This resulted in the relocation of the population in a hostile and alien environment. The design of the new villages according to Western values was ignorant of, or neglected, the peasants' traditional socio-cultural patterns. The families were arbitrarily distributed between the regrouping centres without any regard for their kinship ties (Bourdieu and Sayad, 1964). This complicated the social adjustments of the relocated families to the new environment. The disintegration of the extended family initiated by the regrouping policy was aggravated by housing design. The houses were standardised, and in most cases were basic shelters. Apart from being too small to accommodate the large families, they did not offer any possibility for extensions. They were composed of 'two rooms of less than 18 m^2, a small kitchen of 2.40m^2, a toilet and occasionally, a tiny courtyard' (Planhol, 1961).

The urban values of the planners and designers failed to understand the peasants' way of life and its design implications. Many manifest and latent activities associated with animal rearing were banned in the new villages due to hygiene requirements. This had dramatic consequences on a family's income and restricted women's activities. The courtyards were often too small to accommodate the various functions which formerly took place in this setting. 'This house without out buildings, without a shelter for the flock, without a place for the conservation of the harvest or the storage of the tools, would have been ideally appropriate for landless workers who do not need a space for equipment, livestock or harvest' (Planhol, 1961).

The design of the built environment was also characterised by extreme physical determinism. Some planners were not only adamant in their determination to ignore the peasants' cultural norms but also attempted to impose their own norms and values through the housing organisation. They were determined to change the families' way of life through physical manipulation. For instance, their desire to see the native woman evolving as a public person has led to the deliberate suppression of the courtyards. Sometimes it entailed the creation of women's clubs right in the centre of the village (Bugnicourt, 1960). Additionally, the fountains and the wash houses were purposely situated in the centre of the village, in such a way as to generate major social changes. These environmental changes had dramatic effects on women's outdoor activities as they were prohibited in the new setting. In the village of Kerkara, the fetching of water from the well became the duty of the men and children. The new houses were often designed in direct contact with the outside (Planhol, 1961), thus disrupting the villagers' need for privacy. Even when the courtyard existed to obstruct direct visual contact, it was still insufficient to ensure the necessary privacy, as the dwellings faced onto the street.

Peasants' response to the new environment

De Lauwe (1965) suggested that the lack of understanding between designers and users can take various forms: conscious or unconscious, passive or active. Man adapts to his environment in a similar way: consciously or unconsciously, passively or actively. The peasants adjusted to these changes by creating a World of their own, according to their cultural and symbolic patterns. At Djebabra, despite all the amenities and facilities which were located in the main avenues, the men still avoided them. The spaces obviously conflicted with the traditional village organisation, where such facilities would be located on the outskirts to prevent outsiders invading their privacy.

The physical manipulation by the planners to change the people also failed. At the village of Matmata, although the women's social club was relocated away from the centre of the village (far from men's sight), still it was also hardly visited (Bourdieu and Sayad, 1964). Despite the official decision to forbid any modifications to the houses, the rural families adapted their environment to suit their cultural norms. In the village of Dalmatie, they increased the height of the wall surrounding the courtyards by lattice work to ensure necessary visual privacy (Planhol, 1961).

As a result of the independence of Algeria in 1962, the French programme was halted. However, it paved the way for the rural planning policies carried out by independent Algeria.

The Algerian Socialist Villages programme

The Algerian rural development programme had strong ideological and methodological aspects. The Government aimed at development on the basis of socialist principles. The underlying assumption behind the Algerian approach is that traditional patterns and attitudes are seen as major factors inhibiting desired change and development. Therefore, it was assumed that the improvement of rural life entails the destruction of any vestige of traditional rural socio-economic patterns. 'It (the Agrarian Revolution) will not progress if it does not succeed in modifying the peasant's mentality and destroy in him all the archaic structures of thinking, of action, of world view' (Charte Nationale, 1976).

Planning implications of the Socialist Villages

Similar to the French programme, the rural housing programme involved the construction of '1,000' Socialist Villages. The objective of this new policy was to transform the peasantry and to restructure rural space. The villages were constructed to perform a specific role in the rural space. Within this broad classification, a three-fold hierarchy of villages was established: primary, secondary and tertiary (C.N.R.A., 1972). These changes initiated by the socialist villages programme were remarkable as for the first time, they 'formulated the problem of rural housing in terms of Planning' (Brule, 1976). Nevertheless it inherited and repeated the same mistakes that had occurred during the implementation of the regrouping centres policy.

The lack of understanding of the real implication of these planning objectives, has led to severe problems of design and implementation of the new settlements. The preliminary phase involving the collection and analysis of relevant information for the layout and implementation of the Socialist Villages, relied on stereotyped socio-economic and technical surveys. Instead of military imperatives of the former settlement policy, the location of the socialist villages was often determined by bureaucratic and technological presumptions. This resulted in several villages being carelessly located. They were also far too large, with very low population densities. More importantly, they had undesirable locational implications, divorcing the peasants from agricultural activities. (Ministère de l'Habitat, 1981). In the example of the village of El-Kouchia, it was necessary to build a dike to prevent flooding (Lesbet, 1983, p.99). Several villages were unable to survive economically as a result of which many families had recourse to non-agricultural occupations to make a living. Consequently some villages became dormitory centres for industrial workers (Maurer, 1982, p.289). Additionally, many beneficiaries were forced to withdraw from the co-operatives mainly because the land was allocated too far away from their places of residence. This was further aggravated by the lack of transport or any real subsidy.

Socialist Villages policy and its design implications

The Algerian planners ignored the socio-cultural basis of rural life in Algeria and imposed ideological solutions designed to 'change' people. Many mistakes that were made during the French regrouping policy were inherited and repeated. Rapoport (1980) argued that planners/designers and the public represent very different value systems. He also suggested that this cultural and communication

Figure 8.3 A general view of a Socialist village.

gap between designers and users led to difficulty in understanding the culture and its physical implications. He attributed this disagreement to different meanings of environmental quality. The Algerian planners and designers set out to create better living surroundings on the basis of their own understanding of what is a 'good' and 'bad' environment. The attitudes of the rural families were merely ignored, which resulted in different evaluations of places. The planners evaluated the traditional rural housing as substandard and both physically and socially uninhabitable - the standard being new urban housing. Moreover, ideological positions which were designed to eliminate individualistic attitudes often prevailed. 'The creation of the Socialist Village is to eliminate the *gourbi* [traditional house], and the spirit of the *gourbi* with the poverty and individualism associated with it' (Mergerand, 1970).

The policy makers' erroneous attitude towards traditional housing has resulted in the imposition of unrealistically high standards, primarily designed to eliminate eyesores. It led to a strong emphasis on the formal and aesthetic aspects of design (Figure 8.3). The villagers were, for instance forbidden to alter their houses. Ironically, the only space that allowed modifications (a tiny area reserved for the extension of the house) was requested by a Ministry circular to be covered, so that the peasants' initiatives do not spoil the [architectural] harmony of the village.[1]

The planners' attitudes and lack of understanding of how local culture worked socially and physically also resulted in the imposition of a new model of design and environmental organisation, which had both undesirable social and economic consequences. The replacement of the loose-knit spatial organisation by a more compact one disrupted the mechanisms of territoriality. The suppression of some mechanisms, which were used to achieve privacy through distance, physical boundaries and so on, severely threatened the rural families' privacy. This was accentuated when the villagers were denied the right to gather according to criteria such as kinship or even common interests (Mutin, 1982). There was a deliberate policy to distribute the families at random within the village so that they did not develop clan feeling which the authorities feared would clash with the socialist principle of communality. Besides aesthetic, there was also a strong emphasis on health standards. Urban planners failed to understand how rural people preferred to use space. The ban on raising animals dramatically affected the rural families economy, as it severely diminished their incomes. As an alternative, they proposed a communal shed (Lesbet, 1983), which was psychologically and socially unacceptable.

The provision of recreational facilities was heavily based on urban values. It resulted in major gap between the provision of such services and facilities and the peasants' needs and economic affordability (Lesbet, 1983). The designers allocated space in the new dwelling according to a specific function, for instance, a kitchen for cooking, thus disregarding the people's traditional multi-use of space. In any case, the houses were often too small to accommodate the large families. The planners' theoretical standards set the number of six to seven

Plate 8.2 Provision of high rise buildings as a new approach to rural housing.

persons per household. In most cases, the extended families' size was much larger (Lesbet, 1983). Once again, inappropriate surveys resulted in the provision of an environment which was not in harmony with families' social structures.

An assessment of the short experience of the Socialist Villages concluded that this policy has failed to achieve its fundamental objectives. Since the 1980s, the policy makers have become reluctant to continue with this policy. The Ministry of Housing report (1981) concluded that '[the villages] continue to have undesirable implications, divorcing the peasants from agricultural activities.' Since then, this programme has been halted and a modified rural policy introduced.

Adjusted rural settlement planning design policy

The new rural housing strategy supports self-help housing projects and, in a few cases, the construction of subsidised flats. Various steps were taken to improve rural life by the building of new roads and the provision of building plots for sale, provided with water supply and sewage system. These measures have had, in general, a positive impact on the rural quality of life.

Nevertheless, there are fundamental reasons to suspect the approach of the recent planning design policy. First of all, policy-makers have failed to comprehend the underlying causes for the collapse of the previous official interventions. The planners' urban values have prevailed. Their self help strategy consisted of providing high rise buildings or plots for sale, adjacent to the existing villages (Plate 8.2). This approach is similar to the planning policy in the urban areas. The planners' standards and criteria of design and construction were too high to relate to what could be afforded by the rural population. As a result this policy only managed to attract town dwellers, as city building plots were unobtainable or unaffordable (Rahmani, 1989). Once again, the lack of communication between the planners' attitudes and those of the impoverished villagers resulted in the failure to understand the rural culture in relation to planning design.

Conclusion

It emerged from this study that the successive rural development programmes did not work, mainly because all the plans failed to take into account the socio-economic basis of rural life in Algeria and wanted to impose ideological solutions; so one ideology - French - was replaced by another - Socialist. They were also excessively bureaucratic in style and sought deliberately to 'change' the traditional rural life. The psychological aspects of change were also neglected. They attempted to replace the traditional extended family of production with a socialist one, instead of identifying its potentials and using them efficiently. The

Algerian extended family has the potential to adapt to meet the needs of the new system and to form a basic unit of production.

The official attempt to achieve the socialisation of agriculture through social and psychological engineering combined with physical determinism, has turned out to be doubtful. The policy makers asserted that an improved social environment could be fulfilled by reorganising the farmers into socialist co-operatives of production based upon communal ownership of land and property. The cultural and communication gap between designers and users, made it difficult to perceive fully the culture and its design implications in sufficient detail. It was stressed that the French and Algerian programmes failed mainly because they disregarded the variables relating to rural life in Algeria, which resulted in an environment conflicting with the peasants' way of life and which complicated the process of adaptation to the new environment. As Rapoport (1994) has argued, more research and understanding are needed to identify the elements in the built environment which are congruent with the core cultural elements. This understanding may enable us to create environments which are highly supportive of the rural communities' values, norms, attitudes and patterns of behaviour.

Note

1   Minstère de la Planification des travaux Publiques et de la Construction (Ministry for Planning and Construction.)

9 Gender and structural adjustment:
A case study in North-Eastern Ghana

Mariama Awumbila

Introduction

The severity of economic conditions in Sub-Saharan Africa during the 1980s resulted in many African countries adopting structural adjustment programmes (SAPs) sponsored by the International Monetary Fund and the World Bank in an effort to re-structure their economies. In the short term however, some of the policies adopted have worsened conditions for the most vulnerable groups in the population. Widespread concern now exists about the deteriorating standards of living and the severe erosion of the 'human resource' base of the economy following the economic crisis and resulting adjustment (Cornia et al., 1987). A more recent debate however centres around how the crisis has been experienced by different members of the household often having a differential impact on women vis a vis men (Commonwealth Secretariat, 1989; Gladwin 1991).

This chapter examines the micro level impact of macro-economic adjustment policies on women in a village located in Ghana's increasingly stressed North-eastern savannah environment (Figure 9.1). It explores the link between adjustment policies, and the feminisation of poverty through a comparative analysis of women's time use as a measure of changes in gender roles under economic stress.

Fieldwork was undertaken in Zorse, a village in north-eastern Ghana (Figure 9.1). A baseline study of 124 households was undertaken in 1984, when Ghana had just begun implementing a structural adjustment programme, and the same households revisited in 1991, eight years into the programme.

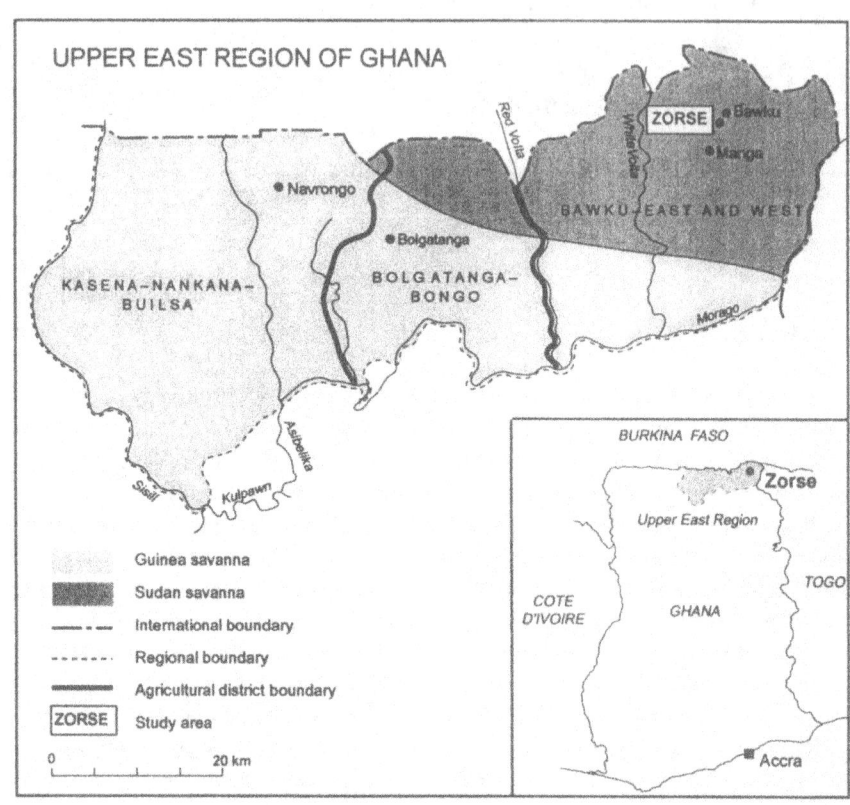

Figure 9.1 The Area of Study.

Economic crisis and structural adjustment in Ghana

After a period of relative progress, the late 1970s and early 1980s were a period of economic crisis for many developing countries. Ghana's economic decline began in the late 1960s. A positive growth rate of 2.1% per annum between 1960 and 1970 declined to - 6.1% per annum between 1980 and 1983 and the inflation rate increased from 9% per annum in 1970 to 122% in 1983. Stagnation or decline characterised almost all sectors of the economy while population increased at a faster rate. The social impact was just as severe with a deterioration in health and educational standards and a reduction in real incomes per head. The result of the economic decline was a general impoverishment of the nation as a whole with about 50% of urban households and 65% to 75% of rural households living below the poverty line by the early 1980s (UNICEF, 1988). Prolonged drought, bush fires and the expulsion of nearly one million Ghanaians from Nigeria in 1983, put severe strain on an already critical food and unemployment situation and exacerbated the crisis.

Faced with the desperate economic situation, the Government of the PNDC in 1983, adopted an IMF/World Bank sponsored structural adjustment programme (SAP) aimed at halting the economic decline and re-structuring the economy to foster growth and development. The programme had as its guiding principle 'the re-alignment of the price and incentive system in the economy *in favour of the productive, particularly the export sectors'* (Government of Ghana, 1987, p.i).

The SAP adopted in Ghana was a fairly standard IMF and World Bank package and included the following policies: demand restraint through cuts in Government expenditure, public sector employment and real wages; price decontrol involving the removal of subsidies on food, consumer items and agricultural inputs; the introduction or increases in user charges for social services; switching policies including trade liberalisation and currency devaluation; long term supply policies aimed at raising the long term efficiency of the economy through privatisation of state owned institutions, and credit reform.

The short term impact of these policies, in comparison with 1982/1983 levels, was the recovery of the economy. Between 1984 and 1989, GDP average annual growth rates were restored to the levels of the early 1970s registering growth rates of 5% per annum, although it has been pointed out that part of this recovery was due to improved environmental factors and improved terms of trade rather than to specific policy (Toye, 1991; Loxley, 1988). Some sectors registered positive growth rates with inflation falling by over 90% between 1983 and 1985.

However the wider social impact has been less successful. Despite the impressive macro-level growth statistics, both absolute and relative poverty increased among both urban and rural populations during the period of adjustment. It has been pointed out that the costs of adjustment are borne most heavily by those with relatively poor ability to withstand such losses, thereby deepening poverty.[1]

The economy of North-Eastern Ghana

An important feature of the Ghanaian economy is the dichotomy between the southern forest zone with its more abundant rainfall and resources, fertile soils and relatively developed infrastructure, and the northern savannah, covering about 60% of the country, with low and erratic rainfall, few resources and a poor infrastructure. Since colonial times the north has remained an area producing largely subsistence crops which are undervalued and under priced in the national market. It is generally thought that northern underdevelopment is not due to the harsh physical environment or lack of resources but rather that it was a by-product of the need for northern labour by the export-oriented mining and cocoa interests of the south (Bening, 1975, Songsore and Denkabe, 1988). Today, the Upper East Region (Figure 9.1) remains one of the poorest, the most rural and the least industrialised regions in Ghana. It has the nation's highest average population density, outside the capital region of Greater Accra, of 87 persons per square kilometre. Densities in the cultivated areas of Bawku District, in which the study village of Zorse is located (Figure 9.1) reach 270 persons per square kilometre.

The area has also been affected by drought conditions since the late 1960s. In the 1980s the major problem for farmers, as evidenced by rainfall records and supported by interviews, was increasing irregularity of rainfall. Field observations in 1991 revealed land shortage, devegetation, soil deterioration and general degradation of the land. (Benneh and Gyasi, 1993).

Compared to the rest of the country, north-eastern Ghana experiences shortages of food with greater intensity because of the single rainfall season and the frequency of drought. The situation is further compounded by the fact that basic cash crops in the region are also food crops and many rural households sell off food crops to satisfy non-food needs often leading to a long pre-harvest 'hungry season' The long season of hunger from about March/February to July is characterised by low food stores, a high demand for agricultural labour and increased incidence of water-borne diseases such as malaria. In Zorse, it was common for meals to be missed in the hungry season.

The impact of structural adjustment policies, with its emphasis on the promotion of exports and the expenditure switching policies it necessitates, has been a reinforcement of existing contradictions between northern and southern Ghana with a further marginalisation of the north.

Impact of the structural adjustment programme in Zorse

The follow up survey of the 124 households in 1991 revealed gender differentiated changes in health and nutrition, food consumption, education and women's workloads between 1984 and 1991 which are linked to some of the policies adopted under the SAP.

Changes in health, nutrition and consumption patterns

Even before the introduction of SAP, the quality of life in northern Ghana, in comparison with the other regions was low. With 19% of the nation's population, the northern sector accounted for only 5% of public health service attendance. The SAP policies of cuts in government expenditure on health-care, the introduction of; or increases in user charges at hospitals; withdrawal of supplementary feeding programmes and increases in food costs which were introduced among other measures, further exacerbated the problem. The impact of these measures on the rural poor in north-eastern Ghana was that health services became expensive and inaccessible to many families. Attendance at the maternal and child welfare clinic in Bawku hospital for example dropped by 15% between 1984 and 1991, and attendance at the three hospitals in the region dropped from 104,447 in 1986 to 91,518 in 1991 (Ministry of Health, 1991).

With the food price rises associated with SAP measures, women as mothers and caretakers of the family have found it very difficult to afford to buy the required food to supplement declining yields from household farms. As a result the general level of nutrition and health of many families declined in the region. Diseases related to dietary deficiencies increased, with anaemia and malnutrition becoming the commonest diseases reported at the Bawku district hospital in 1991. The incidence of child malnutrition in the region also increased from 52% in 1986 to 70% in 1990 (Ministry of Health, 1991).

In Zorse, the data points to a decline in health status during the seven year period. Infant mortality, which can be used as an indicator of the health status and quality of life, increased among the sample in Zorse from 160 to 450 deaths per thousand live births, while infant and child mortality showed a smaller increase form 190 to 220 deaths per thousand live births. This high increase in infant mortality may be linked to the large number of undernourished women who are at a greater risk of giving birth to low birth weight babies who face a higher risk of mortality[2] and to the higher health charges which led to reduced attendance at maternal and child welfare clinics.

Many households made some changes to their diets in response to rising food prices and declining yields from household farms. Fifty two percent of the women were of the opinion that both the quantity and quality of the food they consumed had deteriorated since 1984 because of either lack of money to buy or invest in growing items or the need to sell crops produced and consume only the lowest value products such as millet. Intra-household food distribution which is in favour of men and boys in Zorse implies that when households have to reduce food consumption, it is likely that the consumption by women and girls is reduced more than those of men and boys.

Changes in educational status

The adjustment policies of the introduction of school and book user fees, and housing and feeding charges at secondary schools and universities, worsened the already limited access to education in the region and for girls in particular. Primary school fees of 500 cedis per term were introduced in Zorse in 1985. In addition, parents had to provide school uniforms, a chair, table, books and stationery which, with the exception of uniforms were previously provided free by Government. This was estimated to cost about the equivalent of ten pounds sterling in 1991. The Government has argued that the fees at primary school level are modest but with an average yearly income of about the equivalent of twelve pounds in 1991 for women in Zorse, this means that the cost of educating one child is equivalent to about a year's income thus making education inaccessible to low income families.

Although very few women had any formal education in Zorse, this doubled over the seven year period from 7% in 1984 to 15% in 1991. Despite the increasing number of women with some education, the level of education achieved was lower in 1991. Of the 7% who had some formal education in 1984, 66% of them had more than primary school education, compared to only 17% of the 34 women in 1991. These figures indicate a growing drop out rate for girls particularly after the primary school. National data for the Upper East Region also indicate a drop in school enrolment rates of 6% between 1984 and 1991.

Thus even though the nutritional, health and educational status of the population in the region has always been low, the effects of adjustment policies have reinforced the deteriorating circumstances of many households.

Changes in income-generating activities

SAP policies of retrenchment of workers from the public sector meant increasing unemployment and an influx of retrenched workers into the informal sector at the national level. In Zorse, with only 2% of women engaged in the formal sector, there was very little change in the number of women engaged in an income earning activity between 1984 and 1991. However there were changes in the types of income generating work over the seven year period, with more women undertaking farming and food processing rather than trading in 1991 (Table 9.1).

Table 9.1 Income -earning activities of women, Zorse, 1984 and 1991.

ACTIVITY	Percentage of	Women
	1984	1991
	N=250	N=226
Farming	25.2	36.7
Trading	38.6	20.4
Beer Brewing	9.6	8.4
Food Processing	3.2	9.7
Handicraft Production	4.8	7.1
Formal Sector	4.2	4.4
No Activity	14.4	13.3
Total	**100.0**	**100.0**

Source: Fieldwork, Zorse.

This may suggest that women are cashing in on the higher prices of crops as a result of SAP policies as found in a study among women in southern Nigeria (Guyer and Idowu, 1991). In Zorse however, the incentive to move into farming was not the higher producer prices of food crops, since these are produced at a higher cost, but for survival. As most women farmers put it 'at least with farming one's children would not go hungry'.

Changes in women's time use

The changes outlined above have had a number of important implications for women. In their triple roles as mothers and wives, producers and community managers, women have been most affected by the adjustment policies in terms of increasing workloads and conflicting demands on their time (Moser, 1992). Time use studies can be used as a measure of the degree of involvement in different types of work and help to reveal the daily and seasonal fluctuations in the demand for labour and trade-offs between different categories of work. The assumption is that the amount of time used for work can provide a reliable measure of the workload of various household members. In Zorse, the sexual division of labour is noticeable from the age of six onwards and gradually becomes more rigid with age, with women being in charge of almost all domestic chores.

Table 9.2 Average daily time spent on reproductive work, Zorse, 1984 and 1991.

ACTIVITY	WET SEASON		DRY SEASON	
	1984	1991	1984	1991
	N=250	N=226	N=250	N=226
HOUSEHOLD MAINTENANCE				
Cooking	1.5	1.7	2.3	2.0
Child Care	1.6	1.2	1.4	1.1
Water Collection	1.4	1.1	1.9	1.2
Cleaning/Washing	1.1	0.6	0.8	0.8
TOTAL HOUSEWORK	**5.6**	**4.6**	**6.4**	**5.1**
KITCHEN GARDENING	**1.5**	**1.4**	**0.6**	**0.4**
TOTAL	**7.1**	**6.0**	**7.0**	**5.5**

Source: Fieldwork, Zorse. 1984 and 1991.

Table 9.2 shows that cooking, including food preparation, is the most time consuming domestic chore and also the most gender specific task. It was the activity which revealed the least equitable distribution between members of the household. Of the 180 married women living with their husbands, 72% did the cooking themselves and the remainder had some help, mainly from daughters. In the wet season, cooking is done only in the evenings but in the dry season, when food is more plentiful, a morning meal may be cooked as well. Cooking and food preparation are laborious involving the pounding of vegetables and dried fish in a mortar and the winnowing of millet and sorghum grains before taking them to the mill for grinding into flour.

Collecting water takes about an hour of women's time each day on the average, but this time varies with family structure and size and with the season. The main sources of water supply in Zorse are a bore-hole situated at the centre of the village, a well and a dam located about four miles to the south of the village. Water is carried in wide enamel bowls which weigh about 25 kilograms when full. Firewood collection[3] also takes about an hour each day. The main types of fuel used are dried millet and sorghum stalks and wood obtained from gathering fallen twigs and branches from the nearby forest reserve or from surrounding farms. After the harvesting of the millet grain, the stalks are left to dry on the fields and later gathered and transported to the compound. These are stock piled and serve as the main source of fuel supply from November to about March. When the millet stalks run out, and the twigs and branches from the forest reserve are no longer available, women have to walk long distances sometimes even going into neighbouring Burkina Faso to gather wood for fuel. Women usually organise these trips in groups about once a week and return carrying bundles of wood weighing up to 30 kilograms.

Cleaning, washing clothes and utensils and other housework are the least time consuming activities. The mud huts do not entail much cleaning and sweeping and this is normally shared out among the female children in the household.

Kitchen gardening is a wet season activity. Each married woman cultivates a garden on the land directly behind her hut, growing mainly vegetables for the family's meals. Women also keep small livestock, mainly poultry, sheep, pigs and goats in the compound.

Women's time use and seasonality

The marked seasonality of rainfall that characterises North-eastern Ghana means that the availability of resources changes throughout the yearly cycle and has a profound impact on the types of activities of both men and women in northern Ghana. The seasonal nature of rainfall means that for six months from about May to October, everyone's time and energy goes into producing enough millet to feed the family and to earn some cash for the whole year. At the same time women must take care of and maintain their households. Rural women in the developing world are therefore involved in a 'zero-sum game', a closed system in which time or energy devoted to any new effort must be diverted from another activity, the effect of which is reflected in Table 9.2 in relation to seasonal time use between 1984 and 1991. Cooking and food preparation time increases in the dry season when there is enough food for two meals a day. However the increase was less in 1991 than in 1984 because of other competing demands on women's time. Cleaning the house and washing clothes also take more time in the dry season, as it is a dusty period with trees shedding their leaves thus demanding more sweeping and dusting. Clothes have to be taken to the water source for washing rather than using rain water as can be done in the wet season. Water collection time also increased in the dry season in 1984 as a result of the drying up of the dam and wells. The construction of a bore-hole in Zorse in 1985 meant the availability of water in both seasons in 1991.

Time spent in gathering fuel wood on the other hand is less in the dry season, because of the availability of millet and sorghum stalks stored in the compound. Time use declined from 1.2 hours in the wet season to 0.7 hours daily in the dry season in 1991. At this time of the year, 62% of the women used millet stalks as their main source of fuel compared to only 9.6% in the wet season. This intensive use of millet stalks gathered from the grain fields, leaves the soil bare and exposes it to sheet and gully erosion, thus contributing to the degradation of the environment. Kitchen gardening, also takes very little of women's time in the dry season as it is dependent on rainfall.

In terms of seasonal time use between 1984 and 1991, there was a smaller increase in time spent on household maintenance activities in the dry season in 1991 than in 1984 (Table 9.2). This was compensated for by an increase in the time spent on income earning activities (Table 9.3) with more women undertaking farming and food processing.

Table 9.3 Seasonal differences in average daily time used in Zorse, 1984 and 1991.

ACTIVITY	HOURS PER DAY			
	WET SEASON 1984	1991	DRY SEASON 1984	1991
REPRODUCTIVE WORK	7.1	6.0	7.0	5.5
Household Maintenance	5.6	4.6	6.4	5.1
Kitchen Gardening	1.5	1.4	0.6	0.4
SOCIAL DUTIES	0.9	0.5	2.4	1.7
PRODUCTIVE WORK	3.3	4.1	2.3	5.2
TOTAL TIME USE	**11.3**	**10.6**	**11.7**	**12.4**

Source: Fieldwork, Zorse, 1984 and 1991

Total average daily hours of work between 1984 and 1991 fell from 11.3 hours to 10.6 hours in the wet season, while dry season work hours increased from 11.7 to 12.4 hours (Table 9.3). The total average daily work hours has therefore not changed significantly between the two years, but the balancing of time between women's various roles has been adjusted. These confirm findings from Ecuador during a period of economic crisis (Moser, 1992). Time spent in reproductive work and social duties fell in both seasons between 1984 and 1991, but work hours in income earning activities, increased by almost an hour in the wet season and by about 3 hours in the dry season (Table 9.3). Thus in 1984, whereas in the dry season work hours in household maintenance and in social duties were increased and productive work hours reduced, the opposite obtained in 1991. Reduced time in reproductive work and social duties in the dry season was used to earn more income in 1991 (Table 9.3). This suggests the use of the dry season to generate and diversify income as has also been noted in Burkina Faso (Reardon et al., 1988). The traditional view of the dry season being a period of rest when ceremonies such as funerals and festivals could be organised is changing. As household incomes fall with economic restructuring, women are making more use of the dry season to generate additional income thus increasing their workloads.

When asked if they thought they were working harder in 1991 than seven years earlier, 60% of women thought they were, while 32% thought their workload had not changed as described by Lariba:

> We work more than our mothers in the past. Our mothers in the past only busied themselves with preparing food for the household. After that they sat down and relaxed. They only had to grind the millet and plant on household farms. Our mothers did not weed. Today, we work from sunrise in our domestic tasks and in addition go and work on the farm. We weed and in the evening we have to go home and prepare the evening meal for the family. This is what we do daily from sunrise to sunset. Our mothers in the past never did this. We work and work and we are tired and poor.

Conclusion

The effects of adjustment which have resulted in rising food prices, increases in the cost of social services and declining real and household incomes, when combined with deteriorating environmental conditions obtaining in the savannah north-east, have meant increasing workloads and falling standards of living. There is a visible process of impoverishment taking place in Zorse which is reflected in deteriorating health and nutritional status, changes in the pattern of food consumption, a growing drop out rate from education for girls, and an intensification of women's workloads as shown by increasing work hours especially in the dry season and the intensification of labour inputs in agriculture. In response to the question whether men or women more affected by the crisis, almost all women thought themselves in a worse position relative to men as they felt that women were more concerned with and responsible for household welfare. As one women put it

We know that these problems we are facing are not the fault of our men. They know what is happening at home, that the money and millet is hardly enough to feed the whole family, but they pretend not to see....they go and get drunk in order not to see. I am the one who sees what the children need everyday and I have to think what to do.

Gender inequalities in access to resources of land, credit, capital and labour have increased women's difficulties. Macro economic policies of structural adjustment appear to have given rise to greater gender inequalities and placed heavy burdens on rural women. Like previous development polices, they have been carried out under the assumption that it is a gender neutral process, but as Elson (1991) points out it has an inbuilt gender bias. By ignoring the sexual division of labour in work and intra-household distribution of resources as well as women's triple role, SAP has meant women are carrying heavier workloads in the household. For sustained development, it is important that macro economic policies are undertaken from a gender perspective to make them more responsive to the needs of both men and women.

Notes

1   A 1988 study found that the percentage of the 'hard core poor', defined by the World Bank as the population falling below a per capita yearly income of 18,562 cedis or approximately twenty pounds sterling has been on the increase in Ghana since the mid 1980s (Boateng et al., 1990).

2   A survey in the Upper East Region found that 30% of males and 50% of females were underweight for most part of the year, but during the 'hungry season' this increased to 49% of men and 63% of women. The number of low birth weight babies has also been on the increase since the mid 1980s, more than doubling from 7.3% in 1988 to 19.5 % in 1992 (Ministry of Health, 1992).

3   Data for time spent collecting fuelwood was unavailable in 1984 and as a result is omitted from the 1991 data presented in Tables 9.3 and 9.4.

10 Societal values in development process:
Place-making in Sokoto, Nigeria

Umar G. Benna

The important role societal values play in the process of spatial development is receiving an increasing attention as shown not only by the many contributors to this volume - Rapoport (Chapter 1), El-Sharif (Chapter 7) and King (Chapter 15) - but also by many earlier researchers - Al-Hathloul (1982), Hakim (1986 and 1994) and Akbar (1988). Many of these researchers have indicated the need to develop an appropriate analytical model that can correctly analyse and predict changes in the community. It is perhaps not by accident that most of the efforts by the researcher have focused on the local development processes in Arab-Muslim cities of the Middle-East and North Africa.

This paper drawing from the study of Sokoto, Nigeria, seeks to achieve three main objectives namely (a) to suggest an appropriate conceptual framework for the analysis of spatial development in Muslim cultures; (b) to broaden the discussion of Muslim cities by drawing attention to the cities in many parts of the world; and (c) to extend the level of analysis of Muslim cities from the local built-environment to the regional level. To achieve these objectives the paper first outlines a model which links societal values to major development decisions and actions to the resultant pattern of development. Next the key personalities who were able to bring these values to the level of general acceptability are identified along with the main development instruments they used. Then the patterns of development at regional and local levels are discussed.

Conceptual framework

Many concepts have been advanced to analyse cities in western industrialised societies. Among these are theories of 'good city form' which propose performance dimensions for assessing spatial forms of cities, and economic theories that try to explain spatial structure through the workings of the market in allocating user spaces according to supply and demand relationships in an equilibrium system. From social sciences there are human ecology theories that see market changes producing demographic and land-use regulations changes over time. Political-economic theories focus on the influence of powerful political interest and the resolution of land-use conflicts between and among individuals and groups in the community. Most of these theories have normative components allied with some descriptive elements and would appear to be inappropriate for our purpose.

Clearly there is no theory that is absolutely value-free, but those concepts whose formulations internalise societal value systems stand a better chance. In this regard, we find Walter Firey's (Firey 1947) concept of Social Values, and its later adaptations by Chapin(Chapin 1968pp:29-39), very promising and therefore forms the basis of the following conceptual framework. The simplest form of the model states that motivated by values, ideals and the resultant articulated attitudes held by the various urban individuals or groups, their decisions and actions follow a defined behaviour sequence that culminates in land use changes i.e., societal values → behaviour → development, as illustrated in Figure 10.1.

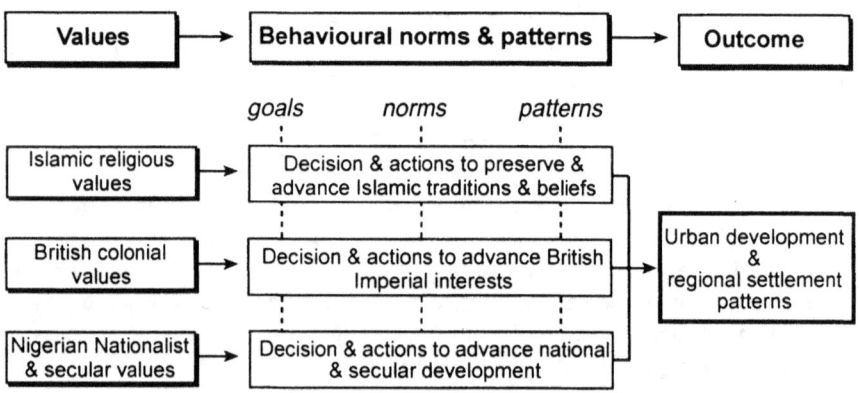

Figure 10.1 Conceptual model for the analysis of Sokoto's Development.

Social values are seen here as deeply rooted convictions and shared community beliefs which give weight to choices on the various courses of action regarding development. Behaviour refers to specific value rooted actions taken by the community through the centralised decisions of the authorities and the decentralised actions of the private developers and users to ensure the appropriate type of development. Development is the tangible result of values directed behaviour (place-making activity) patterns at the local, urban and regional levels. The articulation of new values and their translation into development is assumed in this model to be an interactive and continuous process.

This proposed model for the analysis of development of Sokoto can easily be modified for use in most cultures, especially in the Muslim cultures. In this particular case the model suggests that Islamic religious values, moderated by the indigenous Hausa-Fulani culture, tended to exert influence on the development-related decisions and actions of the Islamic government and its institutions. The decisions and actions, in the one hundred years of the existence of the Sokoto Caliphate (1804-1904), had in turn greatly affected the pattern of both urban and regional development. During the colonial period which lasted about fifty years, the British colonial values, dominated by the concerns for profit-making, had considerable influence on the development decisions and actions of the British colonial administration. After independence in 1960, the nationalist and secular values greatly affected development-related decisions and actions of the government in Sokoto and the outcome of these decisions and actions are the present pattern of development. Thus the Sokoto place-making activities relevant to this study can be seen as the sum of all activities at the various levels influenced by the three distinct value systems.

Development actors and instruments

The term 'Sokoto' has been defined in many ways. Its definitions have been based on its geographic features, its historical continuity, its religious zeal, its political configuration and on the basis of its linguistic style (Benna, 1985). Each of these approaches is valid but the geographical and historical approaches are more relevant to this paper. In its spatial context, Sokoto refers to the new settlement founded by Sultan Bello in 1804, surrounded by defensive city walls and with a central mosque as the focal point of the city. It also included the suburban settlements that grew outside the city walls. A broader definition refers to all the lands whose traditional rulers pay allegiance to the Sultan of Sokoto. This area is often called Sokoto Caliphate.

From a historical perspective Sokoto derived its significance from the Sokoto *Jihad,* an Islamic reform movement that affected most of what is now known as northern states of Nigeria and many parts of West Africa. The Jihad was started in 1804 by Shehu Dan Fodio and continued for most of the first half of the nineteenth century and was directed from Sokoto town which was initially started as one of the many defensive walled towns that served as army bases and rallying points along the expanding frontiers of the Caliphate. The historical analysis in this paper considers the role of value systems in the place-making activities initiated by three waves of intrusion into Sokoto of new value systems introduced by the Islamic reformists, the British colonial administration and the post independent secular government.

While the dominant societal values continued to influence development activities, there was also great pressure for change that must be acknowledged. The interpretation and re-interpretation of the prevailing values was carried out by certain key personalities who tried to nurture the correct intellectual attitudes and established the principles of a self-sustaining development process. Involved in the process were public officials, legal, social and political institutions and professionals all of whom sought to translate societal values into tangible development. Perhaps more important is the pivotal role of the many decentralised actions by private developers and users. The authorities take major decisions which set the basic framework for development within which citizens make their own decisions on house-building activities and on improvement of access to their houses. It is from these that the conventions and codes for urban development evolve which give Muslim cities their identity.

Dan Fodio defined the development instruments under Islamic government

Islamic religious values provided general guidance for development decisions and activities. To ensure that his central message of revivalist Islam was internalised, Shehu Dan Fodio (1754-1817) tried all methods of effective communication open to him. He initially conducted open classes for young and old and then started public preaching as he travelled widely throughout the land. He wrote over one hundred scholarly works in Arabic and in local languages. To ensure that the large and pluralist polity did not revert to its old ways, Dan Fodio (assisted by his brother Abdullahi Dan Fodio, 1763-1829, and his son Mohammad Bello, 1781-1837) established a strong administrative system and a judicial system on the models built by the Prophet Mohammad at Medina in central Arabia (Last, 1967). The institutions provided guidelines and principles, sometimes explicit and often implicit, that have shaped the urban and regional development patterns in Sokoto Caliphate. Regional and urban development issues were handled by the highly trained government officials (*hisba* and *muhtasib*) who operated a liberal land policy and ensured that local and regional commerce was encouraged and conducted according to Islamic laws. The main building codes and conventions were shaped by the Maliki School of Islamic Law and a carefully developed hierarchical system of judiciary.

Lugard set the ground rules for development

Colonial economic values moderated the type and pattern of development the British initiated in northern Nigeria. Although the colonial ideal of promoting civilisation and justice might be used to intrude into the Sokoto Caliphate, yet its potential as a source of cheap raw materials and as a market for British goods had great influence on the development that emerged during British rule.

The three value-laden elements that influenced developments under the colonial system were the strong personalities of British administration in northern Nigeria, the Indirect Rule policy and the land policy. Spatial development during the colonial period bore the firm imprint of Lord Lugard, Sir Winston Churchill and Sir Hesket Bell. Lugard was appointed the first British High Commissioner in northern Nigeria and later, in 1914, he became Governor General of a unified Nigeria. Winston Churchill was the Secretary for the Colonies at the critical period of decision-making which was of great importance to spatial development in northern Nigeria. The Indirect Rule Policy was part of the administrative innovation introduced by Lugard and nurtured by Sir Hesket Bell. The new policy sought to support clearly the authority of the Sultan and his emirs as well as the *Sharia* courts. He introduced the dual mandate concept, based on a symbiotic relationship, which accepted that it was the duty of the colonial administrator to bring benefits both to the citizens of the Caliphate and other Nigerians and 'to his own country's industrial class at home' (Hogben, 1967 p.67). The application of both indirect rule and dual mandate ensured the co-existence of two systems of development, one Islamic and the other British. The means by which urban lands were wrenched into conformity with official development policies were laws, memoranda and official directives. The early colonial laws were mainly concerned with the appropriate location of activity systems within urban areas to ensure health and safety of the colonial officials first and then of the natives. The introduction of physical segregation of people based on race was abhorred by Islam but remained the British official policy for much of its period. However its key element, the quarter mile buffer zone segregating the European and the native area, was redefined over the years in both its function and name.

The British Land Policy introduced innovation to land administration. Under the Islamic system land was considered a resource which was sacred, inviolable and inalienable property of the community and could be subject to individual ownership assigned by the emir, but natural resources such as water and minerals remained under community control. Under the British colonial system the concept of land remained the same but the power to grant land in the townships rested with the Governor. Although there was no free-hold ownership of land, yet the right to occupy or use land can be bought, sold, inherited or borrowed by individuals. The increase in security of title ensured that developers could mortgage their property.

Ahmadu Bello and Post independence developments

Nationalist and secularist values moderated the nature of spatial development after independence. The wave of nationalist fervour and the secularist position of the Federal constitution had considerable influence on the spatial development of northern Nigeria, which was broken into states to reduce its political dominance in the Federation. The instruments through which the values were translated into tangible development included the personality of the first premier of the region, Town and Country Planning Law and Local Government Law.

Sir Ahmadu Bello, the Sardauna of Sokoto, had a great influence in the development of northern Nigeria and of Sokoto town during the post-independence period. The great grandson of the founder of Sokoto town and Caliphate, Ahmadu Bello had the responsibility of forging a new development style within a secular Federal Republic of Nigeria constrained by the values of the Islamic and Colonial governments of the two earlier periods. Because of his Sokoto background many politicians with secularist views carefully watched his use of power. His cautious attitude toward secularism was not shared by subsequent leaders of northern Nigeria. In the area of urban and regional development he enacted the Town and Country Planning Law and revised the Local Government Law both of which reduced the sharp edges of the colonial development approach.

The Town and Country Planning Law placed great emphasis on land management, dealing mainly with applications for development, surveying, beaconing and the registration of titles. The most far reaching element of the law was aimed at rolling back some of the objectionable aspects of the colonial township laws, for example the abolition by this law of the building-free zone around the Government Reservation Areas (GRA) in an attempt to integrate existing GRAs and the institutional areas with the native towns.

The Local Government Law gave local authorities wide powers over planning and development. Unfortunately they hardly had adequate funds or expertise to carry out their functions effectively. There were attempts to improve their performance but with limited success; the state government had more funds and expertise to draw from. This situation often resulted in different quality of development within most urban areas, the details of which will now be discussed.

The patterns of development

This paper has so far tried to identify the main value systems that have influenced the spatial development patterns in the three time periods under review. We have also suggested some key instruments which were used to translate values into concrete development at the urban and regional levels. We shall now explore the resultant changes in development at the regional, urban and built environment levels.

Changes in the relative importance of cities

There have been some changes in the distribution and relative importance of cities over the study period. As the model above suggests, these changes can be attributed to the underlying values of the Islamic, colonial and the nationalist governments. Before the establishment of the Islamic government in Sokoto, the Hausa city-states of Katsina, Kano, Zaria, Gobir, Daura and Rano, were relatively small but autonomous and each of them tried to expand through conquest. By the time the Islamic government was fully established all these kingdoms, along with many neighbouring cities to their south and east, were integrated and brought under the authority of one government in Sokoto. New settlements were created to serve the goals of the Islamic government. Sokoto was initially created as a *ribat*, defensive walled city but it soon became the seat of the Caliphate and many *ribats (or rubut)* were established to protect it.

Some of these *ribats*, such as Kware, Gandi, Silame, Katuru, Shinkafe, grew into large towns. Besides these garrison towns, ordinary new towns were created in the frontier regions to the south and east of the Caliphate. These frontier towns included Gwandu, Kontagora, Bauchi, Katagum and Yola. (This is similar to the development described by Akbar (1988, p.82) of Kufah, Basrah, Fustat, Baghdad and Rabat in the early period of Islam in Arabia). As a result of the establishment of the Islamic government and its activities, the region experienced a profound change in the relative importance of the major cities. Kano, Katsina and Zaria in that order could be categorised as the most important towns in Hausa land before the establishment of Islamic government. However, a new hierarchical system of cities emerged with Sokoto, the capital of the Caliphate as the highest in importance, while emirates' headquarters such as Gwandu, Kano, Katsina, Zaria, Yola, Bauchi, Bida, Kazaure, and Mubi formed the second level. Below them were district headquarters which were also trading centres that had Friday congregational prayer mosques built in them. The presence of Islamic scholars and their role in the spread of Islam can be said to be the criterion for judging a city's importance in this period

Guided by its colonial economic values, the colonial government introduced further change in the regional system of cities. Kaduna was created as a new town deliberately located away from any of the Muslim strongholds and was made the capital of Northern Nigeria, relegating Sokoto to a city of spiritual importance only. Kaduna soon became an important administrative centre with all the major railway lines and roads passing through it. The development of transportation routes in support of the colonial economy helped many towns to grow rapidly and new ones were created to support it. Lokoja, Minna and Makurdi were created by the colonial government at critical transportation nodes. Offa, Gusau, Kauran

Namoda and Nguru owe their importance in the rank of northern Nigerian cities to their position on the railway line. Jos became important due to its tin and columbite industry and its role both as a transportation centre and provincial headquarters (Urquhart, 1977).

Like the Islamic government before it, the colonial government used a number of policy instruments to achieve its objectives. The two policies relevant to the change in relative importance of cities were the development of new towns and the transportation system. Kaduna, Zungeru, Jos, Minna, Makurdi and Lokoja were new towns created to support the colonial administration. Many other towns including Yola, Bauchi and Katsina grew in importance due to their positions as provincial headquarters. The pattern of railway and road developments were designed to link the export crops and mineral producing areas with the ports to serve the colonial economy. Most of the towns along these routes experienced rapid and uncontrolled growth. A notable feature of the colonial transportation system is its change of direction from northward across the Sahara to southward to seaports in Lagos and Port Harcourt thus limiting contacts with the Muslim states of north Africa and opening up new links with Britain and the West.

The political goals of national unity and of redressing imbalanced development had a great influence on the relative importance of cities in the post-colonial period. The most important urban development projects in this period were designed to achieve national, political and economic objectives. The relocation of the Federal capital from Lagos to Abuja, symbolises the national aspirations for unity, national security and ethnic and religious accord. It was also an attempt to correct development imbalance by initiating development in the area of relatively low density population in the middle belt region that had lagged behind the more densely populated southern forest and northern Savannah zones. The creation of new states to reduce the threat of political domination was another policy that benefitted many towns in northern Nigeria. The effects of these nationalistic policies were that the colonial capital of Kaduna suffered the same fate as Sokoto before it, whereby it was relegated to the position of a state capital, and remote towns such as Birnin Kebbi, Damaturu, Dutse, Jalingo and Lokoja are now the headquarters of their respective states, just as are the older cities such as Kano, Katsina, Sokoto, Kaduna, Ilorin, Minna, Makurdi, Maiduguri, Bauchi, Jos and Yola.

Many new towns were created in response to the goals of national economic integration. New Bussa was created to settle people who were affected by the hydro-electric dam built across the River Niger to provide power to satisfy the increasing demand from all parts of the Federation. Shiroro town was built to settle people affected by the development of the dam across River Kaduna. Another major national project is the iron and steel complex in Ajeokuta, as a result of which a new town was built for the people the project would attract. The infrastructure built to serve these projects inevitably helped to tie-in the southern forest and the northern grassland regions into an integrated national entity.

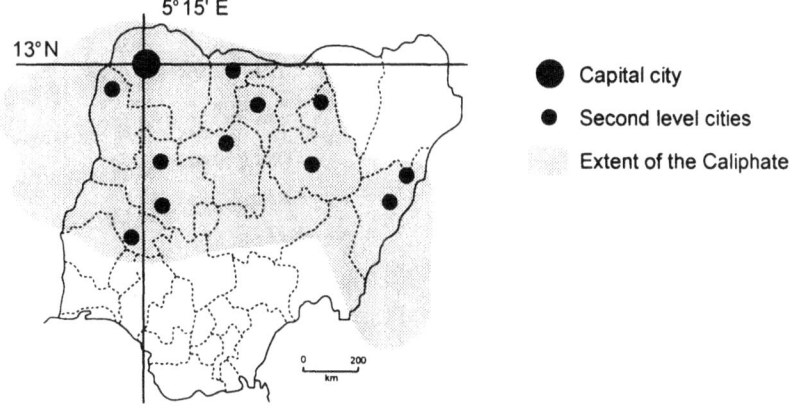

Figure 10.2.1 Caliphate system of cities.

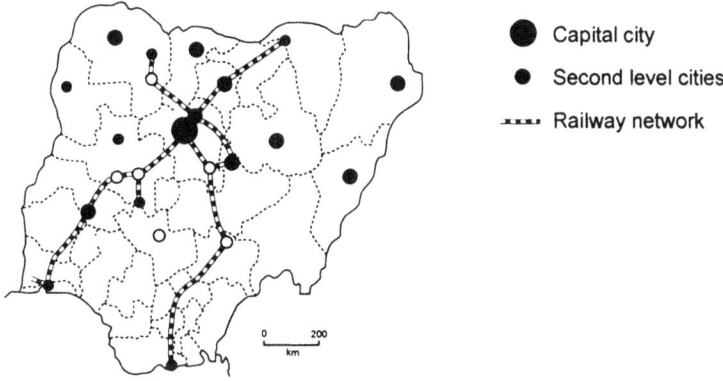

Figure 10.2.2 Colonial system of cities.

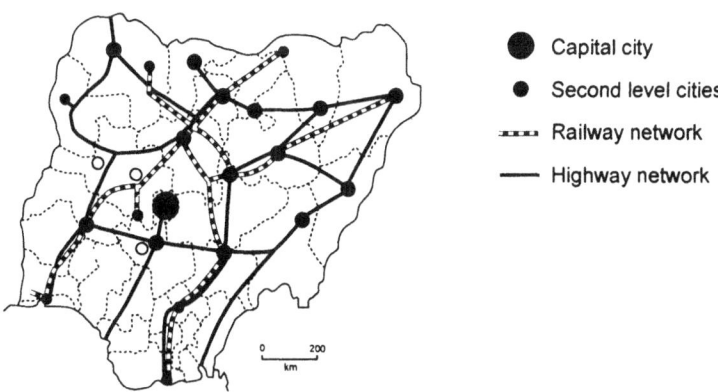

Figure 10.2.3 Post-colonial system of cities.

Changes in the spatial structure of Sokoto town

The early spatial structure of Sokoto town has been defined largely by the city walls, the central mosque and major public buildings, the residential compounds, open spaces and traffic routes. Changes were later introduced to these elements by the Islamic, colonial and nationalist governments to reflect their relative values. The overall effect of these changes is the emergence of dual foci in the city; one in the traditional old city and the other around Government House and Secretariat axis in the suburb.

The major elements of the city during the period of Islamic government were highlighted by Clapperton, an English explorer who visited Sokoto in 1823 and described it as

> The most populous town I have visited in the Interior of Africa; for unlike most other towns in Houssa, where houses are thinly scattered, it is laid out in regular well built streets. The houses approach the walls which are between twenty and thirty feet high, and have twelve gates.. There are two large mosques, .. a spacious market place in the centre of the city and another large square in front of the Sultan's residence. The dwellings of the principal people are surrounded by high walls, which enclose numerous coozies, circular huts with thatch roofs, and flat-roofed houses built in the Moorish style.

Thus the elaborate city walls of enormous size, with its many gates and watch towers, were built for defensive reasons but also as an important city-structuring element during this period. The wall and its associated elements (ditches, gates and towers) were often changed to fit new circumstances. For example when Bello succeeded his father as the leader of the Caliphate in 1818, the walls of Sokoto were rebuilt to include Sabon Birni, the suburb in which the Shehu had his residence (Last, 1967, p.183). Another change is in the number of gates which was initially eight but was increased to twelve, and later changed to nine (Urquhart, 1977, pp.69-72). However, the mud walls melted back into the earth during the colonial and nationalist periods when the purposes for which they were built were no longer valid.

The major public buildings of the Islamic government included the palace, the mosques and compounds of the officials, all in central locations. Both palaces of Bello and Shehu were large and incorporated many sections. For example, they had their private quarters near the eastern wall, with a garden on the north, and reception halls and courts to the west (Last, 1967, p.184). Near each of these palaces, was a mosque used for both daily and weekly prayers. The houses of the senior officials might have been smaller but had their own mosques and large reception halls. All these public buildings have remained virtually in their present locations and were in fact rebuilt using permanent materials. A new mosque has recently been built near the state secretariat outside the old city to meet the needs of the increasing suburban population.

The main public open spaces, as Clapperton described above, included a spacious market in the centre of the city and a public square in front of the Sultan's palace. With the increased trade with North Africa and the Guinea coastal regions, the location of the main market kept on changing and became bigger. For example in 1912 under the colonial administration it was relocated a mile from the western gate and in the 1970s a new larger modern market was built outside the city to the west. Besides the changes in the locations of the market, a new system of retail was introduced to reflect new economic values. In 1919 the Canteen Area was developed to cater for largely British firms trading mainly in red goat skin for which Sokoto had become famous.

The public square in front of the Sultan's palace had become an important area where the Sultan met the general public on ceremonial occasions. In the colonial and nationalist governments' period such functions continued to take place in the same place, but if the governor was involved, the function took place in the Polo ground outside the city.

Most of the growth outside the city was initiated by the colonial government and continued by the nationalist government, culminating in the emergence of a second focal point for the city around the axis between Government House and the State Government Secretariat. The British expeditionary force arrived in Sokoto town in 1903 and they built a fort south-west of the city and this developed into the government station. When in 1917 Sokoto was declared a Third Class Township, a building-free zone around the government station and a separate area for European traders' plots were laid out in accordance with the colonial Township and Public Health Ordinances.

The spatial layout of Sokoto was further modified by educational, health and other institutions inspired by the values of the colonial administration. Typical of such institutions was the School for the Sons of Chiefs, opened in 1905, which became the first school in Hausaland to be built on the British public school model. Later an Industrial Arts School opened in 1919, followed by clerical school, Arabic teachers school and many others that were all located outside the city walls on large land parcels at low density.

Post colonial developments, which tie Sokoto firmly into the Federation, include financial institutions e.g., branch of the Central Bank, commercial institutions e.g., National Supply Company, shops, stores and offices of the Federal and State Governments mostly located in the area bounded by the Government Residential Area (GRA), the walled city and the canteen area. More recently several large Federal Government institutions were built, including the Federal Government College (known as Unity School), the Federal College of Arts and Science and the Usmanu Dan Fodio University.

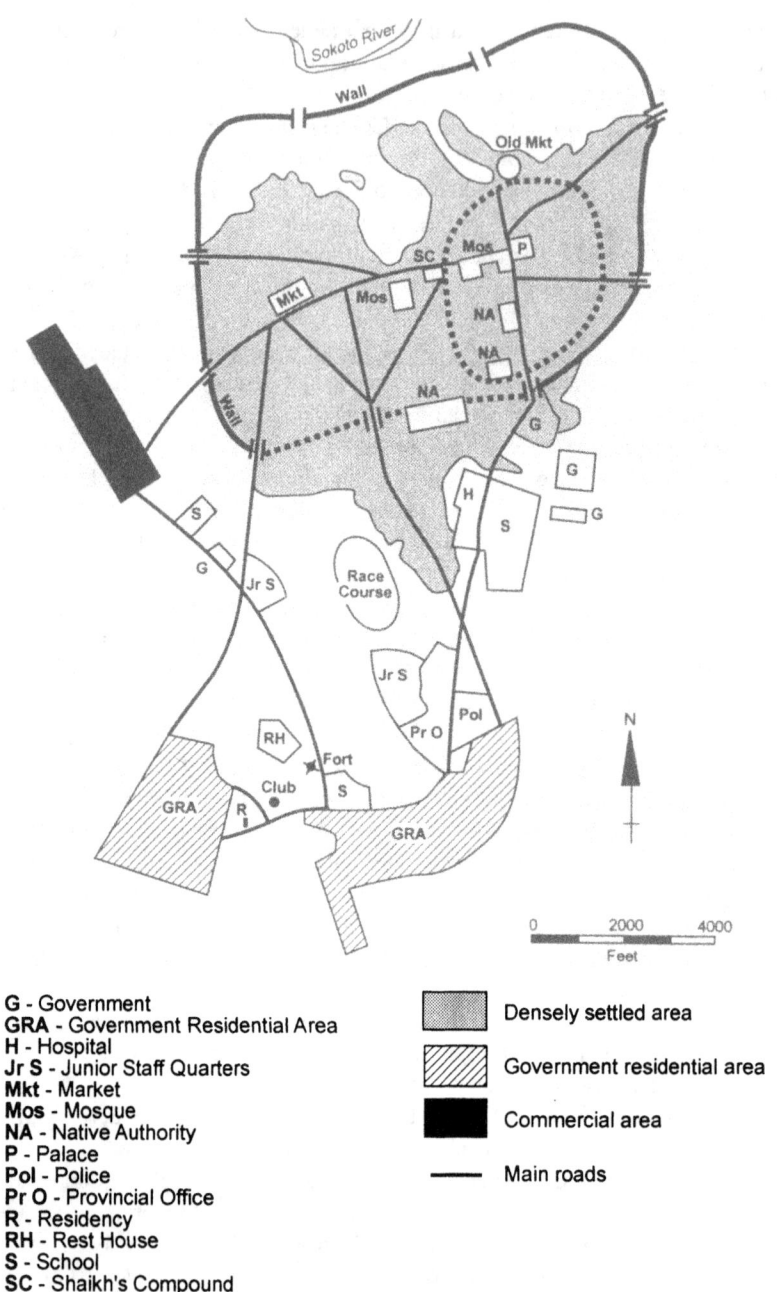

G - Government
GRA - Government Residential Area
H - Hospital
Jr S - Junior Staff Quarters
Mkt - Market
Mos - Mosque
NA - Native Authority
P - Palace
Pol - Police
Pr O - Provincial Office
R - Residency
RH - Rest House
S - School
SC - Shaikh's Compound

Source: Urquhart, 1977

Figure 10.3 Sokoto urban area in the 1960s.

The character of Sokoto is determined not only by its city walls, the focal spots such as the major public buildings, the roads channelling pedestrian and vehicular movements, and the open spaces, but also by its districts, which are dominated by compounds of various sizes.

Changes in the types residential units

The changes in residential development in Sokoto culminated in the emergence of three basic house-types in Sokoto urban area, each type inspired by the values of the government of the time. There is the Old City type the development of which was influence by the values of the Islamic government. The GRA type was inspired by the British colonial administration and the nationalist government influenced the Modern Development type.

Old city type Previous studies have shown that the compound arrangement reflects constantly changing family patterns as well as economic, social and aesthetic values, tastes and abilities of the Hausa people (Moughtin, 1964, 1985; Schwerdtfeger, 1971; Urquhart, 1977; Nwanodi, 1989). Schwerdtfeger (1971, p.78) suggests some five factors that influenced the form of the residential unit in the old city of Zaria. The factors he mentioned appear also to influence the form of Sokoto compounds, especially the local application of the law and rules of Islam.

The laws and rules of Islam and their local interpretations had a profound influence on the residential form and pattern in Sokoto. The application of the traditional building rules of behaviour left a deep imprint on the individual and the community and had a great influence on behaviour in the process of renovations, conversions, additions, demolition and erection of new buildings. Knowledge of one's place in the extended family system keeps the individual alert to the need to avoid harming others in the exercise of one's full rights. The concept of interdependence encourages self-regulatory behaviour, the seeking of collective problem solving and demands respect for the privacy of others, to mention just a few social conventions relevant to development activities.

Typically the perimeter of a plot is marked by a high wall and entry is made very explicit through the 'zaure' from the street. The *zaure* acts as an entrance hall the doors of which are designed to ensure maximum physical and visual control of the compound. It is very flexible in form and it has many economic and social functions. Clearly, the greatest asset of the present building practice is undoubtedly the flexibility of the compound that can quickly respond to any change in family structure and size.

Another change which emerged in response to the influx of labour needed by the colonial economy, to which Sokoto contributed especially in livestock and hide and skin production, was the development of the multiple household type of home. In many areas of the old city there are multiple household types that existed in response to the need for multi-family housing. These were built for newly arrived migrants and were, in a sense, apartment type dwellings within the compound structure. The basic unit was the two-room arrangement that was repeated many times depending on the expected number of households, each with separate entrances, all sharing a central set of common facilities. In spite of the multiple nature of the interior units, the site is still walled in the traditional manner.

G.R.A. types As a product of the colonial value system, this type of house differs from the old city type in its internal layout, social orientation and general approach to design. The location of the house on the plot was very much as an object set in a garden atmosphere. The house was usually set well back from the street frontage, approached by a driveway, with the bulk of the single storey structure placed across the width of the site. The internal accommodation consisted of a pattern of room types that clearly suggest its European derivation. This type of house form introduced into the Sokoto community the concept of the nuclear family and the master-servant housing which was of very different qualities of services and buildings on the same plot.

The Old City type houses subscribed to specific rules of conduct that are proscriptive in nature. The new GRA development introduced the concept of setback, which is a prescriptive regulation to which every new development had to conform. The zoning of activities, and the accompanying specifications of street sizes, densities, building height and materials were a radical and somewhat constraining change. This approach of imposing preconceived form contrasted with what was happening in the old city. The social conventions proscribe certain rules of conduct and the physical form is left to the builder who is free to choose from many possible options. Al-Hathloul (1982, p.76) and Rapoport (1977) suggest that new development regulatory instruments by telling residents what is allowed tend to limit the emergence of a reciprocal and possibilist relationship between form and use, thereby severely constraining the variety of urban forms.

Modern developments Some areas at the periphery of Sokoto are experiencing rapid residential development. These houses are being built as either speculative developments to meet the needs of the expanded managerial class or as 'sponsored' housing for specific government agencies or commercial institutions. They tend to emulate the intentions of the colonial GRA layouts, but the plots are considerably smaller and the house types more eclectic. Typical of this type of residential development is the duplex, two houses sharing the same site. The plot layout shows a tendency to place the building in the centre of the site, with a small planted area in front and the rear devoted to service and 'boys' quarters, much as was done with the GRA. While this type is more entrepreneurial and pragmatic than the GRA type in economic terms, it is devoid of any cultural connotations.

Summary and conclusions

In this paper we have proposed a conceptual framework that can help us to analyse the process of development in urban areas especially where socio-cultural and historical contexts are important. The model can be simple or made more complex to deal with the research problem at hand. We highlighted the development process in an African-Muslim city in northern Nigeria. The pre-Islamic Hausa cities accommodated Islam, Muslim cities adjusted to the British Indirect Rule and more recently they have accepted the changes and even the false promises of the nationalist government. This triple urban heritage probably marks the African-Muslim city from the Arab-Muslim city, but one can claim that both types of cities possess a continuity and a wholeness that makes them exciting and challenging places to live in.

It has been shown that Sokoto city, like many northern Nigerian cities, has never functioned as a separate entity, but it has served as the pivot of an expanding political, religious and economic system of values. The activities of individuals, institutions and governments were all organised on the broader scale of the city into the regional system of cities. This fact was hardly changed by the British colonial administration nor tampered with by the nationalist government. Thus the relationship of the components of the model seems to bear up well in this paper as the development changes resulting from the introduction of new set of values were predictable, yet more research is needed to ensure its general applicability. There are many other questions which are not raised by the model. For example the issues of quality of development, the impact on institutions as new values are introduced and ability of the system to absorb new values. All these, and other questions yet to be raised, need to be resolved through careful research.

11 Community self build in Britain:
The potential and the reality

Christine Holman

Introduction

Throughout the world the majority of households have had some form of direct involvement in the provision of their homes. The importance of self built housing in the developing world has long been recognised (Turner, 1976) whilst cogent criticisms have been levelled at its limitations (Marcuse, 1992). More recently Duncan and Rowe (1993) have demonstrated the extent to which self provided housing forms a major contribution to supply in the developed countries of Western Europe, North America and Australia.

In Britain self provided housing has played a smaller role than in many other comparable countries. Using a wider range of data sources Duncan and Rowe (1993) have estimated that, inter alia, in Belgium 60 per cent of total house completions are self provided, whilst in Norway, Finland and pre re-unification West Germany the proportion is 45 per cent. In contrast they estimate that a comparable figure for Britain is about 8 per cent. It has elsewhere been estimated that approximately 15,000 self provided homes were completed in 1991 in Britain. This compares with published sales figures in the same year from the major commercial house builders of 8,500 properties by Tarmac, 6,600 by Wimpey and 5,000 by Barrett (Armor, 1992). More recently it has been claimed that self build completions approached 30,000 in 1993 as land availability improved as the result of lower activity by commercial house builders (Gallilan, 1994).

In Britain self provided housing uses a range of methods of production. Only a small proportion is at least principally self built by the occupying household. The majority could more accurately be termed self promotion as the household contract out the actual construction of their home. Indeed the recent entry of the Bradford and Bingley Building Society to the self build finance market has been specifically targeted at people who will not be 'planning physically to build'

(Built It, 1994, p.2) Proponents of self build estimate that significant savings can be made on total scheme costs, confirming evidence from in countries where self provision forms a significant factor in housing supply. Typically the self providing household enjoys a middle range income, the adults are aged between 30 and 45 years old with, or planning to have children, although in practice a wide variety of household types participates (Duncan and Rowe, 1993). Most participants in self build housing in Britain will be already in full time work. Indeed this is normally an essential precondition before lenders will consider making an advance.

Much recent directly self built housing in Britain has been initiated by self build consultants who have developed schemes on a commercial basis. Potential self builders have been required to demonstrate an appropriate level of expertise in a skill useful to the group and sufficient financial security to guarantee being able to purchase the completed home. Most group self build schemes require participants to contract to provide a minimum number of hours on site per week. Normally this can be achieved by working at weekends or in the evenings. Alternatively the assistance of friends or relatives can be used to avoid a potential shortfall in commitment. However this sector experienced a significant collapse as the late 1980s housing boom came to a dramatic conclusion. Many self builders, finding themselves unable to finance their progression through the housing market, walked away from incomplete projects. As a result the then major lenders for self built housing, the Halifax and National and Provincial Building Societies, withdrew their support. Additionally several firms of consultants ceased trading.

Access to self provided housing in England has until recently been denied to those people most likely to be in housing need. Without secure employment, construction related skills and access to credit it proved impossible to negotiate the complicated pathway to self help. However the gradual evolution of a Housing Corporation programme has allowed some groups in housing need to bring together the components of a viable and achievable self build scheme.

This chapter will describe the evolution of community self build in England and assess its attempt to marry the provision of training and low cost housing for unemployed people in housing need.

Community self build in England

Community self build in England was initiated in Bristol in the early 1980s with the Zenzele project. This originated in intensive community development work in the aftermath of the 1980 St Paul's riots in the city.

The pioneering work of a local team led by Stella Clark JP, brought together the necessary components to facilitate the construction of a block of 12 flats by a group described by the local press as 'young, disadvantaged and unemployed'.

The scheme's ethos was 'to provide incentives and work experience for the young unemployed so that skills acquired will improve their job prospects' (quoted in Armor, 1991, p.163).

Although all Zenzele's self builders were unemployed at the start of the project some had previous construction industry experience. With the exception of specialist sub-contractors who installed a concrete slab first floor, designed to maximise sound insulation between flats, the group was responsible for all aspects of work on the traditionally built block. Building was supervised by a working site foreman whose services were funded from scheme costs.

Development finance for the project was arranged via a local housing association. After agreement had been reached with the then Department of Health and Social Security to meet interest only repayments through benefit payments, the Bristol and West Building Society approved in principle individual mortgages on the completed flats. The DHSS were instrumental to the success of the project by accepting that it was possible to be both engaged in building a home and 'actively seeking work' as defined by the Department of Employment's regulations. This decision ensured that self builders were eligible to claim benefit payments.

The Zenzele project was so successful that by the time construction was complete in late 1985 all but one of the self builders were in full time employment, mostly within the building industry (Levine, 1989). Further evidence of their material success can be demonstrated by the rapidity with which the flats were sold as their owner-builders took advantage of a rising housing market to trade up (Armor, 1991).

Despite widespread and enthusiastic support, including the Prince of Wales' imprimatur, the Zenzele project proved difficult to replicate. Several groups, including at least two in the North of England, began the long struggle to co-ordinate a self build scheme. For one of these, Front-line Self Build Housing Association, it would be over seven years before the group made a start on site. The other, Youth Self Build North Tyneside, would eventually complete their homes in early 1994 after only six years. Quite long enough for the sobriquet 'youth' to no longer be so appropriate.

In 1989 the Community Self Build Agency (CSBA) was established, funded largely by grants from the Housing Corporation and the Thames Television Trust, to pursue two complimentary objectives. The funders anticipated that the CSBA would promote self build for owner occupation among groups normally excluded by their financial status either because they were in low paid employment or were in receipt of benefit. In addition the CSBA would also work with statutory, voluntary and financial agencies to dismantle barriers in the path of emerging self build groups.

Unfortunately with hindsight, it is perhaps hard to imagine a more difficult time to have launched an organisation predicated on the expansion of owner occupation, albeit at low cost, for households unable to afford orthodox entry to the tenure.

Financing community self build

The development of community self build in this country has been led by the availability of funding. During the 1980s some self build schemes for outright ownership were able to gain support from the Housing Corporation in the form of a guarantee for development finance already provided by a private funder. Housing Association Grant (HAG) was not available to self build schemes at that time although it had already become the major source of public subsidy to social housing in England. HAG is administered by the Housing Corporation, on behalf of, and in line with, the priorities for social housing identified by the Department of the Environment.

In 1989 the Housing Corporation negotiated a new arrangement. Two major building societies, the Nationwide Anglia and the National and Provincial, agreed to make available £160 million at competitive rates of interest in development finance over the following five years (Housing Corporation, 1989). The Housing Corporation expected this arrangement to enhance scheme viability, to allow greater flexibility in tenure arrangements and to promote alternative construction methods (Holman, 1991).

As the property market collapsed the two building societies suffered considerable losses from their exposure to traditional self build. Many group members abandoned arrangements that were no longer attractive. In consequence the societies withdrew their previous commitment, leaving community self build without any financial backing.

During the late 1980s the Housing Corporation was lobbied by those agencies actively engaged in promoting community self build including the CSBA, the Walter Segal Trust and CHISEL a secondary housing co-operative active in South East London. These organisations sought to have HAG made available for schemes where participants wished to build their own home but were unable to afford to rent or buy without subsidy. The Corporation, convinced by arguments that access could genuinely be widened to encompass low income groups, opened negotiations with the Department of the Environment during 1990.

By October of 1990 the then Housing Minister approved, subject to four conditions, a three year pilot programme for HAG funded self build shared ownership schemes. The conditions were that :

i projects would be able to demonstrate at least 20 per cent savings over equivalent costs of a contractor built scheme;
ii. associations would target both traditional shared ownership groups and those whose incomes were below that level;

iii. expenditure on self build schemes would not exceed 5 per cent of the total low cost home ownership programme;
iv. the Corporation would constantly monitor and review the programme before comprehensively evaluating it after three years.

In addition from 1991 at its board's direction, the Housing Corporation initiated a revolving fund to provide a minority percentage (initially 40 per cent, later raised to 49 per cent) of development finance for community self build schemes for outright ownership. It was anticipated that, secure in the knowledge that a substantial element of risk was borne by a statutory body convinced of a project's viability, financial institutions would be prepared to advance the remaining development costs and to grant mortgages to individual self builders upon completion.

The final piece in the jigsaw came late in 1991 when agreement was finally reached between the Department of the Environment and the Housing Corporation to allow regional offices to enter into agreements with housing associations sponsoring self build for rent. At first these agreements were negotiated under tariff arrangements and subsequently under the revised Cash Programmes. Both of these financial systems, available only to the larger more financially secure housing associations, allow for the negotiation of a programme of housing within defined limits of size, location, client group and level of subsidy. Self build groups act as the contractor working in collaboration with a registered housing association able to access HAG. When construction is complete self builders rent their homes from the association.

By the end of 1991 it was theoretically possible for a group of people in housing need to choose to construct their homes for rent, shared ownership or even outright ownership whatever the initial financial status of its members. However groups still encounter considerable difficulty in achieving their objectives.

Most community self build groups experience a long gap between their inception and the time when work can start on site. Although there are many other contributing factors to the length of delays, gaining financial approval is a major element. The slump in the property market combined with financial institutions' reluctance to consider mortgages, particularly for a relatively high proportion of value, for unemployed people has severely restricted the number of schemes for outright ownership able to succeed.

Schemes aiming at shared ownership have struggled to adapt their projects to ever changing procurement and contracting arrangements at the Housing Corporation. At first, groups had to juggle and pare at their designs to bring scheme costs to 20 per cent below the Total Cost Indicators (TCI) which represent the maximum acceptable cost of construction for accommodation bidding for subsidy. TCIs vary according to location, size and dwelling type. Then morale was further sapped by a new requirement for self builders to purchase a minimum of 50 per cent, rather than 25 per cent, of their homes.

When all costs are included, few completed schemes have achieved significantly more than 20 per cent 'sweat equity'. Individual self builders must negotiate with financial institutions to borrow perhaps £15,000 on an average home at a time when their only income is solely from social security benefits. This has proved a complex, time consuming task, often the final obstacle before construction can begin.

Mortgages have been obtained successfully from two sources. Firstly, establishing good informed relationships with smaller locally based building societies has proved more beneficial than negotiating with the market leaders. Secondly, in some areas especially the North East where self build has achieved a significant public profile the use of local lenders' panels has allowed the risk to be spread amongst several institutions.

Raising money to fund self build for rent schemes has proved easier than in projects where some element of ownership is involved. Sponsoring housing associations are able to access their usual Cash Programme borrowing arrangements. The financial complications in rental schemes have become more closely concerned with finding legitimate ways of rewarding self builders. Three methods have been proposed, sometimes in combination. The most straightforward option would be to employ self builders to construct homes in which they will live. Alternatively the sponsoring housing association could agree to levy a reduced rent on the accommodation, either for the length of the tenancy, or for a pre-agreed period. The major disadvantage of this method occurs if a self builder does not find paid work when construction is complete. In this situation the beneficiary would be the Department of Social Security as less housing benefit would be payable. Finally, and most practically, a premium tenancy as permitted under the Housing Act 1988 could be created. At its simplest this would allow the sponsoring housing association to pay to the self builder a sum equal to 'sweat equity' when the tenancy is terminated. A refinement of the arrangement may permit the release of some money when the home is first occupied, to enable furniture and carpets to be purchased.

Inevitably, given the complexity and novelty of community self build schemes, financial decisions are not the only difficult ones to be faced, but they are perhaps the least tractable. Other crucial considerations include the choice of housing association, arranging and funding suitable training, finding a suitable site, arranging experienced, knowledgeable and committed professional help and, obviously, the size and membership of the self build group (Holman, 1994).

Community self build in 'northern' England

Community self build groups have now been established throughout the country. Some owe their existence to a wish to emulate Zenzele's success, others have developed in response to a particular funding opportunity, for example City

Table 11.1 Self build schemes in 'Northern' England, July 1995.

Completed Schemes	Location	Number of Units	Tenure	Construction
Nova Terra	Bolton	8	O.O.	New Build
LATCH	Leeds	2 completed	Rent	Rehab
Cowgate	Newcastle	14	Rosehaugh model (a.)	Rehab
Youth Self build	North Tyneside	8	S.O.	New Build
Openshaw Young People's Housing Project	Manchester	4	Rent	Rehab
Brunton's Manor	Middlesborough	22	S.O.	New Build
Tough Links	Liverpool	10	S.O.	New Build
Freshrootz	Hull	10	Rent	New Build

Schemes on Site	Location	Number of Units	Tenure	Construction
Bodmin Square	Sunderland	14	O.O.	Rehab
Keyskills	Middlesborough	7	Rent	Rehab
LATCH	Leeds	1	Rent	Rehab
Frontline	Leeds	12	S.O.	New Build
Maltby Rainbow Project	Rotherham	9	Rent	New Build

Schemes with 93/94 HAG Allocation	Location	Number of Units	Tenure	Construction
Woodways	Sheffield	4	S.O.	New Build (Segal method) (b.)

Table 11.1 Self build schemes in 'Northern' England, July 1995 continued

Schemes Awaiting Funding	Location	Number of Units	Tenure	Construction
404 Housing Co-op	Middlesborough	10	rent	New Build
Holmewood	Bradford	8	S.O.	Rehab (decapping 3 storey flats)
Belfast Self Build	Belfast	to be decided	O.O.	New Build
North Benwell	Newcastle	10	O.O.	Rehab (decapping 3 storey flats)
Homes for Change (c.)	Manchester	50	Rent	New Build
Sandsend Crescent	Hartlepool	14	Rent	New Build
St Helens Young Persons SB	St Helens	12	Rent	New Build
Kirklees MC	Huddersfield	15	Rent	New Build

Key: O.O. - outright ownership   S.O. - Shared ownership

Notes

a. The Rosehaugh model was a short-lived funding proposal devised and promoted by Rosehaugh plc as part of a social action programme. The funding arrangement sought to remove the immediate cost of land purchase from development costs.

b. Segal construction is a particular form of timber frame housing suitable by participants without traditional craft skills.

c. Although Homes for Change hope to eventually produce 50 homes, they will be partially self built. The bulk of construction will be undertaken by contractors. Homes for Change's partner co-operative, Work for Change, expects to obtain a contract to fit out some elements of the interiors.

Challenge, and some have grown from a focused attempt to meet individual or perceived housing need. This section will consider the state of community self build in the area of England broadly serviced by the Northern Regional Forum of the CSBA. Although there is no centralised register of community self build groups it is possible to collate details (see Table 11.1) about those community self build groups which have had contact with the CSBA. Usually representatives of the group will have attended at least one Regional Forum meeting. It is possible that other, unrecorded groups are active in the area.

In July 1995 there was a total of 22 community self build groups known to exist in 'northern' England. Of these, eight groups had completed construction, five were still on site, one had obtained a confirmed commitment of HAG funding to allow building to begin during 1994/95 and eight groups were still engaged in raising money. A total of 78 homes have been produced and a further 47 should be completed within the next twelve months. The future of these schemes without committed funding must be considered less certain although the growing interest in City Challenge areas gives grounds for optimism.

Balancing costs and outcomes

The provision of something over 120 new homes throughout the region does not represent an impressive return on the enormous investment of time and effort by self builders and their diverse professional partners. A superficial analysis would suggest that community self build has proved an extremely expensive way of providing nominally low cost housing. To qualify for HAG funding, shared ownership and rental schemes must demonstrate that costs will amount to 80 per cent or less than final value. Groups aiming for outright ownership can normally expect to have to meet even more stringent financial criteria from their lenders. To comply with these targets many of the real costs of community self build are hidden under what has become a rather lumpy carpet. These items will need further investigation to consider whether they have been a necessary component of community self build's lengthy birth process or whether they form an intrinsic element of replicable schemes. Yet it is important to emphasise that both the future survival and potential growth of community self build in this country depend upon assessing not only housing outputs but also the broader range of gains to participants.

Members of community self build groups receive training in the craft based skills essential for the construction of homes. They learn to manage a large project and, receive the considerable boost to self confidence and self esteem that follows from the successful completion of a demanding task, although this can be less readily quantified. The ad hoc evolution of community self build has allowed for the participation of group members and, indeed, whole schemes, without previous construction industry skills or training. Inevitably this leads to increased costs. In comparison the traditional model of group self build has been more prescriptive about the level and mix of skills necessary within a particular project (Armor, 1991).

Several paths have been taken to developing and enhancing a skill base in group members. Priority can be given to either a training or a product based approach. This more relaxed approach has made it possible to allow entry to projects to be based simply on housing need and a willingness to participate. As a result it has been possible to attract some, although admittedly as yet few, women in their own right rather than as partners of self builders. Additionally some schemes have been designed as a response to the particular housing needs of young unemployed people.

The use of design and construction methods advocated by Walter Segal can further reduce reliance on traditional construction skills, relying instead on a level of expertise people might acquire through basic DIY projects (Broome, 1986).

Some decisions will be influenced by the project's 'buildability'. At the design stage an architect experienced in the limitations of self builders, or in other circumstances low skill trainees, can opt for simpler but notionally more expensive techniques which will reduce the level of expertise necessary to complete a task (Skillbuilding, 1992). A practical example of this approach might be the specification of a plastic snap together water supply system in place of the more usual method of soldering joints on copper pipe. There is a clear comparison here with many decisions taken in DIY stores where customers may decide to purchase a more expensive product to eliminate the cost of employing a tradesperson. At a personal level this may still result in a clear net saving. In contrast the specification of a higher cost component in a self build project inflates total scheme costs because the cost of labour does not enter the equation. Some reduction may be possible if a group can obtain sponsorship from product manufacturers.

If a self build group's future homes have been traditionally designed all members will need training in basic construction site practices and some, at least, will need to demonstrate proficiency in particular skills. Two methods have evolved. In the first members of the group follow a Training for Work programme in a skill which they refine as the scheme progresses. Most trainees are able to gain a qualification at the appropriate NVQ level. This form of training has, with some adaptations, been available from local TECs. However, problems have been encountered as funding for TECs has come to depend upon their ability to move trainees into paid employment. Additionally it has been argued that, given the very high level of construction skills trained personnel currently registered as unemployed, there is not a need to supplement their number with fresh entrants to the industry. A possibly more useful training programme has been implemented in some schemes, where self builders are trained in the specific techniques of building their homes. For example, they will learn to plumb one particular bathroom suite rather than becoming competent to tackle the whole range. This training frequently takes the form of a preliminary 10 week off site block, supplemented by input from a site manager as construction proceeds. Although self builders will gain transferable skills, their potential path to employment will not be as direct. It must, however, be remembered that not all self builders want a future career in the construction industry.

Inevitably, whichever methods of skill enhancement is chosen, some work will need to be sub-contracted. Many groups employ a specialist contractor to clear the site, dig foundations and lay over site concrete. This is often a sound investment partly, to ensure the accuracy of the floor slab, and partly because this forms the most disheartening part of any building project. Most groups also have to employ an electrician to provide necessary certification.

Ultimately any training for self build will have to be funded by external sources, usually the local TEC. Funded training formalised into a Training for Work package also ensures that self building households have an assured income equivalent to their social security entitlement enhanced by a £10 per week premium. Where this has not been arranged a satisfactory agreement must be reached with local Department of Social Security offices to ensure that it is acceptable for participants to be considered coterminously to be actively seeking work and building their own home.

In addition to arranging practical training self build groups must audit for project management and inter personal skills. However speedily and successfully the essential components of the scheme coalesce, members will be together for a long time. The group must agree ways to monitor and value diverse contributions, to discipline errant members and, importantly, to resolve disputes. The process of developing these skills can be painful. Some groups have been able to benefit from the services of a development worker to ease this process.

Charity Projects, the charitable foundation initially established with the money raised during national Comic Relief days, set aside £300,000 to promote community self build with young people. The bulk of this money was spent on funding development workers in ten projects where the majority of members were under 25. Although there is no definitive concept of this role, it is clear that the presence of development workers has facilitated the particularly harsh transition young people without experience of work face when joining a community self build group (Levine, 1994). Without an input of charitable funding it is difficult to imagine how this pivotal role can be provided in any future community self build schemes designed to accommodate young people.

Housing Associations partnering community self build groups are aware that the costs that they incur in developing schemes are far in excess of their norm. Typically, a development manager has admitted that 'the file is three times the thickness I would expect'. The extra costs accrue because each project has presented novel problems in development, as association development staff master unfamiliar procedures and often new methods of working with community based groups. Frequently extensive negotiations have been required with associations' legal representatives to ensure a watertight development agreement.

Housing Associations which have embarked on involvement (in community self build schemes) have most often been precipitated by a wish to broaden their social role or because the project was located in a geographical area where the association hoped to raise its profile (Levine, 1994).

The future of community self build

As the Housing Corporation considers its own evaluation of the self build programme and many of the 'first round' schemes approach completion it is appropriate to questions whether community self build has a future in this country.

Without undertaking a detailed research exercise, it is not possible to measure the extent to which community self build provides outputs in excess of housing per se. From observation it is clear that for at least some participants the programme has provided a valuable and life changing combination of training and personal skill development which has lead to employment, often after many years without work.

The success of the initial Zenzele scheme has been well documented (Armor, 1991). Group members were fortunate to have acquired new skills in a time and place of increased activity in the construction industry. There are huge differences in the economic climate of Bristol in the mid 1980s and North East England in the mid 1990s. However it has been possible to observe the beneficial effects of community self build on the lives of one set of young people in North Tyneside.

Youth Self Build North Tyneside was rooted in a conversation which took place between young people attending a local drop-in project. One participant asked 'if we have nowhere to live and no work, why can't we build our own homes?' The eventual response to this simple question was a project to build eight semi-detached houses for shared ownership, which were completed in early 1994. Here is not the place to record the difficulties overcome by the group of young people and the development worker employed to facilitate the scheme, save to mention that at one point their frustration lead to a lobby of Parliament.

All of the young people found re-entry to life post self build difficult. Inevitably the completion of a project, which had dominated their lives for six years, left a vacuum. Initially this resulted in an unusually high level of neighbour quarrels and disputes. One year after completion it has become possible to view the beneficial effects of the experience of community self build. Both individually and as a group the ex-self builders are visibly more confident and assertive. Of the eight participants, seven have found work, of these three are employed in the construction industry and the remainder elsewhere.

Community self build has not proved a cheap method of providing social housing, but the value of the additional personal outcomes is even higher when consideration is given to the severely depressed nature of most areas in which schemes have been established. Long after Ward's advocacy (1976) the potential effectiveness of a comprehensive self build programme has achieved political recognition from the Green Party (Bailey, 1994).

In the short term the future of community self build will depend on three important factors.

Demand

Until recently the Housing Corporation considered that almost all viable community self build groups in the north of England had been allocated HAG funding. Despite the submission of an ultimately unsuccessful Self Build Housing Volume Bid in 1993 (CHISEL) there does not appear to be much substantive evidence of demand for community self build. Certainly there were few emerging groups in the North of England. It can, however, be argued that there is a need for greater awareness of the potential benefits of community self build. In the absence of a sufficiently large critical mass to allow organic growth, there may be valid arguments to support some form of special promotional facility to encourage participants, housing associations, financial institutions and prospective self builders, to investigate the potential viability of a scheme. In the last few months evidence of further interest has been demonstrated as both St Helens and Kirklees Metropolitan councils have initiated feasibility studies for potential self build schemes.

Funding

Future funding for a community self build programme will be contingent on the outcome of the Housing Corporation's evaluation. Although both the Department of Environment and the Housing Corporation have expressed commitment, their primary concern is to obtain value for money in housing provision. The lack of cross-departmental measures to assess costs and benefits may bode ill.

At present there is no method of assessing the additional benefits of an individual moving into employment after completion of a self build scheme or valuing the worth of a sense of community and self esteem. The lack of a more sophisticated analysis may bode ill for the financial future of community self build.

Partner Agencies

Housing associations and, to a lesser extent, other partner agencies have at an individual level amassed considerable expertise about community self build. This knowledge has been gained at some cost. The future of community self build will in part depend upon those agencies being willing to repeat their involvement and hopefully be rewarded for their initial investment.

Community self build in England has experienced a fertile but anarchic growth as each project followed a highly individual path. The future sustainability of community self build may depend on considering alterations to the existing pattern.

A change is occurring in the genesis of community self build schemes. Early projects often grew out of a broad community work framework which emphasised the benefits of bottom led, top fed initiatives. More recently some local authorities have begun to investigate the role of community self build within their broader urban regeneration strategy. A change of direction could lead to a more prescriptive format in which an element of participation was sacrificed, in exchange for a more efficient and cost effective method of producing homes. The major benefit to all participants would be a guarantee of a more efficient strategy that minimised delays.

Currently most community self build groups only make minimal use of sub-contractors. Inevitably this slows down the construction process which in turn increases costs. Stockholm City Council has a long history of municipally co-ordinated self build programmes. Over time the self build element has been reduced until now self builders take over a house shell. They contract to complete the interior work within a 16 week period supplying a minimum of 40 hours per week labour per household (Nord and Persson, 1994). The potential costs or savings of this approach require careful calculation.

Britain has an extremely tight system of regulation controlling the provision of housing. Self build fits less comfortably within this framework. Experience in the developing world has shown that when occupants have clear title to land homes in spontaneous settlements are improved over time as households' income increases. Arguably this process could, and would, be repeated in this country if self builders were given the latitude to make staged additions to their homes. In this way after completing a core to a specified standard and within a time limit they would be able to combine construction with other activities, including earning a living.

Finally, although the overall output in this country exceeds that of any individual volume producer, self build is a low profile activity, little known by non-participants. Greater awareness and publicity of self build's benefits could increase awareness, interest and involvement by people wishing to be actively responsible for improving their housing conditions.

Conclusion

Community self build can be shown to be an effective way of providing homes for people in housing need, who, as a result of the experience and the training they gain, are able to boost their self confidence and frequently enter employment perhaps for the first time. These multiple benefits are difficult to value in a climate which emphasises the compartmentalisation of costs, allocated each to a specific heading rather than viewing the worth of the whole.

Community self build in Britain, at the end of a five year period of funding, is being evaluated by the Housing Corporation. The future of this method of housing provision will depend in the short term on a continuing demand from groups willing to invest significant outlays of time and effort, a continued commitment to funding availability and the willingness of other actors, particularly housing associations, to continue their involvement.

In the longer term the sustainability of community self build may be dependent on a wide ranging review of the formal control structures within which it operates. This might involve a move towards a more prescriptive regime which might or might not include a greater use of subcontract labour. Alternatively the potential to promote community self build may lie in a reduction of the regulatory environment which dominates house construction in this country.

12 Understanding user transformation of public housing

Rafik Salama

Introduction

Public housing represents a significant percentage of the housing stock in many developing countries. Its shortcomings have been identified and examined by many scholars and experts in an attempt to investigate the possibilities of growth and adaptability in future projects. Yet, for many years and through their own initiative, public housing dwellers have been engaged in alteration and extension activities aimed at adapting their dwellings to better suit their needs. These activities have resulted in the transformation of entire housing developments in many parts of the world. Understanding this phenomenon is a prerequisite for any attempt to provide better housing environments and to improve existing ones.

Therefore, this paper examines the development of transformations in different public housing projects in Egypt and attempts to identify some of the implicit factors that control change at both dwelling and community levels. It was found that user transformation of public housing projects should not be considered as a simple space enlargement process, but rather as a result of a complex set of inter-related determinants associated with both context and dwelling characteristics.

Background

The increasing demand for affordable housing in many developing countries has urged governments during the last decades to commit themselves to provide completely finished housing units for medium and low income families. In an exaggerated concern over physical features and standards, government officials have pushed forward their systematic approach, underestimating its socio-economic and cultural shortcomings and excluding low income groups from participating in the formal housing production.

As a result of the inappropriateness of public housing and its failure to respond to users' needs, many families decided to take over their housing and started engaging in informal[1] building activities inside the formal sector. This engagement was embodied through a variety of modifications and extensions - referred to as user transformations - carried out in government-built housing projects. The phenomenon was first observed in four and five storey walk-ups after ownership of flats was transferred to the occupants during the early 1980s. Given the scale of 'illegal' building activities, local authorities had difficulty in maintaining a firm attitude towards transformers and usually ended by ignoring them. Transformations have resulted not only in an increase of the actual housing stock, but in changing entire housing environments into dynamic, mixed-use developments where daily activities overlap and maximum use of the available space is made.

The new environments created have gained some of the advantages of informal settlements such as more suitable dwellings and an effective use of outdoor spaces without losing the advantages of formal projects such as proper infrastructure and services; and could be described as a combination of formal and informal housing, since they assimilate characteristics of both types. Therefore, it seemed most important to try and comprehend these new environments, and to understand the factors that control change and determine the outcome of transformations in different environments.

The case study

The research is based on a field study conducted in twenty public housing projects in Egypt[2] where there has been evidence of informal user transformations. The projects were randomly selected in the cities of Cairo and Alexandria. The field study revealed that all of the twenty projects surveyed had been and were still undergoing some kind of transformation activity. These activities were classified into two main categories: interior and exterior transformations.

Types of transformations

Interior transformations

Among the examples observed in the surveyed sample were the following:

- Modifying the use of spaces such as kitchens converted into bedrooms or workrooms (Plate 12.1), balconies converted into kitchens, and toilets used for dish washing, keeping poultry, or storage.
- Modifying interior walls so as to change the size of a room.
- Smaller modifications such as: repositioning doors for privacy reasons, and providing extra storage space by building wall closets or false ceilings.

Exterior transformations

- Closing up parapets of exposed balconies for privacy.

- Making openings in flank walls of blocks for new windows.
- Enclosing balconies for use as an extra room or as an extension of an existing room (Plate 12.2).
- Appropriating public open spaces for extensions which were basically carried out in two directions: vertically and horizontally.

Plate 12.1 Kitchen used as a workroom.

Plate 12.2 Variation in balcony enclosure.

Plate 12.3 Roof top extension.

Plate 12.4 Underground extension.

Vertical extensions

Roof top extensions These were usually carried out by top floor dwellers and used for keeping animals, storage, and as a living space. Access was gained through an opening made either in the ceiling of the existing dwelling or in the roof of the public staircase (Plate 12.3).

Underground extensions After ground floor dwellers had extended horizontally, they later extended downwards to accommodate a basement. This was done by excavating the ground beneath the existing extension down to the foundations level and building retaining walls (Plate 12.4). Basements were generally used as storage places and to keep animals, and usually had a separate access from the street.

Horizontal extensions

Ground floor extensions Ground floor dwellers would often start by appropriating a piece of public land surrounding the dwelling unit to make a private garden; later, they would start building extensions inside their gardens. Extension activities varied from expanding an existing room up to building several additional rooms or even adding a complete new dwelling to the existing unit. In general, sufficient clearance was left between extensions for access to public staircases and maintenance of vertical pipework. Ground floor extensions located on main streets were often used to accommodate a shop or other business (Plate 12.5).

Plate 12.5 Ground floor extensions used as shops.

Upper floor extensions The most common types observed were cantilevered balconies, room extensions, cages and porches fixed on buildings' facades (Plate 12.6). Porches and cages were generally used as an additional space for storage or poultry breeding. Most balconies and room extensions were made of steel and supported on steel girders fixed in the floor slab, but in some cases they consisted of a concrete cantilevered slab.

Multi-storey extensions These tended to start incrementally with upper floor dwellers extending on top of already existing ground floor extensions. But this tendency has been subsequently replaced by the erection of concrete frame multi-storey stacks which allowed pre-planned and organised extension activity for all households sharing the same vertical section. If one or more families are reluctant to join the others, and that their reluctance doesn't stop the process, the support structure will only be used by participating families. In some cases, occupants of top floors will build a complete support structure for their own extension leaving out the neighbours below (Plate 12.7), and families who wish to join later will have to pay their share of foundation and structure costs. In other cases, stacks have been erected simultaneously as a single structure covering the total width of a block, thus reflecting both vertical and horizontal co-operation amongst neighbours (Plate 12.9).

Plate 12.6 Upper floor extensions.

Plate 12.7 Multi-storey extension.

Plate 12.8 Individual transformations.

Plate 12.9 Collective transformations.

Patterns of transformations

Originally, the appearance of most public housing projects was similar, but presently, and after more than a decade of transformations, each project has gained a character of its own, resulting from common tendencies in transformation activities; these tendencies are defined, in this study, as 'patterns of transformations' and classified into two categories following the way they reflect whether activities have been carried out on an individual or on a collective basis (Plates 12.8 and 12.9).

Individual versus collective transformations

Individual transformations can be considered as the main trend in 75% of the surveyed projects. The individuality of these transformations is evident from the fact that they have been carried out independently, even though they might have occurred simultaneously in adjacent dwellings.

On the other hand, collective transformations were comparatively more limited in their occurrence and mainly represented in the form of multi-storey extensions. Other forms of collective activities were also observed such as: building community market places (El Zawya el Hamra and El Sharabeya), planting public gardens (Helwan and Shubra), and renewing sewage networks (El Amiriya).

Out of the twenty surveyed projects, five (El Teraa el Bulaqiya, Imbaba, El Amiriya, Ain el Sira and Helwan) had large-scale collective transformations (Figure 12.1). Whereas in the remaining fifteen projects, transformations were mainly carried out individually, except for a few cases of newly built multi-storey extensions observed in five projects (Bulaq, Ahmed Helmy, El Zawya el Hamra, El Sharabeya, and El Wayli). This suggests a possible sign of the beginning of a widespread deployment of collective transformation activity in those areas as well. Finally, it should be pointed out that in several of the surveyed projects a combination of individual and collective transformations were observed.

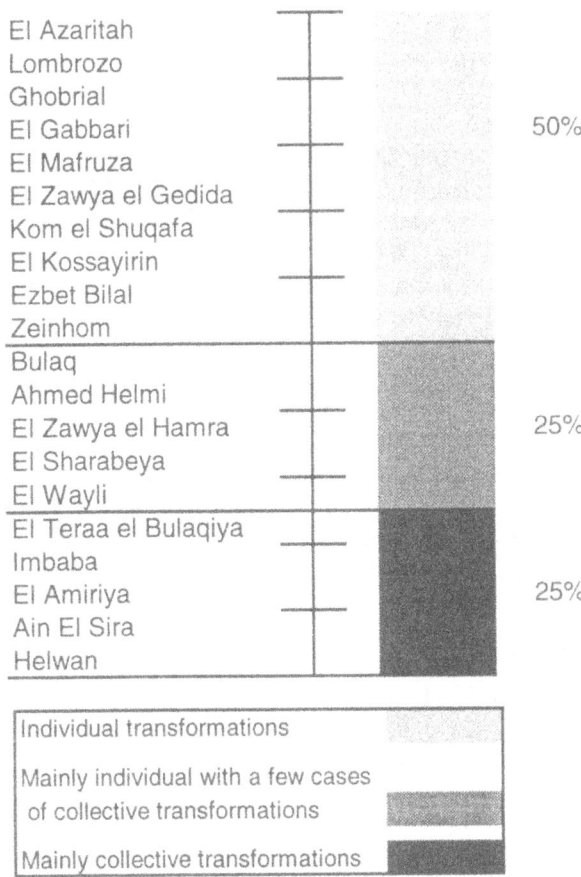

Figure 12.1 List of projects by order of size of transformation activity.

The decision making process which determines whether transformation activities will be carried out on a collective or individual basis was found to be affected by the following factors:

The level of co-operation between residents This is a key factor in the process of negotiation in order to reach a consensus for collective activity. It was found that stable communities with similar cultural backgrounds along with strong social ties are more capable of working collectively (e.g. Imbaba, Ain el Sira, and Helwan).

The location of the project In projects located on major streets or in proximity to the city centre (e.g. Bulaq, El Kossayirin, Azaritah and Lombrozo), where local authorities generally adopt a tougher attitude, transformations were found to be carried out individually. On the other hand, collective transformations were concentrated in projects located on peripheral and marginal sites (e.g. Helwan and Ain el Sira).

The role of local contractors This has proven to be one of the mobilising factors of collective participation in Helwan (Kardash and Wilkinson, 1991). A successful contractor usually convinces households to follow their neighbours' example by extending. The contractor's control over a neighbourhood is also a factor: in areas where cantilevered steel balconies are the common trend (e.g. in parts of El Amiriya and El Zawya el Hamra) it would be more difficult for a new contractor to introduce concrete frame structures.

The dwellers' financial capability The cost of a typical two room extension (of about 30 sq.m.) in a concrete skeleton multi-storey stack can range from L.E. 2000 to L.E. 3000, the same extension, carried out individually, could cost less than L.E.1500 if cheaper building materials were used (e.g. brick and tin sheet). On the other hand, the cost of a typical steel balcony or cantilevered room extension varies from L.E.500 to L.E.700; and although it has a smaller area, it is considered as an additional room at an affordable price.[3]

Resulting environments

By comparing the built environments resulting from individual and collective transformation activity, differences in the following aspects were found:

Variety of types More variety was found in projects where transformations were carried out individually (e.g. El Zawya el Hamra and El Sharabeya), since these reflected each family's own needs and aspirations. Collective transformations, on the other hand, being the outcome of a compromise between different households, tend to be less representative of each family's particular needs.

Regularity of patterns Transformations carried out individually vary in terms of size, form and function from one household to another; while on the other hand, households participating in multi-storey extensions usually decide collectively on aspects such area, shape, location sometimes even the colour of finishing of extensions. Consequently, the patterns resulting from multiple individual interventions (e.g. Ezbet Bilal and El Zawya el Hamra), tend to be less regular than those resulting from single collective interventions (e.g. El Teraa el Bulaqiya and Helwan).

Gained floor area The percentage of area added to the original dwellings varied according to their location and floor level. This was a determining factor in the case of individual transformations where only ground floor and top floor dwellers had the opportunity to built relatively large extensions, while upper floor extensions were usually more limited in size (e.g. El Zawya el Hamra). On the other hand, multi-storey extensions usually allowed relatively large extensions for all units within the same vertical stack (e.g. Ain el Sira and Helwan). Hence, from a cumulative standpoint, the total area gained from collective extensions, could be significantly more important than the one resulting from individual extensions.

Viability of structures Dwellers who build on an individual basis were usually less capable of financing expensive structural systems. The resulting structures were often less viable than the ones produced collectively. Several single-storey extensions were built of scavenged lightweight materials and a few cantilevered extensions had clear deviations as a result of insufficient support (e.g. El Zawya el Hamra). Whereas when dwellers joined together, they were more capable of financing the construction of sound and durable structures. Most multi-storey extensions observed were built from concrete skeleton frames and were usually of better structural quality than other types of extensions (e.g. El Teraa el Bulaqiya and Helwan).

Quality of living conditions Overall, collective transformations have resulted in higher quality environments and have offered better living conditions for residents. By comparing transformed environments in areas like Helwan, Ain el Sira and El Teraa el Bulaqiya with the ones in Kom el Shuqafa and Ezbet Bilal, it was found that not only did collective transformations create better housing and more regular block patterns, but other activities such as planting public gardens, building market places and improving sewage networks contributed in upgrading whole neighbourhoods as well.

Problems resulting from transformations
- Problems of obstruction caused by extensions which blocked the view of neighbouring flats.
- Problems of access to infrastructures for maintenance, caused by extensions covering exterior pipework leaving too little clearance for access.
- Problems of poor natural light and ventilation in areas where large multistorey extensions have developed on both sides of blocks.

- Problems of cross-circulation and lack of privacy in the internal layout of dwellings (e.g. access to new rooms through existing ones) which were caused by the fact that original designs were not meant to allow transformation.

Factors affecting transformations

Understanding transformations implies identifying implicit factors that affect the extent of transformation developing in different projects. This study has set as an objective to examine these factors. For this purpose, transformations were recorded in different selected areas and by analysing data collected through frequency distribution and percentages of different transformation activities, it was possible to measure the extent of transformation in each project. By examining correlations between different variables, two categories of factors were identified: factors related to housing environments and others related to housing units.

Factors related to housing environments

Area The most extensive transformations were generally observed in projects which cover areas of more than 300,000 sq.m., whereas projects smaller than 40,000 sq.m. were generally less affected by transformations. A possible explanation could be that the size of projects is likely to affect the level of the local authority's control over the area.

Number of dwelling units Large-scale transformations were generally concentrated in projects of more than 4,000 units, while more limited activities were found in projects of less than 1,000 units. This could be due to the fact that the large number of households living in a project could strengthen local opinion within the community, and thus undermine the attitude of local authorities towards transformers.

Density Transformation activity seemed to be inversely proportionate to density. In projects where densities were less than 220 units per hectare, extensive transformation activities have taken place; whereas, with only a very few exceptions, the rest of the projects (with densities exceeding 220 units per hectare) were less affected by transformations. It could be argued, therefore, that low density could be an important incentive for dwellers to carry out extensions. Density was also found to affect the degree of greenery in different projects. More public and private gardens were observed in projects with densities of less than 240 units per hectare.

Built-up area With a few exceptions, transformation activity was generally affected by the percentage of built-up area in each project. Projects with less than

20% of built-up area, had undergone more extensive transformations than those where the built-up area exceeded 24% of the total area.

Duration of existence Projects built in the late 1970s were less affected by transformations than ones built during the late 1950s and the early 1960s. In the absence of housing mobility in Egypt, older projects have generally more stable communities with stronger social ties among residents. These ties could be an important catalyst to the spread of transformations, in addition to the positive role of socio-economic networks among residents in the building process.

Distance from city centre It was noted that building activities tended to decrease in projects located near the city centre where local authorities control is generally stricter, while large-scale transformations were usually observed in remote areas. However, some projects with extensive transformation activity were situated within the city's limits, but their locations in not easily accessible areas and on marginal sites made them less subject to government control.

Level of existing services There was almost no correlation found between the level of existing services (i.e. communal facilities and transportation) and transformation activity. However, it was found that the lack of existing commercial facilities has resulted in the emergence of a huge multitude of shops, small businesses, and home-based economic activities in several projects.

Conditions of open spaces Very limited extension activity was observed in projects where all streets, sidewalks and open spaces were paved. Whereas the most extensive building activities occurred in projects where open spaces between blocks were unpaved but demarcated. This could suggest that households were more encouraged to extend after clear limits were set between public territory (streets) and what is viewed as 'private' territory (sidewalks around blocks) which is usually appropriated by residents.

Socio-economic conditions of the resident population Extensive transformations were found to be carried out by populations consisting of a combination of different income groups (e.g. public sector workers and employees). This could be due to the fact that in many cases of multi-storey extensions, wealthier families have helped out those with lower incomes by financing the major part of the structure costs. On the other hand, communities which mainly consisted of only one income group (e.g. low income groups such as resettled populations from slum clearance projects) were found to be less active in terms of engaging in co-operative building activities.

Factors related to housing units

Location of blocks Transformations seemed to decrease in blocks located on the outer border of projects, while at the inside, more extensive transformations usually took place.

Open space between blocks Large extensions were more frequently observed when the distance between adjacent blocks exceeded 12 m. On the other hand, where spaces were less than 8 m., extensions were much more limited and did not exceed 1.5 m. in depth (Plate 12.10).

Layout of blocks Among the most common patterns identified in the sample (Figure 12.2), the first, which consists of vast open spaces created by arranging blocks in parallel lines, has resulted in an enormous waste of land which could have been used for extensions. The second, which represents a more compact layout achieved by arranging blocks in parallel and perpendicular rows with relatively narrow spaces between blocks and has resulted in higher densities and less available open space for extension activity. Finally, the third pattern, which consists of small groupings of blocks clustered around semi-public squares, proved to be the most efficient in terms of land use (23% of the total area used for housing); and was found to allow relatively large extensions, to promote collective participation and to enhance dwellers' control over common open spaces.

Plate 12.10 Narrow spaces in Ahmed Helmi have limited the scale of extension activities.

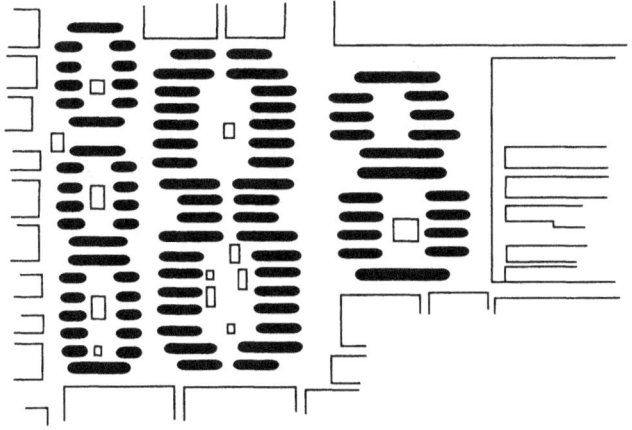

El Zawya el Gedida - 16% of area used for housing.

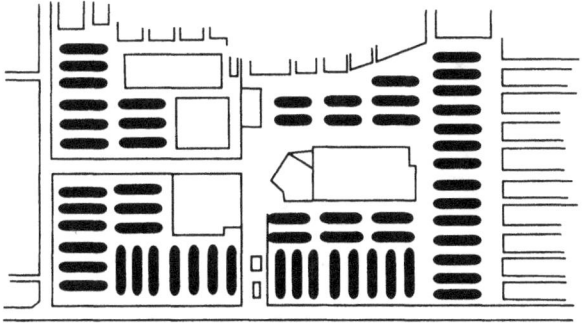

El Zawya el Hamra - 20% of area used for housing.

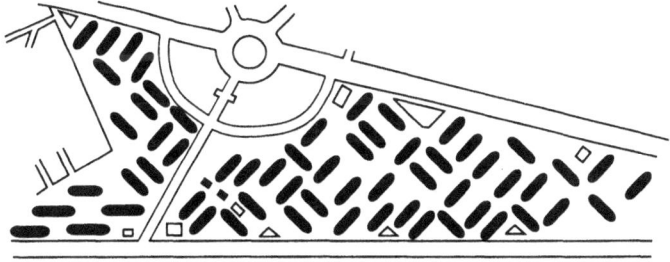

El Teraa el Bulaqiya - 23% of area used for housing.

Figure 12.2 Different layout patterns used in the surveyed projects.

Design of blocks Different extension profiles developed out of different block designs (Figure 12.3). Blocks with open corners and accentuated facade projections were found to encourage extension activity which took place by filling-in alcoves and open corners. Double loaded blocks with flats arranged back to back, have lead to the development of extensions at both sides of blocks, resulting in higher densities and limiting future extension possibilities. Finally, in some projects (e.g. Zeinhom), blocks were raised too high above ground level which significantly reduced the number of ground floor extensions observed.

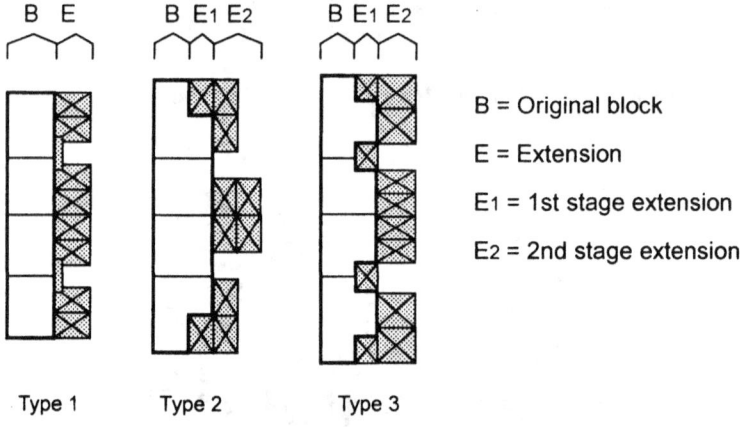

Figure 12.3 Different extension profiles develop from different block designs.

Location of flats within a block The largest and most frequent extensions were found at the ground floor level, followed by top floor units which usually extended on roofs. The remaining floors were found to have lower rates of extension activity. Corner units were also found to have generally larger extensions than mid-block units.

Design of flats Figure 12.4 shows how some of the different protoypical designs of flats have resulted in different configurations after transformations took place. Wasted circulation space and narrow rooms have resulted from the transformation of flats type 1b and 2, while wider rooms, but with problems of cross circulation through existing rooms, have resulted from transformations in flats type 1a and 3.

Summary of findings

This study has shown that transformations can vary widely according to different housing situations. Most of the projects surveyed included a combination of different types of transformations as described earlier.

However, two main patterns were identified based on whether transformations were carried out on an individual or on a collective basis.

Individual transformations, which usually required less co-operation between neighbours and fewer financial resources, were found to be more widespread in the surveyed sample; collective transformations, on the other hand, were more limited in their occurrence and were a function of neighbours' agreement, contractors' ability and users' financial capability. A given project's location in an area where local authorities maintained a firm attitude also limited the extent of collective building activities.

While individual transformations created more variable and irregular patterns, reflecting individual needs and aspirations, collective transformations resulted in more uniform patterns, with more impressive effects on built-environments as well as a significant increase in total area used for housing, higher quality structures and improved infrastructures and services.

It was found that various factors related to both housing and household characteristics have affected the extent of transformations observed in different projects. At the level of housing environments, the most extensive transformations were concentrated in vast projects with relatively large populations, whereas smaller projects were less affected by transformations. Lower densities and less built-up area, on the other hand, were found to encourage transformation activities. Older projects were usually more affected by transformations than more recent ones, and the further a project was located from the city centre the more likely it was that large-scale collective transformations would occur. The level of finishing of streets and open spaces within the projects also played an important role: unfinished but demarcated spaces between blocks seemed to have encouraged large multi-storey extensions in many of the surveyed projects, while totally paved streets and sidewalks were found to have discouraged extension activities in other projects. The lack of commercial services has also encouraged the emergence of shops, small businesses and home-based economic activities in several of the surveyed projects. Finally, socio-economic conditions of public housing populations have also affected transformations. The most extensive collective transformations were carried out in projects which combined different income groups. On the other hand, collective activities were found to decrease in projects in which residents mainly belonged to only one group (i.e. the low income group).

At the level of housing units, transformations were found to increase in blocks facing relatively large open spaces and located towards the inside of projects.

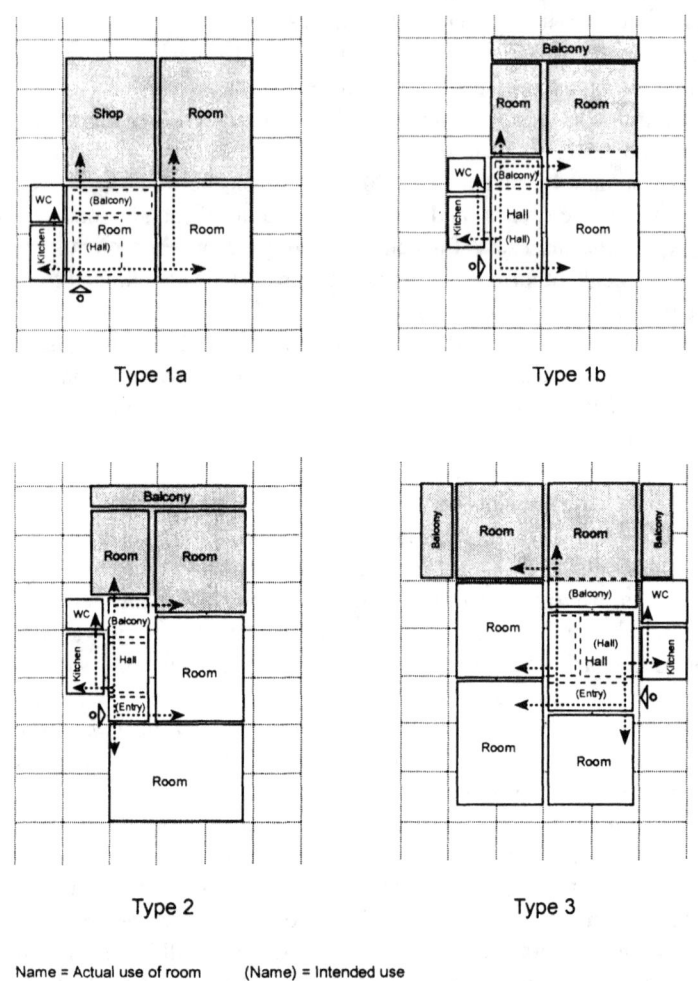

Name = Actual use of room   (Name) = Intended use

Figure 12.4 Different design configurations observed in the surveyed sample as a result of transformations.

Flats grouped in small clusters around common open spaces were found to be the ultimate setting for the development of collective transformation activities such as multi-storey extensions and public gardens. Accentuated facade projections were found to encourage extensions, and ground floor extensions were much more limited in blocks where ground floor flats were raised too high above ground level.

In general, extensions were larger and occurred more frequently at ground floor and roof top levels than on other floors, and flats located at corners of blocks allowed larger extensions than those in the middle. Finally, it was found that layouts of transformed flats largely depended on their original designs which determined the size, direction and arrangement of new rooms.

Conclusions

User transformation of public housing projects is likely to continue in Egypt as long as its benefits outweigh its costs. All of the projects showed signs of ongoing building activities regardless of the variable stages of development observed in each project. Overall, transformations have created more housing accommodation better suited to household needs and provided families with opportunities for income generating activity.

The attitude of local authorities has, in many instances affected transformation activity. While strict attitudes adopted by local authorities did not stop the spread of transformations, it has affected the scale and pattern of transformation activity as described earlier. Hence, governments should play a more positive role as 'enablers', by legalising existing transformations and allowing - if not encouraging - future transformers to undertake building activities, as long as they are carried out within acceptable standards and do not represent a hazard to other residents.

Since it is the author's belief that governments in many countries will proceed with the production of public housing, it is therefore recommended that new projects should take into consideration the possibility of future transformation activity from the early planning and design stages:

- Allowing different income groups to co-habit in small groupings within relatively large developments could promote the development of socio-economic ties, strengthen local feeling and facilitate collective building activities.
- An efficient distribution of open spaces, which would reduce the percentage of public space and increase the size of private space between blocks without necessarily increasing density and built-up area, could encourage transformations and reduce its negative effects as poor lighting and ventilation.

- Demarcating spaces between blocks, while leaving sufficient 'unpaved' space for private use, could promote extensions and help avoid conflicts between neighbours.
- Locating infrastructure networks in suitable vertical and horizontal positions could prevent hindering future extensions and ensure easy access for maintenance.
- Choosing clustered layouts of blocks could enhance dwellers' control over common open spaces and encourage collective transformation activity.
- Using appropriate designs for both blocks and flats could facilitate future expansion and rearrangement of internal spaces.

More important than these proposed 'design guidelines' is the change in the attitude of professionals resulting from the experience of user transformation. Existing housing policies and codes of practice should be reviewed in the light of actual transformations in different projects through empirical in-depth studies.

Finally, housing should be seen as a process of constant transformation and endless variation. There is certainly a lot to be learned by looking at user transformation as it unfolds in a continuing open-ended process of unexpected developments.

This paper has presented some of the results of a broader study on housing transformations which includes detailed case studies from different public housing projects in Egypt. More detailed information can be obtained by writing to the author.

Notes

1 In this study, user transformation is referred to as an 'informal' activity because constructions are built on public land, without construction permits, and therefore considered illegal by local authorities.
2 The twenty surveyed projects are: 1) Alexandria: El Azaritah, Lombrozo, Ghobrial, El Gabbari, El Mafruza, Kom el Shuqafa. 2) Cairo: El Zawya el Gedida, El Kossayirin, Bulaq, Zeinhom, Ezbet Bilal, Ahmed Helmi, El Zawya el Hamra, El Sharabeya, El Teraa el Bulaqiya, El Wayli, Imbaba, El Amiriya, Ain el Sira, Helwan
3 To low income households, what matters most is the number of rooms or spaces added to their dwellings rather than the area of extensions.

13 The making of territories:
A case study in South Africa

Maano F. Ramutsindela

Introduction

It is not sufficient to explain the choice of location by a community in terms of needs such as shelter, food, security, etc. Factors from outside a community can also play a vital role in determining the location of people in particular territories. Different authors in this book have acknowledged the central role played by the government in controlling space. This chapter focuses on the role played by the government in the construction of territories and the location of communities in order to promote the separation of racial and ethnic groups in South Africa. It demonstrates the role of the state on the location of communities by drawing examples from the Northern Province, South Africa. The Northern Province is chosen because it consists of four adjacent ethnic territories which were created in accordance with separate development (apartheid). The drawing of boundaries around the adjacent ethnic groups illuminates a variety of strategies used by the government to lay the foundation for ethnic territories.

The chapter adopts a particular meaning of 'territory' in order to advance the argument of the author. Although the concept 'territory' has spatial and legal connotations (Taylor, 1993), its use in this chapter is limited to the political and ideological significance. Lefebvre, as cited by Sayer (1985, p.60), summarised the use of space in these words: 'Space is not a scientific object removed from ideology and politics, it has always been political and strategic ...'. This view of space is relevant to the topic under discussion because race relations in South Africa were regulated by use of space. Massey (1985) is right when she considers space as a social construct. The sense of belonging to a particular place can be created and nurtured by exploring existing power structures in society. In support of this idea, Sack (1986, p.5) regarded territoriality as 'a primary geographical expression of social power'. Taylor (1993, p.153) presents a vivid picture of the geographic expression of social power when he says: 'The establishment and disestablishment of states represent victories for some social groups and defeats for others'. Whites in South Africa as the wielders of political power could arrange territories unilaterally (Ramutsindela, 1993). The arrangement of territories were in line with the political ideology of the time - separate development of races and ethnic groups.

Territories were used to foster ethnic identities especially among Blacks whose numerical strengths threatened the implementation of separate development. Ethnicity and territoriality were properly mixed to produce desired 'ethnic nations'. Such a mixture was important because 'people are given their identity by the state within which they find themselves' (Knight, 1985, p.248). Ethnicity would not have been easily mobilised without territorial focus because 'one's conception of himself and of his place in society is thus subtly merged with his conception of the spatially limited territory of limited social interaction' (Urry, 1985, p.32). Slowe (1990) shares the same opinion with Urry because he considers ethnicity as an important feature in facilitating territorial organisation. The way in which the then South African Government fostered the relationship between Black ethnic groups and their territories is demonstrated throughout the chapter.

Views on the separation of territories

There are two dominant views on the separation of racial and ethnic groups and their territories. The view of the apartheid government is that the location of communities is a result of history and has nothing to do with the state. The government argued that the land surface of the country was not divided by the South African Government, but by history. In the words of the government (Republic of South Africa, 1983, p.197),

> the scattered and fragmented nature of these traditional Black territories was not due to any legislation or action on the part of Whites. By and large, the Blacks had settled the areas of their choice and this choice was determined by one of two factors or both; the nature of the land and each tribe's wish to have a buffer strip to separate it from the next.

As a result of this view, authorities who encouraged the partitioning of South Africa saw the division of South African society as a natural outcome of cultural diversity. This was evident in the Assembly Debate on 13 October 1966 when the Minister of Bantu Administration and Development (Republic of South Africa 1966, p.147) said: 'Our Policy is based on the facts ... (of) the separateness and the diversity of the various Bantu (Black) nations and other nations in South Africa as separate national entities set on separate destinies'. The opinion of the Minister was realised when separate national states for Blacks were established.

The opposing view is that the government created separate territories for different racial and ethnic groups and had the political and legal power to determine the location of communities. Supporters of this view argue that settlement patterns for Blacks and Whites are a result of government intervention and planning. Typical of such planning was the removal of Blacks from areas which were earmarked for Whites and the resettlement of different ethnic groups to separate territories. In 1983, the total number of people removed was 1, 297, 400 while 542, 000 was under threat of removal in the Transvaal (Platzky and Walker, 1985).

The construction of territories

Various methods were used by the government to construct territories in South Africa and the Northern Province in particular.

The law as an instrument of place-making

Since the legal power was in the hands of Whites, the law became an instrument of land acquisition. As Rogers (1933) correctly pointed out, the Transvaal native locations are a result of the recommendations of the Native Location Commission. The Commission had the powers to define the boundaries of the native tribes. Using its powers, the Commission located related tribes together. The separation of land rights was advocated by the South African Affairs Commission of 1903-1905. After the annexation of the Transvaal by Shepstone, the land and any Black population it carried submerged under White ownership and all land tribally owned was registered in the name of the Minister of Native Affairs (Rogers, 1933; Benyon, 1974). Competition for land ownership necessitated a strong mechanism to separate land for Blacks and Whites. Consequently, the Natives Land Act of 1913 was passed to enforce territorial segregation and to 'freeze' the then division of land between Blacks and Whites (Kirkwood n.d.). The Natives Land Act provided measures to control, specify and define areas for occupation by the population groups of South Africa.

The effects of the Act on Blacks is succinct in Rev. Mtimkulu's comment cited by Bundy (1992, p.6), 'There are many natives who have already been removed from the farms on account of this Act (Natives Land Act of 1913) '... There are others who have farms, but titles are refused to them by the government ...'.

Developing a sense of belonging to territories

The Native Administration Act of 1927 and the Bantu Tribal Authorities Act of 1951 made provision for the delimitation of tribal areas and the establishment of tribal authorities. The delimitation of tribal areas was not an easy exercise for the government because certain areas had a mixture of tribes and ethnic groups. In cases where the tribal area was 'mixed' in terms of ethnic classification, the government decided upon the ethnic group and tribe which should occupy the area. A case in point is the determination of ethnic classification for the rural village of Senwamokgope in Lebowa homeland (Republic of South Africa, 1957). Tribal areas were grouped together to form regions under regional authorities. Vosloo, Kotze and Jeppe (1974) maintain that a regional authority consists of all chiefs and other heads of tribal authorities in the region as ex-officio members. According to a Survey of Race Relations, the Polokwane regional authority was established for the North Sotho around Pietersburg (South African Institute of Race Relations, 1960). Two or more regions formed a territory which was administered by a territorial authority Territorial authorities were established for each ethnic group in the Northern Province in order to allow ethnic groups to govern themselves in separate reserved areas. The Black Authorities Act of 1951 and the Promotion of Black Self-Government Act of 1959 made provision for the establishment of territorial authorities. Territorial authorities for the North Sotho were established on the 10th of August 1962, for the Venda and Shangaan-Tsonga on the 9th of November 1962 (Cloette, 1982). Territories created for different ethnic groups were aimed at developing a sense of belonging to certain places. It was expected that the Venda would, for example, feel that they are citizens of Venda and not of 'White' South Africa.

Social Engineering

Social engineering is a concept used in South Africa to describe the creation of racial and ethnic territories and the resettlement of Black communities by the state in order to achieve separate development of races and ethnic groups. The establishment of territories for ethnic groups could not have succeeded if members of these groups were not resettled. Wilson and Ramphele (1989) maintain that the removals were aimed at segregating one ethnic group from another and the consolidation of people living scattered through the reserves into villages. The political motive is one of the common explanation of resettlement (South African Council of Churches and the Southern African Catholic Bishops' Conference, 1984; Platzky and Walker, 1985; and Murray and O'Regan, 1990). Certain steps were taken to facilitate resettlement programmes which were carried by force. According to Madima (1971), the first step was the counting of people. Secondly, areas for different ethnic groups were identified and their boundaries drawn. Areas were scheduled and released for occupation by ethnic groups

(Figure 13.1). This was followed by the third step, the relocation of residents who were found on the wrong side of ethnic boundaries. The novelist Madima (1971) describes the resettlement of the Venda and Shangaan-Tsonga ethnic groups in the district of Sibasa as 'Operation Sibasa'. Some of the resettlements carried out among the North Sotho appear in Figure 13.2.

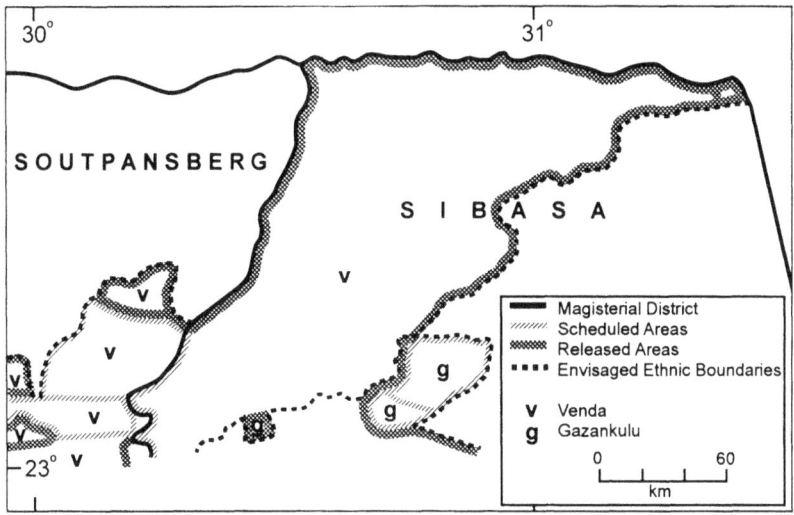

Figure 13.1 Creation of ethnic territories.

Administrative procedures as a basis for ethnic compaction

After the formation of the Union of South Africa in 1910, administrative procedures of the Province of the Cape of Good Hope, Natal, Orange Free State and the Transvaal were made uniform. The Magistrates' Court Act was passed in 1917 and gave the Governor-General powers to 'create districts and declare the name by which any district shall be known ... define, increase or decrease the local limits of any district, ... annexe any district or detach portion of a district or portions of two or more adjoining districts as a sub-district, ...' (Union of South Africa, 1917, p.468). The jurisdiction conferred to native chiefs by Article Four of the Transvaal Law No. 4 over the subjects was to be placed under the districts created by the Governor-General. This was made possible by the Native Chiefs' Jurisdiction Act of 1924. This Act placed the chiefs' jurisdiction under the court of the Native Commissioner of the area within which the native chief exercised jurisdiction (Union of South Africa, 1924).

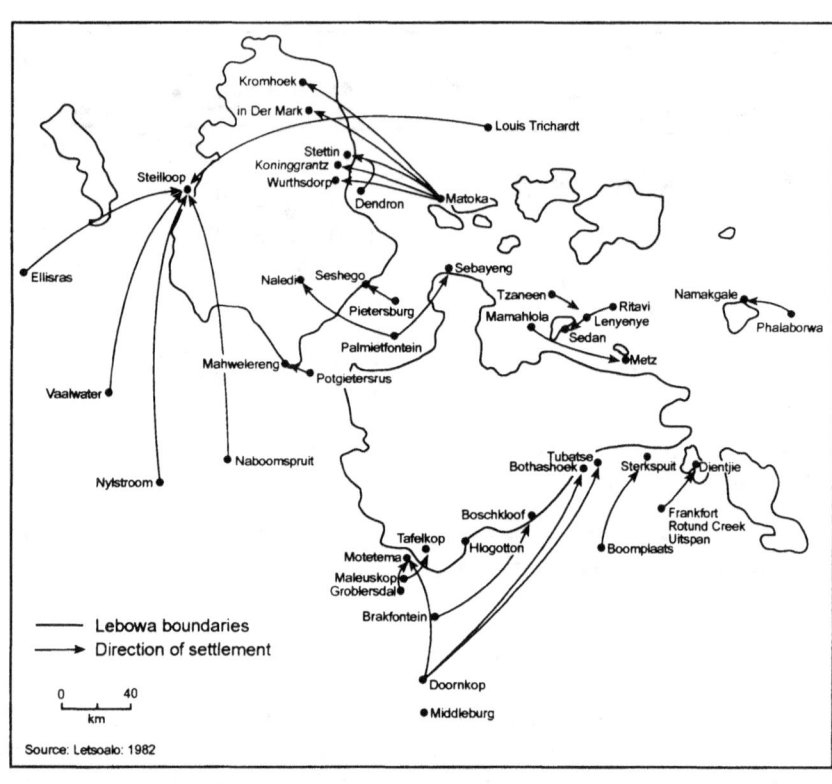

Figure 13.2 Resettlement of the North Sotho.

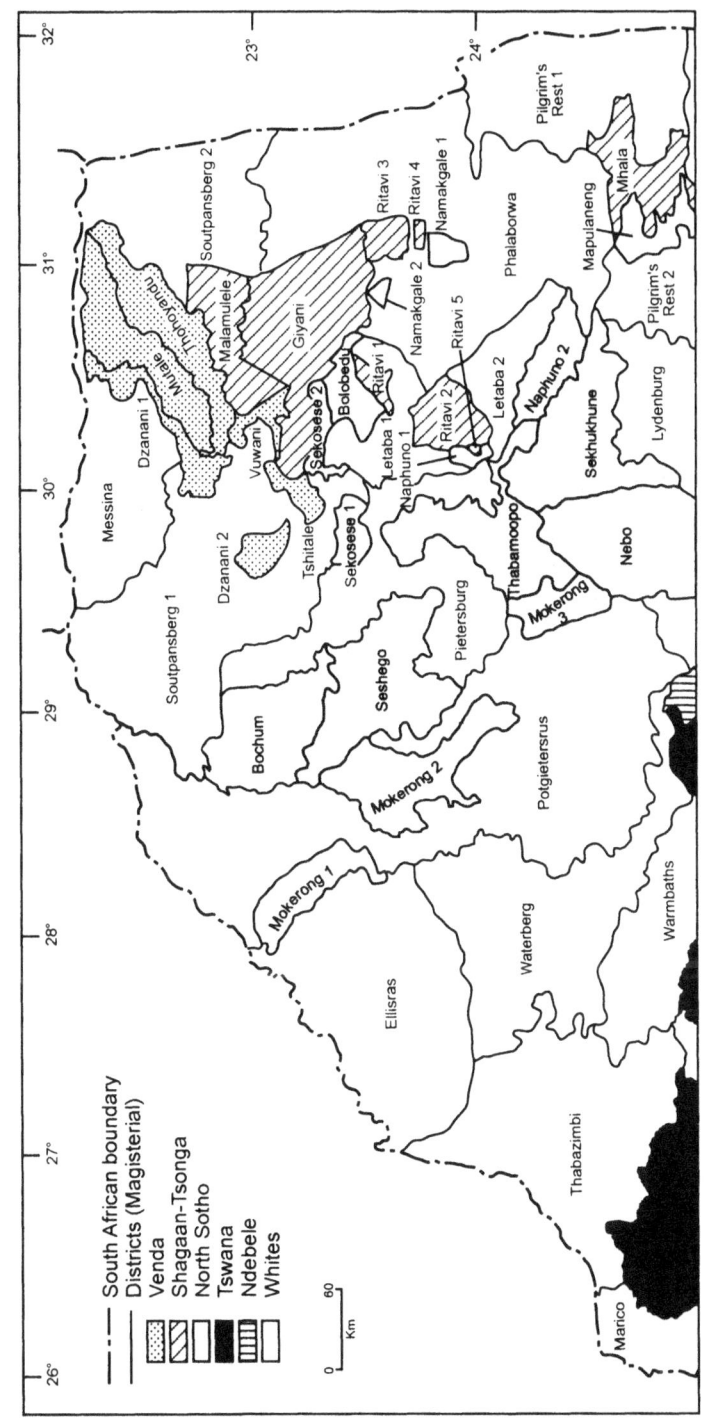

Figure 13.3 Ethnic and racial magisterial districts.

The powers conferred on the Governor- General by the Magistrates' Court Act of 1917 were shifted to the minister of Justice by the Magistrates' Court Act of 1944. In 1944, the Northern Transvaal had non-ethnic and non-racial magisterial districts. Since these districts were non-ethnical, separate administration of justice was not possible. Consequently, ethnic magisterial districts were created and named in accordance with ethnic territories, e.g. a district created for the Shangaan-Tsonga was given a Tsonga name in preparation for a Tsonga homeland (Gazankulu). The district of Sibasa represents the beginning of ethnic magisterial districts in the Northern Province. Its local limits were defined by Government Notice No. 356 of 1953, amended by Government Notices No. 768 of 1953 and 1932 of 1959 (Republic of South Africa, 1972). The creation of districts in 1953 implies the realisation of the policy of separate development in general and separate administration of territories in particular. The district was located in the then Northern Transvaal (called Northern Province in this chapter), the location which was dominated by the Venda and Shangaan-Tsonga.

The location of the Venda, Shangaan-Tsonga, North Sotho and Whites within the boundaries of the district of Sibasa was an obstacle to separate administration of the Northern Transvaal. This obstacle was removed through the use of scheduled and released areas for Black occupation (see Figure 13.1). These areas were concentrated on the western side of the district of Sibasa. The concentration of Blacks, namely, the Venda and Shangaan-Tsonga on one part of the district enabled the state to reserve the eastern side of the district for occupation by Whites. Consequently, the local limits of the district of Sibasa were redefined in 1959, thus excluding the eastern part of the original district. This exercise culminated in the creation of ethnic magisterial districts (Figure 13.3).

Furthermore, when magisterial districts for a particular ethnic group were combined to delimit the area belonging to a homeland, magisterial district boundaries became homeland boundaries except in the case where the boundary divides districts belonging to the same ethnic group. For example, the boundary between the district of Vuwani (Venda) and Soutpansberg (RSA) forms the international boundary between the two 'states' whereas the boundary separating the districts of Vuwani (Venda) and Thohoyandou (Venda) is a district boundary. Merrett (1984) correctly observed that homeland boundaries were originally intended to mark the limits of magisterial districts. He argues that the international boundaries of homelands were largely founded upon a pre-existing pattern of magisterial districts. Following the same idea, Prescott (1979, p.21) argued that the homelands of South Africa 'were originally defined in terms of Magistrates' districts and the limits of such areas were not fixed with the precision necessary for effective international boundaries'. If magisterial district boundaries had only administrative functions without political motives, there was no need to establish part 5 of the district of Ritavi in Gazankulu. The said part occupies 113.82ha within the district of Naphuno in Lebowa. Christopher (1982) correctly pointed out that the drawing of boundaries around ethnic groups was a significant element in the implementation of the policy of separate development.

Conclusion

It is logical to conclude that the construction of artificial ethnic territories in the Northern Province has become a geographic reality. This geographic reality remains intact even after the scrapping of laws which promoted separate development. These territories have inherited unequal development. It is true that 'even if the ethnic borders (boundaries) are removed, what remain are the frontiers of deprivation' (Cross Times, 1990, p.1). As Christopher (1993) observed, the heritage of the past is more of a burden than an inspiration in South Africa.

The greatest challenge facing the final constitution to be drawn up by the elected Government of National Unity will be the reordering of South African territorial space, if a united South Africa is to be built. The reordering of space will remain meaningless to disadvantaged communities if development remains racially and ethnically skewed. The Northern Province, which has inherited four different territories, requires strategies to build a regional iconography. These strategies are important since the geographic separation of ethnic groups has created perception patterns which can become a nation-destroying factor in the region (Ramutsindela, 1991). The withdrawal of the Bushbuckridge area (Mhala and Mapulaneng) from the Northern Province is an indication of the continued existence of perception patterns developed and nurtured by past political strategies. According to the Star (1994, p.2) 'the area (Bushbuckridge) should be included in the Eastern Transvaal provincial territory with immediate effect, ...'. The reconstruction of the Northern Province in the new political dispensation demands the development of a new meaning of regional territoriality.

14 Upgrading of townships in South Africa after apartheid

Ola Uduku

Introduction

> Meanwhile the South African urban areas are menaced by the four horsemen of the urban apocalypse: namely poverty, overcrowding, homelessness, and unemployment - all of which impact most directly upon the urban Black population.[1]

Images of the poverty and depravation of the South African township as described by social critics and writers was required introductory reading for all who wanted to join the struggle. Now that the fundamental battle for equal rights seems won, the more intricate questions surrounding public welfare needs, housing, health care and sanitation for example, are likely to be no less vexatious. The cost of social infrastructure, its equitable distribution, and its future management, are some key issues which require serious consideration in the new dispensation. The State's success or failure in ensuring the adequate provision of welfare facilities and services for the local population will prove a major indicator of national development.

This chapter discusses future strategies for more widespread infrastructure provision in South Africa. It does this by first considering the history of social infrastructure provision in deprived areas of South Africa. It then goes on to give an analysis of the present transient situation of townships and other residential areas of South Africa in the period during and after the transition to democratic rule. Next it discusses possible infrastructure provision strategies which might serve to address problems of equity, economic cost and efficiency in the new era. It compares these strategies with those attempted in two other countries, Nigeria and Britain, which have both similar and contrasting problems to South Africa in terms of effective social welfare policy. Finally the chapter attempts a critical analysis of the unity government's most likely approach to ameliorating the crisis.

Effectively the chapter is written in two parts, the first gives a brief history of infrastructure provision to current times. The second part deals more analytically with the 'pros' and 'cons' of infrastructure provision strategies and related policies. This is done from both a local and national perspective, which ultimately influence final choices from a political viewpoint. Sociological and physical problems associated with infrastructure planning are also considered within the unique South African context. The cost, organisation and management implications of large scale infrastructure provision is the final aspect covered in the analysis.

Throughout this section, comparisons have been drawn from Nigerian and British experiences. Both these countries have contextual similarities to South Africa and therefore their experiences give more concrete evidence of the effects of various policies on social infrastructure provision elsewhere.

The conclusions the chapter arrives at are only tentative, pointing mainly to the need for further integration of research, planning and documented infrastructure provision projects, in order to appreciate research and methods which might be used to deal with the problem rather than the prescription of specific solutions. What is presented then is very much an exploratory discussion which the author hopes will lead to a more rigorous analysis of the problems associated with infrastructure provision in South Africa and elsewhere in Sub Saharan Africa.

Section One

A history of neglect

> White South Africans were as prosperous as the middle and upper classes in Europe and America .... they owned cars lived in substantial houses or apartments in segregated suburbs .... the state provided them with excellent public services: schools and hospitals, parks and playing fields, buses and trains, roads, water, electricity, telephones, drainage and sewerage.

> Public services for Blacks were characteristically inadequate or non-existent. .....in homelands women still walked miles every day to fetch water and firewood: in the towns people crowded into single sex compounds, leaky houses or impoverished shacks. Schools, hospitals and public transport.[for Blacks].was sharply inferior. Electricity, running water, public telephones, sewage systems, parks and playing fields were rare.[2]

South Africa's modern or 'European' history begins with the Dutch East India Company's establishment of a victualling point in Cape Town. This was to provide essential needs such as fresh water, fruit and vegetables for ships on their way to or from the Far East. Prior to this the area had an indigenous local population which used the land for daily activities. It could be argued that South Africa's development has been shaped by the continued struggle for access to natural, and more recently public, resources by the majority.[3]

In the early years land on which to live and farm was the main scarce resource. Public services comprised essentially of access to rivers for adequate water supply, and possibly to roads on which the rudimentary post service might have been run. With the finding of diamonds and later gold, however commenced the development of South Africa both economically and socially.

Economically the wealth being generated from mines in Kimberly and on the Rand created major urban centres and the development attendant social infrastructure required both for the sustenance of the local population and also for the transportation of the product to the ports.

Social segregation in this period also gained ground, as employers had differentiated pay based on race, which subsequently led to segregated housing. In mines this usually constituted all male, same 'tribe' dormitories known as 'hostels'. In towns also the significantly lower earning power of Blacks meant de facto segregation took place between racial groups. Black settlement became concentrated in poorer locations with less reliable services which would have been all that was affordable within their means at the time. This form of segregated second class service provision characterised the development of Black areas or townships in South African cities.

The first early townships originally called 'locations' were state planned at the turn of the century.[4] The first townships, (such as Orlando, Johannesburg) were state-built in the 1930s to attempt to house the rapidly increasing African population. Up until the 1940s there was a government policy to provide housing in designated townships to help house the backlog of inadequately housed Blacks in shantytowns bordering White cities, and inner city mixed residential areas with poorly built housing (Calderwood, 1953).

Although these measures did help to reduce the backlog in housing even at the end of the era, in the early 1950s, there was still not enough housing for Blacks. This contrasted with the government's ability to provide adequate low income housing for poor whites. In terms of urban infrastructure provision the original townships were provided with the bare basics, initially the State built two room houses, with a kitchen and outhouse provided on a small individual plot of land.

Pipe-borne water was provided free from a standpipe in the backyard, whilst human waste disposal was by means of bucket latrine. Electricity was generally not provided, and roads were dirt tracks. This was an improvement from the earlier shantytowns - which had no service provisions at all - although of a substantially lower standard to the often adjoining White cities.

Rural conditions were often worse as, with most workable land owned by White farmers, rural housing tended to belong to the farmers who employed Black labour. Thus 'free' housing was included as part payment of wages for farm labour. Effectively then farmer landlords could evict at will with little government involvement. Services provided were also determined by the farmer; electricity, water and school provision for black farm workers and their families were thus directly controlled by the farmer and not the State.

Urban areas such as District Six - Cape Town, and Sophiatown - Johannesburg however remained areas of racially integrated housing until the formal 'apartheid' legislation banning various forms of inter-racial mixing was put in place.[5] Such areas attracted Whites and Blacks of various classes. Although some housing in these areas were indeed slums, they were still substantially better provided for with social services than the black shanty towns or housing estates of the day.

In the 1950s there was a more intensive drive to eradicate the 'Urban Black Problem', by the provision of site and service plots the government was able to 're house' thousands of blacks in newly developed townships like South West Town, near Johannesburg [6], Nyanga, near Cape Town, and New Brighton near Port Elizabeth. However Frescura (1981) suggests that by 1945 there was a Black population of 395,000 in the Johannesburg municipality, for which there had been provided 9,573 (usually two-room) houses. This housing stock was estimated to house 50,000 inhabitants or approximately five inhabitants per house. Effectively 345,000 inhabitants remained unhoused in shanties.

The era of apartheid began with the election of the national party into power in 1948, however actual apartheid legislation took some years to come into force. Indeed the mass 'site and service' urban housing projects reached their apogee in the 1950s. However by the 1960s, apartheid ideology began to place emphasis on the need for a separate 'Bantustans' or Homelands policy.

What this meant was that all South Africans who were not White were classified by race, Africans by their historical 'tribes' were thus subdivided into smaller 'nations' whose 'Bantustans' were in the old reserves and some newly created ones. Other racial groups were classified as initially Indian and Coloured, and had specific townships demarcated as their 'own areas'. Effectively all non Whites were legally barred from living in the designated 'White' cities. Thus began the re-zoning and re-classification of most of urban South Africa.

The forced re-locations and evictions which followed re-created the shantytown problems earlier government policies had begun to redress. Because the ensuing apartheid policy effectively devolved most responsibility of infrastructure provision and housing to 'native' homelands, little was done in the 1960s and early 70s to increase, or upgrade existing urban Black townships. Instead intricate political and economic arrangements were made to help 'develop' the Homelands into self-governing-territories (SGTs) to which all Africans, rural or urban were supposed to belong.

Evidence suggests that generally these Homelands had not much better facilities than urban Townships.[7] With the non arable land on which most Homelands were sited, the migrant labour system worked in full force. Female-headed families often lived in poverty, and 'development' was mainly dependent on South African funding.[8]

By the early 1970s the 'unworkability' of grand apartheid planning had become clear. There was considerable dissatisfaction and protest about the condition of housing and other social infrastructure in Black Townships. This culminated in the rent boycotts, the refusal of families in townships to pay council rents, or bills for public utilities where they were provided. Significantly also during this period was the marked re-appearance of large Black squatter camps in areas such as Crossroads (Cape Town), Umlazi (Natal), and the Winterveld (PWV). Aside from these near self-created squatter camps there were also large numbers of squatters on marginal lands near the earlier constituted townships such as Soweto, Nyanga, and Ibhayi.

The 1976 Soweto riots, started by school children in protest about the introduction of the government's 'Bantu' education policy, marked the most determined and sustained period of militancy in Black South Africa. The interest it generated globally and the sustained group protests which followed, resulted in the commencement of the gradual but definite dismantling of apartheid.

In the area of social infrastructure provision, Churches, NGOs, Local and International Corporations and, most importantly, Community organisations known as 'Civics' all became involved in the planning and implementation of local infrastructure provision projects.[9] The national government began its transformation of various parts of the apartheid state also.

In terms of infrastructure development this resulted in the marked increases in government and corporate investment in school building projects in Black areas. NGOs and churches also became involved with some construction projects and also in local development efforts such as small business development schemes, and adult literacy programmes. The repeal of some of the more offensive 'petty' apartheid laws in the 1980s and the government's apparent sanction that civil servants turn a blind eye to the entry of Blacks into previously 'White' schools and housing zones also took place.

In the 1980s therefore, before the release of Nelson Mandela in 1989 and the commencement of the CODESA talks, the state of social infrastructure in some of Black South Africa had already undergone a period of irreversible transformation. This began with the removal of 'petty apartheid' such as by laws prohibiting non-Whites using public facilities such as beaches, WCs and restaurants which were officially designated 'Whites only'. The repeal of the 'mixed marriages act' and subsequently 'group areas legislation' meant that the government began to acknowledge multi-racial living.

Social infrastructure began to improve substantially also specifically in urban areas where the government and local corporations became more involved with school and health centre provision, as well as road rehabilitation, and electricity provision in established black townships. The 1991 creation of the 'Model C' schools from the old White state schools went as far as the then government would go in allowing some Blacks equal access to privileged white facilities.

The marked poverty and deprivation of most of Black South Africa was however not alleviated. Farm schools still remained owned by local farmers, African education remained fee paying, and the provision of social infrastructure like electricity and adequate pipe-borne water was lacking for most Africans in townships and rural areas. Furthermore de facto desegregation laws were not always upheld. An African who took ill in a 'White' neighbourhood might not get admission to the local White hospital because she would be expected to seek treatment only in her 'own' neighbourhood.

The short era between the release of political prisoners and the negotiation of a new South African constitution brought few changes to the state of local infrastructure provision.

More corporate and government capital went into further provision of electricity, schools and roads for selected communities, but long term plans were subject to the policies of the then yet to be elected new government of national unity.

Four months after the election of the ANC-National Party 'Unity Government' things are yet to change. There have however been the launches of prominent programmes and policies which, with the earlier negotiated Kempton Park draft constitution, all impinge directly on social infrastructure provision in the new South Africa.[10] The new draft constitution embodies in it the key principles on South African administrative matters for the next five years.

Crucial to infrastructure provision, the new constitution's support of the right to self determination of (existing) communities in this context gives certain support to the continued differentiation of infrastructure on a 'self determined community basis'.

This might mean the constitution's guarantee of every citizen's right of equal access to social infrastructure could be difficult or contradictory to carry out. For example the interpretation of all cultural groups being entitled to promote their culture might mean the exclusion of non Afrikaner children from classes in a predominantly 'Afrikaner' area.

In the run up to the elections the various parties presented policies on social infrastructure provision. The ANC specifically published an Educational Renewal Strategy, and a sketch Public Works Programme (PWP). Various other parties had similar policies, with similar themes; hoping to increase infrastructure provision to deprived areas. In summarising the main policies, all policies presented were agreed that education was to become unified and free to a certain level. Health care was also to be increased to cover all South Africans. However the way in which this would come about differed with various party policies. The provision of improved local infrastructure such as roads and electricity was also agreed unanimously. Policies differed as to the efficacy of the PWPs versus more conventional methods in bringing about infrastructure development (ANC, 1955; ANC, 1994a; ANC, 1994b; and also Emmett, 1993).

The history of infrastructure provision in Black South Africa was indeed one of sore neglect. Although the past discussion dealt specifically with the African situation, the history of infrastructure provision for Asians and so-called 'Coloureds', although better than for Africans, was similarly lower than for Whites. The position of 'Coloureds' is a case in point. Much has been written about (Coloured) attempts to 'pass for white', or be re-classified racially from being 'Coloured' to being 'White'.[11] This was done by Coloureds and other racial groups in order to secure a better standard of living and access to social infrastructure which the Apartheid system had denied them in their original racial categories.[12]

Infrastructure provision for White South Africa, although not discussed in detail, remains of the highest standard found in urban areas in sub-Saharan South Africa. Given the relatively late development of the mining cities of Johannesburg, and other cities in the PWV the quality of real estate built there and in the Cape is impressive. There is little distinction between social infrastructure provision in White suburbs in South Africa and elsewhere in the Western world, except for its foundation and continued dependence on the use of cheap Black labour for its maintenance.

The segregation of schools and hospitals begun at the turn of the century continues as a form of economic segregation in the new South Africa.

The few Africans who can afford the privilege of a relatively expensive White State education are admitted, whilst until the new education policy is in place, the State continues to subsidise White South African children who cannot afford the school user fees which the model C (former White) schools now charge.

Similarly basic South African health care in cities has only in the new dispensation become free for citizens without a medical insurance policy. However the maintenance and auxiliary staffing in private schools, hospitals, and other services has remained predominantly Black. Private sector salaries in this area remain disproportionately lower for South African Blacks than their counterparts in the Western world.

Electricity, pipe-borne water and roads in White South Africa remain of a high standard. Towns founded in the 1920s at the same time as the black townships have always had full electricity and piped water to each individual household, as opposed to the minimal provisions the governments of the past were able to provide for the 'natives'. Current policies as begun with the RDP similarly will not substantially alter the quality of roads, electricity or pipe-borne water supply for this minority. Proposed electricity and pipe-borne water schemes for Black South Africa will depend more on external loan finance as well as local contributions, and to ensure cost recovery will be metered for 'pay as you use supply', a more expensive scenario than that found in White South Africa.

The male bias towards social infrastructure planning has also remained constant in the development history of South Africa. Although in the Homelands and SGTs females have for generations become heads of households by default due to the migrant labour system, real economic and political power remains male-dominated. Social infrastructure provision such as housing, schools and roads are designed and built predominantly by White males. Where community development projects do take place, often the experts remain male representatives of NGOs. Alternatively they are placed in the hands of male village or township heads. There has only been a slow transition to more representative forms of consultation.

There had been a number of (White) Women's movements during the apartheid era. They reached their apex in the militant protest days of the Black Sash in the 1970s. They have also however failed to 'engage' effectively with the Black female constituency with which they had claimed 'solidarity'.[13] Black female participation in the key South African women's pressure groups today remains substantially unrepresentative of the numbers of Black females who remain amongst the most oppressed by the old system.

Thus the social infrastructure development programmes which were and are being planned have often failed to alleviate the root problems facing females in shanty towns or deprived urban areas.

For example the evening classes which were planned by liberal educationalists to help redress educational imbalances were inaccessible to most females. This was because many had been afraid to go out at night to schools located in Police and Internal Security Unit patrolled rough neighbourhoods, often the case in Black townships. Also the provision of kindergarten or creche facilities for small children in townships was minimal until ANC pre-primary policies spearheaded by Nelson Mandela were introduced in the new dispensation.[14] As most White South African households have traditionally had Black South African domestics and 'nannies' in their employ, and thus had not had to bother about pre-primary education or care for their infants, this oversight might be better understood.

From the following it is clear that there has never been equitable distribution of social infrastructure in the South African state. The structure that was consolidated by the 40 years of the National Party rule has yet to disintegrate in any substantial way since the transition period came into being. Although there has been a considerable improvement in infrastructure distribution since the 1960s and 70s, the move to address the backlog of infrastructure provision in areas has yet to bear fruit.

Thus there has been little progress in addressing the scale of the problems involved in basic health and education provision, as well as pipe-borne water and electricity supply. It is not certain that with the new government of national unity installed, equity in infrastructure provision will be achieved. There is a great will to provide for the masses, as amply illustrated in the RDP plan however the issues of ownership, state versus private cost, state subsidised or free market, and equity are yet to be addressed. The possible future scenarios which the new dispensation might produce is discussed in the next section. It is hoped that the past section has provided the background to this.

Section Two

Tomorrow's South Africa

> ...more than 60% of South Africa's population (3m households or 23m people) had no access to domestic electricity in 1993 ....
>
> in May 1993 ... Eskom raised funds to electrify some 1m households by 1998....[15]

The new South Africa is certainly different from Vorster and Voerwood's vision. The current new government of National unity's vision of development would seem to suggest a form of free market socialism. The ANC, the majority party in the new government campaigned on a platform of access to social infrastructure such as housing, pipe-borne water, electricity and free education to the masses, the majority of whom were Africans and Coloureds.

In the current scenario, there is unlikely to be considerable change to the current state of affairs. The government will do as best it can with the limited resources it has to provide infrastructure to needy communities. There will be a continued emphasis on contributions from the voluntary and private sector, and local communities. The backlog already discussed in infrastructure provision means that it will be unlikely that there will be full provision to all with such a piecemeal approach.

The evidence at the moment suggests private and voluntary sponsors are willing to contribute to projects with potential 'success-features'. Thus the trend is towards private sector sponsorship of infrastructure provision in more respectable areas rather than the ghettos. In Cape Town for example projects are concentrated in Athlone and not Manenberg.

Increased community participation is also unlikely - definitely not amongst the more needy groups who are the poor Africans and Coloureds, who barely have the wherewithal to survive above the poverty line let alone produce the finance and time required for community projects. There is the chance that the affluent minority with 'own rights' safely entrenched in the draft constitution might set about constructing their own community schools in affluent catchment areas. This however at present is unnecessary as the government owned former White State (Model C) schools exist to take up the White middle classes and affluent

Blacks. The independent (private) schools, remain more exclusively White and the preserve of the extremely rich (Tikly, 1994).

In other areas of social infrastructure provision the same precedents hold. Most middle and upper class South Africans have adequate state-provided facilities, whilst the poor live in ill-provided townships, or survive in shanties on marginal land. Thus without government support, it is unlikely that the poor will be able to command the resources needed to provide power, pipe-borne water or basic health care facilities in their localities.

Scenario two would entail the State's increased dependence on private and free market forces to invest in infrastructure provision. In some ways South Africa has already begun to follow this line. It has a substantial number private medical facilities, and health insurance is a standard feature in most middle income white collar jobs. The National Health Policy draft paper also envisages a form of basic national health insurance plan to provide healthcare for all. It is however uncertain how much more the private sector might want to be involved in less profitable, quasi state health infrastructure investments.

South Africa has evolved from a historically dual-track, heavily government controlled economy into a multi-partite, class based, subsidised economy. The free market works for the South African entrepreneur who already has the wherewithal and in areas where there is inelastic demand, such as transportation, in townships.

Electricity and pipe-borne water are wanted by many, but can be and is done without in most Shanty towns. Unlike Nigeria, there is no well developed illegal grid tapping network, or cheap diesel generator distributorship supplying the demand for power, neither is there an organised trading network in water provision. Effectively the demand is not there and where it is in existence it is not profitable for the private sector. Private sector schools and health care facilities suffer similar problems: there are no profits to be made providing private infrastructure in poor areas.

The 'Pretoria-will provide' socialist state, the third scenario is also highly unlikely. Basically the government cannot afford this. The ANC in earlier years had certainly hoped it could deliver infrastructure to all, through the hoped nationalisation of all private concerns. Well before the CODESA talks and Kempton Park negotiations however this policy was shelved. The demise of the communist block and backing for socialism in the West would seem to have made this approach untenable.

In the area of infrastructure provision also the main loan agency, the World Bank, advocates 'cost recovery' approaches over free state provision. The state controlled structure of the South African state however means that there will still remain substantial involvement in infrastructure use such as schools and health facilities. Possibly the state might be able to provide bare bones facilities for many of the poorer communities, but not without external voluntary agency help or soft loans.

Given these options, the provision of tomorrow's South African infrastructure is likely to be particularly problematic. The conditions for equity have yet to be seriously addressed, and the current policies in place seem to sanction this continued oversight. The structure of bureaucracy inherited on the 10th May 1994 is likely to remain in place for most of the five year transitional government period.

Caution, and low taxation have been deemed necessary economic policies to espouse in order to attract investments and prevent capital flight. The effect of this status quo policy has yet to be felt; the honeymoon however might soon be over. That the immediate effects of a lack of social infrastructure will hit the poor and vulnerable such as women and children has already been highlighted.

The further consequences on development however are equally serious. South Africa's manpower cannot reach the competitive edge they seek to become Africa's success story without a properly educated, housed or fed workforce. The concluding section explores issues which might alleviate the current status quo, and areas which might need further research.

Conclusions

The people shall govern ....[16]

All solutions to any problem need to centre on those on whom these decisions will have an impact. The consultative process entrenched in the new government's RDP scheme will need to be used to the full, to hear the views of the unspoken for women and children in rural as well as urban areas. The agenda for the future if there is one will need to acknowledge fully the rights of all to basic facilities.

Finance is probably the most crucial factor determining infrastructure development. There are no easy ways in which the new government can fund its plans without considering considerable restructuring of the current taxation system. High taxation however is a sensitive policy to push in any country. Possibly methods of cross subsidisation can be devised whereby area rates are paid for services supply. Thus more affluent suburbs would pay more in service charges for their better quality regular supply than would township dwellers. The known revenues from 'grey area' production of commodities such as armaments might be re-ploughed into development projects in order to reduce the ethical questioning of arms sales to the continent.

The willpower to institute such change is also lacking. However there are various examples of economies which have managed in the past or more recently to improve drastically their infrastructure coverage - with and without the sanction of the IMF: Cuba and Tanzania before the end of the cold war and more recently Ghana and parts of Southern Nigeria. The former two tried (and failed) to use classic socialist forms of development, whilst the latter two took more of a mixed approach - with mixed results.

Two countries which have distinct similarities to and differences from South Africa are Nigeria and the United Kingdom. The former, a one time British colony like South Africa, has a population estimated at between ninety and one hundred million of considerable ethnic, religious and class diversity. In the 1970s it experienced an upturn in its economy due to profits from oil revenues during the energy crisis. This enabled the government to provide and upgrade local infrastructure extensively throughout the country. Education, health, power and sanitation projects were implemented with varied success.

Initial infrastructure was provided on a quasi socialist model: the government proposed to finance and provide infrastructure to all citizens. Political, religious and class conflicts however soon ensured that equitable provision was never achieved. However considerable increases in provision were achieved in the two decades, (Figures 14.1 and 14.2) and translated into increased human development in the areas of literacy and health. With the downturn of the economy in the 1980s the government could no longer provide or maintain these facilities.

The adoption of structural adjustment policies by the then government resulted in the withdrawal of government involvement or subsidisation of many services and privatisation. This also encouraged community development projects in regions renowned in the past for their local organisation and motivation in self help issues. Human development indicators in the 1980s show a substantial decrease in literacy and health in Nigeria. These figures however are global for all of Nigeria.

When regional figures are examined, the disparities are however more glaring. Generally Southern Nigeria suffered less decline than the North due to the 'community motivation factor', which they are renowned for. The new free market infrastructure provision mode which the country now espouses has however begun more gradually to have effects in the North.

Britain, or more specifically England and Wales, has the closest relationship in the developed world to South Africa, as up until 1910 it was a British Colony. Social infrastructure provision started late during the industrial revolution. Prior to this the vestiges of the feudal system of land tenure meant that peasants had no ownership of property and had minimal services provided at the whim of their employers.

The health and sanitation acts which were drawn up in the mid 19th century set the stage for public service provision. Initially many public services were privately or municipally owned. However by the post-war years the Beveridge reforms resulted in the public infrastructure system becoming fully state owned and provided.[17] Based on socialist theory, state built public sector housing was also built.

By the late 1970s with a change of government the dismantling of the state infrastructure began. Currently most public utilities have been privatised, and there is evidence to suggest this process will continue. This change to privatisation has resulted in financial hardship for significant numbers of the population. The state burden of paying for the indigent is also considerable. Furthermore the unit costs of provision of most privatised services has worked out considerably more expensive to the local consumer.

These two country discussions show the hazards of privatisation, in both developing and developed economies. Although the privatisation trend is global and supported by many of the financial institutions like the World Bank, its success in the area of social development remains questionable. Ghana the world bank's financial 'success story' in Africa had to have specially designed 'safety net' programmes to alleviate the effects of privatisation and free market economics on social welfare activities such as education and health.

South Africa's RDP acknowledges the historic deprivation and neglect of most of the Black population. Its programme objectives will need to evolve more flexible approaches to infrastructure development, as this is the most important step in future planning approaches. It is likely that there could be much better co-ordination and planning of non governmental and private institutions' contributions towards this (for example see Holland and Ashley, 1993 and Prey 1994). To begin to attack the problem, adequate financial resources, better communications and flexibility would be crucial.

In all, infrastructure will continue to play an important role in development. It has already, in most of the world, become more complex and wide-ranging with the introduction of telecommunications and the 'information superhighway'. This development threatens to revolutionise work modes and forms of production, as evidenced by Indian based computer programmers working by satellite with multinational firms in the USA.

For South Africa and indeed the rest of sub Saharan Africa to 'catch up' in development terms, it is necessary to ensure that much more is done to close the growing gap between the affluent few and the poor majority. Affordable, equitably distributed services and social infrastructure are a basic human right which every government has a duty to provide to all its citizens. Until this is done 'these freedoms' [18] will still need to be fought for.

Notes

1   Beavon K, in Drakakis Smith (1992, p.67).
2   Thompson (1990, pp. 200- 201).

3 Not being an historian, all historical references are from secondary sources; mainly Davenport (1987), Thompson (1990) and also Bundy (1983).
4 In the 19th century, mission stations in 'Reserves' were already segregated, and there had been some 'locations' initially for Asians but the first Act of Parliament establishing the basis for this was the 1902 Native Reserve Location Act.
5 District Six was proclaimed as a white group area, (renamed Zonnenbloem) in 1966/7, whilst Sophiatown had been 're-zoned' as a White Group Area and renamed Triomf since 1956.
6 Better known as Soweto, substantial contributions from a mining house helped in the construction of approximately 750,000 houses in gridiron layout on the original site and service plots.
7 Statistics in the Race Relations Survey, (SAIRR, 1994) and information in Legassick (1983, pp. 175-200) bear this out.
8 Remittances from husbands working in South Africa were often irregular and contributed very little in real terms to development programmes.
9 For more on 'civics' see Seekings, J. in Moss, G. (1992).
10 For example the National Health and Education Policies, (launched in June and August 1994 respectively). (See ANC, 1955; ANC, 1994c; ANC, 1994a; and Horen, 1993)
11 The classic book describing this is 'Passing For White' (Watson, 1970). More recently Christopher (1994) has a section devoted to this.
12 Blacks in Natal for example often converted to Islam to be reclassified as Indians, and thus gain admission into Indian schools which guaranteed better access to higher education than Black schools.
13 Evidenced by the author whilst in South Africa from January to April 1994. Attending a series of workshops and conferences the dearth of Black women delegates and speakers was very noticeable.
14 The ANC's Education Renewal Strategy (part of its manifesto for the 1994 elections) and the new White discussion Paper on Education, both have substantial sections on pre-primary education.
15 SAIRR (1994, pp. 350-351).
16 Part of the ANC Freedom Charter, related in the Kliptown Declaration in 1955 (ANC, 1955).
17 The Beveridge Plan was developed between 1942 and 1944, and the Welfare State legislation came into being between 1944 and 1948.
18 Paraphrased from the Freedom Charter 'These freedoms we will fight for side by side, throughout our lives until we have won our liberty' (ANC, 1955).

Plate 14.1 Shanty Housing in Port Elizabeth.

Table 14.1 Access to electricity amongst South African households.

TYPE OF HOUSEHOLD	% WITH ELECTRICITY
URBAN	59
RURAL	10

Source: Van Horen et al Saldru, South Africa, 1993.

Table 14.2 Inadequate sanitation and water supply in South Africa.

REGION	% WITHOUT PIPE-BORNE WATER	% WITHOUT SANITATION
PWV	15	23
WC	10	10
NC	17	63
EC	15	27
OFS	22	42
N	27	36
ET	17	40
NT	62	73
WT	32	49
AVERAGE	19	31

Source: Van Horen et al Saldru, South Africa, 1993.

15 Modernist housing policy and tradition

Peter King

Introduction

The purpose of this chapter is to examine the manner in which current housing policy, dominated by a modernist epistemic, threatens the traditional and habitual relationship of dwellers with their environment. We shall analyse the nature of modernist housing policy and suggest that its essence is the problematisation of housing. Modernity's attempt to solve the 'problem' of housing is effectively to nationalise provision through a concentration on material aggregations. We shall go on to explore the conditions whereby traditional - or vernacular - dwelling may be protected and nurtured. We shall show that we cannot experience and maintain our implicit relationships and practices without the 'whereness' of place (Relph, 1985).

Modernist housing policy

We can characterise housing policy as being concerned with the solving of problems. It is about the eradication and prevention of the problem of 'bad' housing; the problem of the provision of a sufficient quantity of 'good' housing; the problem of who pays for housing and how much; and so on. Housing policy, it is presumed, exists because these problems exist. We need a policy of action and reaction because of the problem of 'bad' housing.

Such a characterisation depends upon three suppositions. Firstly, it assumes that problems can be properly and meaningfully identified and it assumes we can differentiate the 'good' from the 'bad'. Secondly, it assumes that once a problem is identified it can be solved through specific actions - it assumes that a technology of intervention is possible. Thirdly, and following on from the above, there is the assumption that the identification of problems makes them predictable.

Problems are thus reducible by the efficacy of the technology of policy into technical questions.

However, it has become increasingly clear that this technicality merely disguises the normativity of the process of policy making, rather than eradicating it (Foucault, 1980, 1988). Policy making is a technology of power and domination based on the normative prescriptions of those with authority. As Foucault (1976, 1978) has described it this is a process of normalisation aimed at reducing the subject to a specific model of subjectivity. We could almost say it is the objectivisation of the subject - the construction of Humanity out of our individual humanity.

Housing policy, when it is implemented, thus goes beyond the solving of technical problems. It attempts to construct, contain and control processes within the bounds of a normalising universalism. In short, it is a process which aims to suggest one solution and one means of implementation.

This has led to a policy whose major concern is for the material aggregation of dwellings. It has emphasised material standards and the technical issues of control and management of dwellings to ensure they maintain such standards. Housing is often judged according to standards deemed necessary to undertake a civilised life. The problem for policy makers is thus that there is a deficit of housing to a particular standard. The problem is frequently phrased in terms of the 'need' for such housing, to which all citizens are deemed to have a right. The practice of housing management - as a process of policy implementation - is thus about placing households in 'need' in suitable accommodation according to some rationing system.

This determination of 'need', and the attempt to meet it, is effectively nationalised. The level of resources deemed to be necessary to meet 'need' ensures that government takes on the role of policy maker and provider. Problems are seen as national ones, and accordingly solutions are also posited on a national basis. Solutions are determined, in part at least, by the results of aggregation. The result is a homogenising process whereby needs are generalised within standardised categories whose significance is determined by the results of aggregation.

The results of this process of aggregation, as critics such as Power (1987), Turner (1972, 1976) and Ward (1985, 1990) have pointed out leads to monolithic structures and heteronomy. Decisions are taken out of the control of the users and placed with technicians deemed to have expertise in the 'problem' of housing provision. Solutions are seen as being exclusive and total, and consequently resources are provided overwhelmingly for one particular policy.

However, because these solutions have a normative basis (they are based on 'ought' statements that cannot be justified by a non-circular argument), they are liable to frequent change. We have seen this, for example, with the switch in resources in many countries from direct provision, to site and services in the

1970s (Skinner and Rodell, 1983). One complete solution was replaced by another, apparently with no sense of irony.

These totalising solutions are typical of a policy based on the modernist ethic. The concern for the overarching principle or metanarrative (Lyotard, 1984) formed the core of public policy. Problems were to be permanently solved by the use of rational and scientific techniques. These would deliver the correct solutions, which could then be implemented by those experts with the requisite skills.

A further aspect of the modernist epistemic is the attempt to re describe subjectivity as isolated from history. As Kolb states, modernity was:

> the attempt to institutionalise an individual or social subject free from traditional restrictions. The modern individual or community is supposed to be able to make its life and places as it chooses them to be; in the strictest sense it would have no traditions or places, since nothing would locate it except facts laid out for judgement and manipulation. (1990, p.6)

Modernity sees traditions as restrictions that distract from the project of developing a universal individual essence (Berlin, 1969). Thus the traditions of urban communities were, and are, seen as a hindrance to progress. In place of traditions and accepted practices modernity insists upon a calculating rationality that allows the individual to determine their best interests, presumably with the assistance and direction of experts. We can see this modernist totalism in Kemeny's description of household decision making:

> Households acquire a dwelling with a view to match existing and projected household budgets and the life cycle space needs, and to harmonise and compromise between the sometimes conflicting priorities of household members concerning space and facility needs. (1992, p.11)

Households are thus deemed able to make, monitor and evaluate choices on the basis of specific isolatable purposes. The purpose, implied in Kemeny's definition, is that of the rational maximisation of utility. This is to describe households as positive entities which have no historical baggage to encumber their decision making. Moreover it is a definition that apparently internalises the interests of households, describing them as a self enclosed unit separated from the locality and community.

However, as commentators such as Power (1987) have shown, the consequences of this positivistic approach is by no means value neutral. Power has described how the combination of slum clearance and delays in redeveloping led to the dispersal of urban communities in Britain. This dispersal saw the destruction of forms of interaction that had developed and been nurtured for generations. Instead the diversity of these vernacular communities was replaced by rigid forms of provision that were uniform in their purpose and appearance. The tragedy of this policy was that the destruction of certain dwellings and the preservation of neighbouring ones was largely arbitrary (Ward, 1985).

The result of modernist heteronomy was to homogenise systems of housing provision, firstly across the developed world, but increasingly into all parts of the globe. Forms of provision have become globalised, but according to a rubric determined by a eurocentric hegemony. Illich (1992) has described this process as the creation of residents, who reside in garages, provided by a central authority:

> Housing provides cubicles in which residents are housed. Such housing is planned, built and equipped for them. To be allowed to dwell minimally in one's own housing constitutes a special privilege: only the rich may move a door or drive a nail in a wall. The vernacular space of dwelling is replaced by the homogenous space of the garage. Settlements look the same from Taiwan to Ohio and from Lima to Peking. Everywhere you find the same garage for the human - shelves to store the workforce overnight, handy for the means of transportation. Inhabitants dwelling in spaces they fashion have been replaced by residents sheltered in buildings produced for them duly registered as consumers of housing, protected by the Tenants' or the Credit Receivers' Act. (1992, pp.57-8)

The particular effects of such a policy has been shown graphically by Turner's discussion of the 'supportive shack' and the 'oppressive house' (Turner, 1976, pp. 54-59). Turner shows that a dwelling built to modern standards of amenity in Mexico City in 1971 may not actually benefit the household, despite the fact that it provides higher space and amenity standards. This is because it does not fit the particular lifestyle and lifecycle needs of the household. The household consisted of a middle-aged mason, his wife and son. The house was situated away from their network of friends and from the mason's employment. He paid 5% of his income on transport to and from work, in addition to 55% spent on rent and utility charges. In addition, his wife had previously run a small vending business from home, and this was forbidden by the tenancy regulations. Thus not only were they incurring greater housing costs, but they were forced to live on a reduced income (p. 56). This situation was despite the fact that the dwelling was subsidised and aimed at meeting housing need.

This particular dwelling proved to be an imposition on the household. It was not, and could not be personalised, and it did not arise out of the interaction of the household with the community or the local environment. It took no account of the specific needs of the household and offered them no opportunity to correct this situation. The dwelling offered a uniform and inimical framework for dwelling. It did not respect the traditions of the households and the community. Finally, it did not really assist the household, or improve their material conditions. It rather dominated them and restricted their ability to function creatively and autonomously. Turner compares this dwelling unfavourably with the 'supportive shack', a self built temporary dwelling, which is close to the dweller's place of work and allows them to save for something better in the future. Whilst this dwelling is of relatively poor quality, it allows the household the maximum level of autonomy they could expect in their current circumstances.

The form of heteronomy, typified by Turner's description of the 'oppressive house', destroys local tradition, and with it both the social cohesion of the community and the significance of dwelling for the individuals within the community. We now need to look at these traditions and their significance to dwelling, and consequently why they should be protected, developed and maintained.

The habitual, implicit and the traditional

We need not, however, restrict our description of housing to the conceits of modernity. Housing need not be seen in terms of a problem that is seeking to be solved. We can see housing as a holistic concept concerned with possibilities determined by use. Housing can be seen as the possibility for fulfilling our purposes - as a process within which the technology of the self may operate (Foucault, 1988). Housing is here described as an activity and not as a facility, and thus it is better described by the term dwelling, which also emphasises the holism of this concept. Dwelling is more than 'to house'. It is to live on the earth as humans (Heidegger, 1993). Dwelling encloses our activities of settlement, interaction, dialogue and privacy (Norberg-Schulz, 1985).

Dwelling differs from the model of housing policy in a further fundamental respect. Housing policy, through its technology of problem solving, treats the practice of living as an explicit process. Housing is something that we can identify, quantify, grade, select and generally decide upon; it is where our needs, preferences and desires are apparent, and having been expressed, may be met by the appropriate response. Yet housing - as dwelling - is not something that we experience in this explicit sense. We do not hold the significance of our housing in consciousness. It is rather an implicit relation that manifests itself when the activity of dwelling is either displaced or disrupted. Dwelling, at least for those with the requisite freedom of action, is determined by habitual and implicit processes, limited only by the particular context in which these acceptable forms of behaviour operate.

Successful dwelling is not planned, manufactured and imposed on communities and households. It rather develops out of the practice of living as households within communities. It is more than the production and consumption of houses, but rather relates to the way in which households, individually and collectively, interact with the environment.

However, this interaction is not a conscious process. We do not relate to the community or the environment in a necessarily deliberative manner. The relationship rather takes place at the level of 'practical consciousness' (Giddens, 1991) where we do not consider or question our actions directly. We rather experience this interaction implicitly through our involvement in recognisable and understandable processes. One such process is that of dwelling. We do not consciously dwell because we cannot exist outside of this process - our dwelling encloses us. The ends which dwelling fulfils hides its obvious functioning. As Heidegger states dwelling:

> remains for man's everyday experience that which is from the outset 'habitual' ... For this it recedes behind the manifold ways in which dwelling is accomplished. (1993, pp.349-350)

Dwelling is an everyday experience and we live through it. Dwelling does not exist separately from us. It is therefore more than the physicality of housing that offers us shelter. Dwelling is rather the layered process in which our private refuge is linked to public institutions, urban space and human settlement generally (Norberg-Schulz, 1985). It thus relates the personal with the social - the individual and the community through the mutual interdependence of each layer of dwelling. The public level that serves to establish and maintain common values is in part determined by the nature of settlement within the surrounding environment; in part by the exchange of ideas and goods within the institutional space above it; and in part by the value individual households attach to their dwelling which allows them to contribute to the creation and perpetuation of these values.

The implicit nature of dwelling is particularly significant in this holistic notion of dwelling. Dwelling, in its interconnectedness, relies on tradition for the transmission of meaning. Traditions can be seen as developing out of implicit practices. The implicit is that which develops non-consciously into the recognisable, the comfortable and the secure. As a result of these features the practice becomes one of habit. We repeat the practice habitually as it reinforces our desire for security and basic trust (Giddens, 1991). Through interaction at the public level these habits are woven into traditions that form the cultural support to dwelling and which dwelling itself supports. Thus, by a process of public dialogue and discussion our habits become referenced with acceptability through social interaction. This process, like dwelling itself, is an implicit one. We do not create traditions consciously and deliberately. Traditions are invented, but only through the practice of interaction in dwelling.

Traditions are often perceived as being backward looking and reactionary. Even such writers as Foucault and Heidegger who emphasise the implicit and local character of inter subjectivity are suspicious of tradition. However, traditions should not be seen as conservative or static. We do not propose a description of dwelling based on the rigidities of existing practice. Rather, traditions should be seen as both conserving and dynamic. They preserve those elements of a community and culture that reinforce the values and practices that are meaningful. This significance alters over time as the nature of interaction and its context changes. The implicit practices that determine traditions develop and change over time and this will leak into communal activities and values. Traditions may appear to be static because of the implicit nature of their development. Consciousness of tradition is by definition a retrospective action.

The importance of traditions are therefore in their relation to everyday practice - in terms of what they allow and facilitate. We can suggest a number of reasons, relating to the practice of dwelling, for the stressing of traditions. Firstly, to emphasise tradition is to be anti-elitist. Traditions embody the mechanics of daily life and what is recognisable to the dwellers. Secondly, the traditional is readily understandable and thus inclusive. Thirdly, traditions are localised through reference to a specific community and its history. In this sense traditions are inimicable to generalised and universal standards. Instead provision is linked to a particular local context. Fourthly, traditions emphasise participation: they are the practices of the users. Fifthly, and perhaps most significantly, traditions in the dwelling process - in its widest sense - are important because they show us the means by which needs are fulfilled. The particular ways in which the dwelling process operates are the results of vernacular attempts at fulfilling needs. Traditions can therefore be seen as implicit means of fulfilment. They are expressions of the expectations of individuals mediated through communities in the form of often formalised behaviour and the expression of hopes and beliefs. They offer effective limits across which an individual will be reluctant to transgress. Traditions can be seen to express a framework of acceptable agency that binds individuals into communities through a tacit recognition of needs, duties and responsibilities. These interrelations are part of the dynamic public discussion on which public dwelling is based.

Thus traditions are related to a community - they are social traditions. Indeed, it is fallacious to suggest that we can exist beyond or outside of the social. As Gross (1992) has suggested, all socialisation and enculturation relies on tradition in the form of tacit knowledge. Communities exist within traditions in as much as they are social entities. The notion of dwelling recognises this basic axiom. Yet this does not signify that the individual is reduced to a cipher of communal imperatives. The levels within dwelling are not hierarchical, but rather co-equal and co-determinant.

Tradition and location

The needs, duties and responsibilities tacitly recognised within traditions are not universal. They are rather contextualised by their implementation and the practical possibilities exhibited by this process. This context forms the conditions by, or more precisely, in which needs are fulfilled. The exact nature of the fulfilment will differ temporally as traditions develop and change. But they will differ also spatially. Dwelling, to reiterate, is the interaction of household within the environment. It is not an abstraction derived from a totalising discourse, but rather the practice of living within specific conditions. These conditions are determined by location.

Human dwelling cannot be pursued without place. Casey (1993) suggests that we would find it both difficult and disturbing to conceive of a placeless world. Dwelling needs to be located, and this location should be recognisable and reinforcing. A recognisable place helps the individual to identify with the community and the wider environment. It offers a permanence and sense of meaning to relationships with those sharing the location. In addition a place can orientate the individual by offering a centre and boundary from which to journey out of and return to (Norberg-Schulz, 1985).

This identification and orientation can be traced through the levels of dwelling. It locates the individual within a specific dwelling that is meaningful and helps to secure the individual within a community. The dwelling provides both a boundary - a refuge - and a secure platform from which to enter into the public domain. It gives public life meaning through the definition and relationship of institutions in which daily practice can occur and common values can be maintained. Communities identify with urban space as a focus for interaction and exchange. They are orientated through the cultural focus of collective dwelling. Finally identification and orientation occurs at the level of settlement through the relation to the natural environment which we live alongside.

Therefore, location is the medium in which traditions operate. It is literally the space in which our implicit practices grow into social traditions. Thus the value of traditions cannot be separated or abstracted from the place in which they have developed. Households and communities are tied to a place because this is where practices are recognisable.

But traditions also mould the places in which we dwell. Traditions, as a frame limiting acceptable moral agency, help to determine how we use, create and mould place. Traditions thus shape the expression of our identification with and orientation towards our environment (Norberg-Schulz, 1985). Thus we can suggest that traditions assist us in creating *our place* out of the surrounding environment.

We again must resist any conclusion of conservatism or stasis in this description. The significance of location relates to the meanings attached to it. As traditions develop and practices change so will the boundaries of significance. Location can be perceived as the nation, the locale, household space and so on. We live in different spaces concurrently (Massey, 1994), which do not contradict because they are separated by the distinct meanings we attach to them. Our perceptions of location will alter with the context that locates us. Thus traditions are dynamic.

Indeed the importance of traditions is precisely this dynamism, and this is why they should be conserved.

The conservation of tradition

The importance of our discussion of tradition and dwelling is that it offers an opening towards an alternative to the modernist conception of housing policy. We have presented a description of located traditions that differs by the context in which they have developed and continue to operate. They have been described as being developed and maintained through an implicit process that is definitionally local.

However, we could also suggest that such traditions are threatened, if not already dead. Such a view would be misleading as the logic of the above argument has indicated. Communities exist within traditions in as much as they are social entities. They are therefore capable of the development and support of traditions.

The issue is not of the death of tradition, but rather the domination of a particular tradition that has overcome others. We can suggest that the erstwhile implicit practices of certain Northern European communities have become dominant and been reified into intentional globalised practices. The economic and technological dominance of the West has allowed its traditions to be seen as permanent and universal prescriptions applicable to all communities regardless of context. Post-enlightenment traditions of rationality and scepticism are not seen as the condition of humanity.

The issue is therefore one of breaking the dominance of certain overarching traditions now operating as metanarratives. This is essentially a matter of redistributing the control of resources and the break up of dominant centres of power. It is only through localised control of, and access to, resources that communities will be able to conserve and activate their implicit processes into traditions. In doing so they will greatly enhance the stability and sustainability of the dwelling process. The nature of housing as an existentially significant activity (Turner, 1972) implies that it should be under the control of the users. It is only dwellers who are able to judge the viability of the process simply because they can determine provision according to their implicit practices.

Conclusion

Two issues stand out as being of particular importance to the process of place-making. The first is to suggest that the major means of protecting tradition is to foster *informal processes* and to place modernity and its attendant technologies and processes at the service of communities. Modernity dominates by the technologies of control it commands. The informal is thus a threat to it as it implies that certain processes are beyond this control. The central issue is the notion of control and the consequent limits that are placed on technologies and processes.

The second issue, which is a necessary prerequisite for a re-determination of control, is to recognise the ubiquity of tradition, not as a series of restrictions, but as necessary to a community. This involves the recognition of modernity as a particular set of practices which deny their own temporality. Thus the problem is not with tradition itself, but in the ossification of a particular tradition of progress perversely based on the very denial of the possibility of progression beyond itself.

16 A study of a house type with an open space

Aysu Baskaya and Martin Symes

Research Overview

The main goal of this paper is to examine the typology of a house type with an open space as a part of the urban structure. In this work, as in the work of Aldo Rossi (1982), dwelling is seen as the major component of urban structure. The form in which residential building types are realised is closely bound up with the urban form and with the way of life, the latter being more easily transformable.

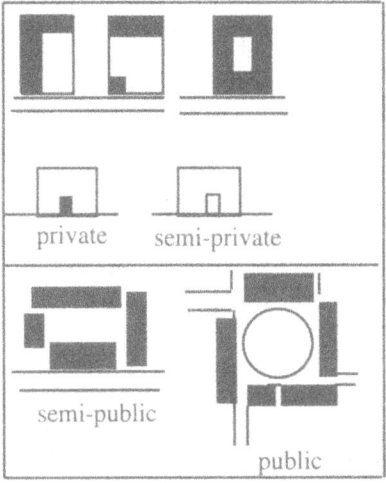

Figure 16. 1 Different uses of open space.

The study focuses on vernacular housing traditions and particularly multi-family use of the type in Ortigia. This is examined as an alternative to the single family house type with an open space in Gaziantep. The appropriateness of multi-family use of the type and urban design components of vernacular settlements are analysed. Particular attention is given to the study of the process leading to the organisation and use of private and semi-private open spaces. These fill a unique niche in vernacular settlements within the city, functioning as a transitional link between the inside and the outside world (Figure 16.1). The contrast between individual and collective use is one of the principal viewpoints from which the open space of the type is considered in this paper as it manifests the relationship between these spheres.

The study explains the conceptual framework of socio-spatial structure and helps us to understand how the house type with an open space fits cultural requirements. Its ability to satisfy the cultural desire for privacy is studied. It looks for the relevance the type has for contemporary development and gives a perspective in terms of how the designed and built environment can better serve the needs of human beings and different populations. The study also considers whether the open space concept can be combined with modern housing design criteria.

The impetus behind the use of this study is to return to the same quality of design as in previous vernacular architecture. As McHarg indicates (1957, p.74), the introverted house facing upon one more internal courts can provide a residential environment in an urban world. It is believed that the house type with an open space does meet the criteria of providing a milieu for family life within the city, and an appropriate environment for favourable interactions. Especially for the survival of the traditional cultures dealt with in this study, it is assumed that a central organisation is required in the building. This means life organised around an open space. Accordingly, the traditional house type, with an invisible or partly visible open space, provides clues to direct and improve the functional design and quality of contemporary dwelling units. Finally we can argue that the major problem of modern housing and its most conspicuous failure lies in the distribution and design of this open space. The question is: how can this open space concept be incorporated in multi-family living?

The study referred to shows some applications of the diachronic development of the typological process. The main purpose of this typological work is to promote the value of establishing associations between the cultural heritage and new design proposals. In this work, typology can be broadly defined as the study of the artefacts based on form and content, that is, cultural meaning. In this process of experience, history is the necessary condition as a system of time-spatial relations. Following a system of diachronic and synchronic variations, we can recognise that the typological process, generally, does not involve only transformation of function but also spatial transformation of the type. Hence, by reading the typological process with the help of recent data and inherited traces, we may understand the type better.

It can be postulated that every solution is based on past experience and is an interpretation of the archetype. As is argued in the works of structuralists (Levi-Strauss, 1966; van Eyck, 1961, pp.26-28; Hertzberger, 1967, pp.14-18; Tice, 1993, pp.162-163; and Broadbent, 1980, pp.125), man has for thousands of years repeated himself and re-evaluated the existing in order to make it more suitable for current circumstances. In this process, despite the changing environments and culture, the continuity of basic requirements e.g. the need for privacy, access to light and air, and proximity to nature have given rise to distinct housing types in diverse cultures that remain relevant today. Accordingly the continued livability of traditional housing patterns such as terraced houses, semi-detached houses, courtyard houses support this hypothesis.

According to Caniggia and Maffei (1984), these house types are the result of the human experience and of the homogenous development systems of a culture, in adherence to inherited culture, which they called *spontaneous conscience*. It is easy to find a gradual modification of these housing types in different periods. That means that in every period we can come across different concepts of types drawn from the previous ones. That is why it is worth knowing the cultural dimension of architecture. This helps us to understand how the ones we have are informed by our recent past (Robinson, 1991, p.162). This regularity lets us discover a considerable degree of continuity between similar products. The result of this process might help us to produce alternative products for different cultural realities and enable us to generate new building types, modifying existing cultural values.

Definition of the problem

Although the main section of this paper reports on housing in Sicily, the context of the study is given by the problems perceived in Turkey. In the last twenty to thirty years, south-eastern Turkey, particularly the town called Gaziantep, has undergone rapid urban development. The process of urban dynamics destroyed habits, customs, functions and interests and unavoidably changed the use and the form of old city structures. The dwellings are renewed according to new cultural standards. They are added to and altered with new technologies. This paper draws on the need for suitable housing by examining what is left of traditional housing. In addition it defines the problem in relation to the use and organisation of vernacular settlements and rapid urban development.

The main difficulty comes with the use of the vernacular single family house which does not fit either the requirements of dense urban pressure or the requirements of present users. The single-family buildings with capacious open spaces on very large plots mean extremely low densities. The spatial organisation no longer fulfils the socio-cultural requirements of the households. For instance, the main living parts of the house i.e. *liwan* and living room are away from service units i.e. kitchen, toilet, etc. which causes some inconvenience especially in winter. Apart from this, the huge increase in population creates an intense demand for housing. In the last twenty or thirty years, people started giving their land in suburban areas to self-builders to construct a block of flats. In this way traditional houses are being destroyed to be replaced by high rise building blocks. So we can say that self-built housing dominates the urbanisation process in south-eastern Turkey.

The ratios are set by the government to prevent over utilisation of land in dense urban areas. However, these limited regulations have resulted in development of new housing typologies completely different from vernacular ones. Owing to economy in plot areas, in many cases high densities with five to six floors have been achieved where gridiron layouts tend to create monotonous and rigid patterns. Hence a similar arrangement of large blocks of flats with front and backyards has been repeated. The emergence of the block of flats as a standard contemporary house design has failed to meet some cultural needs of the people and the demands of the local climate. These multi family blocks have never been liked by most of the inhabitants in the south-eastern part of Turkey where people prefer to live on the ground with their open spaces, ensuring maximum privacy and a "surrounded" space for outdoor activities.

In contemporary organisation, the outdoor living is left outside of form, surrounding the dwelling, and the use of space turns inside out. As Kenneth (1986) describes it space in traditional form is introverted, and the open space becomes inside which means we are *inside* the house. In contemporary design, the form of the house is placed within a space and the space is defined by the form it surrounds. This concept has been enforced by zoning regulations. The open outdoor space is no longer protected and sheltered by the dwelling's structure; it is totally exposed. We are *outside* the house (Figure 16.2).

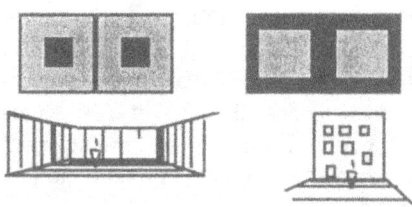

Figure 16.2 Traditional and contemporary organisation of space.

Adoption of the new model has created a conflict between the architectural outdoor design and the physical and social needs of the residents. This process may be regarded as inadequate because of the lack of continuity with the old urban fabric.

The people forced to live in contemporary multi-family dwelling blocks say that a flat in a block is more appropriate for living: it is convenient, useful, comfortable and better planned with all spaces arranged on the same level but they also say it is small in size and closed in character. They say that they cannot breath there and describe the place as a "modern prison". On the other hand, vernacular houses are warmer in winter, cooler in summer, restful, inviting, spacious, large and durable but need more organisation, are poorly planned, uncomfortable and not convenient. It can be said that despite the apparent modernism and changing culture in the area, the urban population is still very traditional and keeps some of traditional values going. That suggests that the main traditional design features are still required in contemporary design. The people are still looking for a new housing typology which is well-balanced with their requirements regarding socio-cultural necessities and thermal comfort. It is intended to establish in this study which housing characteristics are suitable to the people living in the towns of the south-eastern part of Turkey, particularly in Gaziantep.

According to research in the old traditional settlement of Gaziantep, housing components such as open space, multi-functional rooms, and *liwan,* and urban components, such as narrow streets, cul-de-sacs and small squares can be considered as the main characteristics of traditional settlements. And hence it can be postulated that these may make it possible to achieve contemporary user requirements particularly in terms of privacy and comfort within the neighbourhood (Figure 16.3).

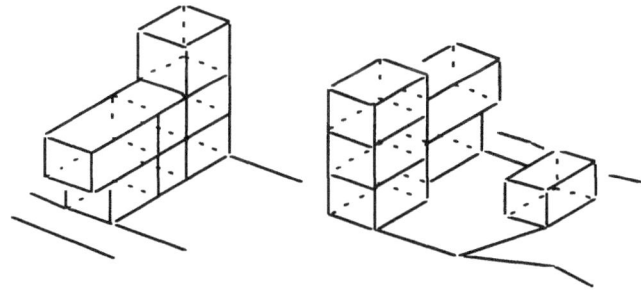

Figure 16.3 Schematic drawings of the house types in Gaziantep .

Taking into account basic housing components and the enforcement of urban design principles achieving privacy and security, and aiming to save urban land, it is possible to achieve the formation of appropriate housing design in the area. Some indications that this is feasible may be drawn from the research undertaken in Sicily, which will now be described.

Example of Ortigia

The objective in this part is to assess the current organisation and use of traditional dwellings and settlements in Ortigia. This is achieved through an analysis of information about housing typology. Then, socio-cultural impacts on the continuity of vernacular forms of the house type in the town are considered and the need for suitable housing is established by examining what is left of traditional housing. The earliest one is one hundred or one and fifty years old. The current users living in these traditional dwellings are questioned and interviewed. The place Ortigia is selected for a number of reasons, but principally because of its connections with the history of the type, from the ancient period till the present. It is the first Greek settlement on the island of Sicily and gives examples of the house type called *casa corte*.

Historical Analysis

There is no typology given about Ortigia houses which can explain how the space has been transformed over time. However it is known that the need for multi-family houses produced the railing house called *la casa ringhiera* (Caniggia and Maffei, 1984). This is the result of several transformations from the *domus* type, that is, the Greek-Roman house into the higher density Roman apartment building called *insula* type. This is seen as the generator matrix of the type with an open space or without. The house type in Ortigia has been drawn both from the single family house *domus* and from the *insula*. In these examples, the common dominator is a prevalence of internal residences formed around an open space, the type is a basic element creating the model and it is a microcosm of the city constituting the urban structure, either in its regular or irregular form (Figure 16.4).

Many of the features of this house type, with Greek and Roman origins, in Ortigia remained little changed for a long time. The population growth has played an important role in this process, since it was built in a walled city on an island. Therefore, expansion outward was limited and new growth was accommodated vertically in the form of third and fourth floors and through the vertical and horizontal subdivision of existing units over time. We can understand this vertical addition by looking at the cornices on the facade.

The changes in social values are related to changes in architectural values, and the form, function and meaning of the architectural product. During the course of time buildings are not only transformed, but also their meanings in relation to use may alter. For instance in ancient periods the ground floor of the insula was a prestigious place to live. Later on, status was established through height. The floor above street level provided privacy and a degree of relief from the pressures of street activity. The previously prestigious place of the type, with one or two rooms on the ground level, was used for service purposes, for storage, for horse and car and servants. The ones facing the street were sometimes for small shops. However today mostly low income families and the people over the age of sixty are accommodated there.

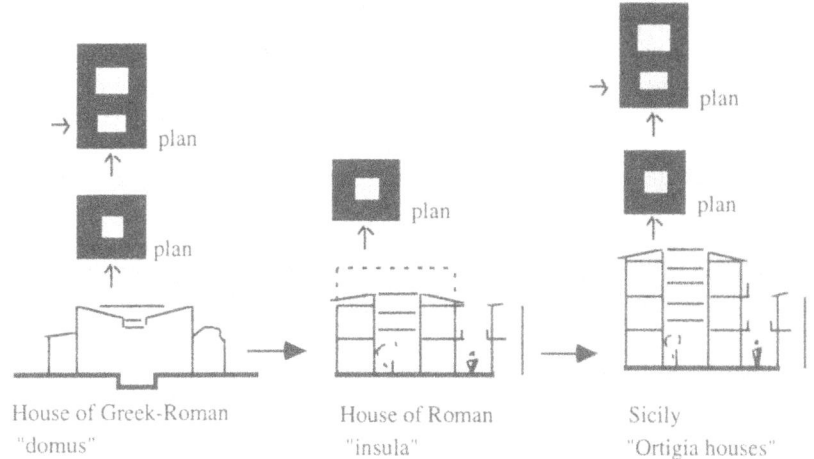

House of Greek-Roman "domus"   House of Roman "insula"   Sicily "Ortigia houses"

Figure 16.4 The evolution of the house type from ancient times till the present.

Dato (1986) gives the typology of house types with an open space in Catania. According to him the first one, dated around 1700, consists of several house blocks where an extended family was living. In a later example the open space was used as a square for the people living around to meet. In 1800, they added two floors on top of this example and the entrance was given an arch to control the open space better. In these semi-public and semi-private relationships, the open space is created over time by the organisation of the living units, mostly terrace houses, around it. It is the result of uniting two basic types into one, preserving an open space inside the physical body. In particular the general shape derives from a doubling frontal body and a second body around the open space. Another type is houses of the wealthy in which a whole block encloses a private open space (Figure 16.5).

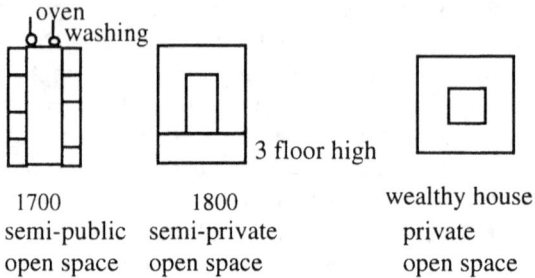

Figure 16.5 The evolution of the house type given by Dato.

The examples of these types can be found very easily in Ortigia. According to oral information given by Liliane Dufour regarding the houses now existing in Ortigia, in the last hundred years only the houses of the well-to-do had an extended family structure. They had servants assigned to a variety of tasks in the house or outside. Even in the changing structure of the town, it is possible to find examples of single family use with two or three stories occupied by more than one family.

In the area of Graziella, in Ortigia, Giuffre talks about the house type called *casa terrena* that was built after the earthquake in 1693 (Giuffre, 1993). This is the house type with one story and with a private open space. Later on in the eighteenth century, new flats were built on top of this single story house to accommodate other families. By that time the wall of the private open space facing the street was demolished to convert the use of space from private into semi-public or semi-private.

After 1861, wealthy people started to leave the area and their houses were subdivided and occupied by many families. However, even today it is possible to find relatives of these people who keep on living in their grandparents' houses. Today, some very large houses have open spaces emphasising the interior of the wealthy house. It is typical for one wealthy house to accommodate between seven and ten families. The open space in such situations is highly decorative; there are big plants and fountains to help cool the air through evaporation. As a result, it becomes a space to be shared sometimes.

By comparing the maps we can understand that, since 1875 the amount of open space on the island has been reduced by more than 60% in order to build more living spaces. This house type with an open space was built by the end of the nineteenth century not only in Ortigia but also very close to Ortigia, in the south part of Siracusa in the area called La Borgata but today it is no longer being built there.

Analysis of the current organisation of the type together with urban components

There are two different house types in the town of Ortigia and the main difference between the two comes with the open space. In this study the blocks with an open space are considered.

Each block is divided into different flats to accommodate more than one family. In order to establish the proper characteristics of this traditional block of flats and to check the appropriateness and usefulness of these in terms of current users' requirements in the area, some building blocks were physically analysed and some households were interviewed and questioned, on different occasions, at different periods of the year in 1993 and 1994. A sample of forty-seven blocks of flats in different locations, were compared and in total fifty households in thirty-five blocks were asked questions about the organisation and the use of their dwellings. The type of difficulties they come across in using the house type was established. The remaining twelve blocks were inaccessible and hence were physically analysed. This was carried out to understand whether the type fulfils contemporary user requirements or not.

Regarding the example, the enclosure of each space is determined by the form of the building and the house is oriented both to the street, on one hand, and to the open space on the other. Hence, the dwelling type is characterised by the definition of a unitary form that encloses an open space and provides multi-family living. In this organisation, the open space of the type is placed, usually, in the centre as a dominant element of the form, kept small and overshadowed by the flats around it (Figure 16.6 and Figure 16.7).

That sort of outdoor place surrounded with flats acts as a ventilation shaft and exposure of vertical surfaces to the sun is minimised. This is partly because of the climatic requirements and partly socio-cultural and economic requirements.

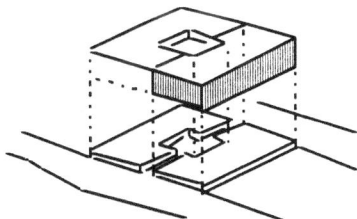

Figure 16.6 Example of the house type in Ortigia.

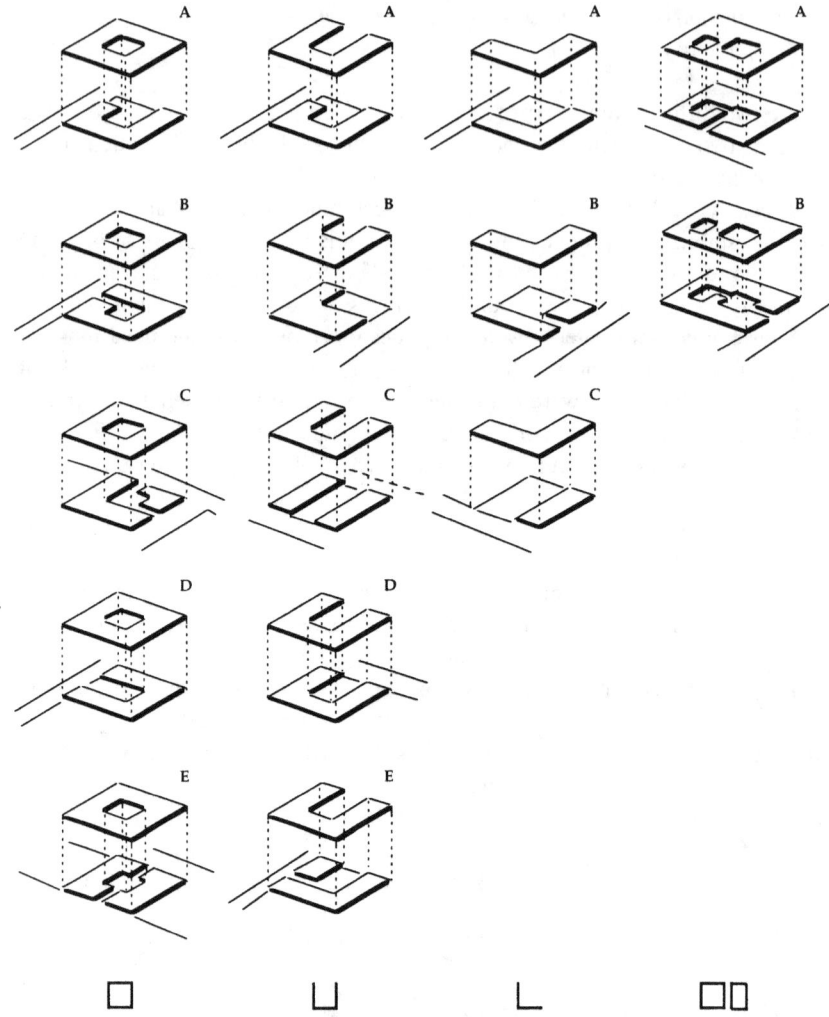

Figure 16.7 Typology of the house type in Ortigia.

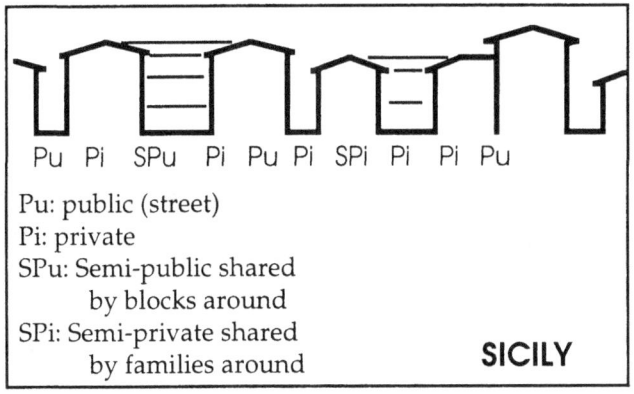

Figure 16.8 Section showing the relation of domains.

The city characteristically comprises public, semi-public, semi-private and private open spaces, varying in the degree of accessibility and enclosure. There are some thresholds such as entrances dividing them into separate quarters as can be recognised in the section of the urban pattern (Figure 16.8). However, the outward looking type of housing and its multi-family use do prevent drawing a clear line between the public and the private spheres. The distinction between public and private spaces is not always clear or consistent. Owing to the fact that all spaces are homogenised, their position is relatively unimportant. Masonry architecture prevails, floors and walls as well as streets are made of hard materials such as stone, giving inside and outside much the same physical appearance. Naturally, where masonry construction prevails, shoes are worn both inside and outside.

To be in visual contact with the outside and to gather direct sunlight and appropriate ventilation, usually the flats have two facades, one to the street and the other to the open space. This is mostly because of the land use that the street and the open space are the only places to get through. For this reason, there are a lot of openings to the outside and to the inside outdoor areas. The house type opens up its facades with big windows and balconies in order to get light into the individual units and extend their constricted space. However, not only the windows and balconies in the facades but also the narrow space between the buildings on both sides of the street neglect privacy and protection. The interior of the house is usually concealed from the street by net curtains, lattices, symbolic objects, a plant etc. These objects that mark the boundary between the street and the buildings, impart a sense of fluidity between the inner and outer order. Visually the lattice functions like one-way mirror, in that it is possible to see from the dark side to the light side but not vice versa. Apart from that these windows do not protect from dust and noise. In consequence, a habitable indoor climate relies entirely on window shutters which are rarely opened.

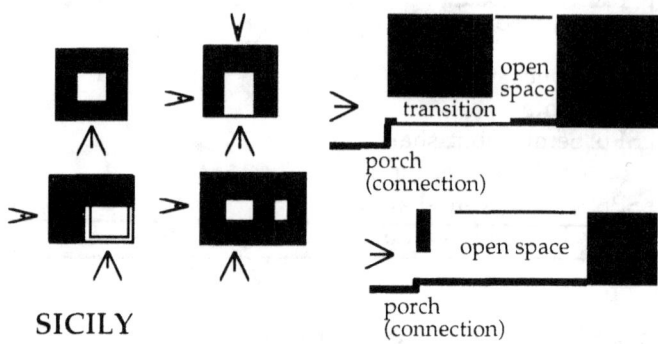

Figure 16.9 Position of main entrance.

The house in Ortigia itself shows many functions within it by its variety of window size and placement of entrance. The position of the main entrance controls the layout of the building and controls the movement to and from the building, determines the configuration of the pattern of the activities within the space behind. The house usually has one entrance that can range from an elaborate to articulated gateway depending on the size of the dwelling (Figure 16.9).

Monumentality can be understood by looking at the dimension of plans and facades. When the house becomes monumental, because of its scale, there is not much difference between the vernacular multi-family house of Ortigia and vernacular public buildings, appearing like an office building rather than a residence. However, the importance of the type in Ortigia does not depend on its monumental qualities but rather arises out of its being repeated as many times as necessary in order to define the city. In this whole building block, open spaces become the constituent cells. Guidoni (1982, p.6) indicates that open spaces and urban components such as narrow streets, *vicolo* (cul-de-sacs), *cortile* (open space) and small squares still exist because they are involved in the structure of the society, they are functional and fit the requirements of the town. We can say that people from Ortigia make these elements an internal part of their daily life and they are crucial elements of their way of life.

User Evaluation Analysis

As a part of the questionnaire survey, households were asked about their satisfaction in terms of organisation and use of their space and thermal comfort.

Table 16.1 Ownership of households.

Ownership	Num	% of total
tenant	11	22
inheritor	3	6
owner	36	72

Table 16.2 Original place of households.

Place	Num	% of total
Siracusa	10	20
Ortigia	29	58
Italy	6	12
others	5	10

Table 16.3 Number of families residing in each block.

Number of families	Num	% of total
1	6	17
2	5	14
3	5	14
4	9	26
5	9	26
6	1	3

Table 16.4 Number of families around the open space on the ground floor.

Number of family	Num	% of total
0	15	43
1	15	43
2	4	11
3	1	3

The majority of the householders questioned, that is 72%, own their houses and their average age is over 50 years. Owning the house and being originally from Siracusa especially from Ortigia, seem the basic reasons for staying there (Table 16.1 and Table 16.2)

The economic and social conditions of the original households are reflected in the size and quality of each housing block. Although the size and complexities of dwellings may change depending on their first owner's economic power and social status, they are inward looking through their open spaces. Hence, regarding the size, the houses are grouped as small, middle and monumental. The monumental ones were wealthy houses originally with two open spaces or two houses around the same open space.

Today the average number of families living in blocks of middle size is four to five (Table 16.3). The access to each flat is mostly from the internal open spaces but some blocks might also have another access from the street leading to the flats upstairs or on the side of the street on the ground floor. In some cases, when there is an independent access to upstairs, enclosed within a volume or subtractive interior stairs (as described by Ching, 1979, p.288) then the ground floor can be occupied by only one family. As a result of this, the open space of the block is a private area being overlooked by the neighbours upstairs. Some of the blocks may accommodate only one family and the open space of the block might be used as a private component of the house (Table 16.4).

The questions about open space are concerned with the need for it and its use. It is important to note that it has not been considered as a place to spend the day. In fact, the internal open spaces in full view of neighbouring houses are unsuitable for private family activities. For that reason 52% of residents prefer to do private housework inside and use the space just to pass through. The interaction amongst the households only occurs when it is necessary to use the open space. For example when the washing had to be put outside to dry (Table 16.5).

As Pagnano indicates, it is possible to distinguish the different use of open space in different groups of houses. It is mainly a transition point between the external public domain and the domestic private domain and functions as the only link between the house interior and the street. It is used in the summer as an extension of ground-floor living rooms, provides for inhabitants to carry on some activities in the open while remaining in comparative privacy between inside and outside, and seclusion from the outside world.

However, not only in the origin but also today, it is difficult to say that the open space was or is private or semi-private or semi-public. In multi-family use, it is an ambiguous space, neither public nor private, neither in nor out. It is clear from the observations that, sometimes a semi-private open space might be considered as exposed semi-public transition space depending on its size, the number of the residences around and the existence of the entrance directed to the open space. In some cases, there is no strong demarcation between the domains. The relationship of the house to the street has undergone significant transformations; either it is direct or the definition of the physical barrier delimiting public from private space is not explicit most of the time. In some cases, the open space is set apart from the street by an iron gate which permits the open space to be read as a partial extension of the city. It might be completely blocked by a wooden gate to make this area invisible from outside.

Table 16.5 Use of open space.

type of use	Num	% of each.
only to pass	26	39
to sit together	16	24
to dry clothes	21	32
to wash clothes	3	5

Table 16.6 Use of balcony.

type of use	Num	% of each.
to dry clothes	19	41
to sit & to have a rest	15	33
don't use (very small)	12	26

Table 16.7 Use of roof.

type of use	Num	% of each.
to dry clothes	19	58
to sit & to have a rest	9	27
do not use	5	15

It is interesting to consider the necessity and use of balconies in Ortigia. The balcony appeared to be as unpopular as the open space. Because of being overlooked by the inhabitants around, residents said that they did not have enough privacy on their balcony because they are too close to other flats. The households who had an open space to use as well as balcony said that the balcony was "not a necessity".

The other factor is the size of balconies. Accordingly, 24 percent of the householders questioned agreed that balconies are small in size and do not permit people, usually, to sit and to have a rest. Most of them are used to dry clothes only (Table 16.6).

Both of them, open space and balcony, might be considered surprisingly as a minimum-functional house component. This is partly due to the fact that neither of them gives enough privacy because balconies are exposed to the outside public domain and the open space to the households around it. Thus, from the sample analysis it appears that in the use of both housing components, open space and balcony, privacy in relation to passers-by, neighbours or guests was a determining factor in their use and that both are used either occasionally or rarely.

It is interesting to recognise that roof tops are places widely used: households which have no chance to sit in their balcony or open space prefer to use their roofs (Table 16.7). They can be shared by all families living in block or just by the family on the top floor given private access to the roof. It can be observed that most of the problems of open space are solved not only within the open space but also on the roof tops which are provided externally and disassociated from the street scene. Either private or semi private these places are the most valuable features in the house, however sometimes they are not suited for outdoor family activities, because privacy is not maintained for example by overlooking.

A flat in a middle sized block is comprised of two or three rooms of similar size. The lack of space has a great influence on the arrangements and functions of the rooms inside the dwelling. For instance when there is enough space, some living spaces are usually allotted to a fixed specific activity, and there is consistently a clear demarcation in between the rooms that functionally differentiate them such as the room for guests and for daily use by the family and for sleeping. However, when there is not much space in the house, the living room is considered as a multi-functional space; it might be used for sleeping, eating, relaxing and also receiving guests. They are based on a non-fixed arrangement, with flexibility in the arrangement of the rooms. It is difficult to identify each room because of its non-fixed furniture arrangement and it is easy to shift the use of one space to another. In this both non-fixed and fixed arrangements, some prestigious rooms, especially the room for guests, have exterior walls and windows. In some cases one room might be oriented both towards the street and the open space. The other rooms for family use are mostly dark and small, sometimes without any windows. To get some amount of light, daily living spaces are grouped around the open space.

User evaluation analysis and observations on the site show that entrance halls are noticeably popular and useful, even more than the balcony or open space or roof top. After the shared open space, the entrance hall can be considered the second centre of the type around which the other spaces are distributed around. It is usually square with one exterior wall and is a transitional space connected to most rooms, to the open space and gives privacy to the family inside the block. The main semi-private spaces in the house e.g. guest room, kitchen, etc. are easily accessible to the entrance. It is multi-functional due to its location within the dwelling, particularly within the block. In some houses most of the days, sometimes the night, are spent there by the residents.

At the end of the questionnaire, in order to help define major characteristics of appropriate housing in Ortigia in particular, households were asked questions related to their housing requirements. Analysis of the survey identified various disadvantages concerned with the dwellings occupied. In fact 18 percent of the households questioned found their dwellings too small for their needs. The same amount complained about insufficient light. Most of them were not happy with the size of the open space; they found the place crowded, noisy and less private (Table 16.8).

Table 16.8 The things which the inhabitants do not like.

Dislikes	Num	% of each.
small house	15	18
insufficient light	15	18
small open space	20	24
crowded & no privacy	21	25
small balcony	12	14

Table 16.9 The type of house in which they would like to live in in the future.

Preferences	Num	% of each.
happy with the present	13	15
bigger house	15	18
bigger open space	21	25
same but close to ground floor	9	11
private single family	4	5
less families	2	2
bigger balconies	20	24

An analysis of the user satisfaction regarding organisation and use of their space has revealed that only 18 percent of households are satisfied. The choices for the house to live in in the future are very diverse but we can say that most of them wish to live in a bigger flat and in a block with a bigger open space and bigger balcony than they have at present. It emerged that some households over the age of 60 would like to live close to ground level and around the open space to be to the far from the traffic (Table 16.9). It is a fact that today in Ortigia most of the households living on the ground floor around the open space or on the street side of the block are around the age of sixty. The family on the ground floor lives outside the open space or alongside the main access road with all its associated problems of noise and lack of privacy.

In Ortigia multi-family use of shared open space, as developed since the nineteenth century, continues to be valuable. It is not as favourable as single family use of a private open space but some important functions can still be carried out in these spaces. They may show how higher density urban areas can retain valued aspects of social traditions as well as of inherited urban forms.

A final view

It is recognised by this cross-cultural-historical perspective that open spaces are cornerstones in the lives of the societies considered. They are created by the intimate relationship between indoor and outdoor spaces, where nearly every movement between the elements of the house begins, ends or passes through. In this organisation, whether it is individual or collective the open space of the type retains some important socio-cultural elements and offers many advantages.

It has a dual function of both providing privacy to the family and accessibility to social life and reconciles the need to be close to or away from other people by forming a passage, a transitional area, a threshold between the 'public' and the 'private'. The right and obligation of the family to live enclosed in its house has led to a clear separation between public and private life. If thought of only as a form, this house type can be given as an example of a good social and physical boundary controller. In this introverted arrangement, it works as a boundary controller between public and private spaces. It offers security and acts as a buffer against street noises. Achieving privacy and security, there is a hierarchy of spaces not only in the organisation of the house in itself but also in the organisation of the vernacular settlement pattern. The concept of boundary having both physical and social connotations, served as a foundation for the research on the social significance of the house type with an open space.

It is indicated by McHarg (1957, p.75) that the court house type can achieve densities perfectly consonant with central locations and central residential values. The interposition of flats with court houses can provide the maximum densities required for central locations (March and Trace, 1968). However there are some disadvantages. When the open space is designed in the centre no correct direction can be given to the space during the day time, especially in the summer. As Gropius (1956, p.125) mentions the form results in unfavourable orientation with inevitable northern exposures for a large number of units, inadequate illumination, as well as unsatisfactory corner solutions, with overshadowed living units. Additionally, when it is shared by other families who are not related to each other, the required privacy can not be provided with this house type. These facts show that the building type needs revision, particularly in respect of the zoning laws.

Lessons drawn from the work described here may indicate how such changes should best be made. Most of this study has shown that there is an important association between the number of the flats and the number of residents using the block, and the size of the open space which fulfils user requirements in relation of housing requirements. It was found that when the open space is deep, narrow and crowded, it is unable to give the required privacy and comfort and it may act only as a ventilation shaft and a light well without bringing any cool air to the surrounding or letting people have company in it. However the type in its multi-family use can associate with internal functions to provide a living environment and to provide valuable open space absent in all other plan types. The dimensions of the open space must be carefully considered in relation to its widths and depths so that the necessary climatic advantages can be achieved. Fundamental to the success of flat living with a shared open space is the balance between form and open space so that a level of proximity is maintained by neighbours.

Acknowledgements

This paper arises from part of the work carried out by the author. She acknowledges the inputs of tutors and assistants from Sicily during case study, in particular Prof. Giuseppe PAGNANO, Prof. Liliane DUFOUR, Maria Pia GALIOTO (std.in arch), Agata LO TAURO (arch), Mario LO TAURO (Eng.), Barbara MICA (std.).

17 Is informal housing the destiny of the urban poor?

Gülsün Saglamer, Hülya Turgut, Meltem Aksoy, Arda Inceoglu and Nurbin Paker

Introduction

In recent decades the squatter phenomenon has been studied and interpreted by different researchers from various perspectives. As these researchers have taken into account different aspects of this phenomenon in relation to their backgrounds, their definitions and interpretations they have differed widely from each other. This differentiation demonstrates the complexity and the multidimensional nature of the problem. The first definition we have chosen is 'Squatterisation is a transition process from rural to urban life, a transitional life style and its reflection onto space utilisation'. The second defines squatterisation as a matter of distribution of wealth (income), social structure and social security rather than only being a shelter (Arslan, 1989, pp.34-37). The third approach takes into account the aspects related to ownership, legislation and construction processes and defines this phenomenon as 'the casual buildings which have been built on lands or plots without having any ownership and/or the right to built on it in terms of building legislation and laws.' These definitions show that the fact of squatter settlements and the squatting process itself are complex because of their socio-cultural, psychological, economic, political and physical attributes. We cannot isolate these different attributes from each other; for example, we cannot study the subject as if it were only a social problem or just a shelter or socio-economic or political problem. We have to have a holistic approach in order to reach much more comprehensive definitions and interpretations.

Squatterisation is also a matter of development closely related to the speed and style of urbanisation which has emerged from the economic and social structure of our country. The available housing stock, meant to meet the housing demands of the increasing population is insufficient in big cities. In the legal housing development areas, personal, individual ownership is one of the basic requirements. Therefore it is clear that especially in big cities like Istanbul, land prices and construction costs in these legal development areas are much higher than that which the newcomers can afford and, as a consequence of this simple fact, the migrants tend to settle on the periphery of the legal settlements where no development plan or ownership exist (Suher, 1989, pp.42-43).

After having summarised the different definitions and the interpretations of squatter settlements and the emergence of this phenomenon in big cities, we would like to focus on the ownership patterns which have been used throughout the history of the Ottoman Empire and the Republic of Turkey in order to develop a rather distinct approach to the problem.

The ownership patterns within the historical process

The concept of ownership and its patterns with respect to technological, economic and social developments have been developed and refined throughout the centuries. In this connection, ownership has been defined as 'the entire legal relations between the owner and the property, influenced and shaped by legal, social and political systems and psychological behaviours within a certain place and time' (Örücü, 1976, p.1).

Starting from its establishment in the 13th century and continuing on to the 19th century, the Ottoman Empire had had no private ownership pattern in its unique system. During this period, it was accepted that all the land under the Ottoman rule belonged to the Sultan. Ottomans inherited the land distribution system from the Seljuks. In this so-called 'Dirlik' system, there were three different types of land: *has, zeamet, timar*. 'Has' denoted the largest and most valuable type and its income exceeded 100,000 akçe (Ottoman money). This type of land was only allocated to rulers and their relatives and vizirs. 'Zeamet' is the second type. The level of income for this type of land was supposed to be between 20,000 and 100,000 akçe. Zeamets were only allocated to high level pashas and governors. The third type, namely 'Timar', was the type which had income less than 20,000 akçe and these were allocated to soldiers. All the people who had received the right of using these types of lands from the Sultan had to provide a certain number of soldiers for the Sultan. Although it had been inherited from the Selçuks, Ottomans developed and adjusted the system according to their conditions and this system lasted until the 17th century.

At the beginning of the 17th century as the Ottoman Empire reached its largest borders, the 'Dirlik' system lost its efficiency because of the many political problems which arose all over the empire. A kind of feudal system began to flourish and this so-called 'Ayan' system provided opportunities to some people to gain private properties illegally. This chaos lasted more than two hundred years in the Ottoman period and continued up to the 19th century.

The transition from the Sultan's land to private ownership emerged in the 19th century because of the dissolution of the economy and the land management systems of the Ottoman Empire.

The authority of 'temlik' *temlik yetkisi* (to give or sell land to individuals to be taken as property) of the Sultan was used to privatise the land when the treasury was in debt. The transition of the Sultan's land to private ownership or, in other words, the establishment of the right of ownership of private land, was realised by the 'Arazi Kanunnamesi' law issued in 1858. According to this law, the five different types of land were as follows: (Sirel, 1993, pp.10-13)

1. Land under private ownership (Arazi-i Memluke)
2. Land belonging to the state (Arazi-i Miriye)
   This type of land was agricultural land, the ownership of which belonged to the state. The public cultivated the land and the state collected the tax.
3. Foundation land (Arazi-i Merkufe)
   This type had been established by the allocation of a certain part of state land to a specific foundation for particular public welfare use.
4. Land belonging to the public (Arazi-i Metruke)
   This type contained the public places such as streets, squares, fountains, places which belonged to the state and was used by the public.
5. Land which was not used for any purpose (Arazi-i Mevat)
   This type of land did not belong to anyone but was later used for privatisation.

The 1858 'Arazi Kanunnamesi' which gave a new direction to the Ottoman system, transformed state property into private property. In 1910, a second law was passed to transfer state land into private land through inheritance. In the Republican period, the civil law which was passed in 1926 defined the true private ownership patterns and gave the opportunity to distribute the title deeds of the land to the people who had the right to use them at that time (Cin, 1987, p.20).

The private land which had not been divided into small pieces through inheritance according to the Seriat (Religious Law) was used until the end of the 19th century in the Ottoman period. The Republic of Turkey had the opportunity of transferring these large properties into state properties.

There is an ambivalence in the legal regulations of today in relation to these properties serving directly or indirectly the activities of the state or the public. Public ownership is divided into two: *domain public* which has been assigned to the use of the public but under the rule and possession of the state, and *domain private* which is under the possession of the state.

The public ownership in the second group is divided into three:

Ownerless Property: properties which are not under the private ownership of the people but are in the use of the public (shores, forests, etc.)

Public Property: places which can be used freely by the public and the state or any other legal entity (streets, squares, parks, etc.)

Service Property: properties assigned to a public service by the related institutions (schools, hospitals, etc.)

The private properties of the state are those properties that have no direct use for the public but have indirect use to the public due to the revenue (profits/ income) they provide. The private properties of the state are those properties that have not been allocated to any public service but are allocated to foundations or other institutions by a special administrative procedure (the properties allocated to KIT *Kamu Iktisadi Tesekkülleri*). According to the inventory study carried out by the Ministry of Finance and Customs, the total amount of this type of land is 5,300,697 hectares which has been registered as the property of the Treasury (Kirbas, 1988, p.34).

The public administrations which have been faced with socio-economic and political problems because of the high rate of population increase in the big cities since the 1950s lost some of their properties in order to solve the problem without creating any serious plan. This change brought along with it both land speculation and squatterisation The state has unmanageable amounts of land and has no structured organisation to control it except for the amnesty laws passed for the sake of political concerns and for the opportunity to lay claim (*zilliyet*) by the invaders of more than 20 years of occupation, creating a very fertile soil for the land plunderers and the land Mafia to flourish in the big cities. As a consequence of this process, most of the land around big cities which belongs to the state has been invaded and transformed into private property by these illegal bodies.

The squatterisation and land ownership patterns

The need for shelter, which is one of the most important basic needs of human beings, has not been met in developing countries in recent decades because of unpreventable population increase and its consequence of a high migration rate from rural to urban areas. The newcomers have been left alone to solve their own problems and as a result of this, they have built their dwellings without taking into consideration ownership conditions and building regulations. This type of dwelling has different names in different countries. They are called 'Gecekondu' in Turkey.

Squatter settlements have emerged at the periphery of cities around legal developments on public, municipal and private lands. This process is steadily continuing as the population increase.

Since the importance of these illegal developments had not been very well understood and interpreted by the decision makers in Turkey, no serious step was taken until 1966 when the first law was passed to stop these developments. The main objectives of this law and the subsequent ones were to prevent building new dwellings, upgrading some of them if possible and demolishing others. The period between 1945-1960 was the period in which the construction of squatter dwellings was prohibited and attempts were made to pull down existing ones. In the period between 1945-1960, prohibition of construction and the demolition of squatter dwellings were the main characteristics. Between the years of 1965 and 1980, the government institutions assumed much more tolerant approaches towards these settlements (Turgut, 1990, pp.56-59). However, the measures taken at different times were not sufficient to solve the problem and the number of squatter houses continued to increase.

The legalisation and the long term planning approaches of squatter settlements have been made possible by the law which was passed in 1984 and afterwards it was decided to provide an infrastructure in order to improve the conditions in these areas and then to integrate them into the existing city structure. Just before elections, when the increase of squatter settlements cannot be controlled, the governments mostly preferred to legalise them by giving title deeds or at least to supply an infrastructure for these settlements to attract votes. The conversion from public land to private ownership has been realised through the legalisation of these settlements and other lands have been allocated to squatter inhabitants in order to empty certain areas of the cities.

According to the 1983 law (No. 2805) and the 1984 law (No. 2981), the squatter houses which were built before 1981 were legalised. This law gave the opportunity to the inhabitants to ask for their title deeds from municipalities or government offices within 6 months. This law also made it possible for the inhabitants to use the land which belonged to municipalities, foundations or the state by payment of the land prices. The squatter houses which were built on private land were to use this opportunity of remission by the approval of the land owner (Keles, 1990, pp.390-392). This law gave the right to the inhabitants of the squatter dwellings which were built on the state and/or municipality owned land to obtain the title deeds. Thus it was decided that until the completion of the improved settlement plans, as a guarantee of the inhabitants' ownership, a 'Deed Assignment Certification' (*Tapu Tahsis Belgesi*) was given.

By modification of the remission law (No. 3290) in 1986, the process of giving deeds to the squatters was made easier and 'Deed Registration' procedures were put to use without waiting for the completion of the development plans. By the last remission law (No. 3414) which was passed in 1988, all the rights which had been used before by different institutions were transferred to municipalities and the conditions which were defined in the Law (No. 775) about the assigned lands or buildings which could not be transferred or sold within 20 years were cancelled. Thus the land to be sold or transferred in short periods could be developed by builders.

Summarising the developments: at the beginning the squatter houses which were built on state, municipality, foundation or private lands were given title deeds in one way or another. From the very beginning, the newcomers gradually began to accept the urban life style and flats have become for them the symbol of being an urbanite. As ownership gave them comfort and as they wanted to obtain rent through their land, they have tended to build multi-storey buildings on their plots in order to rent them out. The squatter inhabitants who have not obtained the title deeds of their plots tend not to build multi-storey buildings because of this problem.

This simple and basic pattern has been converted to another pattern: the great potential of the newcomers and the strong housing demand created a new type of developer in big cities to provide land for 'shared deeds'. In this case, inhabitants own the land but have no right to build on it. This type of development is called 'semi-squatter' settlements. As inhabitants feel themselves secure in terms of ownership and as the land prices are very high for them even in these areas, the settlements tend to be multi-storey in nature.

In the following section, two case studies will be summarised as examples of the first type of different development patterns.

Case studies

The aim of the case study is to compare differences between two squatter settlements that have experienced different development processes with special reference to land distribution and ownership patterns.

Pinar case study

The Pinar settlement is one of the oldest squatter settlements in Istanbul and was started at the beginning of the 1970s (Table 17.1). The first settlers came from the Black Sea part of Turkey and settled on land where there was wood belonging to the state. After having built their own houses they dissected the land into small plots and then began to sell them to migrants. Another group of people again from the Black Sea part came to the area with some 40 families to settle soon after the first settlers. The Pinar area started to be attractive in the mid-1970s.

Table 17.1 Pinar settlement by years.

Years	Number of families
1972	100
1978	500
1981	890
1990	1500

The population boom took place after the 1984 law which legalised most of the squatter settlements like Pinar. The inhabitants of Pinar mainly came from the Black Sea region and the eastern part of Anatolia. Kinship has played an important role in these developments. The newcomers settled by their fellow villagers or relatives thus receiving emotional and financial support. There is a strong feeling of solidarity in these areas (Saglamer and Erdogan, 1993). At the beginning they had extended families but later families became smaller.

None of the settlers have title deeds but 'Deed Assignment Certification' (Tapu Tahsis Belgesi) which means that they are not the owners of the land where they built their houses. The interesting point is that when they came, they paid a certain amount of money to buy the land from the ones who had come first and had set up the illegal land market here. A survey was carried out in this quarter and 50 families were chosen to be interviewed (Turgut, 1994; Saglamer et al, 1994). Observations have been carried out to understand the dynamics of the existing system. Infrastructure such as transportation, water, sewage and electricity have been provided by the municipality. Even green spaces and sports facilities have been organised as if the area were a legal one. Schools, mosques, market places, health services, post offices, police stations and social clubs are also in use. The waste disposal system is one of the inadequate services that the municipality provides here.

Most of the people in this quarter who work are labourers and there is a very small number of civil servants. They work outside the area. Most of the inhabitants, especially the first generation, has only primary school education. The second generation has high school and even university education. The settlers' previous houses were mainly in villages in Anatolia or in another squatter settlement in Istanbul.

People in Pinar obtained a 'Deed Assignment Certificate' in the mid-1980s. They had the right to own their houses to some extent. This development encouraged people to improve and extend their dwellings. Consequently the 1984 law (No. 2981) encouraged more people to invade the land. Since this assignment certificate has not been sufficient for obtaining financial assistance from banks or the Mass Housing Fund, which is a government institution, Pinar inhabitants have had no access to financing. However, single storey houses tended to be extended vertically after 1984 because of the deed assignment certificates. As crowding has become a problem in this quarter, people are complaining about the insufficiency in services. This situation has also encouraged land speculation in this area. The increase in land prices has exceeded the inflation rate.

Plate 17.1 General view of Pinar.

Akatlar Case Study

Akatlar was started by the settlement of a family from the Black Sea region of Turkey in the 1930s to set up a nursery. When the first migration movement commenced, this family settled in this area and began to trade with plants. Afterwards this family, its relatives and their villagers followed them to move here from their villages or the other squatter areas in Istanbul during the 1940s (Table 17.2). In the 1970s the settlement was called Karanfilköy (Carnation Village) and at that time it demonstrated mostly village characteristics. In the second wave, another group who originated from Sivas, a city in central Anatolia, came to settle in the area from other squatter settlements in Istanbul.

Table 17.2 Akatlar settlement by years.

Years	Number of families
1970	50
1979	300
1994	800

The settlers do not have title deeds or a 'Deed Assignment Certification' (*Tapu Tahsis Belgesi*). Like Pinar, the inhabitants are not the owners of the land. The first settlers had paid no money when they settled and as the first group of followers was from the same family or village they did not pay anything either. But the second group, who originated from Sivas but had moved to the area from other squatter areas at the beginning of the 1980s, bought the land from the existing settlers.

A survey was carried out in this quarter and 10 families were chosen to be interviewed. As this settlement shows uniform characteristics, a limited number of families was chosen. The infrastructures such as transportation, water, sewage and electricity have been provided by the municipality. Transportation is not sufficient in this area. Green spaces and sports facilities have also been provided by the municipality. Schools, mosques and market places are also in use. The waste disposal system is one of the inadequate services that the municipality provides here.

Most of the people work as private entrepreneurs in this quarter. They work outside this area. Most of the inhabitants especially the first generation has only a primary school education. The second generation has a high school and even a university education in this area. The settlers' previous houses were mainly in villages of the Black Sea region or in other squatter settlements in Istanbul.

Unlike the Pinar case, people in the Akatlar area did not obtain Deed Assignment Certificates after the laws which were passed in the 1980s and were trying to legalise some of the squatter settlements in the big cities. Therefore, they have no rights to own their houses. Contrary to the Pinar case, the inhabitants in the Akatlar area tended to improve their housing quality instead of extending their houses vertically although they receive no financial assistance from banks or the Mass Housing Fund. The level of rents is much higher in Akatlar than in Pinar in relation to housing quality.

The Akatlar area is very near to the fairly new part of the city and this part has many commercial, leisure and social facilities. These facilities and the developments created very high rents and land speculation in this area. As the land prices have been and still are very high in this area, the central government and the municipality have not been willing to offer 'Deed Assignment Certificates' to inhabitants in this area. This situation helped the settlement to keep its density relatively low until now.

Plate 17.2 General view of Akatlar .

Before settlers in Pinar were given their certificates in 1984 and 1986, the two areas (Pinar and Karanfilköy) did have similar developmental patterns: in both of the areas the majority of the buildings were single storey structures. Since the assignments gave a certain sense of land-security, the density of Pinar has increased greatly.

It may be useful to have information about the characteristics of the populations in these areas to make sound comparisons before we start discussions.

The average household size is 4.4 in Pinar and 4.6 in Akatlar. Having similar household sizes this factor will not be influential in analysing the differences between these settlements. Income levels are 2.0 million TL in Pinar, 2.4 million TL in the Akatlar settlement which may indicate that in Akatlar they have enough income to extend their houses vertically, but it is not the case. As in the Akatlar area the quality of the housing environment is better than in Pinar, the level of rental prices for a house is higher than in Pinar (2.0 million TL per month in Akatlar, 1.2 million TL per month in Pinar).

Table 17.3 Educational level of the inhabitants.

Settlements %	Uneducated		Primary School		High School		University	
	H	W	H	W	H	W	H	W
Pinar	20	25	50	50	20	13	10	12
Akatlar	0	0	55	70	22	30	23	0

Key: H - husband   W - wife

Table 17.4 Employment status.

Settlements %	Government Sector		Private Sector		Self-Employed		Retired		Housewife		Unemployed	
	H	W	H	W	H	W	H	W	H	W	H	W
Pinar	22	10	22	0	11	10	45	0	0	80	0	0
Akatlar	12	0	66	0	11	10	0	0	0	90	11	0

Key: H - husband   W - wife

Discussion

What kind of ownership existed in Turkey until now ?

Although we have no exact figures about the percentage of the distribution of land in Turkey, it has been stated many times that over 60% of the land belongs to the central government and municipalities. This figure is much less in most of the European countries and North America. As a result of the impossibility of establishing control over such waste areas, especially in big cities, all of the squatter settlements were founded on such property. With the increase of the number of inhabitants in squatter settlements over time, the voting potential of those areas started to be influential in politics: local governments look for better relationships with the settlers, giving or promising deed assignment certificates before elections.

In order to stop these illegal developments in big cities, the central government passed several laws in the 1980s. The state expected to prevent the invasion of the state land by newcomers by giving them deed assignment certificates.

Was the 'Deed Assignment Certificate' helpful in solving the problem?

The first two laws which were passed in 1983 and 1984, were for the remission of squatter houses constructed before 1981. According to these laws people who obtained the certificate to own the land were not allowed to sell or to transfer their plot to anyone in the coming 20 years. Unfortunately, this condition was removed in the 1986 law. The implementation of deed assignment certificates created new problems that the central and local governments did not expect to face. This approach gave opportunities to inhabitants to have land security and, as a consequence of this fact, they began to extend their houses vertically and invest more money than before.

As the urbanisation rate is gradually increasing parallel to economic developments, people have a strong tendency to migrate to big cities to obtain better jobs, better facilities and for better living conditions. Therefore migration is a fact in Turkey and the following factors characterise settlement:

the greatest share of the land belongs to the state and the state has no policy to distribute the land to encourage planned settlements in big cities;

the dwellings which were built for the low-income groups by the state are not accessible for the urban poor because of their prices;

the state or the municipalities have no intention of building rental housing for this group;

land developers construct expensive dwellings;

migrants are very ambitious to obtain not only shelter but rent;

people who migrate from rural areas have no option other than to invade the land;

therefore, informal housing is the destiny for the urban poor.

Acknowledgements

We would like to express our appreciation to the British Council for its support of the Academic Link Programme between Istanbul Technical University and University of Newcastle Upon Tyne, through whom we were able to conduct these case studies.

References

Abu-Lughod. J. (1971), *Cairo: 1001 years of the city victorious*, Princeton, Princeton University Press.

Abu-Lughod, J. (1981), 'Strategies for the improvement of different types of lower-income urban settlements in the Arab region', in *UNCHS The residential circumstances of the urban poor in developing countries*, New York, Praeger Publishers.

Acioly, C., Jr. (1994). *Urban Poverty Alleviation and Neighbourhood Upgrading: The International Agendas Versus A Sub-Saharan African Context*, 2nd Symposium Housing for the Urban Poor 11-14 April, Birmingham, United Kingdom.

ACMPP. (1984), *Alexandria Comprehensive Master Plan Project, final Report*.

Adams, M. J. (1973), "Structural bases of village art", *American Anthropologist* 75 (1 (Feb)): 265-279.

Adebisi, B. O.(1989), 'The Challenge of Independence: Major Issues Before and After', in Tamuno, T.N. and Atanda, (eds.), *Nigeria Since Independence*, Ibadan, Heinemann.

Aguda, T. A. (1989), 'The Judiciary and the System of Law', in Tamuno, T. N. and Atanda, (eds.) *Nigeria Since Independence*, Heinemann, Ibadan

Akbar, J. (1988), *Crisis in the Built Environment (The case of the Muslim City)*, Singapore, Concept Media; Mimar Books

Al-Hathloul, S. (1982), "Cultural Conflicts in Urban Pattern: A Saudi Arabian Case Study" In Serageldin, I. and El-Sadek, S. (ed.) *The Arab City: Its Character and Islamic Cultural Heritage*, Riyadh , Arab Urban Development Institute.

Al-Turabi, H. (1992), Global View *Saudi Gazette* January 13

ANC. (1955), Freedom Charter (as adapted from the Congress of the People, 26th June, Kliptown, South Africa).

ANC. (1994a), *Educational Renewal Strategy*, February, Johannesburg.

ANC. (1994b), *The Reconstruction and Development Programme*, Johannesburg,
ANC/Government of South Africa. (1994c), *National Health Policy*, June, Johannesburg.
Antoniou, et al. (1980), *The Conservation of the old city of Cairo*, Paris, UNESCO Technical Report serial No FMR/CC/CH/80/182.
Armor, M. (1991, 1992), *Building your own home*, Bridport, Prism.
Arslan, Rifki (1989), 'Gecekondulasmanin Evrimi.' *Mimarlik*; Vol.89/6 No.238, pp. 34-37.
Ayres, R. U. (1969), *Technological Forecasting and Long-range Planning*, New York, McGraw Hill Book Company.
Barnard, B.(1984). 'Cultural Facades: Ethnic Architecture in Malaysia'. *USFI Reports* (No.5, Asia), Hanover, N.H., Universities Field Staff International.
Bailey, R. (1994), *Homelessness: what can be done*, Oxford, Jon Carpenter.
Bell, J. (1992), "Ecologically Integrated Land Use Planning: A Strategy for Sustainable Development", In Walter, B. Arkin, L. and Crenshaw, R. (ed.) *Sustainable Cities: Concepts and Strategies for Eco-City Development*, Los Angeles, Eco-Home Media
Bening, R. (1975), *Colonial Development in Northern Ghana 1898-1950*, Bulletin of the Ghana Geographical Association, 17 pp. 65-79
Benna, Associates (1985), *Sokoto Master Plan 1983-2003*, Sokoto, Govt. of Sokoto.
Benna, U. G. (1989), 'The Federal Capital: The Debate and the Planning', in Tamuno, T. N. and Atanda, J. A. (eds.) *Nigerial Since Independence*, Ibadan, Heinemann.
Benneh, G. and Gyasi, E. (1993), *Farming and Land Degradation in Stressed Environments: The Case of the Upper East Region*, Second Congress of African Geographers 19th April, Rabat, Morocco.
Benyon, J. A. (1974), "The Process of Political Incorporation", in Tooke, D.W. (ed.) *The Bantu Speaking Peoples of Southern Africa*, London, Routledge, pp. 367-395.
Berlin, I. (1969), *Four Essays on Liberty*, Oxford, Oxford University Press.
Bianca, S. (1982), 'Traditional Muslim Cities and Western Planning Ideology: An Outline of Structural Conflicts', *The Arab City: Its Character and Islamic Cultural Heritage*, Riyadh, Arab Urban Development Institute.
Blake, P. (1956), *Frank Lloyd Wright: Architecture and Space*, Harmondsworth, Middlesex, Penguin Books Ltd.
Boateng, et al. (1990), *A Poverty Profile of Ghana 1987-1988*. Washington DC, World Bank, SDA Working Paper No. 5.
Bookchin, M. (1987), *The Rise of Urbanization and the Decline of Citizenship*. San Francisco, Sierra Club Books.
Bourdieu, P. (1962), *The Algerians*, Boston, Beacon Press.
Bourdieu, P. (1973), The Berber House. *Rules and Meanings*, M. Douglas, New York, Penguin.

Bourdieu, P. and A. Sayad. (1964), *Le deracinement - La crise de l'agriculture traditionnelle en Algerie*, Paris, Edition Minuit.

Boxer, B. (1969), "Tsuen Wan: A case study of Chinese response to urban growth" *Annals, Association American Geog* 59 (1) p. 174.

Broadbent, G. (1980), 'The Deep Structures of Architecture', in Broadbent, G., Bunt, R. and Jenks, C. (eds.) *Signs, Symbols, and Architecture*, John Wiley & Sons Ltd: London.

Broome, J. (1986), "The Segal Method" *Architects Journal*, (5.11.86).

Brown, L. R. (1987), Sustaining World Agriculture, *State of the World 1987*, L. R. Brown, New York, W.W. Norton.

Brule, J. C. (1976), "Transformation recentes de l'espace rural en Algerie." *Bulletin de la Societe Languedocienne de Geographie* 10 (No.1, Monpellier).

Bugnicourt, J. (1960), *Les Nouveaux Centres Ruraux in Algerie*, Direction de l'Agriculture et les forets en Algerie: Algiers.

Built It. (1994), *Building Your Dream Home*. Kingston-upon-Thames, Build It Publications Ltd.

Bunce, M. (1982), *Rural settlement in an urban world*, London, Croom Helm.

Bundy, C. (1983), "The Transkei Peasantry, c 1890-1914", *The Roots of Rural Poverty in central and Southern Africa*, Palmer, R. and Parsons, N. (ed.) Heinemann, London.

Bundy, C. (1992), "Land, Law and Power in Rural South Africa" *New ground: Journal of Development and Environment* 8 pp. 6-8.

Burgess, R., M. Carmona, et al. (1994, June), *The Hidden Assignment, Position Paper prepared for the International Seminar*, Faculty of Architecture, Delf University.

Calderwood, D. M. (1953), *Native Housing in South Africa*, (PhD Thesis), Government Publisher, Pretoria.

Calthorpe, P. (1993), *The Next American Metropolis: Ecology, Community and the American Dream*, New York, Princeton Architectural Press.

Caniggia, G. and G. L. Maffei. (1984), *Composizione e Tipologia Edilizia*, Marsilio Editori.

CAPMAS. (1990), *Final Results of 1986 Census: Governorate of Alexandria*, Cairo, CAPMAS Publications

Casey, E. (1993), *Getting Back into Place: Toward a Renewed Understanding of the Place-World*, Bloomington, Indiana University Press.

Chant, S. (1995), "Gender and Development in the 1990's" *Third World Planning Review* 17 (2).

Chapin, F. S. J. (1968), *Urban Land Use Planning*, University of Illinois Press: Urbana First Edition.

Ching, F. D. K. (1979), *Architecture: Form, Space & Order*, Van Nostrand Reinhold, New York.

CHISEL. (1993), Self build housing volume bid: submission to the Housing Corporation, June 1993, CHISEL: London.

Christopher, A. J. (1982), "Partition and Population in South Africa." *Geographical Review* 72 pp. 127-138.

Christopher, A. J. (1993), *The Burden of the Past: Geographical Perspectives on Current Affairs*. The Chairman's Address, Annual General Meeting of the Society for Geography, Stellenbosch, South Africa, 28th April.

Christopher, A.J. (1994), *The Atlas of Apartheid*, Routledge, London.

Cin, H. (1987), *Miri Arazi ve Bu Arazinin Ozel Mulkiyete Donusumu*, Konya, Selcuk Universitesi.

Circulaire. (1976), Ministere de la Planification et des Travaux Public and de la Construction.

CRNA (Commision Nationale de la Reforme Agraire)

Commonwealth Secretariat. (1989), *Engendering Adjustment for the 1990's Report of a Commonwealth Expert Group on Women and Structural Adjustment*, Commonwealth Secretariat, London.

Cloette, J. N. N. (1982), *Central, Provincial and Municipal Institutions of South Africa*. Pretoria, Van Schaik.

Cohen, M. (1994), "Will the World Bank's Real 'New Urban Policy' Please Stand Up?" *Habitat International* 18 (4) pp. 117-118.

Coleman, D. A. (1994), *Ecopolitics*, New Brunswick, NJ, Rutgers University Press.

Conway, M. (1993), "Tomorrow's Supercities for land, sea and air" *The Futurist* 27 (3, May-June).

Cornaton, M. (1967), *Les Regroupements de la decolonisation en Algerie*, Paris, Ouvriere.

Cornia, G., Jolly, R., et al., (eds.) (1987), *Adjustment With a Human Face. Protecting the Vulnerable and Promoting Growth*, Oxford, Clarendon Press.

Cross Times (January, 1990).

Daly, H. E., Cobb, J. B. (1989), *For the Common Good*, Boston, Beacon Press.

Dato, G. (1986), *La citta' Catania*. Catania.

Davenport, T.R.H. (1987), *South Africa, A Modern History*, Third edition, Macmillan Press, London.

DeLauwe, C. (1965), *Des Hommes et des villes*, Paris, Payot.

Delp, P. et al. (1977), *Systems Tools for Project Planning*, Bloomington, International Development Institute.

Department of Housing. (1994), *A New Housing Policy and Strategy for South Africa - White Paper*, Pretoria, South Africa.

Dewar, D., (ed.) (1993), *The DeLoor Task Group Report On Housing Policy For South Africa: Some Perspectives*, The Urbanity and Housing Network, Faculty of Fine Art and Architecture, University of Cape Town.

Dewar, D. (1994), *Urban Housing in Southern Africa: The Need for a Paradigm Shift*. 2nd Symposium Housing for the Urban Poor - Housing, Poverty & Developing Countries 11-14 April, Birmingham, United Kingdom.

Doxiades, C. A. (1986), *Ekistics: An Introduction to the Science of Human Settlements*. New York, Oxford University Press.
Drakakis-Smith, D. (1992), *Urban and Regional Change in Southern Africa*, Routledge, London.
Duncan, J. S. (ed.) (1981). *Housing and Identity: cross-cultural perspectives*, Croom-Helm, London.
Duncan, S. and A. Rowe. (1993), "Self provided housing: the first world's hidden housing arm" *Uban Studies* 30 (8).
Eidt, R. C. (1971), *Pioneer Settlement in Northeast Argentina*. Madison, University of Wisconsin Press.
El-Hamamsy, L. S. (1982), The Assertion of Egyptian Identity, *Cultural continuities and change,* Devos, G. and Romanucci-Ross, Chicago, University of Chicago Press pp. 39-63.
El-Nagar. (1993), *'Interview with chairman of the Gomrok District, Alexandria'*.
El-Sherif, A. (1992), *Values and development thinking in the Arab city: Barriers and Limitations for professional interventions in old quarters*, Unpublished paper presented at the 10th Interschools Conference on Development, DPU, UCL.
Elson, D., (ed.) (1991), *Male Bias in the Development Process*, Manchester University Press.
Emmett, A., et. al. (1993), *Water Supply and Sanitation Services in South Africa*, SALDRU, Cape Town.
Faludi, A. (1976), *Planning Theory*, Oxford, Pergammon Press.
Fiori, J. and Ramirez, R. (1992), "Notes on the Self-Help Housing Critique - Towards a Conceptual Framework for the Analysis of Self-Help Housing Policies in Developing Countries", In Mathey, K. (ed.) *Beyond Self-Help Housing*, London, Mansell.
Firey, W. (1947), *Land Use in Central Boston*, Cambridge, Havard University Press.
Food and Agriculture Organization, F. A. O. (1983), *Fuelwood Supplies in the Developing Countries*, Rome, FAO.
Foucault, M. (1976), *Discipline and Punish: The Birth of the Prison*. London (trans), Penguin.
Foucault, M. (1978), *The History of Sexuality*, London (trans), Penguin.
Foucault, M. (1980), *Power/Knowledge.* London (trans), Penguin.
Foucault, M. (1988), "Technologies of the Self", In Martin, L., Gutman, H. and Hutton, P. (ed.) *Technologies of the Self.* London, Tavistock.
Frescura, F. (1981), *Rural Shelter in Southern Africa*, Ravan Press, Johannesburg.
Fromm, E. (1965). *The Art of Loving*, New York, Bantam.
Gallilan, L. (1994), Build me up, *The Guardian Weekend*.
Giddens, A. (1991), *Modernity and Self-Identity: Self and Society in the Late Modern Age*, Cambridge, Polity.

Gilbert, A. and P. Ward. (1985), *Housing, the state, and the poor: policy and practice in three Latin American Cities*, Cambridge, Cambridge University Press.

Gist, N. P. and Fava, S F. (1974), *Urban Society*, New York, Harper and Row, Publishers.

Giuffre, A. (1993), *Sicurezza e Conservazione Dei Centri Storici Il Casa Ortigia.* Catania, Editori Laterza.

Gladwin, C., (ed.) (1991), *Structural Adjustment and African Women Farmers,* Gainesville, University of Florida Press.

Government of Ghana. (1987), *A Programme of Structural Adjustment. Report Prepared for the Fourth Meeting of the Consultative Group on Ghana*, Paris.

Gropius, W. (1956), *Scope of Total Architecture,* George Allen & Unwin Ltd: London.

Gross, D. (1992), *The Past in Ruins: Tradition and the Critique of Modernity,* Amherst, University of Massachusetts Press.

Grubb, M. (1993), *The "Earth Summit" agreements: a guide and assessment, an analysis of the Rio '92 UN Conference on Environment and Development* London, Earthscan Publications.

Guidoni, E. (1982), *Vicolo-Cortine: Tradizione Islanica e Urbanistica Populare in Silicia,* Venezia, Edizioni Giada.

Guyer, J. and Idowu, O. (1991), "Women's Agricultural Work in a Multi-modal Rural Economy; Ibarapa District, Oyo State, Nigeria". In Gladwin, C. (ed.) *Structural Adjustment and African Women Farmers* Gainesville, University of Florida Press.

Hakim, B. S.(1986). *Arabic-Islamic Cities: Building and Planning Principles,* London, KPI Ltd.

Hakim, B. S.(1994). 'The "Urf" and its role in diversifying the architecture of traditional Islamic cities.' *Journal of Arch and Planning Research*; Vol.11, No.2 (Summer), pp. 108-127.

Heidegger, M. (1993), "Building Dwelling Thinking". In Krell, D. (ed.) *Basic Writings, revised and expanded edition*, London (trans), Routledge.

Heilbroner, R. (1980), *The Worldly Philosophers*, New York, Simon and Schuster.

Hertzberger, H. (1967), 'Form and programme are reciprocally evocative.' *Forum*; Vol.7, pp. 14-16.

Hesselberg, J. (1994), *Issues in Shelter Delivery for the Urban Poor: Experiences from India, Indonesia and Mexico.* 2nd Symposium Housing for the Urban Poor 11-14 April, Birmingham, United Kingdom.

Hirschman, A. O. (1975), 'Interregional and International Transmission of Economic Growth', in Friedmann, J. and Alonso, W. (eds.) *Regional Policy: Readings in Theory and Practice.* The MIT Press: Cambridge.

Hogben, S. J. (1967), *An Introduction to the History of the Islamic States of Northern Nigeria.* London, Oxford University Press.

Holland, R. and Ashley, C. (1993), "Let the User be the Chooser" *Appropriate Technology*, vol. 20, no. 3, 3rd December, (Energy edition).

Holman, C. (1991), An alternative solution: self build for rent by young people in Maltby, Sheffield City Polytechnic.

Holman, C. (1994), *Making community self build happen.* London, The Children's Society.

Horen, C. and Afrane-Okese, Y., et. al. (1993), *Energy Research in Southern Africa: Widening Access to Basic Energy Services*, SALDRU, South Africa.

Housing Corporation (1989). *The Housing Corporation and self build for people in housing need.* London, Housing Corporation.

Hundsalz, M. (1994), *Housing for the Urban Poor: Housing Poverty and Developing Countries - Keynote Address*, 2nd Symposium Housing for the Urban Poor 11-14 April, Birmingham, United Kingdom.

Illich, I. (1992), *In the Mirror of the Past: Lectures and Addresses, 1978-1990.* London, Marion Boyars.

Jantsch, E. (1967), *Technological Forecasting in Perspective,* Organization for Economic Cooperation and Development (OECD): Paris.

Jones, G. A. and P. M. Ward.(1994), "The World Bank's 'New' Urban Management Programme: Paradigm Shift or Policy Continuity" *Habitat International* 18 (3) pp. 33-51.

Kani, A. M. (1988), *The Intellectual Origin of Islamic Jihad in Nigeria,* al Hoda, London.

Kardash, H. and N. Wilkinson. (1991), "Development within development: User extensions of 4-storey walk-ups in Cairo" *Open House International* 16 (1) pp. 9-17.

Keles, R. (1990), *Kentlesme Politikasi,* Ankara, Imge Yayinlari.

Kellett, P. (1995), Constructing Home, Production and Consumption of Popular Housing in Northern Columbia, Faculty of Law, Environment and Social Sciences, University of Newcastle upon Tyne.

Kemeny, J. (1992), *Housing and Social Structure: Towards a Sociology of Residence.* Bristol, SAUS.

Kenneth, C. (1986), "Architecture in Space, The Space-Positive Tradition." *Journal of Architectural Education* 39 (3) pp. 17-23.

Kent, S.(1991), 'Partitioning space: Cross-cultural factors influencing domestic spatial segmentation.' *Environment and Behavior*; Vol.23 No.4 (July), pp. 438-473.

Kirbas, Sadik (1988), *Devlet Mallari,* Ankara, Hacettepe Universitesi - Iktisadi ve Idari Bilimer Fakultesi.

Kirkwood, K. (n.d.), The Group Areas Act, South African Institute of Race Relations; Johannesburg.

Knight, D. B. (1985), "Territory and People or People and Territory? Thoughts on Postcolonial Self-Determinism" *International Political Science Review* 6 pp. 248-272.

Kolb, D. (1990), *Postmodern Sophistications: Philosophy, Architecture and Tradition*, Chicago, University of Chicago Press.

Laquian, A. A. (1983), *Basic Housing: Policies for Urban Sites, Services and Shelter in Developing Countries*, Ottawa, Canada, International Development Research Centre.

Last, M. D. (1967), *The Sokoto Caliphate*, London, Longman.

Lawless, R. and K. Sutton. (1978), *Population Regrouping in Algeria-Traumatic Change and the rural settlement pattern*, Durham, University of Durham.

Lee, Y.-J. (1994), Economic Development and the Environment: A Comparison of Green Economics with conventional Economics, Land Economics Annual Publication.

Legassick, M. (1983), "Gold Agriculture and Secondary Industry in South Africa, 1885-1970" in *The Roots of Rural Poverty in Central and Southern Africa*, in Palmer, R. and Parsons, N. (ed.), London, Heinemann.

Leopold, A. (1968), *A Sand County Almanac*, London, Oxford University Press.

Lesbet, D. (1983), *Les 1000 villages Socialistes en Algerie*, Algiers, OPU.

Lesne, M. (1962), 'L'experience de deplacement de population - Les centres de regroupement en Algerie.' *Annales de Geographie*; Vol.71, No.388, pp. 569-603.

Levine, D. (1989), *Building young lives*, London, National Federation of Housing Associations.

Levine, D. (1994), *I've started so I'll finish*, London, Community Self Build Agency.

Levi-Strauss, C. (1966). *The Savage Mind,* London.

Loxley, J. (1988), *Ghana: Economic Crises and the Long Road to Recovery* Ottawa, Canada, North-South Institute.

Lyotard, J-F. (1984), *The Postmodern Condition: A Report on Knowledge* Manchester, (trans), Manchester University Press.

Madima, E. S. (1971),"Ro vha ro dzula", *Tshianeo*. T. N. Maumela and E. S. Madima, Pretoria, Via Afrika.

Mahdjoubi, L. (1990), 'For an improved rural housing to limit distress migration.' *Planning Outlook*; Vol.33 Issue No.1: University of Newcastle upon Tyne.

March, L. and M. Trace. (1968), *The Land Use Performance of Selected Arrays of Built Forms*, Cambridge.

Marcuse, P. (1992), "Why conventional self help projects won't work". In Mathey, K. (ed.) *Beyond Self Help Housing*. London, Mansell.

Martin, R. (1977), "Housing Options, Lusaka Zambia" *Ekistics Journal* 44 (261 August 1977) pp. 89-95.

Martin, R. (1984), "Poverty and professionals" *RIBA Journal* 91 (7)pp. 17-28.

Marx, K. (1906), *Capital. Trans. B. Fowkes*. New York, Random House.

Massey, D. (1985), "New Directions in Space". In Gregory, D. and Urry, J. (ed.) *Social Relations and Spatial Structures*. London, Macmillan pp. 9-19.

Massey, D. (1994), *Space, Place and Gender*, Cambridge, Polity.

Mathey, K., (ed.) (1992), *Beyond Self-Help Housing*, London, Mansell.

Maunier, R. (1926), *La consruction collective de la maison en Kabylie*. Paris, Institut d'ethnologie.

Maurer, G. (1982), Les Villages Socialistes en Algerie. *Formes et Croissance Urbaine au Maghreb*. Paris, CNRS.

McHarg, I. (1957), "The Court House Concept" *Architect's Yearbook* 8 pp. 74-102.

Meier, R. (1980), *Urban Futures Observed*, New York, Pergamon.

Melperri, S. J. (1986), Rent control and housing market equilibrium: Theory and evidence from Cairo, Egypt, Graduate School of Arts and Sciences, George Washington University.

Mergerand, R. (1970), *Les Villages Socialistes en Algerie: Les Influences Occidentales dans les Villes Maghrehine a l'Epoque Contemporaine*, Paris, C.N.R.S.

Merrett, C. (1984), "The Significance of the Political Boundary in the Apartheid State, with particular reference to Transkei" *South African Geographical Journal* 66 (1) pp. 70-93.

Ministry of Health, U. E. R. (1991), *Upper East Regional Health Services Annual Report 1991*, Bolgatanga, Ghana.

Ministry of Health, U. E. R. (1992), *Upper East Regional Health Services Annual Report 1991*, Bolgatanga, Ghana.

Morel, P. and. Ross, H.(1993), 'Housing Design Assessment for Bush Communities', Alice Springs (Australia), Tangentyere Council, Inc./NT. Dept of Lands, Housing and Local Government.

Moser, C. (1992), Adjustment from Below: Low-Income Women, Time and the Triple Role in Guayaquil, Ecuador. *Women and Adjustment Policies in the Third World*. H. Afshar and C. Dennis. London, Macmillan pp. 87-116.

Moser, C. (1995), "Women, Gender and Urban Development Policy: Challenges for Current and Future Research" *Third world Planning Review* 17 (2).

Moss, G. and Obrey, I. (1992), *South Africa Review 6, From 'Red Friday' to Codesa*, Ravan Press, Johannesburg; and the following authors specifically: Swilling, M., Vwada, A., Feldman, M., et. al. (Group known as 'Planact'), "Transition and Development", pp. 201-215; Seekings, J., "Civic Organisations in South African Townships", pp. 216-236; Cedric De Beer, "Health Policy in Transition", pp. 267-278; Chisholm, L., "South African Education in the Era of Negotiations", pp. 279-291.

Moughtin, J. C. (1964), 'The Traditional Settlements of the Hausa People.' *Town Planning Review*, Vol.35 pp. 21-34.

Moughtin, J. C. (1985), *Hausa Architecture,* London, Ethnographica.

Mueller, M. (1990), "Bioregionalism/Western Culture/Women". In Van Andruss e. al. (ed.) *Home! A Bioregional Reader*, Philadelphia, New Society pp. 87-88.

Murray, C. and O'Regan, C. (1990), *No Place to Rest: Forced Removals and the Law in South Africa*, Cape Town, Oxford University Press.

Mutin. (1982), *La Mitidja de colonisation et espace geographiques*. Paris, CNRS.
Nadim, N. (1979), 'The concept of the harah: a historical and sociological study of al-Sukkariyya.' *Annales Islamologique*, pp. 313-348.
National Academy of Science. (1990), *One Earth, One Future: our changing global environment*, Washington, D.C., National Academy Press.
Nelson, J. (1979), *Access to power: politics and the urban poor in developing nations*, Princeton, N.J., Princeton University Press.
Nixon, J. (1972), *The Complete Story of the Transvaal*, Struik, Cape Town.
Norberg-Schulz, C. (1985), *The Concept of Dwelling: On the Way to Figurative Architecture*, New York (trans), Rizzoli.
Nord, M. and Persson, R. (1994), *Unga bygger sjalva i Storbrittanmen*. Stockholm, SMAA.
North American Bioregional Congress. (NABC), Economics Committee (1989) NABC III Proceedings.
Nwanodi, O. B. A. (1989), 'Housa compounds: Products of Cultural, Economic, Social and Political Systems.' *Habitat International*; Vol.13, (4) pp. 83-97.
Okoye, T. O. (1979), "Urban Planning in Nigeria and the problem of slums" *Third World Planning Review* vol.1, no.1 (Spring) pp. 71-85.
Okoye, T. O. (1983), 'The Impact of Islam on the Nigerian Urban Environment', in Germen, A. (ed.) *Islamic Architecture and Urbanism*, Dammam, King Faisal University.
Orucu, Esin (1976), *Tasinmaz Mulkiyete bir Kamu Hakuku Yaklasimi*, Konya, Selcuk Universitesi.
Palmer, R. and Parsons, N. (eds.) (1983), *The Roots of Rural Poverty in Central and Southern Africa*. Heinemann, England.
Payne, G. K.(1979), *Urban Housing in the Third World*, Routledge and Kegan Paul: Boston.
Planhol, D. Z. (1961), *Nouveaux Villages Algerois*, Paris, P.U.F.
Platzky, L. and Walker, C. (1985), *The Surplus People: Forced Removals in South Africa*, Johannesburg, Ravan Press.
Polanyi, K. (1944), *The Great Transformation*. New York, Farrar & Rinehart.
Pollock, N. C. and Agnew, S. (1963), *An Historical Geography of South Africa*, Longman, London.
Power, A. (1987), *Property Before People: The Managemant of Twentieth Century council Housing*. Hemel Hempstead, Allen and Unwin.
Prey, J. (1994), "A conceptual framework for participatory technology development", *Appropriate Technology*, vol. 21, no.1, 1st June, ('Participation' edition).
Prescott, J. V. R. (1979), "Africa's Boundary Problems." *Optima* 28 (1)pp. 3-21.
Proshansky, H. M. et al. (1970), "Freedom of choice and behaviour in a physical setting". *Environmental Psychology*. New York, Holt.
Rahmani, L. (1989), Repartission des nouveaux lots au village El Mouane, University of Setif.

Ramutsindela, M. F. (1991), *Magisterial district boundaries of the Northern Transvaal: Territorial State manipulation by the State.* South African Geographical Society's Quadrennial Conference, 8-11 July 1991, Potchefstroom, South Africa.

Ramutsindela, M. F. (1993), *Boundaries of the Northern Trnasvaal. A Geographic study of the Properties, Functions and Perceptions of Magisterial District Boundaries*, University of the North, Sovenga.

Rapoport, A. (1969), *House form and culture*. New Jersey, Prentice Hall.

Rapoport, A. (1973), 'The ecology of housing.' *Ecologist*; Vol.3, No.1, pp. 10-17.

Rapoport, A. (1975), 'Australian aborigines and the definition of place', in Oliver, P. (ed.) *Shelter, Sign and Symbol*, Barrie and Jenkins, London. pp. 38-51.

Rapoport, A. (1976), "Socio-cultural aspects of man-environmental studies". In *The Mutual Interaction of People and their Built Environment*. Paris, Mouton.

Rapoport, A. (1977), *Human Aspects of Urban Form*. Oxford, Pergamon Press.

Rapoport, A. (1978), 'Culture and the subjective effects of stress.' *Urban Ecology*; Vol.3 No.3 (Nov), pp. 341-361.

Rapoport, A. (1980/81), 'Neighbourhood homogeneity or heterogeneity.' *Architecture and Behavior*; Vol.1 No.1, pp. 65-77.

Rapoport, A. (1981), 'Identity and Environment: a cross-cultural perspective', in J. S. Duncan, (ed.) *Housing and Identity: cross-cultural perspectives*; Croom-Helm: London;pp. 6-35.

Rapoport, A. (1982a), 'An approach to vernacular design', in J. M. Fitch, (ed.) *Shelter: Models of Native Ingenuity*, Katonah Gallery: Katonah, N.Y.; pp. 43-48.

Rapoport, A. (1982b), 'Sacred places, sacred occasions and sacred environments.' *Architectural Design*; Vol.52 No.9/10, pp. 75-82.

Rapoport, A. (1983a), "Development, culture change and supportive design." *Habitat International* 7 (5/6) pp 249-268.

Rapoport, A. (1983b), "The effect of environment on behavior". In Calhoun, J. B. (ed.) *Environment and Population (Perspectives on Adaption, Environment and Population)*. New York, Praeger pp. 200-201.

Rapoport, A. (1983c), 'Debating architectural alternatives'. *RIBA Transactions 3*, Vol.2 No.1 20th century series, pp. 105-109.

Rapoport, A. (1984), 'Culture and the urban order', in Agnew, J. Mercer, J., and Sopher, D., (eds.), *The City in Cultural Context*; Allen and Unwin, London; pp. 50-75.

Rapoport, A. (1986a), 'Culture and built form - a reconsideration', in Saile, D. G. (ed.) *Architecture in Cultural change (Essays in Built Form and Culture Research)*; University of Kansas: Lawrence; pp. 157-175.

Rapoport, A. (1986b), 'Settlements and energy: Historical precedents', in Ittelson, W. H. et al (eds.), *Cross-Cultural Research in Environment and Behavior*; University of Arizona: Tucson; pp. 219-237.

Rapoport, A. (1986c), 'The use and design of open spaces in urban neighborhoods', in Frick, D. (ed.) *The Quality of Urban Life*, de Gruyter: Berlin; pp. 159-175.

Rapoport, A. (1987), 'Learning about settlements and energy from historical precedents.' *Ekistics*; Vol.54 Nos. 325-327 (July-Dec), pp. 262-268.

Rapoport, A. (1988), "Spontaneous settlements as vernacular design" *Spontaneous Shelter*, C. V. Patton. Philadelphia, Temple University Press, pp. 51-77.

Rapoport, A. (1989), "On the attributes of tradition". In Bourdier, J. P., Al Sayyad,N. (ed.) *Dwellings, Settlements and Tradition (Cross-Cultural Perspectives)*. Lanham MD., University Press of America pp. 77-105.

Rapoport, A. (1990a), "Defining vernacular design" *Vernacular Architecture*. M. Turan, Aldershot (UK), Avebury pp. 67-101.

Rapoport, A. (1990b), 'Systems of activities and systems of settings', in Kent, S.(ed.) *Domestic Architecture and the Use of Space (An Interdisciplinary Cross-Cultural Study* Cambridge University Press, Cambridge pp. 9-20.

Rapoport, A. (1990c), 'Science and the failure of architecture', in Altman, I. and Christensen, K. (eds.) *Environment and Behavior Studies (Emergence of Intellectual Traditions)*, (vol.11 of Human Behavior and Environment). Plenum, New York;p. 79-109.

Rapoport, A. (1990d). 'Environmental quality and environmental quality profiles', in Wilkinson, N. (ed.) *Quality in the Built Environment*; Urban International Press: Newcastle (U.K.); pp. 75-83.

Rapoport, A. (1990e), *History and Precedent in Environmental Design*, New York, Plenum.

Rapoport, A. (1990f), *The Meaning of the Built Environment*, University of Arizona Press: Tucson.

Rapoport, A. (1990/91), 'Flexibility, open-endedness and design.' *People and Physical Environment Research (Australia)*; No. 34-35 (Oct 1990/Jan 1991), pp. 53-73.

Rapoport, A. (1992a), 'On cultural landscapes.' *Traditional Dwellings and Settlements Review*; Vol.3 No.2 (Spring), pp. 33-47.

Rapoport, A. (1992b), 'Some thoughts on the future of environmental design' in Kim, S-K. *Proceedings of the 29th IFLA World Congress*, (Seoul), pp. 223-233.

Rapoport, A. (1992c), 'On regions and regionalism', in Markovitch, N. C. et al (eds.) *Pueblo Style and Regional Architecture*, Van Nostrand-Reinhold (Paperback edition): New York; pp. 272-294.

Rapoport, A. (1993), 'Cross-Cultural Studies and Urban Form'. *Urban Studies and Planning Program*, University of Maryland.

Rapoport, A. (1994a), "A Critical Look at the Concept 'place'" *National Geog. Jl of India* 40 pp. 31-45.

Rapoport, A. (1994b), 'Spatial Organization and the built environment', in Ingold, T. (ed.) *Companion Encyclopedia of Anthropology: Humanity, Culture and Social Life*, Routledge, London, pp. 460-502.

Rapoport, A. (in press a), 'Rethinking design (an environment-behavior perspective', in Schaur, E. (ed.) *Building with Intelligence (Aspects of a New Building Culture)*. University of Stuttgart, Germany.

Rapoport, A. (in press b), *On the relation between culture and environment*, ARIS 3 (Carnegie Mellon University).

Reardon, T., Matlon, P. et al. (1988), "Coping with Household Level Food Security in Drought affected Areas of Burkina Faso." *World Development* 16: 1065-1074.

Register, R. (1987), *Ecocity Berkeley: Building Cities for a Healthy Future*. Berkeley, North Atlantic Books.

Relph, E. (1985), "Geographical Experiences and Being-in-the-World: The Phenomenological Origins of Geography". In Seamon, D. and Mugerauer (ed.) *Dwelling, Place and Environment: Towards a Phenomenology of Person and World*, New York, Columbia University Press.

Republic of China, E. Y. (1993), *Taiwan National Income*, Taipei, Executive Yuan (in Chinese).

Republic of South Africa. (1957), *Government Gazette of the Republic of South Africa*, Pretoria, Government Printer.

Republic of South Africa. (1966), *House of Assembly Debates*, Pretoria, Government Printer.

Republic of South Africa. (1972), *Government Gazette of the Republic of South Africa*, Pretoria, Government Printer.

Republic of South Africa. (1983), *South Africa, Official Yearbook of the Republic of South Africa*, Pretoria, Government Printer.

Richards, R. and J. Waterbury. (1990), *A Political economy of the Middle East: State, Class and Economic Development,* Oxford, Westview Press.

Robinson, J. W. (1991), 'Premises, Premises: Architecture as cultural medium', in Rockcastle, G. (ed.) *Type and the possibilities of convention*, Midguard Monograph: New York.

Rogers, H. (1933), *Native Administration in the Union of South Africa* Johannesburg, University of the Witwatersrand Press.

Rossi, A. (1982), *The Architecture of the City,* Cambridge Massachusetts, MIT Press.

Saad, H. T. (1988), 'Urban Blight and Religious Uprising in Northern Nigeria.' *Habitat International*. Vol.12(2) pp. 111-128.

Sack, R. D. (1986), *Human Territory, It's Theory and History*, Cambridge, Cambridge University Press.

Saddiqi, F. R. (1989), *Shaykh Uthman Ibn Fudi: Islam Against Illusions,* Kano, Bayevo University.

Saglamer, G. and Erdogan, N.(1993), 'A Comparative Study on Squatter Settlements and Vernacular Architecture.' *Open House International*; Vol.18, No.1, pp. 41-49.

Saglamer, G., Yurekli, H. et al.(1994),*Comparative Evaluation of Different Approaches in Housing Provision for Low-Income Groups.* unpublished Research Report of TUBITAK,INTAG 104, supported by The Scientific and Technological Research Council of Turkey (TUBITAK) and the British Council.

SAIRR. (1994), *Race Relations Survey 1993/1994*, SAIRR, Johannesburg.

Sale, K. (1985), *Dwellers in the Land*, San Francisco, Sierra Club Books.

Sancar, F. H. and Koop, T. T. (1989), 'Proposing a behavioral definition of the [sic] 'vernacular' based on a comparative analysis of the behavior settings in three settlements in Turkey and Greece'. Paper presented at: *Conference on Built Form and Culture*, Tempe, Arizona (May), Mimeo.

Sastrosasmita, S. and A.T.M. Nurul Amin. (1990), 'Housing needs of informal sector workers (The case of Yogyakarta, (Indonesia))', *Habitat International*, vol.14, no.4, pp. 75-88.

Siegel, B.J. (1970), 'Defensive structuring and environmental stress', *American Journal of Sociology*, vol.76, pp. 11-46.

Sayer, A. (1985), "The Difference that space makes". In Gregory, D. and Urry, J. (ed.) *Social Relations and Spatial Structures*, London, Macmillan, pp. 49-65.

Schwerdtfeger, F. W. (1971), Housing in Zaria. *Shelter in Africa*, Oliver, P., London, Barrie & Jenkins.

Sheng, Y. K. (1995), *Shelter for All: Enabling or Empowering Strategies? The Importance of Habitat II*, International Conference Urban Habitat: the Environment of the Future, Delft, The Netherlands.

Simonds, J. O. (1994), *Garden Cities 21: Creating a Liveable Urban Environment*. New York, McGraw-Hill.

Sirel, A. (1993), *Kent Planlama ve Uygulama Sureci Icinde Kamu Mulkiyeti Varliginin Kent Makroformuna Etkileri* Unpublished PhD Thesis, University of Mimar Sinan.

Skillbuilding. (1992), *The Sponsors Manual*. York, Joseph Rowntree Foundation.

Skinner, R. and Rodell, M. (eds.) (1983). *People, Poverty and Shelter: Problems of Self-Help Housing in the Third World*. London, Methuen.

Slowe, P. (1990), *Geography and Political Power*. London, Routledge.

Songsore, J. and Denkabe A. (1988), Challenging Rural Poverty in Northern Ghana: The Case of the Upper west Region, Ghana, UNICEF, Draft Report.

Sonnenfeld, J. (1976), "Imposing environmental meaning: A commentary". In *Environmental Knowing (Theories Research and Methods*. Moore, G. T. and Golledge, R G. (ed.) Stroudsbury, PA. Dowden, Hutchinson and Ross pp. 254-257.

South African Council of Churches and the Southern African Catholic Bishops' Conference. (1984), *Relocation: The Church's Report on Forced Removals*. Randburg

South African Institute of Race Relations. (1960), Johannesburg.

Standing Committee on Agriculture, Fisheries and Forestry (1984), *Soil at Risk: Canada's Eroding Future*. A Report on Soil Conservation to the Senate of Canada. Ottowa.

Star (The), 26 September 1994 p. 2

Stewart, J. H. (1982), 'The future of planning theory - Whither urban design?' *Planning Outlook*; Vol.24, pp. 74-82. University of Newcastle upon Tyne.

Suher, H. (1989), 'Sagliki Sagliklilastiriyor muyuz? Gecekondu Yerlesmeleri - Plan Disi Yerlesme Alanlari.' *Mimarlik*; Vol.89/6 No.238, pp. 42-43.

Swaney, J. A. (1990), "Common Property, Reciprocity, and Community." *Journal of Economic Issues* 24 (2): 451-462.

Taher, N. A. (1986), 'Social identity and class in a Cairo neighbourhood' Cairo: *Cairo Papers in Social Sciences* Vol.9 No.4,The American University in Cairo Press.

Taiwan EPA. (1990), Taiwan Environmental Protection Administration, Taipei, Taiwan (in Chinese)

Taiwan EPA. (1993), Taiwan Environmental Protection Administration, Taipei, Taiwan (in Chinese)

Taiwan Forestry Bureau. (1993), *A Profile of Taiwan Forestry Bureau*. Taipei, Taiwan, TFB (in Chinese).

Taylor, P. J. (1993), *Political Geography: World-economy, nation-states and locality*. London, Longman.

Thompson, L. (1990), *A History of South Africa*. Yale University Press, USA.

Tice, J. (1993), 'Theme and Variations: A Typological Approach to Housing Design, Teaching and Research.' *Journal of Architectural Education*; Vol.46 No.3, pp. 162-175.

Tikly, L. (1994), *The Future of Model C Schools*, unpublished paper, Education Policy Unit, University of the Witwatersrand, South Africa.

Tipple, A. G. (1987), "Housing Policy and Culture in Kumasi, Ghana" *Environment and Behavior* 19.

Tipple, A. G. (1994), "Employment Implications of Transformation Activity: An Introduction to the Literature on Housing and Employment", *Transformations Working Paper*, CARDO, University of Newcastle upon Tyne. No. 1.

Tipple, A. G. (1994a), "A Matter of Interface: the Need for a Shift in Targeting Housing Interventions" *Habitat International* 18 (4): 2-13.

Toffler, A. (1982), *The Third Wave*, New York, Bantam Books.

Toye, J. (1991), "Ghana - Case Study". In Mosley, P., Harrigan, J. Toye, J. (ed.) *Aid and Power. The World Bank and Policy-Based Lending*. Vol 2. London and New York, Routledge

Turgut, H. (1990), "Homelessness in Turkey as a Result of Squatter Phenomenon" *Open House International* 15 (2-3): 56-59.

Turgut, H. (1994), *Gecekondu Yerlesimlerinde Kultut ve Mekan Etkisinin Saptanmasi, Ornek: Pinar Mahalleso / Determination of Culture and Space Interaction in Squatter Settlements, Example: Pinar Settlement.* ongoing Research Project, Istanbul: ITU Faculty of Architecture:

Turner, J. (1972), Housing as a Verb. *Freedom to build.* J. Turner and R. Fichter. New York, Macmillan.

Turner, J. (1976), *Freedom to Build.* London, Marion Boyers.

Turner, J. (1976), *Housing by People: Towards Autonomy in Building Environments.* London, Marion Boyars.

UNCHS. (1989), *Habitat News* 11 (No.2 August).

UNCHS. (1990), *Habitat News* 12 (No.1, August).

UNICEF. (1988), "Adjustment Policies and Programmes to Protect Children and Vulnerable Groups in Ghana". In Cornia, G., Jolly, R. and Stewart, F. (ed.) *Adjustment With a Human Face. Protecting the Vulnerable and Promoting Growth.* Oxford, Clarendon Press 1 pp. 93-125.

Union of South Africa. (1917), *Statutes of the Union of South Africa.* Pretoria, Government Printer.

Union of South Africa. (1924), *Statutes of the Union of South Africa*, Pretoria, Government Printer.

Urquhart, A. W. (1977), *Planned Urban Landscapes of Northern Nigeria*, Zaria, Ahnadu Bello University Press.

Urry, J. (1985), "Social Relations, Space and Time". In Gregory, D. and Urry, J. (ed.) *Social Relations and Spatial Structures.* London, Macmillan pp. 20-45.

Van der Ryn, S. (1992), "Building a Sustainable Future". In Walter, B., Arkin, L, and Crenshaw, R. (ed.) *Sustainable Cities: Concepts and Strategies for Eco-City Development*, Los Angeles, Eco-Home Media: 62-69.

van Eyck, A. (1961), *CIAM 59* in Otterlo Stuttgart: 'Documents of Modern Architecture'. Vol.1, Congress report, projects and discussions.

Vayda, A. P. (1983), "Progressive contextualization." *Human Ecology* vol.11 no.3 (Sept) pp. 265-282.

Vigier, F. (1987), *Housing in Tunis*, Cambridge, Mass., Havard Graduate School of Design.

Vosloo, W. B., Kotze, D. A. et al. (1974), *Local Government in Southern Africa.* Pretoria, Academia.

Ward, C. (1976), *Housing: an anarchic approach*, London, Freedom Press.

Ward, C. (1985), *When We Build Again Let's Have Housing That Works*, London, Pluto.

Ward, C. (1990), *Talking Houses,* Freedom Press, London.

Watson, G.(1970), *Passing for White*, Tavistock, London.

Wikan, U. (1990), "Changing housing strategies and patterns among the Cairo poor 1950-1985". In Amis, P. and Lloyd, P. (ed.) *Housing Africa's Urban Poor*, Manchester University Press.

Wilson, F. and Rampele, M. (1989), *Uprooting Poverty: The South African Challenge*. Cape Town, David Philip.

Yellen, J. (1985), 'Bushmen.' *Science 85*; (May), pp. 41-48.

Index

a priori, 9
adaptability, 205
adaptable, 19
Algeria, 141, 142, 148, 153, 158
Algerian Socialist Village Policy, 141, 151
alteration, 205
ambience, 11, 14, 15, 16, 17, 18
apartheid, 28, 225, 226, 238, 239, 241, 242
autonomous, 27, 179

Bello, 175, 176, 178, 182
Berber, 158
bioregionalism, 51
British colonial, 177
   administration, 175, 176, 180, 183, 185, 187
   values, 175
buildability, 198
built infrastructure, 55
built culture, 27
built form, 27, 28, 29, 30, 31, 32

centralised decision, 175
change, 11, 17, 19, 27, 30, 41, 51, 56, 57, 62, 63, 64, 65, 90, 93, 95, 104, 105, 123, 126, 131, 132, 138, 141, 142, 151, 152, 153, 154, 158, 173, 176, 179, 182, 185, 202, 205, 206, 207, 247, 252, 257, 263, 266, 267, 274, 279, 284
   agricultural, 151
   climatic, 40
   cultural, 40, 151
   economic, 151
   environmental, 153
   gender role, 161
   health and nutrition, 164, 165
   income generation, 166
   location, 138
   locational, 151
   political, 151
   social, 141, 153
   technological, 40
   tenancy, 138
   topographic, 40
   women's time use, 167, 169, 170, 171
Colonial economic value, 179. *See also* British colonial
complex, 27, 29, 30, 32, 66, 84, 99, 136, 187, 194, 205, 247
complexity, 11, 281
creative synthesis, 19
cultural, 9, 10, 27, 29, 90, 129, 205, 214, 226, 256, 262, 264
   change, 137

syncretism, 19
variability, 10
variables, 11
cultural landscape, 8, 9, 14, 16, 21, 23, 25
culture, 8, 11, 28, 29, 43, 49, 57, 70, 117, 125, 142, 144, 150, 154, 156, 158, 240, 257, 262, 263, 265
    culture change, 19, 21
    Hausa-Fulani, 175
    Islamic, 125,146
    Muslim, 173, 175, 180
    rural, 158
    social, 142
    spatial culture, 85, 105
culture-core
    aspects, 22
    elements, 22, 24

decentralise, 41, 54, 74, 175, 176
    decentralisation, 54, 61, 63
design, 8, 9, 11, 21, 22
design process, 116, 141
development, 7, 27, 28, 30, 33, 60, 66, 77, 107, 117, 126, 136, 138, 163, 172, 173, 175, 176, 177, 178, 180, 185, 190, 192, 199, 205, 220, 223, 225, 228, 232, 233, 235, 237, 239, 241, 242, 243, 245, 246, 247, 257, 262, 263, 281, 285, 286, 289, 292
    ecosystem development alternatives, 43
    human ecosystem, 35, 43
    socio-physical, 35, 36, 37, 38, 40, 41, 43
development alternatives, 40
dwelling, 14, 21, 68, 69, 76, 84, 85, 89, 90, 91, 92, 93, 95, 96, 98, 99, 116, 118, 125, 131, 182, 186, 193, 205, 215, 251, 254, 255, 261, 262, 264, 266, 269, 276, 277, 284, 287, 292
    dwelling unit, 71, 136, 209, 216

economic
    growth, 47
    power, 274
    power-house, 47
Egypt, 81, 118, 121, 123, 125, 132, 137, 205, 206, 217, 223, 224
einfuhlung, 9
El-Hekr, 81, 82, 84, 93, 95, 98, 99, 104, 105, 106, 107, 109, 113, 114, 116, 117
enablement, 27, 32, 43, 59, 60, 61, 62, 63, 64, 66, 67, 68, 71, 77, 121, 124
environment, 7, 9, 10, 14, 18, 50, 55, 62, 65, 68, 70, 71, 74, 121, 161, 164, 170, 173, 205, 206, 215, 216, 221, 251, 254, 256, 258, 262, 279, 290
    environmental upgrading, 81
environmental, 47
environmental function, 58
environmental variability, 10
environment-behaviour
    relationships, 8, 13, 15, 23
environment-behaviour studies, 8
ethnic, 180, 225, 228, 246
    ethnicity, 11, 226
    territory, 232, 233
explicit, 176, 255
explicitly, 37
extended family, 90, 116 *see also* family
extension, 143, 152, 154, 205, 207, 209, 210, 214, 215, 217, 218, 220, 223, 274
extrinsic, 24

family
    compound, 146, 148
    displaced, 151
    economic activities, 151
    extended,143, 146, 150, 152, 156, 158

group, 146
income, 152
member, 146, 148
nuclear, 148
relocated, 152
rural, 144
social structure, 142, 156
structure, 144
Fodio, S. D., 176
function, 17, 37, 41, 54, 55, 85, 89, 90, 92, 95, 98, 104, 105, 112, 131, 136, 146, 152, 156, 177, 178, 183, 214, 221, 255, 262, 267, 272, 274, 276, 278, 279
administrative, 232
functional aspects, 41
functioning, 74

Gaziantep, 262, 263, 265
gender roles, 161
Ghana, 51, 161, 163, 164, 165, 169, 172, 246, 247
glocal, 27, 30, 31, 32, 33
Government Reservation Areas (GRA), 178
grant land, 177
grassroots, 66
grassroots democracy, 54
growth, 49, 50, 68, 72, 98, 104, 163, 180, 183, 197, 202, 205, 266
economic, 60, 65, 72
urban, 60

habitual, 255
relationship, 251
Hausa, 179, 183, 185, 187
city-states, 179
history, 17, 28, 49, 51, 52, 53, 123, 125, 131, 132, 138, 202, 226, 235, 236, 237, 241, 242, 253, 257, 262, 266, 282
house, 90, 91, 132, 135, 142, 146, 169, 182, 186, 189, 237, 254, 262, 263, 264, 265, 266, 269, 271, 287
Arab, 147
assembly, 144, 148, 150
bayt, 124, 125
constituent houses, 81
construction, 203
courtyard, 146
family house, 82, 84
form, 142, 143, 151
gourbi [traditional house], 154
house-building, 176
household, 85
housing, 82, 84, 95, 113, 114, 117, 118, 119, 166
wash house, 153
household, 61, 82, 84, 85, 129, 150, 156, 163, 164, 165, 167, 169, 170, 171, 172, 186, 189, 192, 199, 214, 217, 224, 241, 242, 252, 253, 254, 258, 264, 269, 290
head, 132
head of, 84
type, 185
householder, 59
housing, 56, 57, 58, 59, 60, 62, 63, 64, 65, 66, 68, 69, 70, 71, 72, 73, 74, 77, 82, 84, 95, 113, 114, 117, 118, 119, 121, 129, 132, 135, 136, 138, 166, 186, 190, 197, 205, 206, 221, 235, 237, 238, 239, 243, 247, 251, 252, 255, 259, 262, 265, 271, 281, 286
associations, 193
layout, 81
multi-storey, 125
public housing, 126
rab, 124, 125, 126, *129*
squatter, 285, 292
tenement house, 82
traditional house, 82, 86
type, 124, 185, 186, 261

identification, 251, 258

ideology, 11, 62, 125, 158, 225, 226, 238
implicit, 7, 37, 176, 205, 216
  practice, 251, 258, 259
  process, 259
  relationship, 251
Indirect Rule Policy, 177, 187
informal housing, 292
informal processes, 259
informal township, 81
integrate, 50
integrated, 27, 30, 32, 41, 70, 99, 104, 106, 121, 179, 180, 238
integrated neighbourhood upgrading, 66
intrinsic, 23
intrinsically, 27
Ismailia, 81, 84, 118
Istanbul, 281, 286, 287, 288, 289, 292

Lagos, 180
land policy, 176, 177
Local Government Law, 178

managerial function, 64
modernist, 251, 253, 259
modernity, 17, 251, 255, 259, 260
modification, 13, 53, 74, 138, 153, 154, 205, 263
m-theory, 30, 32, 33
Muslim
  cities, 173, 179, 187
  non-Arab Muslim cities, 173

national
  nationalist and secularist values, 175, 178, 180, 185, 187
  unity, 180
national unity, 233, 240
negative, 121
negative affect, 18
negative effect, 65, 223
  of environment, 9

new towns, 179, 180
n-theory, 31, 32, 33

old city type, 185, 186
open space, 50, 56, 69, 182, 183, 207, 217, 218, 221, 261, 262, 263, 265, 266, 267, 268, 269, 271, 274, 275, 276, 277, 278
orientation, 258, 279
Ortigia, 262, 266, 268, 269, 272, 274, 276, 277, 278

participate
  participating, 205, 210, 214
  participation, 24, 53, 54, 55, 61, 65, 197, 202, 218, 242, 243, 257
physiognomy, 105, 107, 109
physiography, 107, 110, 116
Pinar, 286, 287, 288, 289, 290, 291
policy instrument, 63, 180
Political Economy, 33
Polo ground, 183
private developers, 175, 176
public housing, 205, 212, 221, 223. *See also housing*

race relations, 225, 228, 248
reflect, 13, 27, 40, 67, 132, 138, 182, 210, 214, 221, 274
response, 7, 15, 16, 17, 23, 43, 49, 70, 138, 153, 180, 185, 194, 200, 255
ribat (defensive walled city), 179
rural, 163
  communities, 141, 142
  planning, 151, 153
  policy, 156

self
  self confidence, 197, 203
  self esteem, 197, 201
  self-built housing, 189, 190
  self-provided housing, 189, 190
self built, 255

self-help, 59, 60, 62, 63, 64, 67, 68, 71, 76, 77, 137, 246
setting, 9, 14, 15, 16, 17, 19, 21, 24, 35, 37, 40, 123, 142, 150, 153, 223
settlement upgrading, 59, 70, 72, 73, 75, 76, 77
Sharia courts, 177
Shehu Dan Fodio, 175
Sicily, 263, 266, 280
social power, 225, 226
social space, 27
social structure, 144
socialist village, 153, 156
societal values, 173, 174, 176
Sokoto
   Caliphate, 175, 176, 177, 182
   Jihad, 175
   Nigeria, 173
South Africa, 59, 69, 72, 73, 77, 225, 226, 227, 228, 229, 232, 233, 235, 236, 237, 238, 239, 240, 241, 243, 244, 246, 247
   Institute of Race Relations, 228
space syntax, 119
squatter *see also* housing camp, 239
squatter settlement, 281, 282, 285, 286, 287, 288, 289, 291
structural adjustment, 61, 62, 161, 163, 164, 165, 172, 246

territory, 148, 217, 225, 226, 228, 233. *See also ethnic*
theory, 8, 23, 27, 30, 68, 173, 174, 247
   political-economic, 174

Town and Country Planning Law, 178
township, 48, 59, 69, 73, 81, 82, 177, 183, 235, 237, 238, 239, 240, 241, 242, 244
transformation, 75, 81, 126, 151, 205, 212, 213, 214, 215, 216, 220, 221, 223, 239, 262, 266, 275
transportation, 55, 56, 57, 58, 131, 135, 179, 180, 237, 244, 254, 287, 289
Turkey, 263, 264, 282, 283, 284, 285, 286, 288, 291, 292

unequal, 25, 27, 30, 233
uneven, 27, 30, 32, 98
upgrade, 238, 246
upgrading, 117, 118, 136, 215, 285. see also *environmental upgrading, settlement upgrading and integrated neighbourhood upgrading*
   projects, 60, 63, 72
urban
   growth, 22
   township, 82, 238, 239
urban poor, 11, 65, 121, 129, 292

values
   Islamic religious, 175, 176
variability, 10, 104
vernacular design, 23
vertical extension, 287. *See also* extension
West Africa, 142, 175
zone, 125, 126, 164, 177, 180, 183, 239

For Product Safety Concerns and Information please contact our EU representative GPSR@taylorandfrancis.com
Taylor & Francis Verlag GmbH, Kaufingerstraße 24, 80331 München, Germany

www.ingramcontent.com/pod-product-compliance
Lightning Source LLC
Chambersburg PA
CBHW071234290426
44108CB00013B/1409